# Legacy of Wings

# Legacy of Wings
# The Story of Harold F. Pitcairn
## by
# FRANK KINGSTON SMITH

Jason Aronson, Inc.
New York     London

*For Stephen*

*Three-view plans drawn by Harry Plank.*

*Photographic reproductions: Wilmer C. Baker.*

*Text design: Meryl Sussman Levavi.*

*Library of Congress Cataloging in Publication Data*

*Smith, Frank Kingston.*
    *Legacy of wings.*

    *1. Pitcairn, Harold F., 1897-*
*2. Aeronautics—United States—Biography.*
*I. Title.*
*TL540.P54S57   629.13′092′4[B]   81-20511*
*ISBN 0-87668-485-1          AACR2*

*First printing 1981.*
*Jason Aronson, Inc.*
*111 Eighth Avenue*
*New York, N.Y. 10011*

# Table of Contents

# Foreword

This is an interesting and important book—and one that is long overdue.

The story of Harold F. Pitcairn is an integral part of the development of aviation. He envisioned the future of air transport and courageously started the air mail routes known today as Eastern Air Lines, one of the world's largest air carriers.

Lacking proper aircraft for the first air mail routes, Pitcairn built them: fine, strong open-cockpit biplanes characterized by quality. The first airplane I owned was a Pitcairn PA-6. I can clearly remember the square, steel tubing that made up the frame of the fuselage, and the joy of flying this sturdy aircraft.

But Pitcairn unceasingly pursued a vision of a rotary-wing aircraft—his approach to the safe aircraft—and his entire life was dedicated to the advancement of this important type of flight. Few are aware of his many inventions and the fact that most helicopters flying the world's skies today carry design basics that originated on Pitcairn's drawing board.

This book is a comprehensive picture of Pitcairn, an interesting and complex person, but woven within his story is an exciting look at the history of aviation. There is a true feeling of the early times that brought back to me the days I would land at the Pitcairn factory to look around and talk with Jim Ray, Agnew Larsen, Jim Faulkner and, on a few occasions, the quiet and gentle Harold Pitcairn. On one such trip he invited me to fly an autogiro, my first experience, and I was checked out by Jim Ray.

The author brings into accurate focus the precarious beginning of vertical flight and the tempo and quality of his writing never disappoints as he unfolds the remainder of the narrative.

Everyone interested in aviation will want to read this well-written account of one of its true pioneers; those outside aviation will find it a worthwhile story of an exceptional man.

The bookcase for aviation history has had a vacant place filled at last—and filled well.

Robert N. Buck
Fayston, Vermont

# Introduction

This is the life story of an American aviation pioneer, a dreamer, an inventor, a designer, a businessman, an innovator, and a prophet, Harold Frederick Pitcairn.

On any one of several counts, Pitcairn's name deserves to be familiar. His lifetime spanned the history of heavier-than-air powered flight. In that lifetime, Pitcairn accomplished more than most aeronautical personalities whose names are almost household words, but he did it quietly, choosing to remain in the background. Harold Pitcairn, by nature shy, reticent, and unassuming, shunned the spotlight.

Yet he founded, literally hewed out of the wilderness, an airline that would grow into one of the nation's major air-carrier systems.

One of the fixed-wing airplanes he designed was to become an all-time classic that still elicits comments, articles, and books.

As America's acknowledged pioneer in rotary-wing aviation, Harold Pitcairn was the fourteenth recipient of the highest award in American aviation, the Collier Trophy. The honor was given "for the greatest achievement in aviation in America the value of which has been thoroughly demonstrated by actual use during the preceding year."

An inventor, he was granted almost two dozen patents on rotary-wing aircraft—and he held helicopter patents dating back to applications filed in 1926.

Pitcairn's twenty-five years of dedication to the science of rotary-wing flight prior to World War II was largely responsible for the development of the helicopter industry in the United States.

The Pitcairn name graces no less than three exhibits displayed in the nation's repository for precious, important aeronautical artifacts, the Smithsonian Institution's National Air and Space Museum, in Washington, D.C. Millions of visitors view this shrine of aviation every year.

His creations have been treasured in the Shannon Air Museum, in Fredericksburg, Virginia, and are seen—in flying condition!—at meetings of the Experimental Aircraft Association's Classic Aircraft displays all over the North American continent. One is used every nice day, all day long for six months of the year, to give passenger rides at Old Rhinebeck Aerodrome, north of Poughkeepsie, New York.

The misleading impression given by some books published in the last decade is that Harold Pitcairn was a rich dilettante who used his inherited wealth to dabble in aviation, contributing nothing but his money. No one has told of his struggles, frustrations, victories, and numbing losses—or of his eventual victory over the most devastating blow of all.

I hope this biography will set the record straight.

F.K.S.

## Acknowledgments

I must express my gratitude for the assistance of many people in writing this biography of Harold Frederick Pitcairn and for reviewing the manuscript for technical accuracy: Ralph H. McClarren, W. Lawrence LePage, J. Edward Shinn, Esquire, Raymond and Kenneth Synnestvedt and Carl R. Gunther, archivist for the Pitcairn Corporation. Most of all, I thank Stephen Pitcairn, who gave me total access to every record of his father's life and of both Pitcairn Aviation and Pitcairn Aircraft. Without their help, criticism and suggestions, this book could never have been written.

## Note on Sources

Virtually all of the information included in these pages came either from interviews with persons actually involved or who were eyewitnesses. Most of the details were found in Harold Pitcairn's personal and business correspondence files, or from the daily diary entries of Geoffrey Childs, Pitcairn's vice-president and general manager. Additional details came from personal meetings with Gen. H. Franklin Gregory, Fred W. "Slim" Soule, John Miller, Sterling Smith and Ariel "Gunny" Gunther. Background information was found in contemporary newspapers, aviation journals and anthologies.

# Legacy of Wings

# PART ONE

# The Dreamer

# Safe Airplane

Raindrops drummed on the taut fabric of the Pitcairn Mailwing's fuselage and spattered Atlanta's Candler Field. While ground crewmen loaded canvas bags marked "U.S. Mail" into the bin up front of the single open cockpit, two men looked up speculatively into the gathering darkness. This was to be a night flight to Richmond, with intermediate stops at Spartanburg and Greensboro.

"What do you think about this weather, Johnny?" asked Ben Faulkner, the Atlanta field manager for Pitcairn Aviation, as he helped the pilot to don his clumsy seat-type parachute.

Shrugging into the harness in his preparations to take off for Richmond at the 7:30 P.M. scheduled departure time, Air Mail Pilot John Kytle glanced offhandedly at the gray and dripping skies that had been dumping rain on central Georgia for the last twelve hours and nodded that he thought it was fine.

"How high do you think that ceiling is?" Faulkner pressed on, a note of concern sneaking into his voice.

A seasoned pilot himself, he knew the hazards of flying in bad weather, for in 1928 there were few pilots who could operate safely when visibility became seriously restricted. At that time, virtually all cross-country flight was performed under visual conditions, navigating from point to point by pilotage or sometimes by holding a course and computing airspeed and time to deduce when the next navigation fix would appear. With no radios for navigation or communication, a pilot was totally on his own against the elements—just him and his airplane.

After a few moments of pondering, Kytle responded in his rich southern accent. "Hard to tell looking up at clouds." He turned his attention to fumbling with the harness straps on his chest, clicking them together, then feeling to be sure that the ripcord ring was properly positioned. "But I would guess that we have about fifteen hundred feet. I went up about an hour or so ago to check it out and we had about two thousand feet then. The ceiling

A Pitcairn Mailwing being loaded at Candler Field, Atlanta, for the regularly scheduled night flight to Richmond, 500 miles away. No radio equipment, basic blind flying instrumentation, year round flying in single engine, open cockpit biplanes—that was Pitcairn Aviation during the late 1920s.

seems to be dropping slowly. I might as well go while I can still see something underneath."

He snugged his well-worn flying helmet over his damp hair, perched the goggles on his forehead, and put his left foot up on the mounting cleat behind the lower left wing of the glistening biplane, preparatory to boarding.

"The mail must go through"—he grinned at the worried Faulkner—"even if there are only two small bags of it."

He threw his leg over the rim of the cockpit, stepped down onto the bucket seat, and, supporting his weight on his elbows against the padded sides of the opening, eased down to sit on the hard parachute pack that would be his throne for the next few hours. He wriggled a couple of times to get comfortable. Then he stowed the scroll of his homemade strip chart in a cardboard mailing tube taped to a structural member next to his left leg so that he could retrieve it easily in flight and began to probe the interior of the cockpit with the beam of a flashlight, making sure that everything was in its proper place.

An airmail pilot's working uniform: helmet, goggles, parachute and pistol.

Richmond lay about 450 miles to the northeast. If it did not take too long to refuel and transfer mail at the waypoints, the trip should take about five hours, maybe a little less, if he could pick up a tailwind. Johnny figured that he would be in bed shortly after midnight.

As Kytle was finishing his preliminary cockpit check, the mail-bin hatch cover glomped shut and was latched by a loader who gave it a couple of quick slaps with the palm of his hand as sort of a "there you go" signal before he jumped down from the lower wing.

Kytle snapped off the flashlight and stowed it temporarily in the slack of his parachute harness. Faulkner, standing on the ground alongside and still nagged by doubts leaned into the cockpit and asked again, "Okay?"

The youthful pilot airily waved a gloved hand and nodded his head a couple of times. His mind was made up. He was going to carry the U.S. mail again through the gloom of night, just as the motto tacked on the flight office bulletin board said he should. To Johnny Kytle, a veteran pilot despite his youthful age of twenty-two, it was a routine flight that he had performed many times, in daylight and at night.

He had first flown the route in Pitcairn Orowing training airplanes, to learn the prominent landmarks and the compass headings between them. He had landed at the emergency fields that had been constructed by the Department of Commerce every thirty miles. Then he had made qualification flights at night, using the chain of twinkling airways-marking beacon lights that led pilots over the safest route above the frequently invisible terrain. With those lights located every ten miles, or approximately six minutes of flying time apart, it was easy to keep on course on a clear night; sometimes several flashers could be seen at once, stretching to the horizon. But when heavy ground fog formed or thunderstorms or snow showers moved over the region and obscured the beacons, navigation was a matter of holding precise compass headings, checking the time between fixes, and outguessing the wind. It was a chancy business.

Kytle was not at all concerned that he might be taking off under a ceiling of less than one thousand feet; Pitcairn pilots were used to flying at five hundred feet, sometimes lower. Between Atlanta -and Spartanburg the normal 040-degree heading took them over flat land for an hour or so with only two high points off to the east of the course: Stone Mountain, a monolithic block of granite jutting 825 feet out of the Piedmont Plain some twenty-five miles northeast of Atlanta, then another twenty-five miles northeast of that, the twelve-hundred-foot summit of Hog Mountain. Besides, on that May evening he would have

forty-five minutes of daylight on the first leg of the trip.

Faulkner gave him an almost affectionate pat on the head and stepped back as the pilot and a mechanic began the litany of starting the engine.

"Switch off?" queried the mechanic poised by the big Wright J-5 Whirlwing.

The pilot reached down into the dim recess of the open cockpit and felt to be sure that the engine's magneto switch was in the correct position. "Switch off," he replied.

"Fuel on?"

Kytle moved the selector to the "on" detent, and wiggled it a couple of times to be sure that it was set. "Fuel is on."

"Throttle cracked?"

The throttle was opened about a quarter of an inch and Kytle responded, "She's cracked."

The mechanic pulled the steel propeller over a couple of times by hand to prime the cylinders of the big radial engine, then set it on its compression stroke, moved to the side of the fuselage, and began to crank the handle of the geared starter. "Contact!" he called.

Kytle flipped the magneto switches to the "on" position and engaged the booster mag. The propeller moved for a foot or so, then spun into invisibility as 220 horses began to prance in their traces. A long orange tongue of exhaust flame licked into the dusk.

After a few moments, as the oil pressure built up, the pilot gave his signal to pull the wheel chocks, then fed in enough power to set the plane into motion over the soggy ground. In 1928, Atlanta's Candler Field, little more than a cow pasture dedicated to aeronautical purposes, was totally unlike the sprawling concrete compound known to airline passengers today as Hartsfield International Airport. That evening it was blotchy with marshy areas so that the airplane splashed its way through muddy puddles of every size as it was positioned for takeoff into the southeast wind.

Kytle scarcely noticed the little snakes of water that writhed upward on the windshield and then blew off over his head in the propeller blast, but he was grateful that rain was no longer falling on him and running down his neck. He was feeling better all the time; he could see some ground lights almost a mile away as he rocked and bumped his way across the sodden surface.

Preparing to take off, the cautious pilot once again ran the beam of his flashlight over the switches, selectors, trim controls, and engine gauges and checked out the ignition system. Satisfied that his airplane was ready, he switched off the flashlight and dropped it into the left knee pocket of his flying coveralls, where it balanced the weight of the Colt .38 Bankers Special lodged in his right knee pocket. The pistol was required by Post Office regulations for guarding the mail—from what? the pilots had asked when issued the arms. He cinched up his lap belt, pulled the goggles over his eyes, and opened the throttle.

At first the Mailwing moved jerkily as its tail skid bit into uneven places in the ground, but with the control stick held full forward it was a matter of seconds until the tail came up and the airplane began to accelerate across the turf, blasting puddles into explosions of spray, and then lifted gracefully into its element.

Kytle did not have to look at the airspeed indicator to know when the airplane was ready to fly; he could feel lift developing in its wings and sensed the correct angle for climbing toward the clouds. Rising above the tree line, Johnny was pleased to see that visibility was good except where heavy rain showers dropped their gray veils from the overcast. It was better than he had expected. But only for a moment.

Seconds after takeoff he lost all visual ground contact as he entered the base of the clouds. The very abruptness came as a shock. The ceiling was not fifteen hundred feet, nor one thousand feet. It was probably not even five hundred feet. John Kytle knew that he was in a real bind unless he could descend and see the ground again.

For the vast majority of pilots in 1928, including air mail and military pilots, seat-of-the-pants flying was still the style. As long as an airman could see the horizon or several points on the earth's surface, it worked well, but controlling an aircraft solely by reference to instru-

The Pitcairn Mailwing takes off from rainsoaked Candler Field, Atlanta, for the first leg of its scheduled flight at Richmond.

ments in no-visibility conditions for more than a few seconds at a time was a total mystery and blundering into such a situation at low altitude could be lethal.

When the pilot was in cloud, strange sensations developed: illusions of turning, climbing, and diving. A pilot would respond instinctively to these aircraft movements. He would react reflexively and invariably wrongly, not realizing that he was suffering from a peculiar form of spatial confusion known as "vertigo," which usually resulted in a total loss of control within a few seconds. When this happened at high altitudes, as when climbing or descending through a high cloud deck, pilots frequently found themselves spinning out of the bottom of the clouds. It was not particularly hazardous when there was plenty of room underneath in which to recover—some pilots entered intentional spins when flying above a cloud deck for the purpose of descending through the layer with a known speed. Recovering from a spin at two or three thousand feet was easy, but Kytle knew that entering a spin at five hundred feet

En route, the pilot and his Mailwing were alone, totally out of contact with anyone on the ground.

had only one consequence.

Jim Ray, Pitcairn's chief pilot and operations manager, had cautioned his line pilots again and again that if they entered clouds inadvertently at low levels, they should maintain a steady heading and climb or descend slowly until visibility was regained, but never, *never*, *NEVER* to try to turn at low altitude, especially at night.

Climbing was out of the question for Kytle. The layer of nimbus clouds was undoubtedly several thousand feet thick. His only option

was to descend until he made eye-ball contact with the ground again. It took steely discipline to ignore his thumping heart and all of the illusory sensations that screamed at him to turn, but by keeping the heading nailed on 150 degrees and pulling the throttle back, he was still under control when the bright pinpoints of ground lights reappeared. So far, so good.

While solving his immediate problem, Kytle had created a second one: he had taken off and flown southeastwardly, approximately 90 degrees off his planned course to Spartanburg, and was slightly lost. Not completely lost; he had flown in the Atlanta area for years, but not when the weather was this low, at night.

The rolled-up strip chart in the container by his left knee would be of no use, even if he had a chance to study it under the beam of the flashlight. Air mail pilots had developed their own system of charting in those early days: using ordinary Rand-McNally road maps, they marked the routes and indicated the more prominent landmarks, pasted contiguous maps together so as to form a continuous course line, then cut the charts with scissors for twenty miles on each side parallel to the course. Under normal conditions the homemade scroll charts could be used in flight by unrolling them as the flight progressed to its destination, then rerolling them on the return trip. In his session with the low overcast, Johnny had flown off the area covered by his chart and would have to navigate by memory and experience if he were to get back on the lighted airway stretching to Richmond. To make matters worse, it was getting dark earlier than usual because of the thick clouds, and he could not see anything below that looked familiar.

His best guess was that the bottom of the clouds through which he was nipping were about three hundred or four hundred feet above the surface. Flying at almost two miles a minute, trying to keep visual contact so that he would not fly into an obstruction such as a tall tree or a silo, Johnny did not have time to glance at his altimeter; he was too busy bobbing his head from left to right to see what was ahead, for the long black fuselage and the top cylinders of the Whirlwind engine ten feet in front of his cockpit blocked most forward vision.

Making some quick mental calculations, Kytle estimated that he had flown southeast for perhaps five or six minutes, which would place him about ten miles out of Candler. If he turned left to a northerly heading, he should pass to the east of Atlanta and should be able to see its lights. Keeping close to the city to avoid Stone Mountain, he could proceed north until he intercepted the airway lights.

A glance to the right confirmed that the clouds were lower that way; gently, he turned left, repeatedly bursting through heavy rain showers which momentarily reduced forward visibility to zero, with rain smashing against the windscreen as from a high-pressure fire hose.

Intent on what might lie ahead, Kytle could not take refuge from the pounding rain by staying behind the screen; each time he peered around it, his face, unprotected beneath his goggles, was stung viciously.

After a few minutes, as Kytle continued to stay close to the ragged base of the clouds for terrain clearance, things began to look better. As the compass needle ended its wild swings and settled down on "N," Kytle could see farther off to each side between showers, so he sneaked a quick look at the altimeter. Eight hundred feet! The ceiling was higher as he proceeded northward.

The cushion of altitude gave him a chance to relax. He turned up the instrument panel lights and checked the panel-mounted clock.

"Let's see," he said to himself, chewing his lip in concentration. "We got off at seven-thirty. If we flew southeast for five minutes, we began our turn at seven-thirty-five, or so. It probably took a minute and a half to make that shallow turn and the clock now reads seven-forty-three, which means that we are probably abeam of Atlanta, even if I can't see it behind that rain shower over there. In a minute or two, I should be able to see the lights of the town of Stone Mountain." He settled back in his seat, pushed up his goggles, and began to massage his face.

At 7:44 he saw patterns of ground lights down to his right that looked like the streetlights of the town of Stone Mountain and beyond them, the zigzag pattern of lamps mounted on the stairways ascending the mountain itself, used by tourists to climb to the summit. Confident that he knew where he was at last, he swung around to 040 degrees. In a few minutes he would begin to pick up the airway lights.

When the Mailwing had taken off into the darkening gloom of night, Ben Faulkner continued to stand, hands on hips, out by the loading ramp, squinting at the little black and gold biplane rising toward the clouds, counting to himself, "A thousand and one, a thousand and two, a thousand and three . . ." As he said, "A thousand and twenty," the orange exhaust and wing-tip lights snuffed out, causing the field manager to frown. If that airplane was climbing at the normal 800 feet a minute, the ceiling was about 250, maybe 300 feet high, not very damn much.

Anticipating Kytle's decision to return, Faulkner lingered out front of the flight office for a few minutes, hoping for the familiar sound of the J-5, the radial engine made famous by the *Spirit of St. Louis*'s flight. When it did not come, he entered the little building alongside of the hangar, picked the receiver off the hook of the stand-up telephone on his desk, and called A. P. Kerr, Pitcairn's base manager at Spartanburg.

"Atlanta has a three-hundred-foot ceiling, going down, with intermittent heavy rain. Don't let anyone come this way tonight," he reported. Then he asked about Spartanburg's weather and was relieved to hear that they had a high, broken cloud cover, with some stars peeping through, a good night for flying. Trying to sound casual, as if it were an afterthought, he asked Kerr to do him a personal favor and call when Kytle arrived. He noted the time of the conversation on the office log. It was 7:44.

Now that he knew where he was and behind the protective windshield at last, John Kytle was comfortable and cozy. The engine was humming its mighty song, the air was as smooth as silk; at eight hundred feet, he was barely beneath the overcast, but the ceiling was bound to rise as he flew farther north.

Again, he turned up the panel lights to reaffirm that all the engine gauges were indicating normal operation and that his course was steady. He was as supremely happy as anyone can be who is well paid for doing what he loves to do—and be considered a hero for doing it. In 1928, an air mail pilot ranked right up there with movie stars when it came to glamour. And John Kytle was a bachelor.

Scanning the horizon off to each side of the engine's jutting cylinders, looking for a flashing airway beacon, he saw off to his left a cluster of lights that looked disturbingly familiar. Norcross? he wondered. Milburn?

Johnny glanced again at the panel clock, which read 7:45; then his eyes flicked back to the pattern of lights just ahead of his lower left wing. He sat up suddenly as if jolted by an electric shock. "My God," he said in disbelief as he pulled his goggles down. "*That's* the town of Stone Mountain!"

Leaning out to the side of his cockpit to see better from the Mailwing hurtling through the rainy night, he did not have time to react to the gray mass looming ahead as he flew into seven billion cubic feet of granite.

Faulkner was still cleaning up some paper work when the telephone rang. Too early for Kerr to call, he reasoned as his eyes scanned the clock on the office wall; it was only 7:55. Scooping up the earpiece he said, "Pitcairn, Atlanta."

A strange voice came on the line. "Did you have an air mail plane take off a little while ago?" it asked.

Faulkner's insides turned to ice water as he answered that he had.

"Well," the caller said somewhat haltingly, "someone flying northeast just hit Stone Mountain."

Totally numbed, the Atlanta manager went through the prescribed catastrophe drill: he called Operations Manager Jim Ray at his home in Bryn Athyn, Pennsylvania. When his old-time friend's cheery voice answered, Faulkner blurted out, "My God, Jim. Johnny Kytle's just hit Stone Mountain!" There was no use saying that he had been killed. Anyone would know that it was an unsurvivable accident.

Jim Ray, an old pro in the days when there were few old pros, was well aware of the hazards of flying the night mail on schedule. He had laid out the Pitcairn mail route and knew the terrain along the Eastern Seaboard as well as any man and was sensitive to the thoughts churning through the mind of his friend on the other end of the call.

"Are you *sure* it was Johnny?"

"No one but a mail pilot would be flying on a night like this," Faulkner said, remorseful that he had not put his foot down on the flight. "It *has* to be Johnny."

"Okay, then," Ray said slowly. "I'll be down as soon as I have notified the boss and can get to the airfield."

It was typical of Jim Ray to be on his way whenever there was any kind of operational problem on the airline's system. True to his word, immediately after he called Geof Childs, the company's vice president and general manager, he climbed into his own Mailwing and headed south. When he took off, he knew that he was flying into deteriorating weather and would in any event not arrive until the sun was about to rise.

When the grinding, tearing, scraping, gut-rending impact sounds finally stopped and everything was quiet, two thoughts passed through John Kytle's mind. The first was that he was dead and that this was what it was like: darkness and faint sounds of running water. The second thought was that the running water was from rain and that he was still alive.

Testing himself for injuries, he wiggled his toes, then his fingers, then swiveled his neck. The only unusual feeling was heaviness in his lower abdomen; he released the catch on his safety belt to relieve its pressure—and fell four feet from the upside-down cockpit of his wrecked Mailwing, landing headfirst on the granite surface. It was several moments before he realized that in the minor accident he had gashed his lip and broken the little finger of his right hand—the only injuries he had suffered in the entire incident.

Unsnapping the harness and shucking his heavy parachute, he rose unsteadily to his feet, determined to retrieve the mail sacks from the wreckage. Using the flashlight from his knee pocket and somewhat surprised to find it still in working condition, he took only a few minutes to pry into the mass of splintered wood, fabric, wires, and tree limbs—Tree limbs? he thought. Where did I pick *them* up?—and extricate the two small bags. Carrying the mail over his shoulder, the pilot began a weaving walk back to civilization over the rain-slicked surface of the gigantic boulder.

He did not get far. A few yards from the wreck, he came upon a drop-off as vertical as a high curb. Crouching slightly, he directed the beam of his flashlight downward and realized with a start that he was teetering dizzily on the brink of the north precipice and that the next step was eight hundred feet below. Then he understood the significance of the tree limbs: apparently, he had struck the top of the mountain a glancing blow and his airplane's wild slide had been arrested only a few feet short of the drop-off by hitting a small clump of trees on the summit, the sole bit of vegetation growing on the otherwise bare rock. Were it not for those trees . . . .

Johnny sat down to collect himself before making another move. Pretty dumb to get killed walking off the edge of the mountain after all this, he thought. It would be better to sit here until daylight, when I can see where I am walking. He sat on his parachute pack and waited.

Citizens of Stone Mountain had heard the now-familiar sound of the northbound mail plane, flying despite foul weather, then they heard the sound of the crash. Within min-

Front page of *The Atlanta Journal* covering Johnny Kytle's collision with Stone Mountain.

utes an informal search party had been pulled together and had begun the arduous trip to the crest. God only knew what they would find.

As the search group neared the summit, they saw someone far above waving a flashlight and hollering; reasonably, they concluded that another group had preceded them.

"Where's the pilot's body?" the leader of the lower group shouted between cupped hands.

"I'm the pilot's body," came the faint reply, making the climbers blanch. "I mean, *I'm* the pilot and

I'm all right. Just get me down off this damn mountain."

It took the better part of two hours to transport Kytle to the St. Joseph's Hospital, where they sewed up his lip, splinted his finger, and put him to bed, so that he *was* in bed before midnight, although not as he had planned.

Geof Childs, after receiving the bad news from Jim Ray at about eight o'clock in the evening, had tried to find out more from Faulkner in Atlanta. When he found that there was nothing new, he called Harold F. Pitcairn, the president of the airline, and relayed what information he did have.

"We have had an accident out of Atlanta," he said slowly, trying not to expose his own fears. "We have no details yet, but it looks as if John Kytle has flown into the side of Stone Mountain. Jim Ray is flying south and we should have complete information within a couple of hours. I just thought you should know about it."

Pitcairn sucked his breath in between clenched teeth, taking the news hard. His pilots were more to him than mere names on pay cards. In his little organization he knew almost all of his employees, their families, their children. Their safety was always uppermost in his mind. "Don't fly if the weather is not good," he instructed them. "Don't take any unnecessary chances. Your well-being is more important to me than flying the mail on time. We can always fly another day."

Now, faced with the death of one of his pilots, he realized how emotionally vulnerable he was. He sent his family upstairs to bed and kept a lonely vigil by the telephone in his study. Could anything be worth this, he asked himself.

About midnight the telephone bell jingled.

"Good news," came Geof's cheery voice. "Kytle is all right. The airplane is a total washout, but Johnny says he will be able to take his next regular turn on the line."

It took Pitcairn several seconds to absorb the incredible news. "He hit Stone Mountain and *survived?*" he asked incredulously. "How could that happen?"

The fuselage, mail bin, and cockpit stayed intact," Childs explained. "The airplane was completely demolished but the cockpit area came through in good shape."

"It is a miracle," Pitcairn said feelingly. "Just a miracle."

"Not entirely," responded Childs, somberly. "That was the way you built it."

# The Beckoning Sky

Harold Frederick Pitcairn had been air-minded since he could remember. As a child he had designed and built model airplanes from scratch and had flown them successfully. As he had grown older and approached full manhood, he had become obsessed with the idea of creating the Safe Aircraft, a machine that would be available to ordinary citizens and make personal air transportation as commonplace as driving motorcars. He was driven to do for aeronautics what Henry Ford had done for automobiling; his implacable ambition was to create the Wings of Man. His becoming the president of an airline had been an offshoot of that primary objective.

Born December 20, 1897, the fourth child of the affluent John Pitcairn and his wife, Gertrude, in the tiny religious community of Bryn Athyn, Pennsylvania, Harold Pitcairn was literally a child of the air age. Being born to wealth could have seduced him into a life of indolence and idleness, but his inheritance included more than money.

He was blessed with talent, energy, and imagination, and he was imbued and disciplined in the Work Ethic by his dynamic father.

Long before the Civil War, John Pitcairn had come to the United States from Scotland, a small child accompanying his immigrant parents. Starting from nothing and forced to leave school at the age of fourteen to help support his family, John had by dint of hard work, coupled with an inventive mind, engaged in numerous business ventures, eventually founding the Pittsburgh Plate Glass Company, with worldwide holdings. By the 1880s, through astute business dealings, John Pitcairn had become both a wealthy man and a giant of American industry.

He was also deeply religious; in his youth he had become a member of the General Church of the New Jerusalem (Swedenborgian), based on the theological writings of Emanuel Swedenborg (1688–1772), a remarkable Swedish scientist and philosopher who had devoted the later years of his life to a study of the Bible and had written some thirty volumes explaining the spiritual meaning of many of its passages. After Swedenborg's death a church organization was founded in Europe and soon spread to the United States, and John Pitcairn became a member of one of the most prominent societies of this church, located in Philadelphia. Because of a strong belief in the importance of religious education for the young, an academy had been founded there, but by 1896, the student body had outgrown the school's facilities, making it necessary to relocate where there would be room for future expansion. John Pitcairn purchased several large tracts of land and set about establishing the borough of Bryn Athyn, some twenty miles north of Penn's Greene Countrie Towne. He contributed substantial financial support for building the relocated Academy of the New Church and laid plans for the eventual construction of a cathedral for the society's worship of the Lord. Then he built a mansion surrounded by vast lawns and moved his family to Bryn Athyn so that his children might be educated in the academy.

Shortly after Harold was born, Gertrude died, leaving her fifty-seven-year-old husband with Raymond, aged thirteen; Vera, then ten years old; Theodore, a toddler of three; and the infant Harold. Enlisting the assistance of family and friends within the Church to provide the female love and affection that he believed the children needed, the grieving widower set about the task of raising his family.

Harold's first few years went by in relative isolation from the rest of the world, shuttling mostly between his home and school. In the early days of the twentieth century, life moved at a leisurely pace. Automobiles were rare; most transportation depended on horses and the trip from Bryn Athyn to Philadelphia, which now is measured in minutes, was an all-day affair over dirt or corduroy roads. Telephones were still in the experimental stage. Radio was yet to be invented for civilian use. Homes were illuminated by natural gas or coal-oil lamps and heated by wood fires or cracked coal, also used in stoves for cooking. Cross-country transportation for people and cargo depended on railroads, barges, or oceangoing ships.

But slowly, things were changing. In Europe, then in America, men were flying in balloons and in something new, called "Zeppelins," which were lifted by hydrogen gas and powered by lightweight internal-combustion engines. More and more automobiles and somewhat obnoxious, noisy vehicles called motorbikes or motorcycles were shattering the peace and tranquility of cities and towns. In Michigan a workable, low-cost benzine-fueled engine that was capable of being mass produced was thumping away in the shop of a young inventor named Henry Ford, who was planning to manufacture automobiles on a production line. Two brothers from Dayton, Ohio, were quietly experimenting with gliders, while the famous Professor Samuel Pierpont Langley was pursuing similar endeavors, funded by the United States Government and the Smithsonian Institution.

Harold Pitcairn was six years old, just entering the lower grades of the Academy of the New Church, when the Wright brothers first flew at Kitty Hawk in a powered aircraft. By 1910, as a perceptive teen-ager, he was reading with care and deliberation articles in newspapers and magazines about the exploits of early aeronauts and was soon caught up in the new science of aeronautics.

Exhibition flying was by then reaching its zenith. Virtually every county fair of any size featured a flying show by daredevil airmen mounted on frail machines built by the Wright brothers or Glenn Curtiss, including races between aeroplanes and horses and automobiles and other aeroplanes. Crowds were brought to their feet again and again by performances of "stunting" at low altitude.

Such aeronautical thrill shows had captured the public's attention despite the widely held opinion that, notwithstanding the government's interest in testing the Wright machine at Fort Myer, Virginia, for possible military use, aeroplanes did not—and probably never would—make any significant contribution to society as a whole. Civil aeronautics was considered by skeptics (naturally, they viewed themselves as realists) as nothing more than a passing fancy, a transient craze like six-day bicycle racing, or as a macabre form of entertainment closely related to the then-current insanity of plunging over Niagara Falls in barrels. Flying was relegated merely to being a quick way to achieve notoriety and make a few dollars—if one survived. No sensible, rational person could believe, it was said, that aeronautics held any possibilities as a legitimate form of transportation. It was pointed out that the largest machines in existence could carry only one or two people at a time, for a few miles, at best.

For several years Harold Pitcairn avidly read newspaper reports about exhibition airmen who performed breathtaking gyrations in those crude, delicately constructed aeroplanes. Incredibly (in retrospect), they did so without serious injuries or fatalities. He knew most of them by name: Lincoln Beachey, Arch Hoxsey, Calbraith Rodgers, Eugene Ely, John Moisant, Philip Parmalee; and female pilots, too: Julia Clarke and Ruth Law.

When he was only thirteen years old, Harold Pitcairn's life was again touched by tragedy, this time by the loss of his sister Vera. Only twenty-three years old, she had become his surrogate mother. His austere father had remained somewhat remote and the difference in their ages had kept Harold and his brothers from being close pals. Raymond had by then graduated from law school and had been admitted to the bar and Theo, although only three years older, brooked him merely as a kid brother. With Vera gone, he was left emotionally adrift and turned more and more to his love of flying.

Over the next two years the lethal potential of flying became a matter of public knowledge and concern as newspapers reported with sobering regularity that one after another famous aviation personages had met their deaths while performing. As a result, by 1913 the public's wild enthusiasm for the spectacular aspects of aviation had waned and most people had turned to other interests.

Progressing through the classes of the academy, Harold Pitcairn was never a brilliant student, but he achieved good grades by hard study. An avid competitor, he participated in numerous school activities, represented the academy on its athletic

teams, and belonged to several clubs. After Vera's death, everyone noted that he tended more to be quietly thoughtful, reticent, and reserved to the point of shyness in the presence of adults or strangers. His innate zest showed only when in the company of a small group of his friends from school who knew him to be enthusiastic, vigorous, good-humored, and frequently given to groan-inducing punning, all traits that carried over to his adult life. There was one major difference between Harold and his classmates: while they were off playing childhood games, his main pleasure was delving into aeronautics.

By the time he was fourteen years old, he was spending more and more of his free time with Otho Heilman, a close friend, building and flying model airplanes of original design, continuously experimenting with various airfoil shapes and wing planforms, including radical swept-

The first airplane designed and built by Harold Pitcairn, aged 15. The scaled-up version built the next year led to his training at Curtiss in the summer of 1914.

wings and delta wings, which would one day be commonplace. They were then revolutionary. No one, including his father, who was seventy years old at the time, considered his intense concentration on aviation to be any more than a transient form of technological puppy love that would pass with maturity.

It was not until the summer of 1912, while fifteen-year-old Pitcairn was visiting Atlantic City with relatives, that he saw a real airplane for the first time. A Curtiss flying boat, passing repeatedly overhead along the beach, attracted the youth to join the crowd of curious people hanging over the railings of the famous boardwalk. Time after time, all day long, he watched the perky little biplane land and take off amid clouds of spray from the choppy inlet. Lunchtime came and went, but the fascinated lad never noticed the passage of time; he stayed and watched until the sun went down and the flying was over for the day.

As soon as the family returned to Bryn Athyn, the youngest Pitcairn quietly cleared an area in the rear bay of the estate's large carriage house and set about designing and building a glider large enough to carry him, in the manner of the Wright brothers' early experiments. Over the long winter and well into the late spring, Harold and Otho worked and finally completed the glider by the summer of 1913, when the aspiring pilot pronounced that it was ready to fly.

His plan was to set the contraption on a sledge or pallet normally used for hauling tree stumps, stones, and other heavy objects; the sledge would be drawn rapidly down the rather steep grade by a brace of spirited ponies borrowed for the occasion from the well-stocked Pitcairn stables.

In theory, as the ponies moved off at a smart clip, a brisk wind would be created over the wings and the craft would rise into the air with its youthful payload. Otho's proposed function was to whip the ponies up to speed; two girls of the neighboring Glenn family would be induced to take positions at the wing tips to balance the glider, merely trotting alongside for a few yards until it became airborne and would waft Harold to a gentle landing at the bottom of the hill, three or four hundred feet from lift-off.

As the plan was revealed, Heilman was gripped by towering dubiety, for he had read about spectacular and frequently fatal accidents that had befallen prominent, experienced airmen. But Harold assuaged his fears by pointing out that they had built and flown many small models successfully in the past from that very hill and that, since all he had done was increase the dimensions of the craft to a size that would carry his weight, the forthcoming flight should be equally successful. The lack of any flight controls, he added nonchalantly, was of minor importance; the Wright brothers had at first maneuvered their early gliders by shifting their weight about, and if it had worked for them, it should work just as well for him. The logic may have been assailable to an older person, but Otho's trepidations were sufficiently allayed that he agreed to go along with the scheme.

On a bright Saturday summer afternoon, as squadrons of puffy cumulus clouds were propelled across a blue sky, and with the partly finished Bryn Athyn Cathedral as a background, the launching project was put into action atop the tallest hill in the area. With the tow rope pulled taut on the glider-bearing sledge, the girls positioned at the wing tips and Otho's whip at the ready, the pilot braced himself in hopeful expectation and gave the signal.

Heilman snapped the whip, jerked the reins, and began to dash madly down the hillside, the ponies straining beside him, the girls running at the wing tips with skirts swirling and Harold bouncing violently, holding on for dear life as the glider flounced and vibrated on the improvised launching platform skewing and sliding on the turf.

Never in the wild, hundred-yard dash did the glider exhibit the slightest tendency to arise from the sledge. When he ran out of room at the bottom of the slope, Heilman drew the ponies up abruptly, only to be engulfed by the onrushing glider, sledge, attendants, and its lone occupant, all winding up spectacularly in a heap in the middle of a briar patch at the edge of the tree

line. Except for a few scratches which soon healed, no one was hurt, although the glider was reduced to kindling.

Undaunted by what was to be the first in a long career of aeronautical first-attempt failures, Pitcairn determined to try again and quickly turned to analyzing what had gone wrong so that the next effort would be crowned with success. The move did not pass unnoticed by his father.

John Pitcairn, then aged seventy-three, had watched his youngest son's development from childhood to boyhood with pleasure and satisfaction, for the lad clearly had initiative, drive, perseverance, and personal courage. John also had begun to realize that his son's interest in aeronautics was not as ephemeral as he had hoped it might be and that Harold was determined to try again. The old man was fully aware of the hazards of flying and had already suffered two personal losses, so he could have stepped in and ended the matter then and there. It speaks something for the man that he did not. The senior Pitcairn would not blunt his son's enthusiasm for flying, no matter how much the potential for harm worried him. Instead, he took the venturesome boy aside and gave him some paternal advice about the unproductive and time-wasting aspects of re-inventing the wheel. If anyone is seriously interested in pursuing any project, he counseled, one must first learn everything there is to know about it from the best sources and greatest experts available, prior to embarking on any overt course of action. The unequivocal key to success, he told his son, was thorough preparation as the foundation for making an educated, informed decision; the best way to learn to swim was by taking lessons from a competent instructor, not by jumping into deep water and hoping for the best.

Then the old man demonstrated that, in his characteristically meticulous way, he had done *his* homework. After extensive research, he had concluded that the best place for a young man to learn about aeroplanes was at the feet of masters in the busiest, most successful aircraft factory in the United States, that of Glenn H. Curtiss.

It was common knowledge that since 1911 Glenn Curtiss had been producing a variety of aeroplanes and flying boats in Hammondsport, which is situated at the south end of Keuka Lake, one of the famous Finger Lakes of western New York state, and that he operated full-blown flying schools for military and civilian pilot training. Not so widely known, however, was that sometimes he also employed apprentices to work on his production lines, making both aircraft and engines. John Pitcairn informed his ecstatic son that it had been arranged for him to be employed as an apprentice in the Curtiss aircraft factory during the next summer vacation from school, so that while working on the line he could learn how real, full-sized airplanes were constructed.

That fateful decision would leave an indelible mark on the world of aviation.

# Introduction to Flying

Normally a small community of some twelve hundred inhabitants, in the summer of 1914 Hammondsport had ballooned to many times that size. There were several reasons for its population explosion.

The Curtiss aeroplane and engine factories were going full blast, with several new models in various stages of development. New Curtiss Model J tractor aircraft, both land and floatplane versions, which were gradually replacing the older pusher types, were being eyed with considerable interest by military observers of both the United States and several foreign governments for possible military applications, in view of the fact that across the Atlantic, increasing saber rattling was winding political tensions tighter and tighter.

In addition, large numbers of newspaper reporters were covering all aspects of what promised to be an historic event: the first attempt to fly across the Atlantic Ocean in a heavier-than-air machine. In February, Rodman Wanamaker, a New York merchant—an afficionado of aeronautics, and a pilot—proposed to make the flight in a Curtiss flying boat especially designed and constructed for that purpose. The announcement quickly elicited many other cash prizes for a successful crossing. During the summer of 1914 Curtiss was putting the finishing touches on the flying boat *America* and engaging in preliminary test hops, planning for the nonstop attempt in early fall.

Last, but not least—in fact the most serious activity of all, which drew its own crowd—were Curtiss's efforts to overcome the legal decision in the patent-infringement case that had been brought against him by the Wright brothers. If he could not overturn the judicial findings, he would lose everything—his factory, his personal assets, his future. He would be ruined.

Basically the case turned on the court's concept of a "pioneer" invention. When the Wright brothers had flown their powered aeroplane in 1903, lateral control had been effected by twisting the wings slightly, one tip up, the other down, a system that had been fully covered by their patents. Glenn Curtiss, an engine developer, had established himself in motorcycle racing and then had supplied engines for some of the lighter-than-air balloons of the era. He had also become affiliated with a group of aeronautical experimenters in heavier-than-air machines and had designed a pusher-type biplane with rigid wings, achieving lateral control by small, movable planes, called ailerons, so as not to infringe the Wright patents. Nevertheless, the Wrights claimed infringement and a court upheld their claim, saying that since they were pioneers in the art and science of controllable flight, every subsequent control system would inferentially be based on their original patented format. The court concluded that Curtiss had infringed the Wright patents and directed him to pay a license fee retroactively for every aeroplane that he had sold, an amount far beyond his financial resources.

Curtiss's attorneys believed that they had technological grounds for overturning the decision: a prior-art invention, the Langley Aerodrome, then hanging in the halls of the Smithsonian Institution in Washington, bearing the descriptive placard, "The first powered aeroplane capable of sustained man-carrying flight."

Samuel Pierpont Langley's Aerodrome had crashed ignominiously into the Potomac River a week before the Wright brothers' epic flight at Kitty Hawk, but the crash had been attributed to improper launching techniques, since he had flown numerous small-scale powered models of similar design with great success. According to the legal argument, if it could be demonstrated that, but for the faulty launch, the Aerodrome would have flown, the Langley aeroplane would make its inventor the pioneer, with the Wrights' position being legally inferior. Since Curtiss had so much turning on this narrow issue, he received the approval of the Smithsonian to resurrect the Aerodrome, transport it to Hammondsport where he would rebuild it, and fly it to prove the point. The flight test program of the refurbished Aerodrome was administered during the summer of 1914; hence Hammondsport was awash with observers representing every inventor and manufacturer who had any interest in aeronautics.*

Harold Pitcairn, the eager seventeen-year-old apprentice, was a front-row spectator of these momen-

* The rebuilt Aerodrome flew, but barely, about the same way that the huge flying boat created by Henry J. Kaiser and Howard Hughes was to fly some three decades later: it rose a few feet from the water, flew for a few seconds, then alighted. However, one of the observers was named Lorin Wright—the third Wright brother. Armed with an excellent camera, he took many photographs of the Langley-Curtiss machine and Wright attorneys were able to prove to the satisfaction of the appeals court that the aircraft had been so extensively modified that it was no longer the Aerodrome. The Wright brothers ultimately prevailed in their infringement suit.

tous activities, the effect of which would eventually have a great bearing on his own future in a manner then undreamed of. The deep implications of primacy in applying for patent protection of a mechanical concept were permanently implanted in the young man's mind.

It appears that the youthful Pitcairn did not receive any formal flying instruction during this sojourn in the Finger Lakes region. Occasionally he may have flown as a passenger as a reward for helping to move aeroplanes into and out of hangars or for manhandling floatplanes and flying boats in the chilly waters of Lake Keuka, but most of his time was spent in the factory, learning to bend and glue spruce, hickory, and white ash and to fashion spars and ribs, and to mate wings with fuselages and boat hulls. By actually fashioning subassemblies and rigging wires and control systems under supervision, he began to comprehend the complexities of creating a real man-carrying aeroplane. In the evening when older men were off socializing, the quiet youngster usually retreated to his room in the Lakefront Hotel to make careful notes and detailed diagrams of what he had learned that day. By the end of the summer his notebook was bulging.

The peaceful course of world affairs was to be derailed that summer; as June had ebbed into history, a young political fanatic had shot and killed a duke and duchess in an obscure town in the Balkans, named Sarajevo. With the mainspring of international tensions fully flexed, this pull of the trigger set pre-existing military plans irresistibly into motion in every European capital, and by August German big guns were flattening Liège. With that, the Great War began.

When he returned to school from his summer experience, Harold Pitcairn had matured physically and mentally. Aircraft designs that he drew in his free time were no longer childish doodlings but the drafting efforts of a serious student of aeronautics. Within five months he completed a full set of plans for a small twin-engine hydro-aeroplane, meticulously accurate down to the sizes of screw eyes and rigging wires, based in part on successful Curtiss designs he had observed, but incorporating the dart-shaped planform of his earlier small-scale flying models. Then he moved the collection of horse-drawn carriages, pony carts, and sleighs out of the carriage house on his father's estate and began to build a full-sized aircraft based on those plans.

Otho Heilman was again his chief confederate; as the machine took shape, Otho again became apprehensive about the project's logical conclusion, especially when Harold announced that, come spring, he planned to transport it to the Delaware River at a point some five miles south of Bryn Athyn, and fly it. When Otho mildly inquired how he was going to learn to fly, Pitcairn replied seriously that he proposed to taxi it across the water fast enough to rise from the surface a few inches, fly enough to gain a feel for the controls, and alight again. If anything did not feel just right, all he had to do was retract the throttle and land immediately. Heilman thought it over, and agreed to continue to help. At least there were no briar patches on the river. Nor ponies.

By June, as soon as school had recessed for the summer, Harold was ready to try his wings. Perhaps fortunately, the plan fell short on the important logistics of transporting the ungainly, frail aircraft from his home in Bryn Athyn to the banks of the Delaware: where Wright and Curtiss demonstration aircraft were shipped to exposition sites in large, stoutly constructed, well-padded shipping crates which held them rigidly and protected them from harm, Pitcairn proposed to tote his hydro-aeroplane completely assembled, on the bed of a horse-drawn, unsprung wagon along a route he had laid out over several miles of rough, unimproved dirt roads that crossed rugged farming country. Perhaps it was fortunate that the airplane did not survive the trip. A mile or so from the selected launching site, the wagon lurched crazily as one wheel dropped into a deep rut and another rose high on a tree root, causing its fragile cargo to dance sideways; despite Otho's valiant efforts to save it, the delicate cargo slid off the cart and was smashed into junk.

Disappointed, but not crushed by the accident that had wiped out almost a year's work in an instant, Pitcairn picked up the debris and returned home, vowing to start immediately with the construction of another flying machine. This time the project was quickly short-stopped by his father.

Once again John Pitcairn spoke to his intensely ambitious son—in somewhat more authoritarian, forceful terms—about the time-wasting futility of discovering the techniques that others have already perfected. If Harold wanted to fly so badly, snapped the old man, he should have enough sense to learn how to do so from competent instructors. It was sheer nonsense to do otherwise. Then, with a softened tone, John Pitcairn told his son that since he was so determined to fly, he would help him to go about it the right way. Upon graduation from preparatory school, he would finance the lad's attendance at the Curtiss Flying School located at Newport News, Virginia. First, however, Harold had to finish his formal schooling.

By 1916, flying was very much in the news again. The war in Europe had accelerated the development of aircraft for military purposes, first for observing enemy troop deployments, then for bombing concentrations and routes of movement. In turn, this had led to a new, highly improved generation of airplanes designed to intercept and destroy the opponents' eyes in the sky by what were then called "pursuit" planes. Names like Fokker, Sopwith, Nieuport, and DeHavilland appeared regularly in the American press.

In the United States, Glenn Curtiss's star was in the ascendancy as a result of the growing pressures for military preparation, which had momentarily taken the patent litigation problem off his shoulders. The United States Army was also exploring the military possibilities of aircraft, for in March 1916 General John J. Pershing had been ordered into Mexico because of border incidents involving the bandit Pancho Villa, who had raided Columbus, New Mexico, and killed some American citizens. "Black Jack" Pershing's force of six thousand troops was equipped with several Curtiss "JN" aircraft for aerial spotting, liaison, and fast communications in the wide open spaces of the campaign, with the newly constituted First Aero Squadron commanded by a Major Benjamin D. Foulois.

By the summer of 1916 Curtiss had established several flying schools in various parts of the country, San Diego, Buffalo, and Newport News being the largest, and late in June the newly arrived group of Curtiss students at Newport News included nineteen-year-old Harold Pitcairn.

It was Pitcairn's first real exposure to the rough-and-ready world. Having been reared in the protective environment of Bryn Athyn, where religious training and the nice manners of social graces were the way of life, he did not mesh immediately with the somewhat boisterous aggregation of newcomers, most of whom were several years older than he and were given to rough jokes, needling remarks, and loud talk, typical of young men thrown together. He felt at loose ends for several days, until he crossed paths with another student of his own age, also just out of high school and also from Pennsylvania. His name was Agnew Larsen, from York. Theirs was to be a long and fruitful friendship.

They were attending the school for different reasons. Pitcairn was there to learn to fly, becaused he believed that such was a prerequisite to making a lifelong career in aviation; knowing the problems from personal experience would give him the background to make informed judgments as a businessman in the years ahead. He was convinced that his own future lay in that direction. Larsen, whose background was in drafting and mechanical drawing, was not interested in learning to fly. He, too, had made the decision to follow a profession in what he believed to be the great new industry called aviation. He planned to be an aeronautical engineer.

For the next five weeks, when sessions of flying instruction and engineering classes had been secured for the day, the two young men talked far into the night, speculating about how American aviation would develop and what their roles might be, never considering that within the decade they would team up to make aviation history.

Pitcairn believed that the growth of personal air transportation—"private" flying, as he called it—would be enhanced if it could somehow be made independent operationally from special aviation centers called "flying fields." He had absorbed the fact that Glenn Curtiss had begun to experiment with hydro-aeroplanes and flying boats for just that reason, recognizing that most communities lie adjacent to water in some form: bays, lakes, rivers, whereas there were still only a handful of "flying fields" in the country. But not everyone lived close to water—Harold was still smarting from the disastrous experience with the flying boat of the previous summer—so that was not the answer to flying-for-everyone, either.

Their extended discussion began to center on the idea that aircraft design inevitably had to move away from the fixed-wing concept, which required the entire aircraft to move through the atmosphere fast enough to develop lift in its wings, which in turn meant long takeoff and landing runs—and restricting them to use only flying fields. The future, they agreed, lay in developing a rotating-wing device called the helicopter, which had been imagined and named in the sixteenth century by Leonardo da Vinci, who even created a set of crude drawings to demonstrate the principle of rotary flight. By moving the wings on a spindle, the lifting surfaces could develop thrust so that the aircraft could rise and descend vertically, making possible zero-forward speed takeoffs and landings and eliminating the need for prepared airfields.

A helicopter could operate from one's backyard. Pitcairn and Larsen's youthful enthusiasm was not dampened by the fact that experiments by numerous inventors before them had always led to failure.

Up to that time, experimenters had been successful only in creating devices that would rise straight up, but the ability to translate into controllable horizontal flight was beyond aeronautical technology. Nonetheless, the young students agreed that it should become possible as more was learned about the physics of flight—and that whoever developed the mechanism that could make vertical flight possible would change the course of aviation.

For Harold Pitcairn, the first part of the summer of 1916 was a period of sheer joy. He learned to fly. He experienced that inexpressible thrill of climbing into the sky and wheeling high over Hampton Roads. From the time he first soloed, he experienced a new freedom. He was in love with flying.

Then, when evening came, he joined Larsen and became immersed in discussions about airfoils and thrust and the inherent problems of the helicopter. What more could a young man want?

However, the happy idyll was suddenly shattered: a telegram was brought to him as he returned from a flight. His brother Raymond informed him that their father had died and that Harold had to return home for the funeral.

# Military Pilot

Raymond Pitcairn, then a thirty-two-year-old lawyer, immediately became the titular head of the family and assumed the burden of handling its affairs. Theodore, the second son, was a twenty-two-year-old divinity student preparing to follow the call of his Church; his course through life had already been charted. As far as most people were concerned, Harold, the youngest Pitcairn, was following an irresponsible, imprudent direction. In a quiet conversation Raymond told his younger brother that the time had come for him to forego all that nonsense about aviation. He must buckle down and obtain a formal education that would prepare him properly for the day when he would ascend to the function of administering the family fortune, in accordance with their father's well-laid plan.

Recognizing the reasonableness of the argument, Harold Pitcairn enrolled in the Wharton School of Business at the University of Pennsylvania, intent on preparing himself for his destiny. But his heart was still in the sky.

Plugging along through courses in history, accounting, economics, and business practice, he engaged in regular correspondence with his friend, Agnew Larsen, who in the meantime had become apprenticed to an engineering firm. Pitcairn's fertile mind continually poured out a succession of rotary-wing ideas, illustrated by his own sometimes rough drawings. He paid Larsen a small retainer from his personal funds to refine the drawings and make wooden working models. During the winter of 1916–1917, experimenting with a variety of methods for overcoming the torque problems of rotating wings and the lateral instability created by horizontal flight, they created fourteen purely vertical-lift devices of increasing scale. They were preparing to build a man-carrying version with a twenty-five-rotor diameter, preliminary to addressing the enormous problem of translating to horizontal flight.

The war in Europe, which had begun in 1914 and erupted in all directions on the Continent, had bogged down in a bloody standoff of trench warfare. Far above the pulverized ground of "no man's land," a new type of fierce combat had evolved.

The public looked upon air combat as a type of latter-day knighthood, with one-on-one jousts. By 1917 the names of leading airmen who had accumulated the greatest number of kills had created a new roll of public heroes: the Red Knight of Germany, von Richthofen, was the best known. But there were others, almost as well known: Fonck, Nungesser, Mannock, Bishop, Udet, McCudden, Goering. Except for a few intrepid volunteers, such as Raoul Lufbury, the Rockwell brothers, William Thaw, Norman Prince, and others who donned French uniforms and fought in an all-American group known as the Layfayette Escadrille, virtually no Americans were engaged in the European carnage, except as ambulance drivers and medical aides.

On the western side of the Atlantic, everyone hoped that this would remain the case, for President Wilson had maintained a position of strict neutrality for the United States.

But in the last two years public sentiment in America had slowly begun to change. It began as a ripple of indignation with the sinking of the unarmed ocean liner *Lusitania.* The loss of more than one thousand passengers and crewmen, including 115 American citizens, had horrified and inflamed the nation. With the

subsequent onset of Germany's unrestricted submarine attacks, public sentiment became weighted in favor of joining the Allies and bringing the hostilities to a quick and successful end. Carrying a heavy schedule of business courses, Harold Pitcairn was stirred to join the army. The pressure was building to make the great step, although it would surely change the direction of the rest of his life.

For many months the perceptible drift toward war was finely balanced between isolationist and idealist segments of the national community, and as the national elections began to shape up, the political schism was reflected in the springing up of many antiwar organizations and the major—perhaps the only—campaign posture assumed by Woodrow Wilson, running for his second term, that "he kept us out of the war." However, the Congress, more sensitive to the trend of the great mass of the electorate, had begun to pump financial appropriations into military departments, trying to make up for twenty years of niggling budgets imposed on them. As a result, the U.S. Army Signal Corps suddenly had funds to acquire airplanes for its newly created Aero Service, which formed the First Aero Squadron, composed of low-powered Curtiss JN-model airplanes and had assigned them under a young captain, Benjamin D. Foulois, to accompany General Pershing's strike force into Mexico. With the Air Service beginning to expand rapidly, there was a desperate need for trained pilots to fly them.

Pitcairn was relaxing one evening in his room at the university, trying to catch up with all of the latest developments in the international situation, particularly in the rapid advancements being made in European aviation by reading a recently received issue of *Aviation*, when a headline fairly leaped off the page: WAR DEPARTMENT ASKS ADDRESSES OF CIVILIAN AVIATORS.

Eagerly, the young student began to run his eye down the list of 817 civilians, to see how many of them he might know either from reading in the press or from personal contact at the Curtiss Flying School. Every time he saw a recognizable name, he nodded: Bert Acosta, Vincent Astor, Tom Benoist, Glenn H. Curtiss, Walter Fairchild, Beckwith Havens, Anthony Jannus, Glenn H. Martin, Harold F. Pitcairn!

He looked again. Yes, there was his name in print, listed right along with those of many famous airmen. The reason was clear: U.S. military aviation authorities, woefully unprepared to enter a war that most of them believed was coming, had combed the records of every flight school in existence, trying to locate experienced pilots from whom a basic flying organization could be formed. Pitcairn recounted the names on the list; there were not even one thousand pilots in the United States and many of those listed would be ineligible for military pilot training, either because of age or need in manufacturing plants. Pitcairn's mind was made up that evening. His country needed him and he would be a poor patriot if he did not volunteer to serve in the highly specialized field for which he had been trained and which had been a part of him since he was a small child.

He wrote his current address on a postal card and mailed it off to the War Department, volunteering his services in any capacity within the Air Service. Six weeks later the United States of America formally declared war on Germany.

The United States bureaucracy ballooned with the ponderous transition from peace to a wartime footing. While lofty speeches were made in Congress about deluging the enemy with an overpowering array of men and equipment, the actual effort to put the promises into practice was slow and painful. It was almost another year before Pitcairn donned the khaki uniform of his country and was posted to his first assignment in a hastily constructed military establishment, Penn Airfield in Austin, Texas. It was a tremendous let-down for the energetic volunteer.

Pitcairn had anticipated an open-arms welcome as someone special, a trained pilot. But when he arrived at Penn, he was just another hopeful cadet, one of thousands at a basic training base, where he was required to go through a 460-hour prescribed program which had no

Harold and Clara Pitcairn in the summer of 1918 while he was in training as a military aviator.

terpretation, and radio operation. Finally, he was re-introduced to the theory of flight and the repair and rerigging of slightly damaged aircraft.

When he received his orders for flight training as a member of Aero Squadron 63, at Rich Field, Waco, Texas, his mood improved, only to be dashed again. Since he had learned to fly at Newport News some eighteen months before, aircraft control systems had been changed. The old Curtiss shoulder yoke, by which the pilot turned into a bank by leaning in the direction of the direction he wished to turn, had been supplanted in the latest JN-4 training planes by the European style of Deperdussen controls, which were much the same as the control wheel system used today. Pitcairn had to learn to fly all over again.

By the end of the sixteen-week course, during which he flew three or four hours a day, Pitcairn progressed from fundamental flying to simple aerobatics, formation flying, air-to-air gunnery, ground strafing, and bomb dropping. It was an exhausting schedule, but he enjoyed flying more and more, until he began to experience the loss of some of his newfound friends in airplane crashes, his first real experience with the lethal aspects of aviation.

Even with the slow-motion flight characteristics of the high-drag, low-powered Jennies, the rushing of hundreds of young men through training every day ensured that accidents were almost commonplace.

flying activities. He learned close-order drill, infantry tactics, the care and use of gas masks, map reading, signaling, and camp hygiene. He shot the service rifle courses at all ranges and spent hours on end waiting in lines for food, for mail, for everything.

Toward the end of the basic course, things began to look better. He studied aerial navigation, photography from aircraft and photo in-

That many of them were fatal moved Cadet Pitcairn deeply. As he packed the personal effects of some of his barracks mates, to be sent home to grieving parents, he agonized over what he considered unnecessary deaths in what should have been survivable accidents.

Military specifications still required that basic aircraft structures be of wood, mostly spruce for lightness, essentially as the early Wright and Curtiss aeroplanes had been built. Under the impact of what were frequently minor crashes, airplanes splintered, snapped, and disintegrated into piles of rubbish, usually resulting in death or serious injury for their occupants. Pitcairn was certain that if the airplanes had been constructed of sturdier materials, most of the victims could have walked away unaided from the accidents. He wrote, in his weekly letters to his childhood sweetheart, Clara Davis, back in Bryn Athyn, that someday airplanes would be built stronger and safer, adding perhaps hopefully that it would be done even if he had to build them himself. But first there was a war to fight and he was itching to get into it. He was almost finished with his basic training at the aviation school and would soon be transferred to San Diego for transition into combat types of airplanes, after which he would receive his wings as an Air Service pilot. Then he would be sent overseas to meet the enemy.

Pitcairn never got to fight in it. He was on his way to his final post before an assignment to combat when the Armistice was signed, with which all further military training stopped and the United States began to beat its swords into plowshares. Harold Pitcairn returned home and on January 21, 1919, married Clara.

With his honorable discharge hanging on the wall of the living room in their new home, the twenty-two-year-old Pitcairn had to come to grips with the great decision of what to do with his life. As was the case with many ex-servicemen, he was at loose ends. His formal education had been interrupted by the war, but he had three choices for lifelong careers: he could re-enter school and study for the ministry, as his brother Theo had done, for Harold Pitcairn was also deeply religious and believed implicitly in the ethical philosophy of the Church of the New Jerusalem under which he had been raised. Indeed, for a time he entered theological school, but he could never put aviation out of his mind. He heard the call of the sky more than the call of his Church.

But he was a practical man, which balanced his emotional, enthusiastic attitude about aviation. From his study of the industry in the years following the war, he perceived that the time was not propitious for becoming personally involved. Although United States aviation leaders had proclaimed publicly in January 1919 that the future looked bright for their industry because the public had redeveloped its affection for flying, as a potential investor knowledgeable in the affairs of the industry, Pitcairn had concluded that its immediate future was clouded and that its long-range picture was doleful. From his studies of the financial journals and a few minor investments in some of the leading aviation companies so that he was supplied with periodic financial reports, Pitcairn had seen clearly that the entire aviation industry, which had sprung up during the war nurtured by plush government contracts for military aircraft and engines, had been left hanging by wholesale cancellations of orders that followed the Armistice. From then on aircraft manufacturers would have to look entirely to the civilian market.

But what market? Thousands of JN-4s, the venerable "Jenny"—some old and verging on decrepitude, some brand-new—and hundreds of thousands of factory-fresh OX-5 engines, still swathed in protective Cosmoline and crated in their original factory shipping boxes, lay in military surplus inventories when the war ended. Some three thousand 400-hp Liberty engines, designed to power America's DH-4 airplanes, slated to be the backbone of the U.S. war effort (they never saw a moment of action and were militarily obsolete before they were produced), were still stacked, also preserved in Cosmoline, in government warehouses. Low-cost surplus airplanes and equipment would obviously saturate the civilian market and destroy any volume sales poten-

tial for new machines, no matter how good they might be.

By the middle of 1919, civil aviation in the United States had become the realm of gypsy pilots, many of whom, having learned to fly in the Air Service, had snapped up surplus Jennies for as low as three hundred dollars and began to eke out a happy-go-lucky living by performing at country fairs, bouncing around the countryside, using cornfields and cow pastures as operating bases from which to sell sight-seeing hops for whatever price the traffic would bear. Unregulated, undisciplined, disorganized, it was almost 1912 all over again, with wing walkers, parachute jumpers, thrill show aerobatics featuring low-level antics, frequently ending in disaster. Aviation in America had once again devolved to being merely a form of mass entertainment, rather than developing into a legitimate form of transportation. Considering the disheveled state of aviation, Harold Pitcairn was satisfied to remain on the sidelines, little more than an interested spectator. He took a position with the efficiency department of the Pittsburgh Plate Glass Company in Crystal City, Pennsylvania, moved his new bride to a new home in a strange place, and began to raise a family.

There was more to the momentous move than that: he was also going to learn modern business practices at the feet of older men already skilled in such techniques.

# Businessman

Although it might have seemed that he had put aviation out of his mind, Harold Pitcairn, while plugging away at his business career in western Pennsylvania, kept abreast of developments in the United States as a subscriber to virtually all aviation and financial journals. Fiscally cautious to the point of being leery of investing in aeronautical concerns, he had been following a most interesting trend.

The Manufacturers Aircraft Association, formed during the war for the purpose of cross-licensing aircraft patents, had continued to function after the Armistice to preserve the industry in the face of the government's surplus aircraft policies. MAA had announced with great fanfare a design competition for a new generation of air-mail airplanes, including classes with two-, three-, and four-engine designs, to replace the fleet of single-engine aircraft then used by the Post Office Department's Air Mail Service. Within a two-month span, aviation magazines announced that more than a dozen different plans had been elic-ited by the solicitation, all submitted by aircraft manufacturers with famous names. Harold, with his fingers always on aviation's pulse, recognized, as lay readers would not, that the competition was a ploy, a political promotion to snare the attention of Congress. Aviation entrepreneurs and developers knew that without some sort of direct financial assistance from the federal government, the reeling industry was certain to go broke across the board and that the sole avenue for such financial aid was by way of federal mail subsidies. The announcement of the design competition was the opening gun in the political campaign to obtain it.

Air-mail flying in the United States had an interesting background. In May of 1918, while the Great War was still going on, the Army Air Service had initiated air-mail flights between New York, Philadelphia, and Washington, D.C., using Curtiss JN-3 airplanes to cover the 219-mile route, ostensibly to train military pilots in cross-country flying. The army stopped all such flying after a few months, but as the demand grew for bank-clearing services between the Federal Reserve districts, the Post Office Department took over the route, flying Liberty-powered DH-4s.

From time to time the Air Mail Service extended to additional cities; within a year key routes were well established, some with lighted beacons to support night-flying activities. Large identification symbols were installed on the tops of prominent buildings and water towers at towns along the way, for navigating the daylight legs. Slowly, the Post Office Department was creating the skeleton of an airways system.

It was a piddling exercise compared with reported developments in Europe, where governments had established their own scheduled passenger airlines. Flying the mail, was, however, a strictly government monopoly in what everyone boasted was a free-enterprise economy and, in a move conceived to bring some semblance of financial security and stability to the financially faltering industry, civil-aviation leaders had called upon all their resources and political savvy to eliminate that monopoly and have at least some part of the business of transporting the mail turned over to the private sector. It was purely and simply a matter of the industry's survival.

Harold Pitcairn was diligently applying himself to learn everything about the world of business and his intensity had been awarded by several promotions of increasingly demanding character in a wide variety of administrative and production improvement positions. Brother Raymond and the board of directors had watched his progress closely and were well aware of his development and maturation as a business executive with every new experience in management positions. His diligence and single-mindedness was rewarded by elevating him to the presidency of a struggling, barely profitable company in Michigan, the Owosso Sugar Company. The challenge was to make the little company profitable and productive, objectives that had eluded all prior executives who had held the post. The move was to have a catalytic effect on the younger Pitcairn's career which no one could have possibly foreseen.

The agricultural business was completely new to Harold Pitcairn, but typically he waded into it, not as a desk-bound executive. He studied the profit-and-loss statements, and production graphs—the usual tools of a business administrator—then he put on his old clothes and got his feet muddy learning the absolute fundamentals of producing a crop of sugar beets. Within six months the twenty-five-year-old company president had concluded that the problem was not one of mere business techniques to be solved by theory from a post in the executive offices, but the practical problem of beet-growing mechanics.

Pitcairn perceived the problem in a technique that older company officials had accepted as normal. The annual production of a crop required a two-step process: first, in the early winter they had to plant seeds under a hothouse environment so that they would grow into small plants. Then, in the spring of the year, each of the millions of tiny plants had to be hand-placed into the earth of the huge expanse of open fields in a one-at-a-time, back-breaking, time-consuming manner. Pitcairn's efficiency-expert background had taught him that any business which was labor intensive would have serious problems trying to make a substantial profit. As he analyzed the situation, he recognized that the solution would be to create some mechanical means of doing the replanting job faster, more easily, and with considerably less overhead. There was, he soon learned, no such machine available.

The only answer was to invent such a machine himself.

During the winter of 1922–23, Pitcairn sketched out a number of ideas that demonstrated his ingenuity and culminated in an overall design that he thought might solve the problem. However, to translate his own somewhat crude drawings into refined, formal engineering designs capable of being followed by machinists who would create an actual working device, he realized that he would need the services of a competent mechanical engineer.

Because of what accountants call the "extraordinary, nonbudgeted expense" involved in retaining such an expert's professional input, it was necessary for the young company president to request approval for the

expenditure from the board of directors, which was promptly granted. After all, he had a good track record in his conduct of the company's affairs in various positions and he was the apple of his brother's eye; Raymond was a member of the board. No one asked who the candidate for the drafting job might be, nor did the younger Pitcairn volunteer a name, but the competent engineering draftsman he had in mind was Agnew E. Larsen.

Larsen's career had had a few ups and downs since their last joint efforts in helicopter design before the war had interrupted their association. About the time Pitcairn had joined the Army Air Service, Larsen had taken a position as a draftsman with the Thomas-Morse Aircraft Company in Ithaca, New York, apprenticed to the famous British aircraft designer, Benjamin Douglas Thomas. Thomas, who had gained a great reputation when associated with Vickers, A.V. Roe and Sopwith in England, had been hired by Glenn H. Curtiss in 1913 to be the lead designer/engineer on the then new J and N models, which subsequently evolved into the ubiquitous JN series. He was also personally involved with the design and fabrication of the flying boat *America*, which Curtiss had proposed to fly across the North Atlantic in 1914.

When the United States seemed to be drifting into the war, Thomas had been hired away from Curtiss by the Thomas Brothers Airplane Company and later helped to form the Thomas-Morse Company to produce a U.S. pursuit ship that would equal the best then produced in Europe. Thomas had engaged the services of a young applicant from York, Pennsylvania, as a draftsman: Agnew E. Larsen.

Working under Thomas, the new assistant's first big job was "Americanizing" British engineering drawings of the combat-proven Bristol Scout. As a reward for his excellent work, Larsen was soon promoted to chief draftsman and assistant chief engineer under Thomas on the design of an original first-line fighter to be comparable with the sensational French SPAD. The Thomas-Morse MB-3, which was the product of their work, was destined to be America's first—and only—competitive fighter plane produced in World War I, although it was never to see actual combat. Nevertheless, Agnew Larsen's star was at a high point when the MB-3 was exposed to the plaudits of the military aviation leadership of his country. Then the bottom fell out.

Because of then-existing government policies of making all designs submitted on a contract proposal a matter of public record (and therefore not protected by patents) the army's acceptance of the MG-3 design was only a hollow victory for Thomas-Morse. The award for producing the airplane went to the little Boeing company in Seattle, Washington, which, using the MG-3 plans, had submitted a lower bid to produce the airplane than the bid submitted by the actual designer. The ensuing order for two hundred

MB-3s made Boeing a household name, but without the contract, Thomas-Morse was driven to the wall, and Agnew Larsen was one of the many employees of that company who unexpectedly found themselves out of work. To support himself Larsen then took a job designing parts for a small automobile company named Marmon. That was where Harold Pitcairn had found him and offered him a job.

Larsen was not particularly enthralled by the prospect of constructing anything so pedestrian as a beet-planting machine, but when his old friend told him that, while working together on the farming equipment, they would be able to spend some of their free time together experimenting with rotary-wing aircraft, there was a new dimension to the Owosso Sugar Company project. It would be wonderful to return to the aviation industry in any capacity—even though it seemed to be on its last legs.

Pitcairn knew better. From his constant study of financial reports in authoritative industry journals and investment services, he was aware of an interesting trend. In the face of what seemed to be overwhelming odds, coupled with the towering indifference to all matters aeronautical by the nation's leaders, some hardheaded, unromantic business investors were beginning to exhibit a measure of confidence in the future prospects of aviation. Inside reports showed that entrepreneurs of considerable stature were channeling substantial amounts of fresh money into what the public regarded as a sagging industry. The dominant figure was Clement M. Keys, formerly of *The Wall Street Journal*, later financial editor of the *World's Book* and the founder (at the age of thirty-six) of C. M. Keys & Company, Bankers & Brokers. By 1923, at the age of forty-seven, with an impressive track record of investments and company takeovers, Keys had taken the helm in the reorganization of the Curtiss Aeroplane and Motor Company. At his insistence the company had concentrated on the new design called the Oriole, for the business and pleasure flying markets. The sleek plane, which replaced the JN series altogether, was powered by the 90-hp OX-5 engine that Curtiss had made by the thousands during the war—and of which it still had a warehouse full when the war was over. The Oriole was soon to be followed, Keys had announced, by a three-place flying boat to be known as the Seagull, and he promised that very soon he would introduce a larger four/five-place machine to be called the Eagle, built around the still widely available 400-hp Liberty engine, also of Great War vintage. In addition, new engines were in the design state at Curtiss.

Keys was not the only name to appear on the financial pages in aviation-related transactions. H. L. Talbott and a young executive named Charles F. Kettering were reported to be running the Dayton-Wright Company, while the Wright Aeronautical Company in Paterson, New Jersey, was being operated by George Houston, Fred Rentschler, and Bill Boeing. In 1922, it seemed as if aviation's fortunes were beginning to turn.

Pitcairn had moved his wife back to Bryn Athyn to have their third child in 1923 and she was expecting their fourth, so he spent most of his time there, going to Owosso several times a month to oversee the operation of the sugar beet company, which was slow in the wintertime.

His plan was to set Larsen up in a small drafting room attached to the stained-glass manufacturing building which was supplying the vividly colored glass for the windows of the Bryn Athyn Cathedral only a hundred yards away. There, they could work on whatever problems they would have to cope with. It was not long before they were again exercising their imaginations on the same subjects they had pursued eight years before.

As the beet-planting machinery slowly took shape in the little machine shop adjacent to the stained-glass manufactory on the edge of the Pitcairn dairy's meadow in Bryn Athyn where Larsen had ensconced himself, there also issued a parade of rotary-wing devices of various sizes and shapes. Some were powered by rubber bands, or little steam generators. Trying to overcome the torque, which made the diminutive fuselages rotate in the opposite direction from the whirling lifting blades, the inventive duo created a compressed air helicopter with its power issuing from tiny jets located at the rotor tips. Undismayed by repeated failures, they kept chipping away at the physical problems, their hopes buoyed by the thought that they were making tangible progress with each experiment.

They were not aware that in relative obscurity some thirty-five hundred miles to the east, a young Spanish aristocrat, whose family was politically highly placed, was also experimenting with rotary-wing flight. Don Juan de la Cierva y Cordinu was no dabbler in science. With impressive credentials as an aircraft designer and engineer, and one of Europe's foremost mathematicians, he had experimented with aircraft designs before the Great War, but after numerous failures had turned to the design of military aircraft and had produced a huge multi-engine bomber for the arsenal of Spain. After the war, Cierva's efforts had moved in the direction of rotating lifting planes, which he named the "Autogiro,"* so-called because the wings, or "blades," set atop a pylon-mounted spindle, were allowed to "gyrate," i.e., spin freely as a result of aerodynamic forces—

"relative wind"—created by the movement of the aircraft through the air. As the wings rotated and produced lift, they would permit very slow "slow flight" while practically eliminating the slow-flight aerodynamic hazards of fixed-wing designs. Therefore short takeoff and virtually vertical landing characteristics were possible. Furthermore, if the engine failed in flight, the relative wind produced by the aircraft's descent power-off would continue to drive the rotor blades and produce lift that would permit the aircraft to descend as slowly as a parachute and land at almost zero forward speed—a tremendous safety factor.

Early in 1923, the U.S. press reported that controlled flight in rotary-wing aircraft had been publicly demonstrated at Getaffe Airport, near Madrid. To Pitcairn and Larsen, still concentrating primarily on the beet planter, the news came as an emotional shock. They had believed that the technique of vertical-lift flight was almost within their grasp. Had this unknown Spaniard beaten them to it?

By the spring of 1923 the sugar beet machine had proved to be a huge success; Owosso Sugar Beet Company was headed for a banner year. But something else had happened, too. Harold Pitcairn's renewed investigations of aviation had kindled anew his love of flying, which could no longer be denied.

First, he joined the Aero Club of Pennsylvania, which had been formed in 1909 and incorporated in

---

* "Autogiro" was a proprietory name, owned by Cierva. All other versions of rotary-wing aircraft were variously referred to as "gyro planes," "gyrodynes," or "gyrocopters." However, in time the name became a generic term, spelled with a small *a.* It is also found in the literature of aviation spelled "autogyro" and "autogyreau" (plural, "autogyreaux").

Harold Pitcairn and his Farman Sport-biplane, the first airplane he ever owned. This photo, from the winter of 1923, was taken on the Pitcairn farm, which became the original Pitcairn Field in 1924.

1910 by a group of socially prominent and well-to-do balloonists and aeronauts. It had grown to include several hundred civic, political, and social leaders by the early 1920s, including two old friends, C. Townsend Ludington and W. Wallace Kellett, who had plunged into the business of flying as the barnstorming era was at its zenith. Ludington and Kellett had leased operation facilities at a small airfield near Berlin, New Jersey, a small plot of ground owned by G. Sumner Ireland and his sister and named Pine Valley Field. There, Kellett and Ludington had taken on sales franchises for airplanes, including the American Curtiss line and the French Farman line with Ireland designated as their chief pilot, chief instructor, and demonstration pilot. It required little sales pressure from his friends Ludington and Kellett to induce Pitcairn to attend the weekend get-togethers at Pine Valley Field and when the weather turned balmy, he could not resist the impulse to take some flight refresher sessions with Ireland. Within two weeks he bought for his own use a diminutive two-place Farman Sport biplane and began to edge back into active flying.

Pine Valley Field was an example of the changing face of civil aviation in America, as were the wide-ranging barnstorming pilots, who eked out precarious livings by passing the hat through crowds drawn to watch their aerial antics.

Until then, there were no ground-support facilities. Barnstormers flew into and out of pastures, corn-fields, from beaches, and sometimes from public parks and refueled from the same pumps used by automobile drivers. They did their own maintenance in the field, changed spark plugs and engines, and repaired rents in the fabric coverings of their airplanes. G. Sumner Ireland had been one of the first to settle down in one place and became a "fixed base operator" (or FBO), providing support services to itinerant and based aviators, as well as sales of new and used airplanes. Because new airplanes were so expensive, compared with the used planes sold at surplus, he had leased the sales agencies for factory-new planes to Ludington and Kellett.

As the seasons changed, Pitcairn wandered aloft over the area of eastern Pennsylvania and South Jersey, learning what freedom small airplanes provided. He grew to love the hours-long flights he made in his little Farman.

But weekend flying, or flying on the long evenings of summer, were still merely a form of relaxation, a hobby. Pitcairn's main business interest lay in making a profit with the sugar beet company and working his way up the corporate ladder of the family industrial complex.

When the books were closed on 1923, the profit-and-loss statements showed that he had made a success of his business; to celebrate, Pitcairn packed Clara and himself off to Europe with their old friends, Bishop and Mrs. DeCharms, for an extended vacation away from the pressures of his day-to-day job. They intended to rest on the ten-day sea voyage to Great Britain, then merely to travel over the European countryside.

From the moment the quartet landed in England, Harold was repeatedly astonished at what he found: on the Continent, civil aviation was bursting at the seams.

No matter where they went, government-owned passenger-carrying airlines were operating on published schedules from large airports. One could buy a ticket to travel from any major city to any other large city in big, sometimes multi-engine airplanes, as easily as and sometimes more easily than traveling by railroad—and many times faster. In the face of postwar economic collapse, inflation, and widespread unemployment, the governments of Europe had agreed that commerce must be restored and that the best mechanism was by the use of airplanes.

Starting late in 1918, the Continent was crisscrossed by hundreds of airline routes, all operating under rigid government regulations. People flew mainly for business reasons, including the citizens of

England, France, Italy, Holland, and even those who lived in the economic rubble of Germany.

In every country aviation factories were operating at capacity, producing small, personally flown airplanes as well as large commercial airliners that could carry a dozen passengers at once. There were no barnstormers in Europe; airplanes were for purposeful travel—for on-purpose transportation.

Harold Pitcairn was astounded that European aviation had become so highly advanced, when he knew that the United States, where the airplane had been invented, had fallen so far behind. It was a sobering experience.

But it was also an eye-opening experience, for Pitcairn could visualize that someday similar—indeed greater—strides would inevitably take place in his own country, where air travel would be unfettered and uncomplicated by problems of border crossings, language, and currency differences and where

a single federal government could regulate all flying under one set of rules. He was certain that it would happen, possibly very soon.

Toward the end of his sojourn, he visited the aircraft plant of Henri and Maurice Farman, not far from Paris. The sheer size of their establishment astounded him: a factory two miles long, employing five thousand workers, produced almost a dozen different models, ranging from the four-engine "Goliath" bomber and its two-engine passenger version, down through a number of single-engine fighter planes for the Air Service, a civilian cabin-type airplane, to be used for touring, and the pert little Farman "Sport" biplane.

He could see the potential for small airplanes better than he had ever imagined. When the United States followed suit, the future of aviation would be limitless and he wanted to be, somehow, a part of it. The time for making a decision was near.

# PART TWO

# Fixed Wing

# Career Decision

Still at the helm of the sugar company, Pitcairn found it increasingly more difficult to concentrate on the mundane problems of agricultural production. His mind kept flashing back to compare what he had seen abroad with the potential for future aviation developments he could imagine in his own country. He had a brand-new perspective on aviation. True, the aviation industry in America was still a shambles, but he had no doubts that when flying caught on, it would bloom faster—and with a lot more satisfaction for him—than sugar beets.

While continuing as president of Owosso Sugar Company, Harold lived with Clara and their two children, Joel and John, in the new home he had built in Bryn Athyn, where their third child was born. From his bedroom window he could see the hill that had once been the scene of his first attempt at flying.

Having a home in eastern Pennsylvania and operating a business located in central Michigan created a somewhat difficult logistical prob-

lem for the executive, who had to make the round trip at least twice a month, sometimes more frequently. Normally, this involved an exhausting two-day trip each way, including an overnight train ride with a long, hard automobile trip at each end. The time involved and the discomforts of rail travel—particularly since he had found it impossible to get a good night's sleep on the train as it rumbled across switches through the uncoupling and recoupling operations that seemed to come up just as he was dozing off—deeply impressed Pitcairn. Why, he asked himself, should he have to put up with rattling around all day and night on a dirty, coal-fired railroad train, if he could make the trip by air? Up to the time he had been in Europe, he had thought of flying only as a sporting activity, like sailing. In Europe he had traveled between a dozen cities by air. Abroad, he had learned at first hand that flying, in large aircraft or small, provided excellent point-to-point, straight-line transportation.

Eyeing his travel schedule while

49

sitting in the study of his new home, he pulled an atlas from a nearby bookcase, opened to a map of the United States, drew some lines, and made some quick measurements. From Bryn Athyn to Owosso on a direct course was about five hundred miles, if one crossed Lake Erie just east of Cleveland; it would be about six hundred fifty miles if one detoured around the south end of the lake, which was almost an inland sea. On his ever-present slide rule this trip translated to seven or eight hours in a hundred-mile-an-hour airplane, depending on how many landings were made en route for fuel or because of weather. Certainly, flying would be more time-efficient than interminable train rides with numerous stops, layovers, couplings, uncouplings, transfers, and waits in ticket lines.

To the best of his knowledge, the nearest aircraft charter service using all-new equipment was the recently reorganized Curtiss Company on Long Island. Impulsively, Harold placed a long-distance telephone call, asking to speak to the president, Clement M. Keys, whose name was familiar as one of the financial wizards trying to hold the industry together.

When asked about the possibility of a cash-on-the-barrelhead charter trip covering thirteen hundred miles, plus ferry time between Long Island and Bryn Athyn, plus some overnight waiting time at the destination, the president of the cash-poor company gave the caller his undivided attention. Before the tele-

phone connection was broken, Keys had assigned his newest factory demonstrator, a sparkling new Oriole, for the charter, and his best demonstrator-pilot, James G. Ray.

Jim Ray, a Texan born and raised, had been a schoolteacher before the war. Tall, spare, partially balding, with a quiet nature and a sharply featured face that always seemed to be on the edge of a shy grin, he had been unable to afford to fulfill the dream of flying that had grown to almost unbearable intensity since he was a small boy. He was finally able to reach for the sky when the army's military flight-training program developed in 1916; he was one of the earliest applicants to be accepted.

From the beginning he proved to be a natural flier, born with the talent to feel the wind on his wings. He had been quickly rated as a Service Pilot; then, because of his great ability to teach and his unflappable nature, he had been assigned to flight instruction duties, first for primary students and for teaching advanced trainees formation flying, aerobatics, combat tactics, and aerial gunnery.

While Ray was carrying out his duties at various West Coast bases, Major H. H. Arnold, one of America's top-ranking military aviators, returning from an observation trip to the European battlefronts, had dutifully, albeit painfully, reported to his superiors in the Aviation Section that premature publicity released about the U.S. war effort was an embarrassment to U.S. forces in France. The DH-4, so highly touted in the American press, was a failure in combat comparison fly-offs and the Jenny was looked upon as a joke by fire-tested Allied pilots. His conclusion was that any U.S. contribution to the war in the air would be by pilots mounted in sprightly, nimble European designed and manufactured aircraft which bore only a superficial resemblance to the sluggish American ships in which they had taken all their prior training. What the newly arrived pilots from the States needed was a solid program of instruction from American instructors who were thoroughly aware of their background. Jim Ray had been among the first American instructor pilots to be shipped to France, and had been assigned to fly all the Allied fighter planes as he prepared to take the responsibility of transitioning newly arrived pilots from home.

When the war was over, most military pilots found themselves out of work. Many plunged financially, using their mustering-out pay to buy surplus Jennies, then going into business for themselves as barnstormers. Jim Ray's quiet competence and even temperament had caught the eye of the incomparable Charles Jones, better known to everyone as "Casey," then chief pilot of the Curtiss Company, who hired Ray right out of the service and put him to work as the company's demonstration, charter, and instruction pilot on a full-time basis.

The Pitcairn charter agreement called for Ray to land on a small pasture next to the dairy barn on the Pitcairn farm, then head out for Michigan. The apparently simple concept was difficult to execute. With no marking to show where the Pitcairn farm was located or to identify it from thousands of other similar farms and cow pastures that dotted the rolling hills north of Philadelphia, Ray somehow found the one-thousand-foot-long meadow and landed the Oriole right on schedule.

The two men, Ray and Pitcairn, so dissimilar in background, education, and economic situation, hit it off right from the beginning. They were of the same age and had a common interest in aviation; furthermore, each saw admirable qualities in the other. Although quiet and self-effacing, Ray was quickly recognized as a thorough professional who could confidently embark on a long cross-country trip, casual and unfazed by the total lack of navigational aids, aeronautical charts, or knowledge of where he could obtain fuel or other support along the route of flight. What was more, he made it look easy.

Conversely, Ray was impressed by his client, who was obviously a man of means, although no one would know it when meeting him for the first time. Perhaps Ray's briefing from Casey Jones had led him to expect someone who was formal, dignified, even starchy, but Pitcairn turned out to be a roll-up-his-sleeves-and-go-to-work kind of guy, a leader rather than a driver. Ray was all the more impressed to learn that his companion was also a pilot, that he had learned to fly in Curtiss airplanes and that he harbored the desire someday to get into the aviation business himself, if the right opportunity arose.

As their acquaintance ripened into friendship, Pitcairn invited Ray to join Clara and him in their new home, where the two men often talked far into the night about flying and the career opportunities aviation soon might provide. For Pitcairn the meetings provided an education that he might otherwise never have had about the state of the business.

Since a major part of Ray's job with Curtiss was to deliver new aircraft to purchasers all over the country, he had developed an excellent perspective on aviation in the United States. As they relaxed over a quiet libation together after their flights, Ray turned out to be an almost endless source of information, from which Pitcairn soon acquired a greater depth of aviation knowledge.

Ray casually reported that he too had observed that many former gypsy pilots had forsaken barnstorming to settle down to operate from fixed rather than movable bases, calling themselves "fixed base operators," to indicate their permanence and stability. Some were making a pretty fair living by selling sight-seeing rides—"passenger hopping," they called it—by flight instruction, and from time to time by selling an airplane.

There was a real groundswell of interest in flying, he said, a percepti-ble growth of enthusiasm; people wanted to fly so badly that they would pay five dollars apiece for a ten-minute ride in open-cockpit airplanes, and on good days prospective sight-seeing passengers stood cheerfully in long lines awaiting their turns for the privilege of doing so.

Ray laid out some numbers that intrigued Pitcairn. A two-thousand-dollar Jenny, bought in new condition at military surplus, could carry two passengers at a time in the front cockpit, although it was a tight fit. If a pilot could make four flights an hour, including time for loading and unloading passengers and for refueling, he could take in forty dollars; for an eight-hour day—if they could keep the single-ignition OX-5 engine running—pilots could gross three hundred dollars. By alternating two pilots on long summer days, when daylight lasted until eight-thirty or nine o'clock, passenger hopping could bring in as much as five hundred dollars. In a few weeks of such operations, one could pay off the initial cost of the airplane; from then on, except for maintenance costs—and most pilots performed their own maintenance in those days—passenger hopping was all profit.

Ray had also observed that the public was becoming wise, if not sophisticated, about airplanes and could tell the difference between an old flight-weary Jenny and a new airplane. As a result, successful fixed base operators were beginning to re-equip with factory-new aircraft which had fewer maintenance problems, were more reliable in operation, and, most of all, attracted customers away from their poorly mounted competition. Most of his delivery flights of Curtiss Orioles had been to such progressive operators.

Their discussions fanned the smoldering spark of some personal involvement in aviation in Harold Pitcairn's mind into a flicker of flame that would quickly grow. Late in the winter of 1924, Pitcairn told his wife that he had made the decision to pursue aviation as a career. He proposed to resign from the sugar company presidency and to start his own aviation company. Clara was happy that he was going to do something that he enjoyed, but brother Raymond was concerned and worried that his twenty-seven-year-old sibling was heading for financial disaster.

# The Fleetwing

By any normal criteria, 1924 had to seem the least auspicious time for entering the aviation business. A somber lead article in *Aviation*, one of the principal journals of the time, reported at length the critical state of major aviation companies. The list of plants and their problems was long and scary.

No factory was active when the new year came in. The Curtiss Company, despite Keys's dynamic leadership, was said to be on the brink again financially and in the process of still another reorganization. L-W-F (for Laminated Wood Fuselage), a major wartime manufacturer, was in receivership and shut down. The Glenn L. Martin Company and Aeromarine & Motor Company were idle. Consolidated, Loening, Cox-Klemin, Bellanca, Douglas, and the Thomas-Morse Company had no orders among them.

Contrary to the current rumors, Harold Pitcairn had not decided to take a long walk on a short plank. Before he made his great decision, he had done his homework, as his fa-

ther had taught him.

Through the winter of 1923–24, he had flown his Farman Sport as well as chartering the Oriole with Ray as his pilot. He had ordered a grassy runway cut on the pasture he and Ray used on their Owosso trips and had designed a hangar for his Farman at the edge of the field to create his own private airfield. He had hired a young man named Sterling Smith to act as "groom" for his perky little plane. When spring arrived, he set up a schedule of trips on which, all by himself, he flew the Farman regularly, visiting every public-use airfield and sticking his head into every fixed based operation within a radius of one hundred miles of his home. While most observers of his peregrinations regarded him as merely an aeronautical dilettante out for a good time, Pitcairn had in reality been evaluating the quality of his potential competition and confirming Jim Ray's assessment of the public's attitude toward flying.

He had quickly verified the accuracy of Ray's analysis. There was, indeed, a conspicuous and significant drift toward public acceptance of aviation. Sportsman-pilots had begun to form aviation societies and associations. A number of aviation country clubs, similar in form to golfing's country clubs and to yacht clubs, had sprung up along the East Coast. On weekends, no matter where he flew when the weather was clear, long lines of people were seen patiently waiting to take their turns for short circuits of the airport.

He had also come to the conclusion that many of the fixed base operators were fated to go broke, not because the business was not there, but because they did not know how to operate the businesses they headed; most FBOs were artisans—pilots or mechanics—who were in the flying business because they loved it, which for them was reason enough. But they operated on a cash-drawer basis, not knowing whether or not they were making a profit in the long run, or planning to ride out the ups and downs of the national economy. At heart they were still barnstormers, not businessmen, which would give Pitcairn an overwhelming advantage, because he was by then very much a businessman.

While scouting the potential for his proposed venture, Pitcairn continued his investigations in the realm of rotary-wing flight; he formed a company under the name of Pitcairn Aviation and put Agnew Larsen on the payroll. After hundreds of meticulous experiments, they had almost solved the anti-

torque problems by developing models with counter-rotating vanes, but the ability to control the rolling movement in level flight continued to elude them. For months they reworked vanes, rotors, and control systems, but every time they would solve one problem, new ones would appear.

In the meantime, Pitcairn's highly placed friends in Washington kept him informed of new and interesting developments, indicating that some major changes were coming.

For example, the National Advisory Committee for Aeronautics, formed in 1915 to make recommendations to Congress, had issued a powerful statement condemning the government's total lack of policy on aeronautical developments, pinning the congressional hide to the wall in a scathing indictment entitled *Why Commercial Aviation Lags.* NACA's primary recommendation to bring order out of chaos was that a Bureau of Aeronautics be established within the Department of Commerce. As a result of the blast, legislative bills had been dropped into the hoppers of both the House and the Senate, proposing to regulate aviation by acts of Congress.

The Air Mail Service, still using wartime designed DH-4s as the backbone of its operations, had continued to expand its routes and had established one coast to coast from New York (actually served through Hadley Field in New Brunswick, New Jersey); via Bellefonte, Pennsylvania; Cleveland and Bryan, Ohio; Chicago; Iowa City; Omaha and North Platte, Nebraska; Cheyenne, Rawlins and Rock Springs, Wyoming; Salt Lake City; Elko and Reno, Nevada, on to San Francisco, a tremendous undertaking by any standard but virtually incredible when one considers the archaic aircraft with which the early Air Mail pilots braved the route. As extensive as it was, the air-mail route structure bypassed hundreds of major communities which were thereby isolated from the quick communications air-mail service provided in interstate business affairs. In 1924, the governors of Arkansas, Alabama, Massachusetts, and Utah issued a joint proclamation demanding that the Postmaster General provide their states with air-mail service.

Their voices, endorsing the free enterprise aviation industry's lobbying efforts, finally aroused leaders in Congress. Spearheading the move was Pennsylvania's Representative M. Clyde Kelly, who overcame opposition from well-entrenched opponents to ram through a bill providing that the Postmaster General *must* contract with private carrier companies—including air carriers—to transport U.S. mail to communities in every part of the nation. The wording of the bill was not merely permissive, it was mandatory; a direct order to the Postmaster General to act promptly.

Such a proposal was almost unheard of and was strongly resisted by the entrenched authorities. But Kelly argued strenuously and successfully, after all of the public hearings were over and the positions of

all parties-in-interest thoroughly aired, that such services would benefit the citizens of the entire country. That, more than the arguments of the aviation industry's leaders, won the day, although they had fought with their backs to the wall. Government contracts which would subsidize and therefore bring economic stability to the American aviation industry, then teetering on the brink of calamity, would be the only means by which it would be brought to the level of air service in Europe. It was the industry's last hope.

Pitcairn actively participated in the political maneuvering involved in this vital legislation and knew that things were looking favorable when he made his decision to embark on an aviation career. Having done so, he commenced to draw up a comprehensive master plan, including an operational budget for two years, a preliminary table of organization, and a schedule of target dates for each objective.

His first step was to acquire additional land for his base of operations. He had chosen the cow pasture as a likely site on which to begin, but he and Ray agreed that it was a trifle too small for commercial airfield operations, notwithstanding their own frequent use in the past, so he purchased an adjoining farm, created a two-thousand-foot runway, with a slight dogleg, and arranged to have a large wooden hangar erected as soon as the frost went out of the ground.

He then formed another company, Pitcairn Aviation (a separate organization from the previously formed Pitcairn Aircraft), which would own and operate the field; its first employee—whose job would be known today as "line man" charged with fueling aircraft, moving them in and out of the hangar, and assisting passengers to embark and debark, was Sterling Smith, the young man who had acted in a somewhat similar capacity for the Farman Sport over the winter.

Pitcairn induced Jim Ray to resign from Curtiss and join him in his new venture, to be in charge of field operations and act as chief pilot. Not only could Ray fly and teach flying, he also knew how and where to purchase airplanes the company would need, without being oversold. Ray was also well qualified to hire competent pilots as required by the anticipated growth of operations.

Pitcairn proposed to assume the job of handling the administrative problems of both Pitcairn Aircraft and Pitcairn Aviation and to continue with helicopter experimentation while the airfield was being developed. The target date for the grand opening of Pitcairn Field was circled on a calendar in his study: Sunday, November 2, 1924.

By June 1924, six months before the date so carefully set by the company president, Pitcairn Field was already bustling with activity, for there was no way to keep the planned airfield a secret from the general public. Preparations, including grading and seeding the the enlarged landing area and the construction of a relatively large hangar so close to heavily traveled roads, had created widespread comment not only in Bryn Athyn but in all of the environs of Philadelphia and piqued the curiosity of everyone whose idea of Sunday afternoon recreation was to take a drive in the country.

Jim Ray had quickly set about procuring a suitable fleet of airplanes for sight-seeing, flight instruction, cross-country charters, and contract flying. In addition to Pitcairn's personal Farman Sport, the collection included four Curtiss Orioles, a Standard trainer, and two Martinsyde biplanes of the enclosed-cabin type, which Ray located for an astonishingly low price in Newfoundland, where they had been used for seal hunting before their owner had gone broke. When he was ferrying one of the Martinsydes to Bryn Athyn in frigid March weather, Ray found a sealskin flying helmet tucked under the seat of the open cockpit and appropriated it for his own winter-flying use, an aeronautical chapeau that would soon become his trademark.

Aviation was still a novelty and the almost constant snarl of airplane engines over the Bryn Athyn area quickly whipped up public interest. On every good day crowds gathered at the edges of the little airfield to watch the comings and goings of the Pitcairn escadrille, with real mob scenes developing on spring and summer weekends. Immediately the public began to clamor for sight-see-

Grass roots flying in 1924. Pitcairn Field, Bryn Athyn, already air-marked and in operation before construction began on the hangar. Note the cornfield southeast of the automobile parking area. Five airplanes are visible: two Jennies, a Curtiss Oriole, a Martinsyde and Harold Pitcairn's little Farman Sport-biplane.

ing rides and many applications came in for flight instruction and for charter flights to communities two hundred and three hundred miles away. By July, although the facilities were unfinished, the airfield was in full operation.

To meet the unexpectedly high demand, Ray had to hire a crew of trained, experienced pilots, including the Flying Faulkners—Ben, Jim, and Frank—along with Paul "Skipper" Lukens, to help him handle the volume.

The official grand opening of Pitcairn Field was by no means anticlimactic. Held as scheduled nine months before, it was attended by twenty *thousand* enthusiastic spectators. The major dedication speech was made by one of Philadelphia's prominent aviation figures, W. Wallace Kellett, himself a fixed base op-

Pitcairn Field, Bryn Athyn, viewed from the northwest, a few months later. The hangar has been built, the cornfield has grown and the wheel-rutted track across the middle of the airfield is deeper—a shortcut to Pitcairn's home. The barn in the background is part of the Pitcairn farm.

erator at Pine Valley, New Jersey, and at the Philadelphia Municipal Airport located in the marshlands of South Philadelphia. Following Kellett's remarks, a spectacular air show, like those flown by today's Blue Angels and Thunderbirds, was put on by the famous French war ace, Captain Charles Nungesser, who had won forty victories in the air war over the trenches of his homeland. Aided by Lieutenants André Bellet and Maurice Weiss of his former squadron, a simulated dogfight was part of the show, won—of course—by the dashing Nungesser, mounted in his Nieuport pursuit ship, which was emblazoned with his personal wartime insignia: a black heart surrounding a coffin flanked by two candles. It was a big day for Harold Pitcairn.

When the books were totted up at the end of 1924, Pitcairn Aviation showed a loss of almost twenty-five thousand dollars. Most of the loss was expected and was a harbinger of the high commencement costs of the venture, but Pitcairn was disturbed to discover that his well-used passenger-hopping operation had come up short from his carefully estimated projections. His meticulous records showed that the airplanes used, the Orioles and the Martinsydes, had averaged out about five flights an hour during their busy times, but that did not make up for the slow periods between the weekends. His first priority was to improve the economics of passenger hopping before the next season rolled around.

The "Official Grand Opening" of Pitcairn Field in the fall of 1924. The Aero Club of Pennsylvania's clubhouse has been added to the scene. The largest airplane on the field is a Barling Bomber. The other airplanes include two Martinsyde cabin-style sightseeing biplanes (at bottom of photo near hangar). The three airplanes beyond the Barling (wingtip-to-wingtip) are Charles Nungesser's Nieuports, with the striped vertical fins.

Dedication day at the Bryn Athyn Pitcairn Field in 1924, showing the original hangar and the smaller Aero Club of Pennsylvania clubhouse. The air show drew an estimated 20,000 spectators.

A ground view of dedication day, showing an Army squadron of DH-4s, several Curtiss Jennies and the Nieuports flown in the mock air battle segment of the show.

Captain Charles Nungesser, famous French ace of World War I, in his Nieuport pursuit plane, emblazoned with his personal insignia. Five years after performing at the Pitcairn Field dedication, he would be lost at sea in an attempted transatlantic crossing.

Chief pilot Jim Ray, wearing his famous sealskin flying helmet, and company president Harold Pitcairn on a passenger-hopping day in 1924.

The usual airplanes were too small to make passenger-hopping profitable.

His statistical breakdowns also showed something else: although long lines of people had stood in the Oriole loading positions, the larger, cabin-style Martinsydes drew considerably fewer sight-seeing passengers. The public's idea of flying was to sit outside in open cockpits wearing helmets and goggles, as did their heroes. The first decision was to dispose of the Martinsydes.

This left a problem. Orioles were capable of carrying only two passengers at a time, at most, in the open front cockpit, providing the people were physically small. A large person would fill the hole entirely, which automatically cut down the airplane's cash-flow productivity, which at that time was the key to fi-

nancial success. Pitcairn saw that his immediate problem was somehow to make airplanes at least twice as productive without substantially increasing their operating costs.*

For several weeks he scratched ideas out on a pad of paper. He doodled ways of making an Oriole's cockpit larger, then considered the idea of building an airplane of his own design, constantly referring to the objective of making a profit. He had just finished drawing a biplane with a two-place front cockpit, when a thought struck him. Why not design an airplane that would carry four, perhaps five passengers in open cockpits ahead of the pilot's cockpit? Such an airplane, built for a reasonable cost, could be a hugely profitable investment. He ran his slide rule a few times and raised his eyebrows. If he could load four passengers at five dollars a head every ten minutes for a ten-hour flying day in the five-month period of fair weather, he could make one thousand dollars a day, perhaps as much as twelve hundred dollars. In five months that could come to more than ninety thousand dollars, figuring in the low-volume days in the middle of the week and making allowances for a few bad-weather weekends. As he stared at the figures, he began to believe that such an airplane would be attractive to other fixed base operators who were engaged in selling passenger rides. He began to sketch out what such

---

* Precisely the reason for the modern trend toward wide-body airline jets.

The British Martinsyde World War I single-engine bombers were converted into cabin models for passenger-hopping, but the clients wanted to sit in open cockpits, with helmets and goggles, like the pilots.

an airplane would look like.

Then he had another thought. In 1926, the city of Philadelphia was scheduled to hold a celebration of the hundred and fiftieth anniversary of the signing of the Declaration of Independence, to be called the Sesqui-Centennial Exposition. It had already been certified as an authentic world's fair and in honor of the celebration the Fedération Aéronautic Internationale was apparently going to award Philadelphia the National Air Races for 1926. Considering the hundreds of thousands of visitors attracted to the international affair,

Pitcairn decided that he should bid for the exclusive passenger-hopping franchise to carry sight-seers over the historic sites of Philadelphia and its environs. He believed he could win the assignment, because his close friends in the aviation fraternity of Philadelphia, C. T. Ludington, W. W. Kellett, C. M. Young, and J. V. Dallin had been nominated for the Sesqui-Centennial Aviation Committee. As had he. It was worth the risk.

Calling his confederates Ray and Larsen to an informal meeting in his home, Pitcairn broached the idea of the big airplane and his plan for the Sesqui bid. Ray's eyes twinkled at the idea and he was all in favor of it. But the execution of the plan hinged on Larsen. Could he—in the limited space and with the resources available and from a standing start—draft, engineer, stress-analyze, build, and have ready for flight within a year an original-design airplane like that on Pitcairn's scratch pad?

It was a large order, not the kind to make a snap judgment on. Larsen hesitated, picked up the sheaf of papers proffered by the boss, and examined the crude preliminary sketches for a few minutes, then asked for a few days to analyze the problems involved.

Within the week, he presented his preliminary engineering drawings and specifications to Pitcairn and Ray. Pitcairn smiled when he saw the designs marked PA-1, for Pitcairn Aircraft, design No. 1, for he had never considered that there might be others.

The airplane Larsen proposed would be built around the Curtiss C-6 liquid-cooled engine of 160 hp, for good takeoff performance with a load. The wing structure would be of spruce spars and ribs, covered with tightly doped linen. The fuselage would be built on a frame of chrome molybdenum steel tubing, welded into a basic structure, deeply faired by wooden formers, also fabric covered. The airplane was designed to give a long service life with minimum maintenance, which would keep overall operational costs down. It was designed to operate from unprepared fields, not for speed.

Pitcairn and Ray pored over the drawings for a while, then Pitcairn asked Larsen what gauge steel tubing would be used, eliciting the re-

sponse that he planned to use three-quarter-inch and half-inch tubing for the basic structural members, consistent with normal design practice in the industry. It was not strong enough for Pitcairn, whose mind still carried memories of casualties from inadequately stressed airplanes.

"How about one-inch square tubing?" he suggested, pointing at the drawings with his chin. "Remember, we are going to be carrying families in this airplane, fathers and mothers and little children. I want to have it so strong that, if we ever have an accident, it will hold together." Ray nodded in thoughtful agreement.

Larsen sat back with his arms crossed on his chest and stared into space, considering the novel proposition, for no one ever used anything but round-section tubing in aircraft. But he reasoned that a square cross-section tube would be simpler to weld, would be immensely stronger and therefore safer under impact

Pitcairn-style square-section tubing made for superior strength, especially in welded clusters where the tubing joined in the Warren truss design.

The original PA-1 Fleetwing Warren truss frame. The fuselage was literally built like a bridge.

forces. He agreed. It would take six months.

"All right," said the company president. "Let's get on with it."

Aircraft design was no longer a matter of "cut and fit," then fly it and try it. Technological advances spurred on by the Great War had led to the development of new research and development techniques on the Continent, perhaps reaching their highest state of development by 1925 in England's National Physical Laboratory (NPL), which used no less than nine wind tunnels of various sizes to test airfoil designs under experimental conditions. In the United States the great private academic centers were beginning to learn from their friends across the sea, and one great institution, the Massachusetts Institute of Technology (MIT) in Boston had borrowed from NPL a brilliant young aeronautical engineer, Wynn Lawrence LePage, to assist in the new MIT empirical testing programs. Pitcairn and Larsen promptly made arrangements for a meeting with the MIT testing center for the purpose of re-

serving time in the wind tunnel schedules. The youthful expert with whom they worked was LePage, whose career as an aeronautical engineer would carry him to great heights of aviation achievement.

Within days the drafting tables and walls in the design shop were covered with overall design drawings and detailed engineering layouts involving airfoil shapes, engine mounts, the formation of joints and rigging.

Things were slow in the dead of winter at Pitcairn Field. No passengers showed up to take sight-seeing flights exposed to the chill of open cockpits, nor did aspiring pilots; student activity dropped off to nothing. No one was particularly surprised when Pitcairn announced that he was going to take Larsen to Europe to inspect the latest developments in aviation, leaving the final drawings and fabrication of the new PA-1, called the "Hop-Ship," in the capable hands of the engineering assistants Larsen had brought in, including Jurian Ligett, engineer; John F. Murphy, a master machinist whom he had hired away from Thomas-Morse; and Harlan Fowler, a youthful engineer who would one day become famous for the development of the slotted, extended-flap system that bears his name.

Pitcairn had an ulterior motive for the trip. Several times during 1924, newspapers had carried items about the rotary-wing flight experiments of the Spaniard Cierva, and during conversations with the British aeronautical engineer, LePage, they had learned of some of the successful rotary-wing flights that he had seen at the new Cierva flight-test facility located on the outskirts of London and of some of the wind tunnel testing that he had supervised for the Spanish aristocrat. Le-Page, who understood the intricate mathematics of the radical new development and believed that it was to open the door to a completely new realm of flight within the decade, recommended that Pitcairn, whose absorbed interest in the "Safe Aircraft" he recognized and respected, should investigate Cierva's astonishing progress in a discipline that had been such a stumbling block to aerodynamicists.

While repressing the depth of their reactions to the English engineer's remarks, Pitcairn and Larsen were jolted to full alert. Pitcairn wanted to evaluate the project personally with his resident engineer in the light of their own heretofore unsuccessful experiments. Perhaps Cierva had beaten them to the goal of vertical-lift flight, perhaps not. Until LePage's disclosures they had believed that someone may have been perpetrating a hoax, or it may have been newspaper hyperbole, but with the observer's information in hand they couldn't rest until they knew. The American duo was drawn to Europe like moths to a flame.

With the myriad of problems on his mind during the summer of 1924, Pitcairn had kept up with Larsen on their work on helicopter de-

vices, from time to time flying models in various configurations in the vicinity of the hangar at Pitcairn Field. The openness of their flight tests caught the attention of a young man who was a flight student at the field.

Raymond Synnestvedt was attending law school, preparing someday to join his father's law firm, Synnestvedt & Lechner, specializing in patent law. He ventured the opinion to his good friend Harold that he should forthwith begin to obtain letters patent on all of his rotary-wing inventions, whether they were then successful or not, or *apparently* successful or not, for at that time he was legally a "pioneer" in the field of rotary wing and someday his concepts might be extremely valuable.

Under other circumstances a man in Pitcairn's position might have shucked off such advice as officious meddling, but the words brought back memories of the summer of 1914, when the court had awarded a decision to the Wright brothers against Glenn Curtiss on precisely that basis. He promised Synnestvedt that the next time he had an idea, he would submit it to the patent firm for processing. Before embarking for Europe, Pitcairn sent to Raymond Synnestvedt a set of drawings and descriptions of a "helicopter device."

Pitcairn and Larsen arrived in England on what soon appeared to be a vain expedition. Cierva was not there and they were told that no Autogiros were in flying condition because of modification programs on the prototype. They learned that Cierva's initial experimentation in Spain had been funded by the Spanish government for years, despite disappointing failures. Then, toward the end of 1924, just as he had begun to achieve some success, all government aid had been terminated. When he was offered independent financing from the Lazard Frères in the United Kingdom, he had moved his laboratory there to continue his quest. However, the American visitors were informed somewhat brusquely that since Cierva had returned to his home in Madrid, they might want to inquire of him concerning the status of his device.

Pitcairn and Larsen had not traveled three thousand miles to be shut out; they extended their visit to Madrid, to meet the designer himself. Again they were almost frustrated.

In an interesting but not very productive face-to-face meeting, they noted a certain evasiveness as Señor Cierva discussed the principles of rotary-wing flight in very general terms through an interpreter, which, as the saying goes, lost something in the translation. The language barrier was subsequently diagnosed as a close-to-the-vest ploy, for when their relationship subsequently grew close, they found that the polylingual Cierva spoke excellent English, with only a trace of any accent.

It appeared that Cierva had indeed solved the fundamental problems of controllable rotary-wing flight; no flying models were available, Cierva apologized through the interpreter, but he was willing to show motion pictures of his machine in operation, which the Americans agreed was better than nothing after their long voyage. As it turned out, it was not much. The somewhat fuzzy images flickering on the screen disclosed no details of the inventor's engineering technique, but did show demonstrations of rotary-wing takeoffs, landings, and some short clips of level flight, clearly under full lateral control. It was a convincing, thrilling experience for the visitors, both of whom had noticed two other facts: first, Cierva had shifted his emphasis from true vertical lift, the helicopter concept. Instead he had adapted a small, single-place conventional propeller-driven airplane of the tractor type by substituting rotating wings mounted on a pylon for the original fixed wings. Second, they had both noticed that in the motion pictures, the Autogiro required a considerable ground run in order to turn the rotor blades up to flying speed and hence used as much or more takeoff area than an airplane did.

Pitcairn and Larsen returned home with somewhat mixed feelings. They were greatly impressed by the stable flight characteristics of the windmill-like aircraft; the Autogiro was an extraordinary achievement, an accomplishment not to be dismissed lightly. But they agreed that, as it was developed at that moment, it had no practical value for immediate investment. Although Cierva was onto *something*, they still had a chance to be first with the development of a true helicopter.

Arriving home, they were greeted by wonderful news: wind tunnel tests carried on at the aeronautical laboratories of the Massachusetts Institute of Technology upon scale models of the PA-1 had produced excellent results. Furthermore, stress analysis computations had indicated that the Hop-Ship would be stronger than any airplane then flying. The end of the hangar at Pitcairn Field had been set aside for the actual fabrication and supplies laid in. Already sparks from welding torches were beginning to fly. Slowly the PA-1 was beginning to take form.

On Pitcairn's desk awaiting his return was his first formal submis-sion for a helicopter patent, filed formally on his behalf on March 2, 1925, by the firm of Synnestvedt & Lechner. It was to be the first of thirty rotary-wing patents that would be awarded to Harold F. Pitcairn. It also was the beginning of a lawyer-client relationship that would make history.

When the first flight target date grew near in early spring, the PA-1 was rolled out of the hangar for everyone to see. It was larger than most people expected, yet it was forming into a thing of beauty, with

The original PA-1 Fleetwing, all white and wearing the Pitcairn Arrow design, standing in front of the original frame hangar, which would become the Pitcairn Aircraft factory. The Aero Club of Pennsylvania clubhouse is in the background.

deep, flowing lines. Doped and hand-rubbed to a mirrorlike finish, resplendent in its all-white fuselage and wings, the ship was ready to take to the air as soon as the grass field hardened after the spring thaw.

In preparation for the big event, Pitcairn had retained a hard-driving publicity man to whip up public interest and to alert the metropolitan newspapers, so that when the day finally came for the maiden flight of the large five-place ship, the boundaries of the little field and roads around it were jam-packed with thousands of enthusiastic onlookers.

It was a festive occasion on a beautifully sunny day, warm, almost balmy, with great armadas of towering white clouds sailing overhead in a stately procession. Clara Pitcairn christened the ship Fleetwing, the name that had won out over all others submitted—Harold detested the term "Hop-Ship"—by breaking a bottle of champagne on the steel propeller; little speeches were made by President Pitcairn and Chief Engineer Larsen, who introduced the crew that had brought the design into actual being; then Jim Ray swung up into the cockpit and started the engine amidst the cheers of the crowd.

For perhaps ten minutes Ray ran some preliminary tests on the new, untried airplane, taxiing up and

The PA-1 Fleetwing was a large airplane. Note the boarding ladder built into the left side and the imposing size of the Curtiss C-6 engine. The two occupants are Harold Pitcairn's sons, Joel and John.

down the grassy runway several times, developing a feel for the new controls.

Finally the dramatic moment came. Ray taxied to the far edge of the field, pointed its nose into the wind, slowly opened the Fleetwing's throttle. As the airplane quickly gathered speed, its tail rose and spectators could see the pilot's head swinging from one side of the cockpit to the other for better forward vision as he nudged the rudder to keep her straight down the middle of the runway, then, as he gently tugged on the control stick, the airplane rose gracefully from the ground.

Before it reached an altitude of twenty feet, it became clear that something was dreadfully wrong: the left wing dropped and the airplane began to swerve toward the crowd. As Ray cut the power and hauled back on the stick to kill his forward speed, the pretty biplane reared up at a sharp angle, slowed, fell off sideways and crashed, cartwheeling in a great spume of dust before the eyes of the horrified crowd. For several seconds everyone was rooted to his place in stunned silence. Then people began to run toward the still-quivering wreckage.

Pitcairn, fearful of what he was going to find, was among the first to reach the tangled remains of what a moment before had been a beautiful airplane. With dozens of excited volunteers helping, the body of the pilot, loose as a rag doll, was lifted from the wreck and carried, feet first, to an open roadster which had

been quickly driven to the crash site by pilot Paul Lukens. As soon as Ray's body was laid on the back seat, Lukens, who thought that his cargo was probably dead because of the violence of the crash, slewed around in quick turn and began a wild drive to the nearest hospital, five miles away.

Ray was not dead, merely stunned, and the cobwebs in his head cleared just in time for him to see an express train bearing down on them as the careening car nipped across a grade crossing just ahead of it. Lukens never tired of telling about how his hair stood on end when a soft Texas drawl from the supposedly deceased form in the back seat said, "Take it easy, Skip. One crack-up a day is enough."

Although severely shaken up by the intensity of the impact, Ray had survived unscathed, protected by the bridge-trusslike fuselage structure. In its first real test the square section tubing had indeed proved its soundness. Even though Jim had emerged intact, the accident was a catastrophe, since the company's sole aircraft, on which the bid for the Sesqui-Centennial sight-seeing concession was to be based, was a pile of junk in the rear of the hangar.

Pitcairn called an emergency meeting of all concerned as soon as Ray was back on his feet, to determine the cause of the accident. No one could conceive how an experienced pilot like Jim Ray could become so totally out of control of *any* airplane. Ray recalled that the takeoff run had been quite normal, as

The PA-1 Fleetwing "Hop-Ship" at work, with the company president perched on the edge of the rear cockpit. Note that each passenger had a private windshield. The size of the C-6 engine is obvious in this photograph.

had the liftoff. Once airborne, however, the left wing had dropped slightly, also a normal incident of flight, but when he tried to pick it up by moving the control stick to the right, he had immediately aggravated the situation. Instantaneously, he had intentionally pulled up into a stall rather than taking the chance of plowing into the massed crowd of spectators.

Once Ray had recounted his version of the incident, the answer to the key question was absurdly simple. An examination of the wreckage confirmed his suspicions: somehow, in the hurry to get the airplane flying at the earliest possible date, the control cables linking the ailerons to the stick had been rigged in reverse. It was as simple as that.

In a few days the ad hoc "factory" was back at work on a second Fleetwing, with everyone constantly checking its control rigging, but it was clear that its construction would not be completed in time to make the Sesqui bid, which had to be made well ahead of the affair. This put a severe crimp in Pitcairn's carefully laid plans. Not only had they lost the Sesqui passenger-hopping bid opportunity: Pitcairn had also entered the Fleetwing in a number of so-called efficiency contests against other planes of current manufacture, for air meets of every type continued to draw large crowds, much as automobile races or other athletic contests do today. By participating regularly in such aviation get-togethers, Pitcairn had planned to expose the four-passenger and one-pilot Fleetwing for sales to other fixed base operators who were always in the market for a more profitable aircraft in their business, a substantial amount of which continued to be passenger hopping. Because of the highly publicized PA-1 accident—for the promotion campaign obviously had backfired—Pitcairn had lost the initiative. Somehow he had to regain it.

# The Sesqui-Wing

The Contract Mail Act, sometimes called the Air Mail Act, or the Kelly Act in honor of its sponsor in the House of Representatives, was signed into law by President Coolidge on February 2, 1925, "to encourage aviation by authorizing the Postmaster General to contract with private companies for transporting the United States Mail." Little more than a "feeder line" authorization when it was written, this single piece of legislation was to become the cornerstone upon which the entire structure of American air transportation was to be built, the size of which no one dreamed of at the time. As a sop to its opponents the act provided that the Post Office Department would continue to operate the transcontinental route between New York and San Francisco, still using the well-worn, obsolescent DH-4s with which it had pioneered the service; only a series of new routes branching off from the newly designated "Columbia Route" would be assigned to private carriers. Until the newcomer civilian contractors had proven themselves fully capable of performing the services under the terms of their agreements, the Postmaster General was not going to abandon his important public service.

The first eight feeder routes advertised for bid by the Post Office Department branched north and south from the east-west main stem and elicited bids from all sorts of hopeful operators, from the largest to the smallest. Within seven months—even as Pitcairn Aviation was recovering from the destruction of what was to have been its flagship—five bid-winning routes were assigned. Colonial Air Lines, Robertson Aircraft Corporation, National Air Transport, Western Air Express, and Walter T. Varney, trading as Varney Speed Lines, were the first to be selected. Three of the awardees were well funded, one was marginal, and one was widely known to be virtually insolvent and counting on the mail contract subsidy to stay alive. Everyone in the aviation business was now watching the pattern of the awards by the Postmaster General to discern how the selections were made. The award of an additional five routes shortly thereafter repeated the form of the first five: two routes went to separate divisions of the Ford Motor Company, evidencing the interest of Henry Ford in the aviation business. One went to Pacific Air Transport, on the West Coast, and two more went to Charles Dickinson and Florida Airways, small outfits, new to the business, that probably had organized for the purpose of submitting bids.

It was of particular interest to Harold Pitcairn that the Postmaster General was taking the bids of small operators as seriously as those of large ones; that being the case, his little company might also have a chance. But before he made a move, he had to know more about the way it would work; he had never forgotten the admonition of his father. He made a few more investments in large aviation companies so he could learn from their experience, duly laid out in quarterly and annual reports to their stockholders.

From his experience in efficiency analysis, he believed that many of the successful bidders for Contract Air Mail routes, called CAMs in the trade, would soon learn that they had been equipped with airplanes too large for the loads to be carried, at least for the first few years of operation. Excess capacity, unused, would probably generate operational losses: most of the airplanes selected could carry as much as a ton

of mail, but Pitcairn's analysis was that early operations would require no more than one-quarter of that capacity. After running his slide rule and making some quick calculations, he believed that his group in Bryn Athyn could design a more efficient craft for the purpose.

Studying the routes awarded thus far, he perceived a void of service to the southeast quadrant of the country, leaving the fastest growing section of the United States with no connections south from New York. Atlanta, surely destined to be the economic center of the New South, had been left off the map, except for a short stub-end connecting it with Miami, via Jacksonville and Tampa. He drew a line on the map of the United States from New York to Atlanta and marked off major cities approximately 150 miles apart adjacent to it: Philadelphia, Washington, D.C., Richmond, Greensboro, Spartanburg. Harold was bouncing back from the shocking loss of the Fleetwing; ideas were beginning to perk again.

In February 1926, too late for the Sesqui-Centennial franchise bid, the second Fleetwing was rolled out of the combination hangar/factory and successfully flown without fanfare. Test pilot Jim Ray returned full of smiles, enthusiastic about the plane's sprightly performance, which had erased the blot on its record. Few people knew of the vindication of its design and those who heard about it did not care very much. Pitcairn Aviation was too small for its activities to have much impact on anyone in the industry—a situation that Harold was determined to change.

On March 18, at a company banquet to which all Pitcairn employees were invited, apparently to celebrate the success of the PA-1, Harold unveiled a new overall plan for his organization, not yet two years old. Pitcairn Aviation and Pitcairn Aircraft had been incorporated separately, he announced, and they would no longer operate as before: "Harold Pitcairn, trading as ..." Pitcairn Aircraft, *Inc.*, would manufacture aircraft of its own design, for commercial sales to the industry. Pitcairn Aviation, Inc., would conduct all flight operations and operate airfields which might be subsequently acquired. He was also in the initial stages of creating a third company, Pitcairn Aeronautics, Inc., for helicopter and rotary-wing experiments, development and patenting inventions associated therewith, of which several had already been issued to him and his associates.

All commercial flight operations would immediately be moved from Bryn Athyn to a larger field on property he had recently purchased near the towns of Hallowell and Willow Grove, some ten miles to the north; aircraft manufacturing and rotary-wing testing would completely take over the Bryn Athyn hangar building and would expand its operations to include the manufacture of a new air-cooled radial engine to be designed by Captain Robert W. A. Brewer, to power all future aircraft bearing the Pitcairn name. From then on, Pitcairn's team would be plunging into every facet of the aviation business.

By any criterion, Harold Pitcairn was proposing to take a big bite of an apple that might not even be ripe. While most aircraft companies were still on the ropes, he was proposing to set up a totally controlled conglomerate of his own, to manufacture airplanes and engines, establishing a string of flight schools and possibly an airline. Few people who merely knew him on a social basis realized that the mild, frequently deferential gentleman of the drawing room was such a hard-driving, ambitious, audacious innovator who was determined to make his mark in the business of aviation.

He was always moving, always thinking, always studying the trends and flows of his adopted industry. During April and May of 1926, several air-mail routes that had been awarded almost a year before finally went into operation. Using the wide variety of aircraft listed on their bid forms, they soon found that they were losing money carrying the mail, for precisely the reasons Pitcairn had predicted. He reviewed all of the aircraft specifications available, trying to find what he might be able to use if a route came up for him to bid on.

Meanwhile, the Fleetwing was successful, but had attracted no buyers. Pitcairn was a hardheaded realist who realized that that it would be difficult, almost impossible, for him to break into the market with a salable airplane, no matter how profitable it might be in his own experience, simply because Pitcairn Aircraft was such a tiny, new, and—on a national scale—so relatively unknown a name in the industry. Where names like Fokker, DeHaviland, Curtiss, Douglas, Boeing, Stout, Laird, and Ryan were quickly recognized, Pitcairn drew only blank stares. The situation had to be rectified if he was to sell airplanes. What he needed was to create an instant reputation, an image of solid integrity in the industry.

During a far-ranging discussion of business problems with his closest associates, Ray and Larsen, a possible solution surfaced.

"Why," asked Pitcairn characteristically cocking his head to one side like a bird, "don't we enter an airplane in the National Air Races scheduled to be held in conjunction with the Sesqui-Centennial?"

Except for the fact that the races were only four or five months away, the idea held some merit. Ray suggested that they could enter the Fleetwing in the efficiency race and possibly garner some publicity. Pitcairn shook his head, frowning slightly at the obvious suggestion. What he had in mind was entering the high-speed race, the main event of a week of competition, for winning *that* was a sure-fire way to achieve national attention.

With newspaper coverage from the far corners of the world, newsreel cameramen at every pylon turn, and magazines devoting hundreds of pages to the events, whoever won the major race of the meet would become famous overnight, known everywhere. Not only that: the winning airplane would have its name prominently displayed just as widely. It would be pictured in advertising as well as in editorial coverage. Winning the main event would solve their problems.

But it would not be easy, particularly since they did not have an airplane that was remotely competitive. They would have to face stiff competition, for they would be up against every aircraft manufacturer in America. Knowledgeable people always put their money on the perennial favorite, Casey Jones, dean of the Curtiss contingent. Racing in his record-holding clipped-wing Oriole, no one had defeated him for years.

Undaunted by the obviously overwhelming odds against the ideas he began to lay out, Pitcairn unleashed his resourceful improvisational imagination, devising a way to unseat Ol' Casey. Why not, he urged, design a brand-new airplane, to be called the PA-2, which would be put together in the Bryn Athyn hanger. The fuselage would be built around the square tubing format, except that it would be smaller than the Fleetwing, maybe a two-place ship with wings designed for speed rather than load carrying. The idea would be to keep it clean, for speed. Then he erupted with another provocative idea: The Curtiss C-6, 160-hp engine was widely used for racing planes and the smaller, lighter 90-hp OX-5 was used for economy or efficiency flight events. Pitcairn asked, Why not set the proposed airplane up so that it could use both engines? This could be arranged by installing a quick-change engine mount. The intriguing conclusion was that they should enter the same airplane in both the efficiency race and the high-speed, or unlimited race, both of which were scheduled for the same day, the speed race following the more sedate event. There was method in Pitcairn's apparent madness: as a marketing technique, they couldn't lose; simply by the originality of their design they would attract attention and news coverage, which would take some of the heat off the requirement of winning; simply because of its sheer novelty, it would be bound to achieve wide reception in the industry.

The new airplane, designated as PA-2 on its engineering drawings, was strictly a handmade product, designed and assembled in complete secrecy in a screened-off corner of the hangar. While the basic structure was being welded together, Larsen designed an ingenious engine mount: merely by unfastening four bolts and some snap-on fuel fittings and throttle linkages, the 90-hp OX-5 could be replaced by the 160-hp C-6 in less than forty-five minutes, the time scheduled between the efficiency contest and the speed event. While the trim little ship was growing under one group of artisans, another group had constructed a small crane, easily disassembled and erected, to swing the engines on the PA-2, aptly named the Sesqui-Wing in honor of the occasion. When the airplane was completed, a small crew sequestered itself and practiced for hours on end to effect the change within the allotted time.

In his office, Pitcairn smiled at the note from the entry committee of the National Air Races, inquiring whether or not, by some clerical error, the same airplane had inadvertently been entered in two such dissimilar events.

The Race Committee was having its own troubles. Philadelphia's official Municipal Airport, located southwest of center city and in marshy land near the banks of the Delaware River, was a mudhole, an eyesore, and totally unacceptable as the host site for the prestigious National Air Races. Despite impassioned requests, the Philadelphia administration had refused to spend any tax money to improve it, holding that aviation was not a proper recipient of public funds, since it was of no importance to the city's economy. Nor would the races be allowed at the Philadelphia Navy Yard—close to the huge exposition grounds—which would be thronged with visitors, because of the hazard of airplanes crashing into the built-up area. Besides, the Navy Yard facilities had been leased to the Philadelphia Rapid Transit Company for its proposed multi-engine air transport line which would shuttle passengers between Philadelphia and Washington, D.C., a major operation in itself.

The PA-2 Sesqui-Wing, as it appeared
at Model Farms Field for the efficiency
race at the National Air Races in 1926.
This version, equipped with the 90-hp
OX-5 engine, nevertheless had streamlined wheel covers and wore a racing
number under its Pitcairn Arrow.

As a result, the National Air Race
officials had to move their entire
program to another location on
which agricultural experiments
were carried on, known as the Model Farms. Against this background
of political maneuvering, the PA-2
was rushed to completion, test-
flown, and pronounced ready by
Chief Test Pilot Ray.

On the day of the dual events in
which he was scheduled to participate, Ray flew the innocent-looking
OX-5 powered Sesqui-Wing into
Model Farms Field and taxied to a
stop alongside Casey Jones's Oriole
speedster, being curried and waxed
in preparation for the big event.

Casey immediately began to ban-
ter with his old friend Ray, who a
few years before had been one of the
Curtiss racing team, about the questionable wisdom of the upstart Pitcairn organization pitting a 90-hp
trainer against his all-winning racing plane. Ray smiled sadly, nodding at the obvious truths spouted
by the Curtiss ace. He acted as if he
were almost embarrassed to share
the same airspace with the champion. Some who overheard the exchange actually felt sorry for him.

The efficiency race, which was
run off first, was merely a preliminary bout, unexciting and largely ignored by the huge crowd in the
grandstands. A group of 80-mph biplanes loitering around a measured
course to demonstrate how little
fuel they could consume if flown at

The PA-2 Sesqui-Wing wearing the OX-5 engine is wheeled into position next to the C-6 engine dangling from its specially designed crane.

their most economical power settings were scarcely calculated to stir up excitement. The grandstands were still filling up with spectators who were streaming in to see the main event scheduled to start forty-five minutes after the last of the low and slow fuel savers had been given the checkered flag.

While the efficiency race was in progress, Pitcairn's crew of quick-change artists arrived in a large truck, carrying the crated C-6 engine and the disassembled crane, which they promptly began to put together in full sight of the grandstand. Soon the crowd was beginning to buzz and necks were being craned at the strange doings. Casey Jones was beginning to eye the proceedings with growing suspicion.

After receiving the first event's checkered flag, Ray quickly taxied up to the completely erected crane and the engine hanging from it, whereupon the Pitcairn crew snappily made the complete engine change in twenty minutes, an un-

heard-of accomplishment in those days. When the newly emplaced C-6 roared into life and the contestants taxied to the starting line, Casey was little short of astonished. Well he should have been. In the subsequent hundred-mile race around pylons over a closed course, Jim Ray/Pitcairn just plain wiped the eyes of Casey Jones/Curtiss and won the race, an unexpected victory by a relative unknown which promptly was recorded in the headlines.

Aviators everywhere focused their attention on the new Pitcairn outfit. Anyone who produced a product that could unseat Casey Jones and his Oriole, which had for so long won everything in sight, really had something!

Airline operators who carried mail, maintenance personnel, and aeronautical engineers were attract-

Merely by undoing four bolts and engine lines, the 90-hp OX-5 is swung free so that the 160-hp C-6 can be moved into position.

In a few minutes, the husky C-6's fuel lines and engine throttle linkages are reconnected and the airplane is transformed into a thoroughbred racer.

Jim Ray and the winning PA-2 Sesqui-Wing after the National Air Races of 1926. Compare the lines of this airplane with the subsequent PA-4 produced two years later.

ed by something else. They saw the enormous potential for profit inherent in a quickly demountable, replaceable engine for commercial flight operations. No longer would airplanes have to be laid up while routine engine maintenance was performed. All one would have to do was swing off a sick engine, swing on a fresh one, and send the airplane on its way. The innovation captured everyone's imagination and attention. Pitcairn was no longer an unknown name in aviation circles.

# The Orowing and the Fleetwing II

Sudden success turned out to be a two-edged sword. While the sensational victory at the National Air Races and the revelation of their quick-change engine mount had certainly achieved their objective of raising the company's profile, they had also generated a tidal wave of inquiries about Pitcairn's plans for the future production of airplanes. The one-and-only, handmade PA-2 had gained the company many admirers who believed that Pitcairn should produce a good line of trainers and cross-country charter aircraft—possibly with a basic aircraft equipped with the dual-engine replacement feature. Pitcairn, at first pleased and heartened, soon became frustrated and anguished. There was no way he could fill any orders, nor would he be able to do so for some time.

First of all, the flying school at the newly opened Hallowell/Willow Grove Pitcairn Field No. 2, was flourishing, heavily attended, and required additional airplanes for training programs; hence all of Pitcairn Aviation's production capacity would be absorbed for a long time. No outside orders could be accepted.

Second, to make matters worse, the small dimensions of the so-called factory in the original wooden hangar at Bryn Athyn did not allow separate production lines for wings and fuselages at the same time that helicopter experimental models were being assembled and Captain Brewer was working up an engine. Pitcairn Aircraft could set up a line for wings *or* for fuselages, but not both.

Wrestling with the galling problem one afternoon in the privacy of his office, Pitcairn and Larsen were becoming more and more discomfited by the dimensions of their problem. Short of building a larger factory, there seemed no way out.

At this juncture Ray arrived, fresh in from a charter flight to Long Island, where he had enjoyed spending some free time needling his old pal Casey Jones. When he tuned in to the problem under discussion, he remarked that Casey had mentioned that Curtiss had devel-

Agnew Larsen, chief engineer of Pitcairn Aircraft from 1925 through the development of the airline and into the transition period of rotary wing.

James G. Ray, chief pilot and vice president for operations of Pitcairn Aviation, Inc.

oped some new engines for a new line of airplanes and that they were going to dispose of their sizable inventory of 250 OX-5 engines in the near future. Furthermore, they wanted to sell off a number—he vaguely remembered the figure of five or six dozen—sets of Oriole wings, fully constructed but undoped. He said that he believed that Casey would sell both engines and wings to him for a reasonable price.

Pitcairn and Larsen were elated. That seemed to solve everything. The OX-5, although now being supplanted by newer engines, was time proven, and Oriole wings had made their own reputation for strength and reliability, just the qualities Pitcairn wanted. The safety of Pitcairn's square tubing construction

had been proven beyond any argument in the Fleetwing accident. Now they had a ready-made opportunity to put those tested components together in one airplane. Production based on a fuselage-only factory line was possible, after all. Pitcairn bought everything.

For the next three years the resulting airplane, the PA-3, a three-place open-cockpit biplane, called the Orowing in deference to its geneology, was to be the training mainstay of all Pitcairn flight operations, which were soon to expand enormously. In addition, many of them were sold to private owners and to other flying schools, as well. In 1926 alone, thirty-five Orowings rolled out the door, all powered with the ubiquitous OX-5 engines. It was this

Geoffrey M. Childs, executive vice president and general manager of Pitcairn's aviation enterprises from 1926 until World War II.

Pitcairn's solution: build the PA-3 airplanes by fabricating the fuselages in the Bryn Athyn hangar-factory and mate them to the surplus OX-5 engines and Oriole wings he had purchased from Curtiss. These ten would soon sell for $2,300 each.

airplane that really put Pitcairn into the manufacturing business. But no one project was ever enough to occupy Pitcairn's active mind completely. He continued to work on his helicopters, on the Pitcairn-Brewer engine, and on other possibilities of business development, including the air-mail line.

For several months his interest had been increasingly flirting with the idea that, when the time was ripe, he might make a bid for air-mail business. He had accumulated a huge volume of information about Atlanta, Richmond, and other major southern cities. From studying railroad schedules and Post Office Department statistics, concentrating on the flow of banking and business mail between them and economic centers of the East, he had made some projections.

New York–Atlanta train service schedules showed that twenty-two

Harold Pitcairn and his first financially successful commercial aircraft, the PA-3 Orowing trainer and sportsman-pilot's airplane. It was the Piper Cub of its day.

hours were required to transit the 760-mile distance; by air, he computed, the total time could be cut to eight or nine hours, including stops along the way. His considered judgment was that among them the banking and business communities of New York, Philadelphia, Richmond, and Atlanta would generate three tons of business mail every day, at least one-third of which would use air transport, which would in turn support air-mail service, using the right-sized airplane. It could, indeed, be a profitable venture for his company.

But, again and again, he shoved the idea under the blotter, for the time was not yet ripe and he was already too overburdened with responsibilities. Early in 1926, he had come to realize that he was spreading himself too thin, beginning to flounder around in a welter of intricate business undertakings. He was overseeing four diverse administrative operations: the Bryn Athyn aircraft factory; the operating company at Willow Grove, with its satellite sightseeing operations during the summertime, when it also operated from other fields around delphia's perimeter; the ever-growing expense of engine research and development with Captain Brewer; and his first love, rotary-wing flight.

Moreover, he was carrying the total administrative load himself.

Pitcairn was unable to put a stop to his imagination, no matter how many balls he had in the air at one time. One afternoon, as he was strolling across the tarmac at the Bryn Athyn field, the idea came to him that the public might like to have an airplane with a bit more eye appeal than the somewhat boxy Orowing. He was running out of the Oriole wings that had been stored in the loft and would have to start on a manufacturing line, anyhow, so why not change over the whole thing at once?

He called Larsen in and explained his ideas. Larsen said he would get right to work, but he also said that he thought that they could produce both the PA-3 Orowing and the new plane, which would be the PA-4. Larsen informed the boss that there should be some engineering drawings within a couple of weeks, or so. He would get right on it.

A month later Pitcairn saw the first rough drawings, but as he approved them, he learned that a number of bills had not been paid for factory supplies and that the situation was in a bit of a mess, which he had to straighten out himself.

Gradually, he had begun to realize that the considerable and invalu-

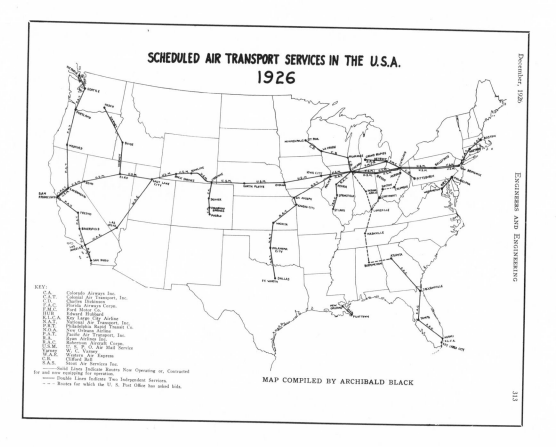

MAP COMPILED BY ARCHIBALD BLACK

able skills of his closest associates were not in the field of business administration. Jim Ray was an accomplished airman, a natural leader of men, highly regarded throughout the organization and in the industry, but he would wither if chained to a desk job. By the same token, Agnew Larsen was brilliant in his profession, inventive and ingenious, with a creative mind, but administrative work was not his forte; in his dedication to solving research or production problems, he frequently ignored the mundane problems of running the factory on a day-to-day basis. As a result Pitcairn found himself enmeshed in an ever-increasing supervisory load and the mere thought of incurring the additional mind-bending burdens of starting and operating an airline daunted him.

The problems he discerned involved in serving a New York–Atlanta route would be formidable. First, he would have to establish support and mail interchange facilities at Hadley Field, New Brunswick, New Jersey (the eastern terminus of the Post Office Department's transcontinental "Columbia Route"), and at the small grass field, more often mud, that had been grandiosely named Philadelphia Municipal Airport. Washington, D.C., the nation's capital, had no civil airport. Worse, Richmond, Greensboro, Spartanburg, and Atlanta had no airports *at all!*

During the period when he and his cohorts were engaged in their secret preparations for the National

Air Races, the harried executive solicited a longtime friend who then held a high post in a trade association, the National Association of Office Managers, to resign his position and join him as the vice-president and general manager of Pitcairn Aviation: the dynamic, irrepressible, keen-minded Geoffrey S. Childs.

To Pitcairn the move seemed to be the perfect solution: as Childs gradually moved in to take over the management of the operating part of the business, the president would be relieved, able to devote more productive time and effort to planning for the future, and to continue his helicopter research. Childs had accepted the position with great enthusiasm, but soon wondered what he had let himself in for.

In September 1926, the Postmaster General advertised four new proposed air-mail routes for bids, supplementing the thirteen CAMs already awarded. Three of the proposals involved service to Louisville, Kentucky, connecting it with Cleveland, Chicago, and Atlanta. The fourth proposal involved the precise routing that Pitcairn had visualized: New York to Atlanta. There were, however, two catches in the proposal: first, the route assignment was for a term of only four years, after which it had to be reopened for new bids. Second, the 760-mile route was to be flown only after banks closed for business, i.e., at night.

Pitcairn found himself in a quandary. For many months he had geared himself mentally to bid for

This 1927 photograph taken at Pitcairn Field Hallowell/Willow Grove shows the lineage of the not-yet-invented air-mail airplane. The two large airplanes are PA-1 Fleetwings; the center air-plane is the PA-2 Sesqui-Wing, in its OX-5 version; and the two airplanes on the end are PA-3 Orowings.

the business of flying the mail over the New York–Atlanta run, but the decision was clouded by the short-term aspects of the award. He saw several serious problems in addition to the obvious ones of no airports, that he had no aircraft in hand to fly the mail, and no pilots to fly the route if he did have airplanes. What would be the state of the industry in four years? Would airlines carry only mail, or would they be trans-porting passengers as well? And, after he had pioneered the route, could some Johnny-come-lately compete and underbid him at the time of the required renewal? Nei-ther the law nor the Post Office De-partment's policy had been clearly defined at the time of the selection of the smallest operators who had submitted the lowest bids.

On the Continent, passenger air-lines crisscrossed every country, fi-nancially supported by their own governments; in the United States, passenger transportation without federal subsidy had been avoided, except for a few sporadic attempts which soon failed. In 1914 Tony Jannus, using a two-place Benoist flying boat, had initiated scheduled passenger service—the first such service in America—between Tam-pa and Clearwater, across the Tam-pa Bay, but it did not last very long. In 1919 Sydney Chaplin, brother of the actor, had opened an air service which also went broke. On the West Coast, Ryan Airlines had modified some old airplanes to carry passen-gers in cabins between Los Angeles and San Diego, a service not heavily used by the general public. More re-cently, the Ford Motor Company had begun to support financially the operations of all-metal Stout single- and multi-engine aircraft over cargo and passenger routes, and Florida Airlines, a new company, apparent-ly formed specifically for the pur-pose of bidding on the Atlanta–Miami air-mail route (which it had subsequently been awarded), was of-fering passenger service, but there were few takers and the industry abounded with rumors that it was in serious financial straits.

Nearer home, Pitcairn had watched the operation of a Philadelphia–Washington passenger air service by the Philadelphia Rapid Transit Company, which ran that city's traction lines, in conjunction with the Sesqui-Centennial Exposition, using ten-passenger Fokker trimotor airplanes. The route was abandoned as unprofitable shortly after the celebration was over; few passengers chose to travel by air when the Pennsylvania Railroad served the same points on an almost hourly schedule, like clockwork, no matter what the weather.

On the other hand, it had been reported that some of the new air-mail operators west of the Rockies were experimenting with mail/passenger transportation in recently redesigned airplanes providing for such service. These planes had turned out to be so large that the mail loads left space for two or three people in the mail bin area, now converted to a cabin. Seemingly, it was merely an attempt to make more use of available, otherwise unused space; carrying the mail was so much more lucrative than carrying people that few airline operators bothered with passenger seats on airplanes or ground facilities to accommodate them.

The possibility of future passenger transportation being a requirement for government subsidy had to be considered, however, before making a bid on the mail-line proposal. Pitcairn, whose memories were clear about the vast development of European air services just after the war, concluded that it was appropriate for him to take Ray and Childs across the Atlantic and make an inspection tour of airports, terminal buildings, factories, airline offices—and flight equipment.

When they returned six weeks later, the decision had been made to avoid passenger service for a few years, concentrating their bid analysis only on flying the mail. If they were successful, the passenger business could be considered later.

What could they use as aircraft over the route? Pitcairn Aviation operated three models of its own design, none of which were really adequate for the task at hand. The five-place PA-1 Fleetwing was too large and too slow; the PA-2 Sesqui-Wing was too small, and the PA-3 Orowing would soon be terminated, for the inventory of OX-5 engines was about to run out and the cache of surplus Oriole wings would soon be depleted.

Burning the midnight oil, the Pitcairn planners analyzed the performance of aircraft then available from other manufacturers, not only aircraft actually in use by mail carriers already in operation, but ships that might be adapted to flying the night mail.

Pitcairn had invested in one of the original air-mail lines, National Air Transport, and as a stockholder was privy to some of the operational problems of such an endeavor. His request for specific information about aircraft on the line and those which had been evaluated was quickly answered by Colonel Paul

Henderson, NAT's general manager, who passed on a memorandum from his engineering department diagnosing the best airplanes for their mail routes when they were planning to bid for the routes they were eventually to receive as Contract Air Mail Route No. 3 (CAM-3).

Double-checking on the somewhat negative analyses, Pitcairn dispatched Ray to the four corners of the United States, arranging for him to fly every air-mail airplane then in use, from the largest to the smallest. Upon his return Ray confirmed that *none* of them fitted into Pitcairn's plans.

After a thorough evaluation of Ray's voluminous flight-test reports, Pitcairn came to the conclusion that his own company could build a better airplane for flying the night mail than anything currently available and do so for considerably less expense in the long run. He set down his own concept of the performance specifications that would exactly meet the requirements he had projected in his analysis of volume and traffic flow, putting down the critical numbers of size, speed, capacity, and operating range.

The theoretically perfect airplane would be single-place, would be able

This photograph of the PA-4, called the Super-Fleetwing and the Fleetwing II, shows that it is totally different from the PA-1 (one of which is silhouetted inside the hangar; note the three open cockpits). The PA-4 was a two-cockpit, three-placer, with room for two in the front cockpit. It was designed especially for the advanced sportsman-pilot. Only ten were built.

to carry 250 pounds of mail at speeds of 100 mph for 500 miles at a stretch so that it could fly a 250-mile leg and be able to return if the weather became unflyable as the destination was approached. He steeled himself for the costs of developing a new design and all that went with such a project. To Pitcairn's enormous surprise, he found his dream plane right in his own backyard.

It was the three-place sports plane he had directed Larsen to design and produce to replace the Orowing, which was running out its string. The design engineering group had fabricated the PA-4 to fill a variety of uses, including primary training, advanced training, and cross-country transportation. But unlike the squarish fuselage of the PA-3 Orowing, its successor had been refined in appearance into a svelte, graceful airplane, attractive to the eye and with the added feature of engine options. The original prototype was equipped with the Curtiss OX-5, 90-hp engine, the same as the Orowing, since Pitcairn had bought 200 OX-5s from Curtiss when he had purchased the Oriole wings. But Larsen had provided that the PA-4 could be fitted with the OXX-6 and the Curtiss C-6 engine, which would give it greater performance—borrowing the Sesqui-Wing (PA-2) idea. And by a simple change in the engine mount, the airframe could be adapted to any size engine, up to 250 hp.

The new design was somewhat confusingly named Fleetwing II, for

Compare this photo of the PA-1 Fleetwing (the Hop-Ship), its bulky construction and big engine, with the preceding photo of the PA-4 Fleetwing II/Super-Fleetwing. As aircraft they are in no way comparable.

it in no way was a variation of the PA-1 Hop-Ship which had begun the Pitcairn Aircraft line. Since he had been so busy with so many diverse problems, the company president had put the PA-4 project in the back of his mind and the first view he saw of the finished plane came when he rounded the corner of the hangar and saw it standing in the sun on the Bryn Athyn field, only a pistol shot from where he had been born. It took only a moment to recognize his ideal air-mail plane.

With the two-place front cockpit replaced by a mail bin, the airplane could carry at least 300 pounds, if it had enough cubic volume. The 90-hp engine could be replaced with a larger engine, as much as 200 or 250 hp. Unfortunately, the Pitcairn-Brewer engine was not yet ready for certification, although it had produced much better performance on the test bench than anyone had hoped for. Until the new engine was available, he could buy and install

This three-quarter rear view of the PA-4 shows clearly the cockpit arrangement, plus the lines that were carried over to the PA-5 Mailwing. Note the ailerons on the lower wing only and the lack of dihedral on the upper wing. The Pitcairn Arrow is still evident.

The Pitcairn-Brewer radial aircraft engine was designed to produce 160 hp. Although it proved out well on engineering tests and in actual airplane installations, Harold Pitcairn elected to discontinue the project and to use Wright J-5 engines already in production.

Profile of the PA-4 Fleetwing II, powered by the OX-5 engine, the direct antecedent of the entire Pitcairn Mailwing line. Compare it with the next photograph.

the Wright 220-hp J-5 engine, the Whirlwind.

Larsen's preliminary engineering computations soon indicated that a revamped PA-4 design would carry 500 pounds of cargo at 100 mph and have a range of 600 miles—more than Pitcairn was looking for, and within days the PA-4 modification, newly designated as the PA-5, was on the way. Everyone agreed it would be called the Mailwing.

In December 1926, just before the expiration of the bid period set by the Postmaster General, Harold Pitcairn transmitted his offer to carry the mail between New York and Atlanta for three dollars per pound. He still had no tested airplane with which to fly the route, no line pilots to fly it, no airfields or support facilities at waypoints or destinations, no navigation aids, no clear definition of the route, and no firm guarantee of the volume of mail that would be carried.

But he thrived on challenges and was resolved that he could make it work.

# The Mailwing

On January 28, 1927, Pitcairn Aviation was notified that it had been awarded Contract Air Mail Route 19, which created a surge of elation throughout the organization.

Initial estimates of the lead time required to begin operating the mail line ranged from six to nine months, based on the experiences of the first ten operators to receive similar awards, so that there was not much time to complete all details required to slip into gear. Childs circled the target date on the large planning calender on the wall of the office: September 1, although both he and Pitcairn had mentally circled October 1 as a realistic slippage date.

For those six months the atmosphere in the headquarters of Pitcairn Aviation was an admixture of frantic activity and frustration, with projects of every kind going on simultaneously. Pitcairn and Childs, aided by Ray, immediately began to shuffle personnel assignments to fill slots that would soon be opening for field managers, supervisors, maintenance men, and pilots, as well as setting up programs to acquire new pilots and train them for service on the line, or to fill in slots vacated by older Pitcairn pilots who would be assigned to flying the mail.

Days were spent closeted with lawyers and real estate experts concerning the terms of leases and operating contracts to be discussed in negotiations with officials of the various cities involved. In the cases of Richmond, Greensboro, Spartanburg, and Atlanta, the Pitcairn group had to persuade the city fathers to create airfields where none had ever existed and then lease them to Yankee strangers. Immediately after the air-mail award was received, Pitcairn had decided that support operations at the municipal airports along the way could be handled by Pitcairn Aviation to everyone's mutual advantage, rather than having local management overseen by local political appointees who might be troublesome. Overtures, carefully couched, were transmitted to the cities to be served.

By March, Vice President and

Chief Pilot Ray was involved in two jobs: day after day he flew up and down the proposed route with Alvin W. Smith, airways extension superintendent for the Department of Commerce, who was officially charged with the responsibility of laying it out, an achievement that soon proved to be far more complicated than anyone had anticipated.

For hours Smith and Ray cruised back and forth, studying largely featureless terrain so heavily forested for the most part that only the largest rivers could be seen from aloft. They took hundreds of photographs to plot the locations of the area's roads, power lines, railroad tracks, farms, and communities in the Piedmont region, but roads were few and, at night, when the flying was to be done, the railroad tracks would be invisible. The only way the line could operate would be with the aid of beacons set up along the route. More trouble, as it soon turned out.

In addition to his aerial survey work, Ray was also responsible for selecting pilots to fly for the company in not-yet-existing airplanes, and at the end of each day's flying was interviewing applicants who professed to be experienced over the areas which one day they would be assigned to fly.

In Philadelphia, Pitcairn's lawyers reorganized the company to perform its multistate functions, creating a number of subsidiary operating companies: Pitcairn Aviation of Delaware, of Virgina, of North Carolina, of South Carolina,

of Georgia. Hours were spent drawing contracts for the construction of hangars on leaseholds as they were acquired, and for access roads and pipelines, including large facilities at the operating bases of Richmond and Atlanta.

Pitcairn's headquarters operation had been streamlined and reorganized by Childs, who had hired as his assistant the English engineer LePage, who had recently returned to the United States again, on loan to the MIT aeronautical laboratories from the British National Physical Laboratory. LePage's job would be administrative, involving engineering advice and sales promotion, for which he had a natural bent, being a writer of no mean ability. One of his functions was to produce the new monthly newsletter and house organ of Pitcairn Aviation, *News Wing.*

Pitcairn's money was flowing outward at a prodigious rate as PA-3 airplanes and pilots were sent to the flight bases under construction. Under the agreements approved by the several cities, Pitcairn Aviation was committed to supply each of its fixed base operations with at least two Orowings and pilots for sightseeing and flight instruction. The government's acceptance of the bid had been predicated on the allocation of at least eight mail-carrying aircraft to the route, with locally based Orowings as backups.

Back at the Bryn Athyn factory, Pitcairn was driving Larsen's group hard to complete the first eight PA-5s, slated to be the line's

The basic PA-5 Mailwing with the 220-hp Wright J-5 engine was quickly sought by sportsmen-pilots in this converted form. The mail compartment was removed and the two-place front cockpit reinstalled, as shown. This airplane, *Yankee Clipper*, was flown coast to coast by a teenaged boy who later became one of the most famous pilots in America, Robert M. Buck. Bob Buck, whose name can be seen on the headrest, retired as a Senior Captain for TWA and was one of the first people to be rated as captain in the Boeing 707 and 747. Note the distinct similarity of the lines of the PA-4 and PA-5S (for Sport).

workhorses. Number one on the production schedule was just beginning to take shape as a beautiful airplane, almost dainty when compared with the ships used by other mail carriers, but the huge Wright radial perched on its nose gave promise of tremendous performance.

And it was going to be a strong airplane: stress analysis computations indicated that the PA-5 would have a strength factor of 7.5, which meant that fully loaded it would be able to handle gust loads that would exert seven and a half times the normal force of gravity. By comparison, the strongest modern lightplanes are stressed to 6.6, and big jets to far less.

The former PA-4's open front cockpit area had been redesigned to create a twenty-six-cubic-foot mail bin and engineered so that the center of gravity, so important to longitudinal stability for ease of

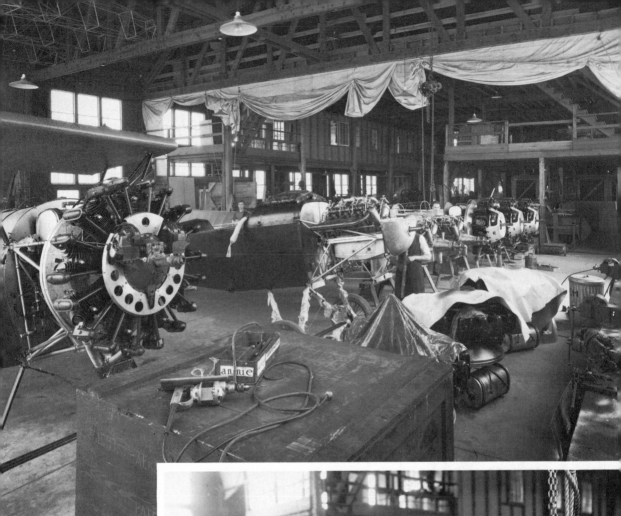

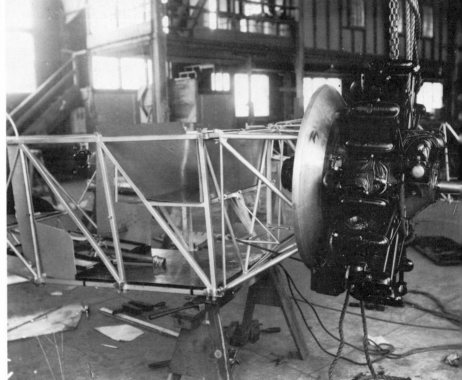

For a few months, PA-4s and PA-5s were built side by side in the Bryn Athyn hangar/factory. Here, two PA-4s (note OX-5 engines) and four PA-5s (with Wright J-5 radial engines) are on the line. The PA-4 line was discontinued soon after this photo was taken.

cross-country flight—especially in bad weather—would not vary by more than an inch, whether the bin was empty or loaded with up to five hundred pounds of mail. The best indication of the PA-5's heritage from the PA-4 was its straight-axle landing gear, retained because of the pressing time requirements to have the ship ready in six months. It turned out that the deadline marked on the calender was optimistic; factors beyond Pitcairn's control were shaping up much more slowly than anticipated.

Once the routes surveyed by Ray and Smith had been recommended to the Department of Commerce and signed off as approved by a phalanx of Washington bureaucrats, it was then necessary for the government to obtain leases, easements, or ground rents for the use of land to be converted to emergency landing

A close-up of the PA-5 quick-change engine mount that was pioneered in the PA-2 Sesqui-Wing. The J-5 could be replaced in less than an hour. In this photo, the Warren truss construction is evident. The fuel tank will be installed in the bin behind the engine mount.

(they called them "intermediate") fields, located every thirty miles along the way. Each intermediate field, according to government specifications, required at least forty-seven acres for the construction of two landing strips of at least two thousand feet in length by six hundred feet in width. In addition, sites had to be acquired for the erection of rotating airways beacons to be erected at ten-mile intervals. This raised a delicate problem.

The Eighteenth Amendment to the United States Constitution, which made the manufacture, sale, and transportation of intoxicating liquors a crime, had soon been followed by an Act of Congress providing for its enforcement by suitable criminal penalties. In this legal environment obtaining title to any property was almost impossible as a short-term matter, for in the bosky dells of the South, where pots boiled and coils dripped as a matter of custom and eventual usage, any strangers were viewed with suspicion; those bearing official credentials were considered—with some justification—as outright enemies. Emissaries from Washington, though they bore sizable checks for otherwise unproductive land, were unable time after time to find anyone to sign anything in those remote wooded and sometimes mountainous areas.

It was a crazy era in America's history. It was the middle of the "Roaring Twenties," a nation rocking along on an economic boom that was creating millionaires overnight—on paper. It was the Flapper Era, the Jazz Age.

Harold Pitcairn was beginning to tear his hair as his company, its operations delayed again and again, was showing appalling symptoms that it might founder in a sea of red ink. He had anticipated a financial loss for the first year, because of the enormous expenses of starting up, normally a concomitance of any new business venture. But he could not see any reversal of the cash-flow picture for months, not being able to see any date when his company would actually begin to fly the mail.

In May 1927, a twenty-four-year-old, Charles A. Lindbergh, flew alone in a single-engine Ryan Monoplane from New York to Paris, an epic flight that fired the public's imagination about flying. His success was soon followed by what the cynical press was to call the "transatlantic air derby," soon followed by "the transpacific air derby." While the public's attention was riveted on the feats of new arising heroes, Pitcairn was going through a period of troubles. The winter and early spring weather of 1927 had halted flying operations at the new Willow Grove field, so that income was nonexistent for almost twenty weeks.

At the same time, costs not only continued for salaries and debt reduction, but were ballooning beyond all expectations. The Bryn Athyn factory staff had been augmented to produce the first Mailwings in time for the projected starting date of the mail line, and bills mounted daily for supplies and equipment to manufacture the airplanes. Legal bills were also multiplying, with the negotiations for additional operating bases in the South, and yet very little progress was being made in nailing down the sites for future operations. Not until May, the month that Lindbergh made his celebrated flight, did Spartanburg select a location for its airfield. Local officials at Richmond and Greensboro were still mulling over suitable locales for their municipal airports. The lease to operate at Atlanta would not be agreed on for weeks, possibly months. By June, the mood at Pitcairn Aviation was gloomy. With only eight weeks to the target date circled on the calender, it was obvious that the carefully scheduled timetable was no more than an empty dream.

Fortunately, as a result of Lindbergh's flight, by the end of May both the Willow Grove airfield and the new satellite operation at Hadley Field were beginning to pick up flight students and sight-seeing rides, which created some cash flow to offset, at least partially, the expenses that were exhausting Pitcairn's financial resources at a rapid clip. Capital was beginning to get tight, almost precarious: the company's president agreed to waive his salary and prepared a directive to cut back entirely on aircraft production after the first ten Mailwings were completed. Pitcairn's personal funds had been depleted by the unanticipated delay in starting the airmail operations.

June was the turning point. On

This is the Number One PA-5 Mailwing as it came out of the factory at Bryn Athyn. Note the straight-axle landing gear and the absence of an exhaust collector ring; exhaust gases came directly out of the short stacks on each cylinder. The noise must have been deafening and the exhaust flames blinding at night.

the seventeenth, the first PA-5 Mailwing was rolled out of the hangar building at Bryn Athyn before a cheering crowd of Pitcairn employees, lifting everyone's spirits like a burst of sunshine on a dismal, cloudy day.

Sleekly beautiful, resplendent with its shining black fuselage and golden wings, a large Pitcairn winged arrow (later to cause hackles to rise in the legal department of the Pierce Arrow Motor Car Company)

emblazoned on its flanks and the words *Pitcairn Mailwing* neatly and optimistically lettered on its rudder, it looked fast just sitting on the ground. It resembled a sleek fighter plane.

After the ground crew had swarmed over it, filled the fuel tanks, and checked the oil level, Chief Pilot Ray stepped lightly into the cockpit, started the engine, and taxied out to the grass runway. After a few moments of waggling the stick and checking the control surfaces, he wheeled slowly around and opened the throttle.

After a run of a few hundred feet, the Mailwing lifted off and climbed several thousand feet over the knot of Pitcairners on the ramp. There its true beauty came out. As the exuberant pilot pirouetted and soared against a background of fluffy white

Mailwing Number One poses for its portrait in July, 1927. This is the Pitcairn Mailwing now hanging in the Main Hall of Transportation in the National Air and Space Museum in Washington, D.C.

clouds, the golden wings flashed the sun's rays again and again, signaling the design's success.

When Ray returned to earth within an hour, his grin told more about the plane's performance than any words could do. When he leaped from the single cockpit to embrace Pitcairn and Larsen, he effervesced about the Mailwing's sparkling performance: it was light on the controls, full of heart, it climbed like a skyrocket, he said animatedly, waving his hands, and flew solidly in every flight attitude, from top speed to hanging on the edge of a stall at the slowest possible airspeed. It had no features that he could recommend correcting—from the beginning, it

This is the Pitcairn Mailwing as modified for actual service, flying the mail at night between New York and Atlanta. Note that the straight-axle has been replaced by the split-axle, with the upper attachments high on the sides of the fuselage (the "long strut" model). An exhaust collector ring has been installed and the hot, flaming gases ducted beneath the fuselage. Two one-million-candlepower landing lights have been added to the lower wings, and in-flight position lights are seen on the wingtips and top of the rudder. This was the typical line airplane.

was virtually perfect, a real pilot's airplane.

Again and again, as the day went on, he circled the field with increasing numbers of sandbags loaded in the mail bin to simulate payload cargo. As Larsen had predicted, weight increments, right up to an excess overload of eight hundred pounds, did not change the Mailwing's flying characteristics or handling qualities, except to lengthen the takeoff run slightly. When the sun declined in the west, Ray stepped out of the ship reluctantly, patted it on the side, and said that it was a winner.

With the prototype's splendid performance, work was continued on the other Mailwings to follow it along the production line, which in turn meant additional expenses for workmen and materials, and further losses on the company's books. Pitcairn and Childs were hard put to keep the company going, but by juggling expenses, transferring funds from one Pitcairn operation to another, and cutting back on nonessential expenditures, they did it, barely. Regretfully, they made the decision to discontinue all manufacturing except the PA-5 line and to dispose of the remaining inventory of OX-5 engines for the best price obtainable. (They sold most of them to a young man in Wichita, Kansas, named Walter Beech, who was manufacturing an airplane called the Travel Air.) They discarded all airplanes not being used more than four hours a day, using the sales money to replenish the company bank accounts.

Flight operations at Willow Grove and Hadley had a few serious problems. From time to time the Pitcairn fleet lost precious airplanes, sometimes with minor injuries to passengers, which brought additional woes to the financially straitened company. After one particularly bad week, Pitcairn and Childs huddled together for several hours, considering the possibility of abandoning the mail contract, closing down the factory, and retaining only the Willow Grove operation until they could build up some cash reserves. Pitcairn had one ace in the hole: the Bryn Athyn operation, still on the family estate, could be kept open to pursue his first love, the development of the helicopter. While battling the relentless financial problems that beset him, Pitcairn also continued to work on rotary-wing experiments and to be awarded additional patents on helicopter devices and systems. Never would he lose faith in rotary wing's potential to make safe flying available to everyone. Preparing for the worst, he reassigned Larsen entirely to engineering research in the helicopter discipline and filled in the vacancy of factory manager thus created with a new man, Carl Chupp.

The Third Annual Commercial Airplane Reliability Tour, sponsored by automobile magnate Henry Ford to demonstrate to the general public that aviation was a legitimate, safe, and ideal mode of travel, was scheduled to visit Philadelphia on its nationwide itinerary. However, the advance route-survey team

had quickly rated Philadelphia's municipal airport as unacceptable and inadequate to handle the huge armada, which included both Fokker and Ford tri-motor airliners, and recommended that the City of Brotherly Love be deleted from the route.

Harold Pitcairn, hearing of this, was aghast and quickly offered an alternative to the tour planners. In the year and a half of its existence, Pitcairn Field No. 2, in the Willow Grove area north of Philadelphia, had become the largest commercial field east of the Mississippi, with almost 125 flight students, numerous

based aircraft, and a substantial sight-seeing business—in the previous year Pitcairn Aviation had carried 16,051 sight-seeing passengers. Up to his ears in his own problems, Pitcairn submitted the idea to the Ford Tour planners that the visit to Philadelphia be transferred to his privately owned facility. Hence, on July 1 Pitcairn Field was deluged with visiting aircraft of every type and size, many flown by famous pilots accompanied by high-ranking officials of leading aviation companies.

As host, Pitcairn took his visitors on a tour of his facilities, including

While waiting for the Post Office Department to authorize Pitcairn Aviation to fly the mail, Pitcairn Field hosted the 1928 National Air Tour (the Ford Air Tour) which brought many famous pilots and airplanes to the Willow Grove field. This was the first occasion for anyone outside of the Pitcairn organization to see the much-rumored Pitcairn Mailwing; it resulted in many orders for the PA-5 from other contract air-mail carriers.

the little Bryn Athyn factory, a few miles away. There they saw, for the first public exposure, the "perfect air-mail ship" that had been rumored about in the industry. Several of the visitors were officers and directors of operating contract air-mail carriers and they lingered for a few moments, looking long and hard at the black-and-gold airplanes inching along the production line. Although none were flying while

The original PA-5 Mailwing continued to fly on the line well into the 1930s, wearing the livery of Eastern Air Transport, as it does now in the Smithsonian Institution's National Air and Space Museum. Note that in this 1931 photo it sported a radio mast and that the original celluloid windshield had been replaced by the flat-section Pittsburgh Plate Glass design, a classic Pitcairn hallmark. (The NASM has displayed this airplane with the original type of windshield, an error.)

the unofficial inspectors were there, they could tell from the very lines of the airplanes that they held promise for the future. As the air tourers departed, they expressed their hopes of seeing Pitcairn Aircraft's exhibit at the forthcoming National Air Races in Seattle, three thousand miles away, across the Rockies.

After the flying flotilla left, Pitcairn and Childs had to make another important decision. Strapped financially as they were, they nevertheless agreed to enter two Pitcairn aircraft, the PA-4 and PA-5 prototypes, in the Transcontinental Air Race from New York to Seattle and to enter two events in the National Air Races as well; logistical planning for the project was assigned to Jim Ray.

While worrying about the day-to-day problems, Pitcairn never stopped planning. Constantly studying statistics obtained from the Post Office Department, he had computed that the volume of mail to be carried on the New York–Atlanta run would be greatly increased if the route could be backed up by extensions to other major cities in the South. His theoretical analysis was soon to be tested. On July 18, 1927, the Postmaster General announced a proposed new route between Atlanta and New Orleans. It was not the route Pitcairn had desired most, for he had been eyeing Atlanta–Miami primarily. But New Orleans provided a possibility for an extension which would enhance his position and protect his investment at the Atlanta airport. He had to make a calculated gamble based on two assumptions: first, he could not believe that the primary route between Philadelphia and Atlanta would not be operating soon—perhaps not by September 1, but by October 1, the "slippage" date he and Childs had agreed on as more realistic. That would mean that he would have the Atlanta operation going and that the New Orleans extension could be quickly piggybacked with little delay. His second assumption was that his bid would be given some extra consideration by the Post Office Department because of the immensity of his expenses in setting up the facilities on the route he had won. He forwarded a bid for Atlanta–New Orleans on the calculated break-even amount of $2.47 a pound. He was, as the saying goes, betting on the come.

Immediately he was faced with an immense dilemma. Hard on the heels of his New Orleans submission, another opportunity arose: the Postmaster General announced that CAM-10, the route between Atlanta and Miami via Jacksonville, originally awarded to Florida Air Lines, had been abandoned because of the carrier's bankruptcy and would be reopened for bids.

Pitcairn was caught in a squeeze. Financially stretched almost to the breaking point by his extensive and expensive preparations for the not-yet-operating New York–Atlanta run, he had put his last chips on the table with the New Orleans bid. Yet for many months he had predicted that a land-development boom in south Florida would create a tremendous economic community of interest between the banking and financial houses of New York, Atlanta, and Miami; bank clearances and business transactions between the Federal Reserve districts of New York, Philadelphia, Richmond, Atlanta, and Miami would surely take full advantage of overnight mail deliveries, rather than depending on thirty-six-hour train schedules, which were seldom met. This development, he concluded, would create huge volumes of mail over what had formerly been a virtually unused route; the original operator whose federal mail subsidy was established on a weight-carried formula had kept going only by mailing bricks up and down the line. When Post Office inspectors caught up with the practice, the operator had gone broke.

Pitcairn really wanted the Atlanta–Miami route, but could not see how he could afford to bid on it in his current situation. He felt like the kid looking in the window of a candy store with no money in his jeans.

The problem solved itself more or less backward. When the Atlanta–New Orleans bids were opened, on July 18, 1927, the award-winning low bidder was a small New Orleans–based outfit, St. Tammany and Gulf Coast Airlines, which had committed to perform for $1.75 a pound, almost half of what Pitcairn had figured as his rock-bottom, break-even price. Pitcairn lost, but

he won; with the New Orleans door shut, the Miami door opened and Pitciarn decided that he had to have it, no matter what the cost, for he believed that in the long run it would prove itself out.

With knowledge of the ridiculously low bid that had won the New Orleans award, he determined to submit a bid for the East Coast extension, "so low that no one could meet it unless he was simply crazy." Sweetening the submission further with the promise to assign five Mailwings for the service plus backup aircraft in reserve at Jacksonville, Daytona Beach, and Miami, Pitcairn on October 22, 1927, transmitted his bid of $1.46 a pound; then sat back with his fingers crossed.

Early in August 1927, the airline leaders, all of whom held air-mail contracts, formed a new trade association, the American Air Transport Association, to deal with a variety of political problems at both federal and state levels; the industry was growing up. Elected as the group's president was Harris M. Hanshue (called "Pop" by his intimates), president of Western Air Express, a West Coast carrier. Clifford Ball, operator of CAM-11 (Pittsburgh–Cleveland), was named vice president and Willard G. Herron, of Boeing Air Transport (BAT), was named secretary/treasurer. The board of directors included Paul B. Henderson, general manager of National Air Transport (NAT); William B. Robertson, president of Robertson Air Services

The last PA-5 Mailwing (a Sport Mailwing) built. It was constructed especially for the personal use of Harold F. Pitcairn. Subsequently modified by installation of PA-7 wings and empennage, it is now owned and flown by Stephen Pitcairn, son of the original owner.

(of which Charles A. Lindbergh had been chief pilot, at the age of twenty-three); George Tidmarsh, vice president of BAT; Walter T. Varney, president of Varney Speed Lines; General John F. O'Ryan, president of Colonial Air Transport (CAT); and Geoffrey S. Childs, vice president and general manager of Pitcairn Aviation. Everyone on the board was already actively engaged in flying the mail except Childs; Pitcairn Aviation was still chomping at the bit waiting to start.

Two weeks later, the Post Office Department wrote that it would be another six to nine months before the New York–Atlanta mail line could go into operation. "We are still having considerable difficulty establishing intermediate fields because of the terrain," the letter said, somewhat disingenuously. Everyone knew that, while heavily wooded, most of the Piedmont plateau was as flat as Florida. Despite the bad news, everyone who saw the letter smiled at the thought of constant face-offs between agents of the Department of Commerce and suspicious locals who undoubtedly were producing personal potables somewhere back in the hills. There was not much to smile about at Pitcairn Aviation's headquarters; they had just gone through six months of serious problems and were hanging on by their fingernails, yet the Post Office expected them to do it all over again. But the picture was changing, possibly for the better.

In September 1927, the Post Office Department stepped out of flying the mail itself, after nine years of incredible pioneering, during which forty-three pilots, flying ancient DH-4 airplanes, powered with war-surplus Liberty liquid-cooled engines, had been killed and twenty-three seriously injured. The western end of the relinquished Columbia Route, between Chicago and San Francisco, was awarded to Edward Hubbard and William Boeing, of Boeing Air Transport; the eastern end, between Chicago and New York, went to National Air Transport.

Other developments, of more direct interest to Pitcairn, had improved the situation: by September 1927, the airways lighting system between New York and Atlanta was largely in place and being tested; Spartanburg's airport was open and Pitcairn Aviation's fixed base operation was starting to do business. Leases and operating agreements had been nailed down and airfields were well under way at Richmond, Greensboro, and Atlanta. Things were still tight but were looking better for the future.

Pitcairn's planning progressed for the New York–Seattle cross-country race, to keep the Pitcairn name before the aviation industry and the public. Ray elected to fly the prototype PA-5 Mailwing, with Ambrose Banks piloting the PA-4 Fleetwing II. They were competing with a

host of other airplanes, including Travel Airs, Curtisses, Boeings, Lockheeds, Bellancas, and Fairchilds, all flown by leading airmen. Starting on September 19, the grueling contest almost turned into a total fiasco for Pitcairn Aviation.

First, Banks was grounded at Bellefonte, Pennsylvania, by engine failure. Then, after repairs had been made, he was forced down again at Bryan, Ohio. On the twenty-first, he disappeared completely for several hours, having made no less than seven precautionary landings because of a balky OX-5 engine. Eventually he left the PA-4 behind and took the train to Seattle; the old PA-2 Sesqui-Wing was dusted off and ferried to the West Coast so that Pitcairn would be able to participate in two events, as advertised. Meanwhile, Ray placed seventh in the coast-to-coast race, losing a higher finishing position because the Mailwing's fuel tank ran dry in flight and after a successful dead-stick landing he had spent several hours obtaining a new supply. Outwardly, all was calm; no one realized the administrative convulsions at Pitcairn's Philadelphia offices which caused Childs to note in his diary, "This race has been anything but a demonstration of the reliability of [our] airplanes."

The PA-4 debacle was soon forgotten in the excitement engendered by the first public flight demonstration of the Mailwing. The fact that Ray won the closed-course speed event in the old PA-2 was of less importance than the effect of

Within a year after their introduction, Mailwings were standard equipment on twelve different U.S. and Canadian airlines. This one flew for National Air Transport between Chicago and Dallas.

the exposure received by the PA-5. Although he took only fifth place in the closed-course race, Banks's subsequent aerobatic demonstration in the saucy Mailwing caught all eyes. To that time, air-mail planes had been like mail trucks, ponderous and purposeful, strictly utilitarian in appearance, heavy on the controls. By contrast, the black-and-gold Pitcairn was a poem aloft, twisting and turning in effortless flight, light and quick on the controls, a scintillating performer, yet obviously with the strength to handle turbulent conditions. It was an impressive, awesome performance. Air-mail operators who had heard about the Mailwing from Ford Tour participants had attended the Seattle meeting to see for themselves what the wonder plane looked like; they came away fascinated by what they saw.

Reaction was immediate. Several mail operators requested delivery positions on the factory line for Mailwings as soon as possible. Until then, Pitcairn airplanes had been sold on the basis of excellent performance, plus low price. The Orowings, the mainstay of the factory for the last year, had been priced at two thousand dollars and the Fleetwing at something less than five thousand dollars. But when the first inquiries came in, Pitcairn put a price of twelve thousand dollars on each PA-5, having made up his mind that he was going to close down the line as soon as Pitcairn Aviation's own needs had been met. When deposit checks came in, showing that the steep price was no deterent, he decided to take a wait-and-see posture for a while and

Texas Air Transport bought a number of PA-5s.

told Childs to put a hold on the factory-closing preparations. Five orders in hand, totaling sixty thousand dollars, would certainly help to turn their cash-flow situation around.

Earlier in the summer of '27, Charles A. Lindbergh, now America's premiere hero, had embarked on a nationwide tour in his *Spirit of St. Louis*, to promote aviation and demonstrate the safety and ease of air travel. Harold Pitcairn, a great admirer of the young man, only six years his junior, invited the shy pilot to stop over at Pitcairn Aviation operations in his swing through the South, promising him that he would be insulated from the petty annoyances of fame. Somewhat to Pitcairn's surprise, Lindbergh had accepted the invitation and adjusted his schedule to visit Atlanta on October 11, then Spartanburg on the thirteenth, Greensboro on the fourteenth, and Richmond on the fifteenth. Which raised another headache.

As late as October 1, Richmond's airport, soon to be named Richard E. Byrd Field (as it is called to this day), was still under construction. At Atlanta, even though the 60-by-120-foot hangar was completed and contained a pair of Orowings and a PA-1 Fleetwing, the field had been only recently graded and seeded and would be unusable until the new grass rooted. Thankfully, both Greensboro and Spartanburg were ready and operating.

Everything came together at the last moment. When the silvery *Spirit* landed on just-opened Candler Field in Atlanta, to be greeted by hordes of newspaper reporters, photographers, and idolizing fanatics, it seemed to most people that the airfield had been there forever. When the most famous monoplane in the world was put away for the night in the large white hangar with "Pitcairn Aviation" over the door, the name was carried in large front-page photographs covering Lindy's progress, so that it went into millions of homes all over the country.

In Spartanburg, Lindbergh saw a Mailwing sitting in the rear of the hangar and was instantly attracted to its beautiful lines. To the astonishment of the Pitcairn crew, he diffidently asked if he could fly it and then put on a sensational exhibition of aerobatics. It was an exuberant performance, the reaction of a seasoned pilot who had been flying straight-and-level for many months

American Airways, the predecessor of American Airlines, flew Mailwings into the 1940 era. Note the AA insignia and the PPG windshield. The fat, low-pressure tires demonstrate the soft field operations the pilots had to cope with. This Mailwing also has a radio antenna atop the vertical fin.

This PA-5 operated by Colonial Airlines had a PPG windshield but no headrest behind the cockpit. The extra-long exhaust stack was designed to prevent the exhaust flames from blinding the pilot on a long, reduced-power descent. By this time, the propeller spinner had been deleted from all Mailwings.

to the scintillating characteristics of the Mailwing. The spontaneous, unsolicited performance garnered extensive newspaper coverage for the Mailwing, in part because Lindbergh was the first person outside of the Pitcairn company to fly it.

At Richmond a few days later, "Slim," as the pilot had invited his new friends to call him, escaped the crowds for a few hours by flying an Orowing over the Virginia countryside, sight-seeing far better than he could in the blind-forward cockpit of *The Spirit of St. Louis*. More newspaper coverage resulted; Pitcairn, already well known within the industry, was becoming known to the public as well.

Toward the end of October, Childs attended a meeting in Chicago of the American Air Transport Association, called to discuss long-range plans for developing the industry. Upon his return to Philadelphia, Childs reported to Pit-

cairn that Bill Robertson had let it slip at an informal get-together that his Robertson Air Service of St. Louis was joining the Curtiss Aeroplane and Motor Company, proposing to build five hundred to fifteen hundred light three-place cabin airplanes to sell for less than twenty-seven hundred dollars. Furthermore, they planned to franchise dealers and distributors in most major cities as sales outlets. It may have been only a straw in the wind; just how much straw and how much wind was the question.

Within a month, things began to jump again at the Pitcairn offices. On November 19, 1927, word came in that they had won the Atlanta–Miami route, now renumbered as CAM-25. Then, in a rush, orders began to come in for PA-5s, accompanied by checks. Colonial Air Transport bought two for its Boston–New York run; Texas Air

During his national tour in the *Spirit of St. Louis* after his New York to Paris flight, Col. Charles A. Lindbergh visited all of the Pitcairn Aviation bases on the not-yet-opened air mail route, CAM 19. This newspaper photo shows Lindy at the Spartanburg base, readying to take off for Greensboro. News coverage on this trip raised Pitcairn's profile tremendously with the U.S. public.

Transport then ordered three, plus spares; Clifford Ball bought two and took an option for a third. Within the week Ball picked up his option. Then Texas Air Transport came back with another order, as did Colonial. Ball ordered still another. Harold Pitcairn tore up his plans to discontinue the production line. Instead he decided to build two dozen Mailwings over his own company's needs, within six months, on speculation.

Orders began to come in from a totally unexpected source, sportsman-pilots. Several wealthy men who had seen the Mailwing in-quired whether a three-place version would be available for personal flying. At first, Pitcairn was loath to change the design as it went through the line, but he pulled engineering drawings of the PA-4 and PA-5 out of his drafting table. A PA-4 cockpit could easily be plushed up and built into the PA-5 in lieu of the mail bin. The PA-5 Sport Mailwing was the result. When the first one was wheeled out of the hanger for Harold to see, he was so smitten that he ordered one for himself.* The

* Harold Pitcairn's Sport Mailwing, NC-6708, serial #30, was to have a curious his-

factory was busy again. Pitcairn Aircraft was over the hump, and Pitcairn Aviation was almost ready to blossom as an airline. On December 12, William P. McCracken, assistant secretary of commerce for aeronautics, wrote that the New York–Atlanta route would be completed by the first of March and that the Atlanta–Miami extension would be ready by September 1, so that the Post Office Department and Pitcairn Aviation should be prepared to operate over those routes on those dates.

Pitcairn's aviation conglomorate had survived its severest test. Although the costs of starting up the airline had created a serious financial drain and the costs of experimenting with the Pitcairn-Brewer engine had exceeded all estimates, the Bryn Athyn factory and the operating company at Willow Grove had combined to save the day. During 1927 they had sold forty-nine airplanes: thirty-two PA-3 Orowings, five PA-4 Fleetwing IIs, and twelve PA-5 Mailwings. The Pitcairn-Brewer engine had passed all tests at the Naval Aircraft Factory and production cost analyses had been concluded, leading to organiz-

tory. Pitcairn sold it in 1930 and it passed through various hands until it was purchased as an antique by Thomas J. Watson, Jr., of IBM, to be included in the Owl's Head Foundation Museum. In 1977, Watson sold the airplane to Stephen Pitcairn, son of Harold Pitcairn. As of this writing it is being flown regularly by the son of the original owner.

ing facilities for its manufacture. During the year Pitcairn Aviation had carried over twenty thousand sight-seeing passengers and more than two hundred flight students were then enrolled. The company's own fleet was up to twenty-three airplanes, with thirty-five pilots on the payroll. Almost eighty-five people were employed, in addition to the pilots and top executives. There would soon be others.

As 1928 dawned, Pitcairn was faced with a new, somewhat unexpected problem: the Pitcairn-Brewer engine tests had been successfully concluded at the Naval Aircraft Factory Engineering Laboratory in a lengthy program of bench runs, and the prototype engine had been mounted in a PA-4 for in-flight tests. Ambrose Banks, who was one of Pitcairn Aviation's top pilots and was slated to be one of its initial airmail crew, conducted the first flights on Febrary 1, followed by Harold Pitcairn himself, who on the same day logged two hours of test-flying the new power plant. When he returned to the Bryn Athyn ramp, Pitcairn was bubbling; soon he would be powering all airplanes bearing the Pitcairn name with his own engines, at great savings over the prices he was paying to Wright and Curtiss. The problem that surfaced was that the notice from the Department of Commerce and his decision to build a fleet of Mailwings was going to tie up all his manpower and production facilities for a long time to come. Two alternatives presented themselves to Pitcairn: he could build a factory to produce the Pitcairn-Brewer engines, or he could farm the project out to a qualified contract engineering firm, guaranteeing it sufficient volume to make the arrangement profitable. He elected to follow the latter course.

It didn't work out. The Light Manufacturing and Foundry Company of Pottstown submitted a bid that rocked Pitcairn back on his heels: the lowest price for a run of 200 engines came to $1,054.65 each. To reduce the cost below $1,000, so the engineering firm advised, required a production run of 500 engines. Pitcairn's thinking had been in the neighborhood of 125 total, which would clearly not make the "nut."

Somehow, the word had leaked out to the industry that Pitcairn Aircraft had a revolutionary engine in development to be unveiled at the next National Air Show, which was scheduled for Detroit. Indeed, Pitcairn had already reserved several booth spaces in the exhibition hall for a pair of airplanes and an engine display, with appropriate publicity from the exposition operators themselves. Determined not to be embarrassed by not having a product to sell, Pitcairn mulled over the idea of buying the Light Manufacturing and Foundry Company so as to recoup his considerable investment in the engine project's research, design, and development—in three and a half years, during the worst business era he had undergone, he had spent $133,000 on it.

He was finally persuaded to drop the matter, for the time being, at least, by his old friend and counselor, Edwin Asplundh, a seasoned businessman and economic planner for the Pittsburgh Plate Glass Company, one of the few people who could look Pitcairn right in the eye and tell him that he simply had too many irons in the fire. It was bitter medicine, but Pitcairn swallowed it. Reluctantly he pulled the engine out of the Detroit air show, although he did plan to have two Mailwings on the floor, as well as at least one flying in exhibitions. The beautiful engine was covered with a tarpaulin in the rear of the Bryn Athyn factory; Captain Brewer was discharged, and Pitcairn turned vigorously to the airline operation.

With the starting date for the airline operation approaching, the mood within Pitcairn Aviation was one of growing excitement. Loose ends were being brought together and operational details arranged. Ray was dispatched to the West Coast to study the workings of experienced mail contractors, including Boeing Air Transport, Western Air Express, and Pacific Air Transport, learning the details of mail handling and route operations. Pilots were selected and each was assigned a Mailwing for his own exclusive use so that he would be familiar with its sounds and individual handling qualities. In accordance with Post Office requirements, Childs arranged for pistol permits for all airmail pilots, field managers, and supervisors.

While Childs was attending to pre-opening administrative details, Pitcairn traveled to New York to attend the annual banquet of the Aviation Chamber of Commerce (ACOC), to which he had been elected a director, a trip that paid off handsomely: Robertson and National Air Transport told him that they were greatly pleased with the performance of their Mailwings and inquired about the possibility of acquiring larger models to carry the increasing volume of air mail that was developing. If the PA-5 could be enlarged, National said, they would purchase another ten immediately. And Juan Trippe, president of a tiny company based in Key West and impressively named Pan American Airways, said he wanted ten Mailwings in one order to carry mail to Cuba on its regular schedules across ninety miles of open ocean.

Rumors eddied around the ACOC hospitality suites. The Seaboard Railroad was said to be proposing a passenger airline between Jacksonville and Miami, and Boeing Air Transport was alleged to be planning extensive passenger service up and down the West Coast, using three-engine cabin airplanes. There was talk of industry mergers and of legislation proposed in Congress which would put a new face on commercial aviation. Pitcairn listened, then tucked the rumors away in the vest pocket of his mind. He had too much to do already without worrying about idle conversation in social settings.

On April 1, airport and airways lights were turned on at every installation along the New York–Atlanta line, so that familiarization flights could begin. The Department of Commerce required that every pilot, to qualify on the route, had to make at least one day and one night landing at each of the thirty or more landing fields strung out over the run. Pilots were required to spot, recognize, and indentify all prominent landmarks, so that they could quickly orient themselves if they strayed off the beeline. Route-check flying consumed another thirty days, but the official word came from the Post Office Department and Department of Commerce before the middle of April: on May 1, 1928, Pitcairn Aviation would commence carrying the mail.

# The Air Line

The opening of the New York–Atlanta air-mail line brought the South a full day nearer the North and hence was enthusiastically celebrated at every city up and down the route. Roads leading to the airports were jammed with automobiles and trucks; ramps, airport borders—even surrounding farms—were congested as people massed to see the big events in their local communities. Civic leaders made speeches. Fireworks flared against the dark skies, and photoflash powder ignited like summer lightning as newspaper photographers recorded tumultuous scenes for posterity.

After a little girl christened his Mailwing, pilot Gene Brown's flight from Candler Field in Atlanta was dispatched by Harold Pitcairn himself—the first flight to get off, quickly followed by Johnny Kytle. About the same time, Sydney Malloy gunned his engine at Greensboro and Ambrose Banks and Verne Treat took off from Hadley Field, New Brunswick, New Jersey, the northern terminus, heading south.

The mail went through as scheduled with only one slight delay: Verne Treat's Mailwing hit a pothole and turned on its back while landing at Philadelphia's disreputable hog wallow of an airport and was seriously damaged. Treat emerged unhurt, transferred the mail to another airplane and continued on to Richmond. Everyone else flew his leg without incident, and three-quarters of a ton of mail was delivered.

With no prior experience in flying on schedule in all sorts of weather, Pitcairn pilots had to proceed on a more or less cut-and-try basis, which led to what were euphemistically called "teething problems." Less than a week after operations began, Verne Treat, bucking unrecognized severe headwinds, ran out of gasoline twelve miles north of Richmond in the small hours of the morning and had to make a deadstick night landing. The mere thought of such a possibility chills the heart of every single-engine pilot, but by great skill and a smidgin of luck, Treat landed in an open

Because Pitcairn Aviation began to operate in June, when the days were long, the pilots had an opportunity to do some of their after-banking-hours flying during daylight. Here, a crowd has gathered at Spartanburg to see the northbound flight out of Atlanta and the southbound flight out of Richmond cross trails and refuel. The third Mailwing, extreme right, is a second section of the southbound flight.

field without damaging either the airplane or himself and quickly arranged to have the mail pouches trucked to Byrd Field. It arrived in Atlanta five hours late.

Three days later Johnny Kytle had the experience with Stone Mountain described earlier. This cost the company a Mailwing. Kytle's accident was so traumatic that hardly anyone realized that Treat, coming into Richmond in the same weather system, had to make another off-airport night landing because of lowering ceilings, this time slightly damaging his PA-5.

On May 19, 1928, all station managers reported that planes had arrived safely despite lines of thunderstorms embedded in the haze blanketing the East Coast. This condition had given every pilot a hectic time, with Syd Malloy arriv-

Gene Brown preparing to take off for a typical night mail run from Spartanburg to Atlanta. Note the butt of the Colt "Banker's Special" revolver in the right knee pocket and the extra cushion tucked between the hard seat-type parachute pack.

Initial flights on any run attracted the participation of top local officials—with appropriate publicity. This view shows the location of the PA-5 Mailwing's mail bin, the "long strut" landing gear arrangement, the old-style windshield and the pilot's headrest.

Mailwings were strong! This one flipped in a night landing and came down on its tail. No personal injuries.

Lost at night in a winter storm, this Mailwing was landed in mountainous country, turned on its back and burned. The pilot escaped uninjured.

ing more than an hour late, shaken by his experience in extreme turbulence and violent downpours.

Pitcairn, perusing the reports, became concerned that his pilots were pushing the weather to keep on schedule and dashed off a letter to all flight personnel, cautioning them once again not to take chances aloft. If the weather was at all questionable, he wrote, they should not fly. If en route when the situation began to deteriorate, they should land at the closest intermediate airport and stay there until things improved. That was what the little fields were for.

Pilots who flew the night mail were a breed apart, fearless and to a man supremely confident of their abilities to cope with any situation aloft. They had listened attentively to Chief Pilot Ray when he cautioned them about flying when ground fog covered the fields, low clouds hung overhead, or thunderheads were popping up all over the place. But few of them heeded his advice. They were Air Mail pilots. The mail had to go through. And they flew, night after night, all alone in the vastness of the sky.

With the airline in operation at last, business was picking up in all directions for Pitcairn's business ventures. National Air Transport had ordered two more PA-5s, notifying Pitcairn that they intended to trade them in on larger models as soon as they became available, which would be soon. Shortly after Pitcairn returned from the Detroit air show, Larsen had begun to concentrate his efforts on a larger Mailwing, the PA-6; the new plane had gone through its stress analysis and wind tunnel tests with a perfect record and the design had been

turned over to Carl Chupp at the factory for production. Pitcairn informed Colonel Henderson at National that the Super Mailwing was on its way.

Trade journals reported interesting new developments. Western Air Express had purchased a ten-passenger Fokker three-engine ship to carry passengers on its Los Angeles–San Francisco run, indicating a trend emerging on the West Coast. The Ford Motor Company was reputed to be subsidizing William Stout in the development of another large cabin ship. People were beginning to elect air travel between points not adequately served by rail, as from Cleveland to Detroit and to offshore islands.

Of more particular interest was the news that early in May 1928, the Senate had passed and transmitted to the House of Representatives a "Revised Air Mail Bill," sponsored by Senators McNary and Watres. The bill contained a provision for government financial support of contract-mail airline operations

The basic Mailwing instrument panel for flying the air mail on night schedules. Modern pilots refer to this as a "primary panel" since it has no gyroscopic-controlled instruments. The two large switches on the lower left panel controlled the million-candlepower landing lights. (Compare with following photo.)

based on an assumption that each cubic foot of payload capacity within an airplane was equal to nine pounds of mail. Strictly construed, this could mean that the amount of cash subsidy would be computed on the volumetric size of a passenger cabin, whether it carried passengers, or mail, or nothing. If the proposal passed, the old subsidy payment basis of actual mail carried would go by the boards.

Three weeks after Pitcairn Aviation's New York–Atlanta mail service went into operation, disaster struck—twice.

At two-thirty on the morning of May 22, 1928, in the face of ground fog and a low ceiling, pilot Edward J. Morrissey took off from Rich-

Pilots designed their own instrument installations. Note how each of the instruments has been canted so that in flight the engine instruments all point in the same direction. If one deviated at all, the pilot's eye would pick up the discrepancy. A clock has been added and in the upper left is a chart of the then-new (1929) low frequency radio range. Most important is the installation of a gyro horizon in the center of the panel. Instrument flying had begun to come of age.

mond, heading for New York. Almost immediately after takeoff, observers in the airport saw him enveloped in blinding fog, so that he totally lost visual contact with the ground. Mailwings were equipped with the latest "blind-flying" instruments: turn and bank, airspeed indicator, magnetic compass, clock. But few pilots who had learned to fly— and had flown for thousands of hours—under visual conditions by the seats of their pants depending on what they could see and feel to keep the airplane under control, used flight instruments for more

than a minute or two at a time. They didn't trust instruments, except to climb through an overcast or descend through an undercast, with plenty of room underneath to make a recovery from any unusual attitudes. They were not trained to make instrument takeoffs.

At full throttle, straining to climb to clear air above the fog, Morrissey apparently became spatially disoriented and lost control. In a classic example of vertigo, he fell off into a descending turn without realizing it, the so-called spiral dive, and flew into the ground full out. Pitcairn's Byrd Field crew heard the screaming engine, then saw a reddish glow in the fog.

Once again the organization shifted into its catastrophe drill. As soon as he was informed of the accident and had forwarded the information to Childs, Ray rolled out of bed, pulled on his flying suit, grabbed his sealskin helmet, and in the same bad weather headed for Richmond, arriving at 5:30, as the sun was just beginning to tint the eastern sky.

Except for picking up the charred pieces, there was nothing to be done.

For Pitcairn, it was Kytle and Stone Mountain all over again, except that this time there was no happy ending. Worse, Pat Morrissey was married.

The company president was devastated. The most difficult thing he had done in his life was to compose a telegram:

TO MRS. EDWARD J. MORRISSEY
563 FENTON AVENUE, AURORA, ILL.

I DEEPLY REGRET TO INFORM YOU THAT I HAVE JUST BEEN ADVISED FROM RICHMOND THAT YOUR HUSBAND WAS SEVERELY INJURED IN AN ACCIDENT SHORTLY AFTER TAKING OFF THIS MORNING. HE DIED BEFORE REGAINING CONSCIOUSNESS. I CANNOT FIND WORDS TO EXPRESS THE DEEP REGRET I FEEL AND THE SORROW OF HIS ASSOCIATES....

Five days later, pilot James R. R. Reid, Morrissey's replacement, was killed shortly after takeoff from Richmond on the same schedule. He had asked to go through, while Verne Treat was waiting at Bolling Field, Washington, for the weather to improve.

The elation of beginning the great adventure dissolved overnight under the sledgehammer impacts of the double tragedy. From top to bottom, morale was at its lowest ebb; everyone was depressed and discouraged. Of all the Pitcairn group, John Kytle was most affected, for Pat Morrissey and Jim Reid had been close personal buddies.

Industry reaction was sympathetic and immediate. Offers of help came in from all quarters, ranging from loans of aircraft to substitute for those lost in the accidents, to pure financial assistance. Paul Henderson of National Air Transport wired:

IF THERE IS ANY POSSIBLE ASSISTANCE WHICH I OR ANY NAT MAN CAN RENDER IN THE MATTER OF YOUR APPARENT EPIDEMIC OF ACCIDENTS, PLEASE DO NOT HESITATE TO COMMAND US. WE WANT TO HELP YOU IN ANY WAY WE POSSIBLY CAN.

Pitcairn responded immediately, thanking Henderson, and wrote: "The loss of two pilots has distressed me a great deal and we are doing everything possible that we know of to avoid loss of life in the future."

Henderson, showing his true colors as a friend, forthwith sent his top instrument pilot to Richmond to demonstrate the technique of needle-ball and airspeed instrument flying, as used by National's highly experienced all-weather pilots over its extensive route structure.

A communication to his friend Clement M. Keys was one of the few times Pitcairn exposed to an outsider the depth of his emotional distress: "The deaths of two of our pilots has given me a blow from

Instrument flight training, circa 1929. The instructor (Gene Brown, here) sat in the open front cockpit of the training plane and the student flew literally "under the bag" in the rear cockpit. Note the late-style Mailwing windshield.

which it will take some time to recover."

Pitcairn regarded the young men who flew for him with a combination of affection and wonder, for he was well aware of the inherent dangers of flying single-engine airplanes night after night, all year, in all kinds of weather. Every night of the week he could see in his mind's eye the handful of tiny airplanes transporting the mail across hundreds of miles of relatively featureless terrain, flown by courageous youngsters totally isolated from the rest of the world. From the moment their engines roared into life until

Pitcairn air mail pilots. Jim Ray, Pitcairn's chief pilot (light suit) selected and trained the men who would fly the mail at night in Mailwings. Two of the famous Faulkner brothers, Ben and Jim (left and right) flank Jim and leather-jacketed Ambrose Banks, insouciance personified.

several minutes after their propellers twitched to a stop, they were alone, out of communication with any other human being, completely on their own. They persisted in the full realization that at any time they might suffer an engine failure or a sudden, unexpected change in the weather, resulting in a forced landing in the dead of night. Yet night after night they would climb into their open cockpits, waggle the controls, and sail jauntily off into the unknown.

The walls at Pitcairn Aviation's offices in Philadelphia were hung with neat charts showing the routes, aircraft and pilot status reports, assignment rosters, timetables, schedule completion records, and volume of mail carried. By looking at the proper chart, an executive could tell who was flying where on any partic-

Air mail pilot Jack Webster flew this Mailwing into the ground one night and suffered only minor cuts high on his back. The cockpit area remained intact.

ular night. No one in the Land Title Building offices, surrounded by neat, orderly, precisely laid out charts and diagrams, really knew *how* the pilots were flying. Actual line operations did not necessarily coincide with the ideal situations set forth at headquarters. They were not so formal. Or neat. Or orderly. Some of them were downright disorderly.

Ambrose Banks, who shared with Verne Treat the duties of flying the New York–Richmond leg, met the schedule from Hadley Field to Byrd on a regular, dependable basis but did not always fly the route as precisely as the line's president and vice president/general manager may have imagined. A superlative pilot, he was nevertheless a lighthearted soul who bore a striking resemblance to Jack Dempsey, then reigning heavyweight champion of the world, and he had a temperament to match: by nature he was gentle and polite, but was always ready for a fight, a frolic, or a footrace at the drop of a hat. He soon acquired a reputation among the pilot group for straying every so often from the straight-and-narrow airways.

There was never any question about when he arrived at Richmond, usually shortly after one o'clock in the morning. Instead of swinging around Byrd Field in a wide turn and making a conservative approach and landing, he invariably began a steep descent from a few miles north of the airport. Leaving his normal cruising altitude of three or four thousand feet with the throttle wide open—which is the way he usually flew—he pointed the spinner on the propeller right at the front door of the flight office adjacent to the hangar. At the last moment he would pull up into a screaming chandelle, which raised the dust—and heads from pillows—for miles around.

One night at about nine-thirty, several hundred distraught citizens of Newark, New Jersey, called the police to complain that a lunatic in a black airplane with yellow wings was performing wild stunts at church-steeple altitude over the heart of town. All the police could do was call all the airports within a hundred miles and raise hell, information which soon got back to the errant pilot. Banks, carrying the mail southbound from Hadley Field, was merely paying his compliments, perhaps excessively, to a young lady of the community who had charmed him. When the complaints reached some lower official in the Post Office Department, for the investigation had soon focused on the air-mail, the reaction was a shrug of the shoulders and the statement that they did not care what a pilot did en route as long as he delivered the mail on time, unharmed. This Banks apparently interpreted as a license henceforth to fly as he pleased.

Since Banks had been assigned his own airplane under the Pitcairn policy that allowed each pilot to have sole care, custody, and control of a Mailwing and to fix it up as he pleased, he took full advantage of his freedom of expression. Other pilots installed cockpit lights, additional instruments, or creature comforts, including pillows and larger cockpit heaters, or armrests; almost every Mailwing bore an identifiying personal insignia of its regular occupant. Banks's whimsical turn of mind, after the Post Office Department's disclaimer regarding the Newark incident, was to mount a wind-driven siren, controllable from the cockpit, on the undercarriage of his PA-5. From time to time, not frequently enough to be caught red-handed, he would hurtle down the main street of Newark, lights off, at 150 feet. In the dead of night that was a noisy feat in itself; when he cut in the siren, thousands of people jumped out of—or under—their beds, undoubtedly thinking that The End had come.

The siren routine came to an abrupt end on a clear night in September, shortly after midnight. Just off Bolling Field, Banks was following the shimmering Potomac River under a moon the size of a silver platter, when he saw ahead, on the right bank, the lights of the Marine Corps base at Quantico, Virginia. It was too good a chance to miss. He reached for the lanyard of the siren, shoved the nose over, and headed in.

Pandemonium reigned as the airplane howled across the drill field, screaming like a banshee, and brought the entire contingent to full military alert. Within seconds thousands of men, in various stages of undress, boiled out of buildings around the compound. The commanding officer, who finally brought some semblance of order to the hullabaloo, promptly fired off inquiries to Washington, asking just what the hell was going on.

As he climbed into the masking darkness, the puckish pilot realized that perhaps this time he had gone too far. The official reaction to a sizzling communiqué from a Marine general was sure to be of a different quality than to complaints of ordinary citizens in Newark: the Army Air Corps, the Post Office Department, and the Department of Commerce would undoubtedly launch investigations to bring the culprit to justice, although their idea of appropriate punishment might fall short of what the general had in mind.

The next morning the siren was no longer to be found anywhere and the expression on Banks's rugged face carried, if not an angelic, at least a "Who, me?" expression, as if he had just arrived from New Zealand or the North Pole.

To demonstrate clearly to possible spies and investigators that he was circumspect in all matters aeronautical, Banks for a time epitomized prudence in flight. His takeoffs were strictly by the book, followed by straight-out climbs to 5,000 feet (where people on the ground could barely hear him passing overhead) and all landings were made power off, circling over the airport in a descending spiral as quietly as a barn owl. He was determined to prove himself exemplary, at least until that Marine general stopped frothing at the mouth.

Except during takeoffs and landings, there was little need for nightmail pilots to keep looking ahead. No other pilots flew at night, so they had the airspace all to themselves. It was customary for mail pilots to snuggle down behind the protection of the windshield, holding altitude and compass heading for hours on end, roaring along, occasionally looking over the side to confirm their progress. Some of them read books or did crossword puzzles as they bored along.

About three o'clock one morning Banks was drilling into the night somewhere near Baltimore, under the pale light of a quarter moon and a canopy of twinkling stars, enjoying the soft little bumps as he popped through the tops of billowing clouds, which broke the monotony of the trip.

Looking for new cloud tops to burst through, he saw ahead a peculiar-looking, long, smooth-topped white cloud just at his altitude. Ordinarily he would have plunged right on through, but for some reaon he elected to pull up and roller-coaster exuberantly over it, whereupon it lighted up, as he subsequently described the scene, "just like a Christmas tree." By the greatest of luck, and the narrowest of margins, he had avoided colliding broadside with the U.S. Navy dirigible *Los Angeles*, which was ghosting along without any lights on a routine midnight cruise—until the lookout stationed on the top of the giant airship heard the sound of an airplane clawing for altitude, realized that they were not alone up there, and alerted the captain, who immediately flipped a light switch. Harold Pitcairn didn't hear about that one for months.

When he recovered from the shock of the fatal crashes, Johnny Kytle's irrespressible nature reasserted itself and he soon was acknowledged as the leading free spirit of the south end of the line.

Unlike the northern segment, between New York and Richmond, which crossed well-populated areas with well-lighted towns and cities always in sight, the hops between Richmond, Greensboro, Spartanburg, and Atlanta were largely over farm country or heavily wooded terrain with relatively few lights below the golden wings of the night-mail planes. Flying for two or three hours at a stretch with no visual diversions made operations even duller routine than they were up north, so Kytle developed the habit of dropping down to low level, when the full moon was shining brightly enough to give some visibility, and hedge-hopping across the endless woodlands of southern Virginia and the Carolinas. Soon he, as did all mail pilots, got to know every farm layout, crossroads, stream, river, and inhabited community—no matter how small—within twenty miles of the center line. Kytle claimed that one time, because a farmer had removed a silo, he had circled for twenty minutes feeling completely lost.

Droning along, night after night, with the coming of spring, Johnny had spotted certain remotely located parking spots, then referred to as lovers' lanes, at the edges of the small towns he overflew, and soon achieved soul-satisfying enjoyment by sneaking along at treetop level, then hitting the twin switches of his million-candlepower landing lights as he burst over the tree lines, flooding the areas with the brilliance of high noon—and shattering moods of amour in all directions. For a time, as a fillip to his act, he tried to buy the no-longer-in-evidence airborne siren from Banks, who merely favored him with a wide-eyed stare and passionately pleaded total ignorance of any such device.

A story leaked back to Ray that one night Kytle, from his perch on high, had noticed a train snaking its way across the flatlands of North Carolina, its locomotive puffing a plume of sparks and black smoke as it hammered over the rails, which showed up under the light of the moon as a pair of silvery ribbons. Easing down to an altitude of ten feet over the straight-as-a-ruler single-line track a couple of miles ahead of the oncoming train, Johnny slid the plane to the right about fifteen feet and flipped on his left landing light. The results were greater than even he had expected.

"You should have been there," he confided to the entranced Pitcairn crew at Greensboro. "I lit the fuse on the biggest sparkler you ever saw! Within ten seconds, every wheel on every car was flat. I'll bet they still haven't found the engine crew; when I went over they were all jumping and running." Strangely, no one ever reported the incident to the Interstate Commerce Commission.

Kytle's endless hair-raising tales of on-the-deck flying eventually induced the other pilots to find some way to make him stop before he met with an untimely end. After one particularly harrowing tale about tree-hopping, they waited until he had left for town, then jammed some pine boughs cut from a nearby grove into the undercarriage of his Mailwing parked out on the ramp.

They had hoped to scare him into abandoning such madness, but it was no use. Nothing seemed to faze him; when the greenery decorating his airplane was pointed out to him the next day, instead of reflecting horror, his face showed elation at the confirmation of his story.

"I knew it, I knew it," he chortled. "I can tell you exactly where I picked them up!"

Many of the pilots had mascots of some sort, animate or inanimate; rabbits' feet and other talismen were common companions as they plied their perilous trade. Henry R. Merrill, known to everyone except his mother as "Dick," carried a pet squirrel in a shirt pocket under his flying coveralls. In flight the little furry head would frequently peek out of the loose neck of the flight suit, sniff the wind, then retreat to the warm comfort of the pocket—until one night, when the bushytailed co-pilot for some reason decided to take a stroll around Merrill's shoulder and strayed into the blast of the slipstream, at which time the state of Georgia and the flying squirrel became one. To this day Merrill claims to be somehow related to most of the squirrel population of Chattahoochee National Forest.

Back in Pitcairn's mail offices, operations were not fun and games. From various indications, the aviation industry was entering another era of change and some major decisions would have to be made soon.

With the mail line functioning in good order, attention turned to other aspects of the total operation. The Orowing line's termination had left Pitcairn without a primary flight trainer; after surveying the field, Pitcairn Aviation became a dealer for the new Kreider-Reisner Challenger, a three-place open biplane. Three of them were assigned to each of the Greensboro and Spartanburg bases.

Contemplating the possibility that there might be a push for passenger transportation when the Congress acted on the pending McNary–Watres bill, Pitcairn purchased a Fairchild cabin model to be used for engineering and cost analyses, just in case Pitcairn Aircraft might have to build similar planes, tentatively to be called Cabin Mailwings. Subsidies for a cabin model would be higher than the actual loads carried by Mailwings, under the pending legislation.

There was money in the airline business, all right: in June 1928, Pitcairn Aviation had received its first check from the Post Office Department, a whopping $25,710.37 for one month—in spite of the traumatic teething problems the company had undergone. Early in June and again in July, the lines on the mail-volume charts in Pitcairn's office had begun to climb, signifying that business was improving rapidly.

Not only by his own records was air mail being embraced more and more by business: Colonial Air Transport had ordered two more PA-6 Super Mailwings on the basis of their experience with the PA-5s,

Pitcairn air mail pilot Dick Merrill ready to take his Mailwing from Atlanta to Richmond in 1929. Merrill remained with Pitcairn Aviation when it was sold to the Curtiss-Keys organization and through its subsequent name change to Eastern Air Transport. He eventually became Chief Pilot for Eastern Air Lines.

although the new, larger model would not be certificated by the Department of Commerce until that December.

Again "showing the flag," keeping the Pitcairn name before the industry and the public, the company president took Ray and Childs to the Detroit air show of 1928, exhibiting a PA-5 adjacent to a skeletonized PA-5 display, which revealed the details of its construction. Their booth area was well attended, but the star of the show was what was at that time a monster of an airplane: the all-metal Ford Tri-Motor, which would carry fourteen passengers, a pilot, a flight mechanic, and a new crew member described as a "flight attendant," who would see to the cares of passengers.

Rumors were flying faster than ever at the meeting. Tony Fokker had responded to the Ford/Stout display by announcing that he was building a thirty-two-passenger airplane and that Universal Air Lines had ordered five of them. It seemed an empty gesture; the word was out that Fokker's company was overwhelmed with financial problems.

Merger talk was again rampant. Gossip had it that Goose Bay Airlines, Interstate Airlines of Chicago, and Scenic Airways of Phoenix had merged to form a holding company called United Aviation Corporation, with $20 million capitalization; C. M. Keys and the Pennsylvania Railroad (PRR) reportedly had put together a deal involving a combination air-rail system, using the Keys-controlled airline, Transcontinental Air Transport, to carry people coast to coast. Furthermore, they had hired Colonel Charles A. Lindbergh as a consultant to set up the combination air-rail passenger route for a two-day schedule between New York and California, cutting train time by one-third. The real bombshell came with an announcement that to carry out the plan, TAT had ordered ten Ford Tri-Motors.

It seemed that almost every airplane manufacturer was planning to take a shot at designing large passenger-carrying planes, spurred on by the favorable reports emanating from Washington regarding the passage of the McNary–Watres Act. Igor I. Sikorsky had developed for Juan Trippe's growing Pan American Airways a thirteen-passenger flying boat, powered by two Pratt & Whitney Twin Wasps; Curtiss Aeroplane and Motor Company had plans for a large land-based passenger biplane to be called the "Condor." Boeing had a three-engine, twenty-eight passenger M-80 in the works, and Douglas engineers were working nights to catch up, with twin-engine high-speed planes capable of toting more than a dozen passengers. Lockheed Aircraft had a ten-passenger twin in preliminary design.

When a high-ranking PRR official casually inquired of Harold Pitcairn about the possibility of working something out in the nature of a plane-train arrangement between New York, Atlanta, and Miami, it was an omen that the winds of change were beginning to reach his sails. Pitcairn's response was that he would have to give it some serious study.

Since Childs and Ray seemed capable of keeping the airline under control and Larsen had the PA-6 prototype in the final stages of construction, Pitcairn announced that he was taking his wife for a vacation from their growing family of five children. It was not to be completely a vacation; he had an appointment to meet Juan de la Cierva in England.

While he was away, the PA-6 Super Mailwing, a "stretched" version

Pitcairn Aviation was the first scheduled airline to use radio navigation aids. The Department of Aeronautics set up low frequency stations at Hadley Field (New Brunswick, N.J.) and at College Park, Maryland; this Mailwing was the first equipped with airborne equipment, including a one-inch-diameter copper mast, well guyed. Another pioneering venture.

of the PA-5, was rolled out for its flight certification program, with Ray in charge of the initial flight tests. Once again, he was delighted with the performance of the ship on its very first flight. Using the same wings and Wright J-5 engine used on the PA-5, Larsen had somehow bettered the handling characteristics and flying qualities of the earlier airplane by lengthening it, thus creating greater longitudinal stability. At the same time, it was able to carry nearly twice the volume of the older Mailwing, with space for 22,500 letters instead of 13,000. It was a delight to fly, and the word about it

quickly spread throughout the industry.

Pitcairn had made the decision before leaving for his European vacation that, if the new airplane met their high standards, a factory run of twenty-five would be initiated to meet the growing demand for mail planes, for volume had more than doubled because of a reduction of air-mail postal rates. Pitcairn Aircraft would commence deliveries immediately after certification of the PA-6, to fill fifteen pending orders, totaling $170,000, from National Air Transport, Colonial Air Transport, Colonial Western Airways, and Canadian Colonial Airways, as well as two Super Sport Mailwings that had been ordered by the Department of Commerce for the use of its top aviation officials.

On August 16, 1928, while the company president was still out of the country, Johnny Kytle hit another mountain and again walked away from it. He had taken off from Atlanta in a light rain which fell

A gathering of Pitcairn eagles at the last line operation of the Mailwing in the background. The man second from the left (in the light suit) is Verne Treat, one of Pitcairn Aviation's original pilots. At the microphone is Capt. Eddie Rickenbacker, then President of Eastern Air Lines. The three-striper to whom he is speaking is Gene Brown, another Pitcairn Aviation pilot; the third man from the right, looking at the camera, is Captain Dick Merrill.

The breed improves. The PA-6 was a "stretched" PA-5, with more capacity. The crank-hole for the inertia starter shows up just behind the engine, as does the chute mounted below the cockpit for emergency landing parachute flares. The PA-6 also had a very short stack on the exhaust collector ring, as seen here.

from a high overcast, and pointed northeast, climbing steadily. Ordinarily it would have been no more than a two-hour hop to Spartanburg, so after three hours, when he did not show up, Pitcairn's search-and-rescue plan was put into gear. Calls up and down the line developed only information that he had last been seen and heard over Jefferson, Georgia, about one-quarter of the way to his next stop. Then he had disappeared.

Two days later the word came to Pitcairn headquarters:

HIT ROCKY MOUNTAIN NEAR OLD FORT NORTH CAROLINA STOP PLANE A WASHOUT STOP MAIL STILL IN WRECK STOP AM OK SGD KYTLE

The cavernous mail bin of the PA-6 increased the Mailwing's capacity from 21.5 cubic feet to 40 cubic feet, making it more productive for air mail operators. In 1928, the old, small-sized windshield was still factory standard. The PA-6 was also the first of the "short strut" Mailwings. Compare the fuselage attachment point with earlier photos.

Rushing to the large wall charts of the states covered by the airline, Childs found Old Fort, right on the edge of the Blue Ridge Mountains, a few miles from Asheville; Kytle was more than thirty-five miles off course!

When he cheerfully returned to work, Kytle told a blood-curdling story. Before he got to Anderson, his halfway point, he was without warning enveloped by a severe wind and rain storm. It was subsequently reported to be a spinoff from a hurricane that had lashed the Atlantic coastline, but no one had warned the air-mail pilots about it. For more than a hour he had flown on solid instruments, lashed by turbulence that kicked his tiny airplane around the sky like a leaf, totally blinded by torrential downpours that made him wonder why the engine didn't drown and quit cold. For an hour and a half he didn't know where he was, or which way to turn to escape the fury of the violent winds. Then abruptly he saw the tops of trees, only an instant before he struck, shearing a swath right into the steep

Many PA-6s came into private ownership when they were phased out of air
mail operations. This one was owned
and flown by an Eastern Air Lines pilot
named Stephen Pitcairn (right) here
shown with his captain, John Gill.

side of the mountain. For seventeen
hours he worked his way through
heavy underbrush, over heavy boul-
ders, and across swollen streams,
with no food or water, soaked
through and severely bruised by the
impact, until he reached the town of
Old Fort and reported that he was
still on the payroll. He was back flying the line within a week in a newly assigned Mailwing. As for his
wrecked machine, neither the U.S.
mail sacks nor the airplane were
ever recovered. The remains still
rest on the side of the mountain.

In England, Pitcairn saw for the
first time how the Autogiro performed: it made steep climbs and
flew straight and level under full
control, even at slow speeds that
would bring a fixed-wing airplane
tailspinning out of the sky. Most
amazingly, it could approach at
well-nigh zero forward speed and
land from an almost vertical descent, rolling no more than a few
feet.

At dinner that night with Cierva,
Pitcairn's mind was stirred and an
abrupt change developed in his
thinking. Clearly, Cierva had made
rotary-wing flight a reality. The
Autogiro was not a helicopter, but
refinements would surely lead to
true vertical-lift flight, since the
Cierva Model Eight, the C-8, would
then do almost everything a theoret-

ical helicopter could. Over cigars and brandy, Pitcairn saluted his host's accomplishment, and suggested that someday they might integrate their efforts and pool their experience for a common end. The foundation was laid for what would be an historic association.

Within a week of his return from Europe, Pitcairn called his top associates to an informal caucus in his living room to enlighten them about the thoughts he had developed on his trip and his estimate of the long-range outlook of the aviation industry.

He believed that he could see a pattern developing, one which indicated that a new era was soon going to replace the one in which they had begun to be comfortable. As the implications of the pending McNary–Watres legislation were perceived, he believed that several well-funded consortia would be formed to dominate the emerging passenger airline business, eventually driving out small operators, as had happened in the automotive industry. His cautious evaluation was that the days of individual-owner entrepreneurs in the airline business were numbered.

It would take a great deal of money to equip Pitcairn Aviation for carrying passengers and to be competitive with the prospective array of large, well-financed holding companies rumored to be sprouting in corporate boardrooms, which in turn posed a problem of serious proportions. Pitcairn Aviation had always operated on his private funds,

and its owner would be hard put to underwrite any program to meet the challenge.

Pitcairn Aviation's executives had to be mentally prepared for him to make a change in the path he had so carefully charted. He could of course follow the airline trend toward carrying passengers, which meant finding new sources of financing, possibly by public subscription—going public—or he could withdraw gracefully from airline operations and concentrate on the fast-growing development of private aviation, zeroing in on the concept of the Safe Aircraft.

In the meantime he urged his associates to exude total confidence in the future of the airline, while he planned detailed alternative strategies as new factors boiled to the surface throughout the aviation trades. For the next few months he would be playing a game of high-stakes poker, and they all had to play their cards close to the vest.

Then he turned to his discussions with Cierva. Since the rather poor-quality motion pictures he and Larsen had viewed on their last visit and the operational shortcomings that had dampened their enthusiasm for the seemingly miraculous piece of equipment, the invention had gone through many refinements and improvements; the new C-8 could take off in one hundred feet or so and could literally land on a tennis court. Cierva had licensed some foreign firms on the Continent to manufacture and sell his machines.

Importantly, Pitcairn said he believed that the experience Larsen and he had accumulated in their own rotary-wing experiments could contribute improvements to Cierva's basic design and that he had already opened the door to further discussions along that line. He proposed to return to England and to purchase an Autogiro for thorough engineering analysis at Bryn Athyn. Only then could he make an informed decision as to the company's future.

Within a week the name of Juan de la Cierva hit the headlines in the United States: he had flown his Autogiro across the English Channel, nonstop from Croydon Airport, London, to Le Bourget, Paris.

# An Industry in Transition

Clement Melville Keys had been one of the first corporate financiers of any stature to envision the potential of air transportation in the United States. As early as 1923, when U.S. aviation was an unregulated, barnstorming, failing circus, he had assembled an investment group to reorganize the fiscally moribund Curtiss Aeroplane and Motor Company. It was considered a major miracle that after a number of ups and downs, he had finally made it a success. As a result he was soon recognized as the prime mover and shaker in the industry.

During 1923 and 1924, Keys was a leader in the political campaign to have Congressman Kelly introduce the Contract Mail bill, for the purpose of extracting the transportation of mail from government monopoly and putting it into the hands of civilian contractors. The Kelly Act was destined to be the turning point for the entire industry.

Shortly after the passage of the Kelly Act of 1925, called the Air Mail Act by most people, Keys, while still president of Curtiss, had assisted in the organization of National Air Transport, Inc., the successful bidder for the Chicago–Dallas route (CAM-3), and was soon elevated to the chairmanship of the line's executive committee. He then induced Colonel Paul Henderson, Second Assistant Postmaster General for airmail, to resign from his government position and become NAT's general manager, thereby acquiring instant expertise for the airline's operations. It was a shrewd move, so everyone agreed.

Soon the NAT fleet of obsolete airplanes was replaced by an even larger fleet of Curtiss "Carrier Pigeons," already designed and built for the purpose of flying mail. The cross-pollination aspects were not lost on one of NAT's original stockholders, Harold F. Pitcairn.

For the next two years, as privately operated mail lines branched off north and south from the coast-to-coast Columbia Route, including the Eastern Seaboard line known as Pitcairn Aviation, Keys had not rested on his oars. Having established the precedent of federal subsidization of air-mail carriage by an act of Congress, his next step was to organize an industry-wide effort to amend the act's original language slightly by adding the words, "one cubic foot of space being computed as the equivalent of nine pounds of air mail."

Then in another momentous move he began negotiations with the Pennsylvania Railroad on a novel concept: an arrangement by which airplanes would fly passengers by day and trains transport them by night, from New York to San Francisco. It was a master strategic move. With one blow he had changed the railroad officials, who had historically been wary of the consequences of passenger air travel on their own business, from opponents to willing, enthusiastic associates. Keys's plan would cut the travel time from East to West by almost half and give the PRR a huge competitive advantage over every other railroad in the country, particularly the New York Central and the Baltimore & Ohio. Then the supersalesman convinced the formerly staid, conservative railroad officials that they could obtain this prime market position merely by investing in a few airplanes. He would do the rest.

No matter how secretive the negotiations, there were bound to be some leaks, hence the rumors of the formation of the new airline, Transcontinental Air Transport (TAT), with interlocking directorates and cross-support from other Keys-controlled companies—NAT and Curtiss Aeroplane and Motor Company. Soon the clandestine organizational plan was unveiled to the press; financial pages reported the development of the "Keys Investment Family" and its plans.

NATIONWIDE TAXI SERVICE PLANNED, blared one headline in *Aviation*, perhaps the country's best aviation publication, in a piece reporting that a new company was to be formed: Curtiss Flying Service, Inc. It would soon establish a number of bases throughout the nation for (air) taxi service and flight schools. C. M. Keys, president of Curtiss Aeroplane and Motor Company, and head of NAT and TAT, would also be chairman of the board of the new service, with Charles "Casey" Jones serving as president.

Financing, according to the release, would be underwritten by Blair & Company, James C. Willson & Company, and the National Aviation Corporation. On another page it was reported that Curtiss Flying Service had ordered 150 airplanes from Curtiss Aeroplane and Motor Company. Pitcairn quickly saw that Keys was entering into an integrated operation like Pitcairn's own—only larger.

Scrutinizing the financial pages, Pitcairn noted other interesting developments in the next few weeks. All of the stock of the Scintilla Corporation, the primary source of magnetos and ignition parts for aircraft, had been purchased on a three-way, even-steven basis by Curtiss Aeroplane and Motor Company, the Wright Aeronautical Corporation, and Pratt & Whitney Aircraft Company; its new directors were Frederick B. Rentschler, president of P&W, Frank B. Russell, vice president of Curtiss, and Richard F. Hoyt, board chairman at Wright. The same names were beginning to pop up again and again, indicating coalescence within the industry.

On September 1, 1928, two days before Pitcairn's briefing session with his top executive assistants, aviation trade journals had reported that the proposed TAT–PRR air-rail service from coast to coast would commence within six months, using Ford Tri-Motors operated by Northwest Airways, "a subsidiary of Transcontinental Air Transport"—hence another Keys enterprise. The TAT–PRR gambit was eyed with concern by other companies which had been left standing at the gate. In what was patently a desperate countermeasure, the New York Central Railroad somewhat lamely announced that it had linked with Universal Air Lines and Harris M. Hanshue's Western Air Express to provide air-rail service to the West Coast, using seven-place all-metal single-engine Hamilton airplanes. Keys immediately stole their thunder by announcing that TAT was ordering ten more three-engine Fords for some $800,000, loudly proclaiming the obvious safety of three engines over one. The New York Central had egg on its face.

Behind its calm facade, the aviation industry was seething with plans, schemes, and combinations. Igor Sikorsky's firm was reorganized and rejuvenated by a heavy infusion of fresh capital underwritten by G.M.P. Murphy & Company, James C. Willson & Company, and the National Aviation Corporation. All rights for commercial sales of Sikorsky aircraft were awarded to Curtiss Flying Service. Pan American Airways, operating between Miami and Havana, then on to points in Central and South America, had been the principal buyer of Sikorsky flying boats; Pan Am was reported to be a subsidiary of the Aviation Company of America (AVCO), recently formed with Richard F. Hoyt as its president. On the Pacific Coast, Boeing Aircraft Company and Boeing Air Transport (BAT) had merged to form Boeing Airplane & Transport Company, a holding company, with directors named Frederick B. Rentschler; K. R. Kingsbury, president of Standard Oil of California; Chance Vought, and others.

Fokker Aircraft Corporation was next to fall into the net. In a somewhat surprising move, Anthony Fokker relinquished all control of his company to a group of financiers led by James A. Talbott, president of Richfield Oil, who became chairman of the board; Harris M. Hanshue, president of Western Air Express, was named new president of Fokker; and one of the directors was L. H. Piper, president of Universal Air Lines. Financial battle lines were discernible; the larger companies were going to get larger every day. The McNary–Watres Act was going to make the airline business extremely lucrative, and the big-money crowd was moving in. Pitcairn's analysis had been proven to be painfully accurate.

So far, all attention had been given by the consortium organizers to east-west routes. Pitcairn began to wonder how soon they would begin to look at north-south routes, as well. He decided to make a chess move of his own, just to see what would happen: he told Childs to prepare a news release announcing that Pitcairn Aviation planned to commence passenger operations the following spring. The first link to be activated would operate between Greensboro and Atlanta, a distance of 307 miles, with rail connections to the north and south of those passenger terminals, connecting New York and Miami. The total en route time would thereby be cut from two and a half days to one full day, beginning in April 1929. Ultimately, the release said, Pitcairn Aviation would serve the entire Eastern Seaboard between New York and Miami, and concluded that the airplanes serving the route would be Ford Tri-Motors, the new "Leviathans of the Air."

Within a few days of his announcement Pitcairn received a number of telephone calls, letters, and telegrams—and several visits from emissaries of C. M. Keys, the Pennsylvania Railroad, and even Pan American Airways. The visitors professed to be interested in reaching some sort of accommodation with him. Pitcairn listened more than he talked, for he suspected that most of the conversations were more in the nature of fishing expeditions than actual overtures. But his gambit had disclosed considerable interest in what he was going to do, which had accomplished his objective. By dangling a morsel of bait, he had discovered for certain that there were hungry fish in the pond. He had a salable commodity.

To keep the waters rippling, Pitcairn dropped another rock into the rumor pond: on November 8, 1928, with appropriate news releases, Pitcairn Aviation ordered three Ford Tri-Motors, at $49,475 each.

It was not all bluff. On December 1, 1928, the Atlanta–Miami line, CAM-25, opened, extending Pitcairn Aviation's route structure from New York to Miami, a total distance of fifteen hundred miles. It was the longest north-south route in the airline business, the largest line operated by one company east of the Mississippi River, and the third longest line operated by one company in the United States.

In the meantime, the big organizational games were still being played. As 1928 was drawing to a close, a massive financial bombshell was dropped with the announcement that nine major aviation companies had consolidated to form Universal Aviation Corporation, to operate passenger and mail service. Some of the companies involved did not mean much in the overall picture, but others did: Universal Aviation Corporation had joined with

Western Air Express to acquire control of the Fokker Corporation of America and would unite the routes of Western Air Express, Universal Air Lines, Robertson Aircraft Corporation, and Northern Air Lines; in conjunction with the New York Central Railroad, the American Express Company, and Greyhound Bus Lines, Universal Aviation would dominate transportation from the northeast to the southwest of the United States. Almost immediately, Keys reported the formation of North American Aviation, Inc., capitalized at $25 million, underwritten by fourteen financing institutions and brokerage firms.

The situation had crystallized.

Three or four giant holding companies soon would control all civil aviation. Piece by piece, they were going to acquire large and small airline operations, either by purchase or by outright intimidation. They would eliminate some and merge a handful of little lines into larger ones. Small operators who did not go along would either be crushed financially or left to die on the vine.

Harold Pitcairn's mind was made up. He would sell at a profit before he would be maneuvered into a defensive position. Besides, the way he viewed the overall situation, he still had at least a year to plan some strategies of his own.

# PART THREE

# The Autogiro

# Turning Point

As were other aviation leaders, C. M. Keys had been keeping a close eye on Pitcairn Aviation's growth and development. In the fall of 1928, he began to exchange personal thoughts with its president about the potential for passenger operations between New York and Miami. Most of their conversations are best described as fencing sessions, as the two men probed gently for the other's true feelings. The fifty-three-year-old Keys must have wondered if the thirty-two-year-old Pitcairn would be an easy mark for takeover by his all-powerful North American Aviation, which had brought many other operators into line. In any closely knit industry, there are few—perhaps, *no*—inviolable business secrets, and Pitcairn's financial burden for the sixteen-month period between the award of CAM-19 and the day it actually went into operation had not gone unrecognized. In the opinion of many, the winning bid of $1.46 per pound for the newly acquired Florida route was suicidally low, would generate losses that Pitcairn

Aviation could scarcely afford and might bring down its entire corporate structure.

In their conversations during the eight months since the route award, Keys knew side bets had been made at aviation get-togethers as to whether or not Pitcairn would *ever* put CAM-25 into gear. Hence, Keys may have felt that he was dealing from totally intimidating strength which would cow the younger man.

However, Pitcairn was not entirely playing a blind hand. The Atlanta–Miami route that had been assigned to him, although not yet in operation, was nevertheless a significant asset in negotiating. Under the existing regulations, it was a protected route, unavailable to anyone else for carrying the mail under a federal subsidy; it was exclusively assigned by the Postmaster General to Pitcairn Aviation for a four-year period, dating from the commencement of service. However, under the language of the Kelly Act, not only was subsidy computed on the basis of actual weight of mail carried, at the end of the four-year cycle the route was up for grabs again. A new, lower bidder could take the route away from the incumbent.

If a financial behemoth like Keys wanted to, he could put on a squeeze play by going into head-to-head competition without subsidy, installing a passenger line to run parallel with Pitcairn's all-mail line. C. T. Ludington had put together a plan for a nonsubsidized passenger line that he was convinced was going to be self-supporting. Would Keys do the same thing from New York to Miami via Atlanta and wait for the rebidding time?

The implications of the prospective McNary–Watres Act were not altogether understood. The primary thrust was to change the subsidy structure from actual mail carried to a presumption that each usable cubic foot of space within the airplane was carrying nine pounds of mail. But the Postmaster General had put in a provision (still being debated in Washington) that he should be empowered to use his own judgment as to the sufficiency and efficiency of service that had been rendered, which would be a major factor in reassigning routes. If that were so, perhaps a lower bidder could not take the route away from a pioneer of the route, who had built it up from the beginning. If adequacy of service would be the key, incumbents might not be dislodged purely on the amount of their bids submitted to the Postmaster General.

To preclude anyone else from electing to step in with such a passenger program, Pitcairn announced his own intention to initiate the combination mail/passenger line in early spring 1929, six months away. It was a calculated psychological stymie until he could make a more informed judgment of what he wanted to do.

Three choices had already presented themselves to Pitcairn: he could continue to run the airline, with passengers or without; he could become more heavily involved with Cierva in commercial development of rotary-wing aircraft; or he could try to ride both of those fractious ponies at once. The issue was money. How much would each of those options cost? Especially, would the airline, with passenger hauling a distinct possibility, be profitable enough to support both itself and the rotary-wing effort?

Within the Pitcairn Aviation family there were three schools of thought. One line of reasoning, led by Jim Ray, was that if Keys and others who had approached Pitcairn really believed that passenger flying without a mail subsidy was a solid proposition, it arguably offered just as much opportunity for Pitcairn's own profitable operation. As the incumbent carrier, Pitcairn Aviation already had its own support facilities along the route. What was more, Pitcairn's long-range alternative plans had included detailed feasibility studies of an air-rail format, which could be initiated in steps; all they needed was the equipment. He had ascertained that Ford Tri-Motors would be best for the loads they had projected. After a period of experimental operations, he could decide intelligently whether to expand or not, making the judgment on the basis of actual experience. At the end of the Post Office Department's route assignment period, he would be in a position to rebid for the route, or elect to drop out. Ray had made some telling points.

Another line of thought, propounded by Childs, was to eschew the passenger line for another year or so—they still had three years to go on their first route assignment period—and stick to the currently profitable style of operating on a mail-only basis. As long as Pitcairn Aviation held the exclusive right to transport mail over the route, any new, competitive operator up and down the East Coast would have to rely entirely on passenger revenue, which had historically been a failure everywhere in the absence of federal subsidy.

Pitcairn had to plan for the long haul. Based on his estimate of the overall industry situation, Pitcairn Aviation would soon become an isolated operation. Despite the size of its route structure and its growing success in carrying the mail, he prophesied that it would soon be a financial pigmy compared with the three or four heavily financed giant consortia, and he was concerned about pitting his personal resources against the endless flood of money in the arsenal of the Aviation Company of America, North American Aviation, General Motors, and the Ford Motor Company.

Pitcairn's thinking was further colored by the fact that his first love had always been the development of the Safe Aircraft, then to make it available to every American. Before making any decision, he had to return to England and see Cierva's latest Autogiro.

This time he not only saw the new Cierva C-8 fly, but flew it himself. After a short briefing by Cierva's chief pilot, Pitcairn was able to make steep, almost vertical descents to acceptable landings, rolling to no more than two lengths of the little Autogiro. He took off after short runs, flew at such low speeds over the ground that automobiles passed him on the roads below, and developed a feel for the amazing abilities of the unusual aircraft. He told the British engineers that he would purchase a C-8 then and there if they could reassure him that the rotor system would function properly were the machine equipped with an American-built Wright J-5 engine, which would turn the propeller in a clockwise direction, rather than the counterclockwise style used in England. When they made it clear that the free-spinning rotor blades worked no matter what sort of propulsive power might be used, Pitcairn said that he would arrange to have a Wright J-5 radial shipped to them for installation and forthwith placed his order.

Then he sat down for some serious discussions with the inventor and his English associates. Pitcairn requested an option that would give him time to return by steamship to the United States and consult with his own colleagues—including patent counsel, although that may not have been specifically mentioned—so that he might consider purchasing all American rights to the Cierva invention and patents. He also raised a proposal in the nature of a reciprocal agreement: he would cross-license all existing and future Pitcairn Aeronautics, Inc. patents on rotary-wing inventions to Cierva's British company, would cooperate fully in all of his future experimentation and development on the Autogiro, and also swap engineering technology. In addition, Pitcairn Aeronautics would be renamed Pitcairn-Cierva Autogiro Company of America. In essence, Pitcairn was proposing a virtual partnership with Cierva. The keystone of the deal, of course, was the scope and validity of the U.S. patent protection that could be obtained on Cierva's inventions. The option period would give Pitcairn's lawyers an opportunity to investigate the patent situation thoroughly.

Pitcairn returned to the United States, as usual brimming with ideas. A few months before, the Guggenheim Foundation had announced that it would sponsor a National Safe Airplane Competition in 1929, offering a large cash prize for an aircraft of the heavier-than-air type that would cruise at 110 mph, glide at 38, land at 35, and stop within 100 feet after an approach over a 50-foot obstruction. As a result, American engineers had been thrashing about, experimenting with variable incidence airfoils, adjustable cambers, slots, and flaps.

Pitcairn had been watching them, but only half-heartedly. He was too busy with the airline, the Mailwings, and particularly in finishing a new home, Cairncrest, on the family estate for Clara and their five children. It was to be a stately, dignified mansion overlooking the hills of Pennsylvania and the towering Bryn Athyn Cathedral, also still under construction. Their new home would have open fireplaces and paneled rooms, with spacious halls and containing enough bedrooms for all the youngsters he and Clara planned to have. He would have a den just off the main entrance and deep within the structure would be a rough-stone finished room where he could entertain his friends and associates. He named it, aptly, the Stone Room. The Guggenheim contest had been far from his mind.

But when he was in England, flying the Autogiro, Pitcairn realized that if with a little practice he could land it on the lawn of his home, the Cierva C-8 would more than satisfy the seemingly impossible criteria set by the Guggenheims. He knew that he had the winner of the coveted prize practically in the palm of his hand. But he didn't want to win in a foreign-built aircraft. He wanted to have at least one rotary-wing craft bearing his own name to enter in the Guggenheim competition.

For three weeks the Philadelphia patent law firm of Synnestvedt & Lechner delved into the records of the Patent Office, while Pitcairn reorganized his business affairs for an immediate move when he got the green light. He brought production genius Edwin Asplundh on board to plan for the future expansion of manufacturing facilities. Pitcairn Aircraft was using all of the Bryn Athyn factory space and in fact had outgrown the old assembly line's capacity. A new plant would be required if he proceeded with the Autogiro program.

Then Pitcairn took Ed Davis, one of the Synnestvedt & Lechner partners, to England to review the option and license arrangements. They returned on December 11, 1928, on the S.S. *Aquitania*, accompanied by several boxes and crates, and within a few days a modified C-8 had been assembled at the Bryn Athyn field. On December 18, twenty-five years almost to the day after Orville Wright's first powered flight at Kitty Hawk, the first Autogiro in America made its first flight. Harold Pitcairn was the first American pilot to fly it.

Industry and public reactions to the flight of the remarkable "windmill plane" were instantaneous and

An historic photograph: the first rotary-wing flight in America, with Harold Pitcairn flying the Cierva C-8 Autogiro at Bryn Athyn in December, 1928. The Aero Club clubhouse and windsock are at the bottom of the picture.

overwhelming. For the first time observers saw a flying machine that took off in a relatively short distance, climbed steeply in a strong, sustained ascent, flew straight and level at high speed, and maneuvered with ease, then came back overhead, almost stopped in midair, settled slowly to earth, and landed with a roll of less than its own length.

For the first time everyone realized why Pitcairn was so enthused with the Autogiro. The strong trend toward social mobility, reflected by the rapid growth of the automobile industry, offered many interesting possibilities for an aircraft that could be operated from confined spaces. But Childs and Asplundh were aghast at the projected costs of acquiring the Cierva license, creating a new production facility, research and development to produce a commercial version of the still-experimental machine, and the problems of financing the entire project. The research and development costs by themselves would be staggering; producing a machine that would be certifiable by the Department of Commerce, which would be necessary before any could be sold to the public, could overextend Pitcairn's already tightly stretched finances to the breaking point, as had the problems of starting the air-mail line.

Pitcairn reviewed three possibilities: he could borrow capital from banks or other lending institutions, using Pitcairn Aviation's considerable assets for collateral; he could convert the company from a wholly privately owned to a public corporation, then sell enough stock to make it financially liquid and able to carry on both the airline and Autogiro programs; or he could sell the airline outright and allocate the proceeds for the new undertaking of rotary-wing aircraft development.

The decision of course was Pitcairn's alone. It was his company, his money, and his future. For four years he had committed his personal fortune to fund several aviation enterprises, including his helicopter research, the development of the Pitcairn-Brewer engine—which he had reluctantly dropped, since no one would build it for the price he believed could be profitable—the creation of a line of airplanes, a string of fixed base operations now stretching from New York to Miami, and the operation of the airline itself.

By the end of 1928, CAM-19 was making a profit, the operations at Hadley Field, Willow Grove, Richmond, Spartanburg, Greensboro, and Atlanta were in the black and new operations at Jacksonville, Daytona Beach, and Miami were beginning to shape up. The scheduled aviation enterprises were operating five flying-service airfields, an aircraft factory, and an air-mail airline, and Pitcairn was seriously considering some kind of a business alliance with Juan de la Cierva to jump into the rotary-wing development, which had been his quest since 1916.

The increasing regularity of communications by telephone and correspondence between Keys and Pitcairn did not go unnoticed in financial circles and spawned all sorts of speculations. Wherever aviation people gathered, the word was that Pitcairn Aviation was definitely going to tie up with Keys. This precipitated a meeting in Philadelphia in which Pitcairn was offered a proposition for a merger with Colonial, Stout, Maddix, Southern Pacific, and Tide Water Oil for a monster airline. Pitcairn respectfully declined. Then the Post Office Department indicated that it wanted Pitcairn Aviation to tie in with Pan American Airways to Cuba and South America. Pitcairn took this under advisement. Another proposal was to merge with St. Tammany and Gulf Coast Airlines and Texas Air Transport. Pitcairn said no. His general posture and demeanor was one of disinterest with any proposal to dispose of or dilute his interest, ownership, or control of the very successful airline he had developed. In March 1929 he had opened the spur line from Daytona Beach to Tampa, was extending air-mail service to five additional cities, and carried almost twenty-eight thousand pounds of mail, a 200 percent increase. He could afford to be aloof He took special satisfaction in the grand opening of CAM-25 on December 1, 1928.

It was not a particularly auspicious beginning. The entire Eastern Seaboard from Jacksonville north was covered with a heavy blanket of ground fog and airplanes were grounded all over the Piedmont region until the sun rose high enough to burn off the mist. All of the mail deliveries were late and connecting flights were delayed for hours. It took several days to get the schedule back on the track, as published.

CAM-25 had been almost as galling emotionally and financially as had been CAM-19 in the start-up delays and expenses. First of all, the bid, submitted October 22, 1927, was awarded to Pitcairn Aviation in the phenomenally short time of one month. Since it also was to be flown at night—the original route holder (Florida Airways, CAM-10) had flown only daylight schedules, and had abandoned the route after less than a year—the newly awarded 615-mile route from Atlanta to Miami had to be laid out and light beacons established literally from scratch. Under the government contract five Mailwings had to be assigned to the route, plus backup airplanes, usually Orowings or Fleetwing IIs (PA-4s).

While CAM-19 was opening, with all of its problems and accidents, Ray had selected pilots for the southern end of the line and had the new cadre of pilots on route familiarization flights. Somehow, Pitcairn Aviation had inaugurated operations on CAM-25 on December 1, 1928, and by the end of the year Pitcairn was in a state of exaltation. It was the best year Pitcairn Aircraft had ever had, with forty-three airplanes delivered for a gross income from sales two and a half times 1927 sales. Mailwings were being used by eight air-mail lines, the U.S. Department of Commerce, the Canadian Department of National

Defense, and Sport Mailwings were in the hands of a number of private owners. The people who had bet that Pitcairn *would* start the CAM-25 operation had already pocketed their money. To all the world, Pitcairn Aviation was a success.

From the stream of visitors and correspondence flowing into his office, proposing mergers or other arrangements, Pitcairn was very much aware that he had a readily salable asset; the only issue was its price. Caution dictated that he should not consider relinquishing the airline until he had complete answers to the status of the Cierva patents, so while his patent attorneys were assiduously chasing down all aspects of the patent situation, their principal intermittently continued his talks with the insistent Keys, but necessarily temporizing on the decision.

In the relative isolation of Bryn Athyn, Larsen and the brilliant Paul Stanley, a new engineer assigned to the project, were running flight-comparison tests of the C-8 Autogiro against the PA-5 Mailwing. They were also investigating all of the intricate design details of the C-8's rotor system, in contemplation of enlarging the scale of the mechanism and improving its aerodynamic efficiency.

C. M. Keys, typically cool, pragmatic, and detached, began a campaign designed to capture the highly attractive Pitcairn air-mail line and to integrate it into his ambitious planning for a dominant position in the airline industry when the McNary–Watres Act would go into effect.

Pitcairn found himself walking a tightrope. Keys kept raising the ante from his bottomless resources of strategy and money, while Pitcairn kept staving him off. He had almost decided that if the Cierva patent situation was strong and if he could recover the million and a half dollars of his own money he had invested in the airline, he would sell. The pivotal issue was the patent clearance from Synnestvedt & Lechner, which was not ready yet. Pitcairn remembered the story about the old maid who every day became more particular and less desirable; he could say no to Keys once too often and wind up with nothing.

The first experiment by Pitcairn was to compare the takeoff and climb performance of the Cierva C-8 Autogiro against that of the PA-5 Mailwing. That the C-8 left much to be desired led to redesign and re-engineering by Pitcairn and his associates.

Keys must have made optimistic progress reports to his own principals; word came back to Pitcairn that someone within the preeminent investment banking firm of Blair & Company, a major Keys group underwriter, had mentioned in a private conversation that the Keys-Pitcairn deal was almost concluded, sparking a rumor that quickly spread throughout the industry.

On a bitterly cold winter day Pitcairn arrived at his office to find on his desk a carefully worded letter from Synnestvedt & Lechner advising him that in their opinion the Cierva patent footing was favorable for his proceeding with the proposition of aligning their forces. As the final details of the proposed business alliance were being solved by frequent transatlantic telephone calls and exchanges of cables, some acrimonious dialogues between the Pitcairn and Cierva groups over royalties to be paid by each firm to the other for the use of licensed inventions almost upset the deal. Not

until Colonel John Josselyn, the managing director of the British concern, arrived in Bryn Athyn with an unrestricted power of attorney to enter into a final agreement, did everyone sit back and relax.

After several exhausting sessions, myriad details were finally ironed out and the agreements were signed on February 14, 1929. For almost $300,000 (in 1929 dollars), Pitcairn Aeronautics obtained the U.S. rights to Cierva's inventions and patents. The agreements provided for technical collaboration between the Pitcairn and Cierva groups in a comprehensive approach to rotary-wing research and development and also for the repository in Pitcairn Aeronautics, Inc., of all resulting U.S. patents.

In less than two months Pitcairn Aeronautics, Inc. was renamed Pitcairn-Cierva Autogiro Company of America, Inc. (PCA); it would be a research, development, and patent-holding (i.e., licensing) company, not a manufacturing company. Ac-

tual production would be the function of licensees who would agree that all patentable developments and improvements would flow back to PCA and thus be available to all of *its* licensees. The objective was to reduce the costs of continuing research and development that would ensure the commercial success of rotary-wing aircraft; it was hoped that no one would have to waste time and effort duplicating what some other licensee had already accomplished—"reinventing the wheel" would be eliminated.

Pitcairn knew that he was embarking on a very expensive venture: with Asplundh, Childs, and Larsen, he had drawn up a pro forma budget for the first year of a million dollars, over and above the initial payment to Cierva Autogiro Company, under their agreement. The budget projection included the cost of designing and constructing an eighty-thousand-square-foot factory building on Pitcairn Field, Willow Grove, where Autogiros would be produced, as well as future variations of the immensely popular Mailwing series. With all further emphasis to be concentrated on the Autogiro and the Mailwing, Pitcairn made the anguished decision to scrap two planes already in advanced design: the all-metal Mailwing and the projected Cabinwing, both of which, as Childs noted in his diary, were simply "thrown into the trash pile." Pitcairn dismissed his feelings about the decision, saying that soon there would be other, better Pitcairn aircraft coming off the line.

No one could disagree with him; the U.S. economy was booming, and people were spending their new wealth on recreation and personal pleasures. Lindbergh's spectacular transatlantic flight, followed by that of Chamberlin and Levine, then by Lindy's widely publicized national tour in his little *Spirit of St. Louis* and his subsequent participation in setting up the passenger routes of Transcontinental Air Transport and other sensational aviation achievements, had once again stimulated the nation's interest in aviation. On March 4, 1929, the United States inaugurated a former secretary of commerce as its thirty-first president, Herbert Clark Hoover, a world-famous economist and humanitarian.

Soon, Pitcairn and Keys were sparring again. The Philadelphian nonchalantly mentioned that the PA-6 Super Mailwing was selling well, having proved itself to be such a real money-maker for several airlines, including some passenger lines that used it to supplement their regular mail services on routes that were not yet heavily used by air travelers; during 1929, more than a third-of-a-million dollars' worth of Super Mailwings would be sold.

At the same time, Pitcairn Aviation's mail loads were increasing on all routes and plans were on the drawing boards for still larger Super Mailwings, the PA-7, to be powered by the 235-hp Wright J-6 engines, which had additional capacity to carry the growing volume of air-mail. Pitcairn's attitude was outwardly bullish, but under the surface he was troubled by the projected expense of the rotary-wing venture. Keys was aware of rumors still being bruited about the industry: that Pitcairn was to merge with

Pan American, with Texas Air Transport, with St. Tammany and Gulf Coast, with Colonial—any or all of which were conceivable to the big-thinking New York entrepreneur. He did not want to lose his tactical position, either.

The Pitcairn PA-7S, the "Super Sport Mailwing," was widely used for racing in the early 1930s. The front cockpit of this one has been covered by a removable fairing and the front windshield stored. A "speed ring" has been installed on the engine and wheel pants have been added for additional speed. With the PA-7 series, all Mailwings sported the slanted plate-glass windshield and many had the high turtleback, instead of the pilot's headrest. This photograph was taken after the disastrous fire at Bryn Athyn, when all manufacturing was moved to the Willow Grove field. The building in the background is still standing and in operation as a heavy equipment factory.

Quietly, the decision was made by Pitcairn to postpone taking delivery of two of the three Ford Tri-Motors that had been ordered with such a splash of publicity; only the first one would be put into service, painted in Pitcairn livery for publicity flights along the route. Because of the solid growth of his airline and the flood of inquiries about the availability of the Autogiro, Pitcairn momentarily harbored the thought that he could continue to operate both the airline and the rotary-wing division of his business, if the latter could be made self-sustaining. In any event, it was premature to make

This Ford Tri-Motor on the Bryn Athyn field in 1929 was one Pitcairn had ordered while contemplating passenger service on the air mail route. The all-metal Ford was to be the catalyst that would change the entire structure of airline aviation and indirectly seal the doom of the Mailwing line.

the final decision. To stoke the rumor mill, Pitcairn announced that it was consulting with Ford's Bill Stout about equipment required to support the operations of the Tri-Motors and that plans and specifications for large passenger terminal facilities were being worked up for all airfields that would have passenger service.

Keys kept sweetening the pot. He had begun his campaign simply by telling Pitcairn that his investment group intended, come fall, to run a passenger line between New York and Miami, no matter what. They didn't need a mail subsidy, he said. They could absorb a considerable loss until the line was established. Pitcairn's response was that he was still planning to commence mail-passenger service himself.

A few weeks later Keys proposed an alternative: his group would work out an accommodation with Pitcairn Aviation, sharing the route's support facilities, for the use of which they would pay Pitcairn a fee. When that proposal was rejected, Keys next proposed an outright merger. Pitcairn kept shaking his head.

Word then came that Keys had held a series of meetings with the Atlantic Coast Line regarding a possible New York to Miami air-rail service, similar to the TAT–PRR coast-to-coast arrangement he was setting up. Pitcairn tended to discount it as a mere rumor, and refused to be stampeded. He still had a couple of cards to play: official figures released by the Post Office Department for January 1929 showed Pitcairn Aviation to be the fourth largest mail carrier from a standpoint of income and third largest in miles flown.

Meanwhile, the aviation industry was kept aware by a series of press releases that Pitcairn Aviation was not content to stand pat; spur and shuttle lines were being added regularly to its main route, so that more cities were being served each month. C. M. Keys was aware that Pitcairn's air-mail line extended almost eighteen hundred miles and was still growing, and mail poundage had almost tripled over the previous year. Industry observers concluded that, no matter how shaky Pitcairn Aviation may once have been, it was well on its way to financial rejuvenation.

Pitcairn's resourceful press releases were giving every outward indication of driving ahead with the passenger operation, but he was actually delaying the project without seeming to do so: the delay was publicly ascribed to Atlanta's failure to purchase Candler Field and improve it for the operation of the Ford passenger ships. No one seemed to notice that a few months earlier, Pitcairn's own Atlanta base had hosted a Ford Tri-Motor, which used the airport without difficulty.

Pitcairn Aviation exhibited the new PA-7 Super Mailwing at the 1929 National Air Show in Detroit and the place buzzed with rumors about a Pitcairn-Keys linkup. These the Pitcairn company's attendees tried to stop, or at least staunch, without success, for it was hard to explain their president's absence at the important aviation gathering. That fact had added fuel to the fires of merger speculations.

Pitcairn was entirely involved with the Autogiro project, leaving him time for little else. He had taken Larsen and a construction engineer to Europe to confer with his new associates on the technical problems of laying out a factory production line, and Larsen was already roughing out designs for an Autogiro considerably larger than the diminutive, single-place C-8, since they had concluded that such a small version would have limited commercial sales potential in the U.S. market. A three-placer, following the lines of the classic Sport

Mailwing series, was contemplated; indeed Larsen's group was planning an Autogiro/Mailwing that would revolutionize air-mail service to small communities that could not afford to build their own airports: with an Autogiro/Mailwing, air-mail could be delivered directly to post offices, using nearby parks or lawns as landing spots for the versatile aircraft.

Publicity generated by the limited flying of the C-8 in the immediate vicinity of Bryn Athyn quickly excited the nation about the potential uses of rotary-wing aircraft, especially high government officials; soon, the army, the navy, the Department of Commerce, the Post Office Department, and the National Advisory Committee for Aeronautics were clamoring for demonstrations of the "windmill" machine that could land on its own shadow. Every request was respectfully turned aside by Pitcairn, who doggedly resisted what he considered any premature exhibitions; he wanted to hold off until he had three or four 'giros flying, his own modified C-8, plus two experimental ships to be built by his own company and perhaps another pair brought over by Cierva. But the pressures brought to bear by high government sources could not be denied.

In the spring of 1929 he dropped everything—including his negotiations with Keys—and flew the C-8 from Bryn Athyn to Langley Field, Virginia, to demonstrate its unique flying characteristics at the annual conference of the National Advisory Committee for Aeronautics. The

Harold Pitcairn test flies the C-8 over his home, left center. The world-famous Bryn Athyn Cathedral is shown at center top of this air-to-air photograph. Compare the wingspan of the Cierva Autogiro with the length of the fuselage; wings were necessary only to provide ailerons for lateral maneuvering.

next morning, he hopped across the watery expanse of Hampton Roads to Norfolk so that naval officials could also see how an Autogiro performed. It was the longest Autogiro flight ever undertaken in the United States up to that time, ranging more than five hundred miles over Philadelphia, Wilmington, Baltimore, Washington, and Richmond. Everywhere, crowds boiled out into the streets to gawk as the wonder-plane passed overhead.

A few days after returning to Bryn Athyn to have the ship thoroughly examined by his engineering staff for any signs of excess wear or incipient mechanical problems, the little Autogiro was pronounced fit for another trip, and Pitcairn

promptly flew off to Washington to make a special demonstration for the Spanish ambassador and a large number of guests, including members of the administration and the Congress. Press reactions were overwhelming, making Pitcairn's decision to proceed with rotary-wing development look better every day. Now the thorny question of whether to expand the airline business or to pursue rotary-wing aircraft development could no longer be postponed. Except for one worrisome development: Keys had been quiet for several weeks. Now the question was whether he was looking in some other direction, or whether he was simply playing possum.

To provide additional grist for the rumor mill, and to move the static situation off dead-center, photographs of a smiling, confident Geof Childs appeared on the business pages of eastern newspapers as he and his wife departed for Europe on the S. S. *Staatendam*, "to take note of European developments in passenger air transport, in anticipation of the inauguration of the Pitcairn Aviation passenger line some time during the coming fall." It was a ruse. In reality, Childs's nerves were twanging like guitar strings; he was taking his wife on a European vacation on the boss's orders, to get away from the relentless pressures of his tumultuous years in the aviation business.

While Childs was away, the Post Office Department released information that Pitcairn Aviation had made a $34,000 profit during the month of May, its largest to date, indicating a steady pattern of growth and financial stability.

A few days later, Pitcairn received in the mail an invitation to have an early meeting with C. M. Keys in his New York offices. Clearly, negotiations were coming to a head.

It was a low-key meeting in high-key surroundings, complete with oak paneled walls and the inevitable pool-table-sized desk. As the two friends discussed the state of the industry and its future, Keys picked a long Havana cigar from a humidor at his side, clipped off its end, lighted it, and blew out a long streamer of blue smoke.

"Harold," he said, picking his words slowly and carefully, "we have reviewed our position relative to acquiring your New York–Miami mail line. My board of directors has authorized me to make a final offer: I can go no more than two and a half million dollars."

Pitcairn said nothing for perhaps ten seconds, while he formulated his

Harold Pitcairn discussing the Autogiro with Orville Wright at the Langley Field meeting to which he flew for the NACA examination. This photo shows the large Wright J-5 engine as mounted on the small Avro fuselage. The C-8 was flown from the front seat: note the round Model-T type control wheel and, above it, the rotor blade tachometer dial.

response in proper language. Then he said contemplatively, "I will have to consult with my own board of directors."

The two men shook hands and Pitcairn departed by train to Philadelphia, hoping that Keys had not seen the yellow feathers at the corners of his mouth.

On June 12, 1929, less than a week later, the hugely profitable sale was consummated in a lengthy written contract, accompanied by a certified check in the amount of $500,000, the balance to be paid within thirty days. The Curtiss-Keys Group had acquired Pitcairn Aviation, Inc., including the air-mail route, all of the

The last Eastern Air Lines Mailwing, as of 1955. Its pilot, Eastern Captain Gene Brown, was one of the Pitcairn Aviation original crew; he later flew Eastern's jet airliners before he retired. This PA-7M posed for its picture at Miami International Airport.

fixed base operations at New York, Richmond, Greensboro, Spartanburg, Atlanta, and on down to Miami, and had agreed to retain all operating personnel for two years. Pitcairn continued to hold the Bryn Athyn factory, his flying field at Willow Grove, and the Pitcairn-Cierva Autogiro Company. The way was now clear for Harold Pitcairn to pursue his dream of providing Americans with personal air transportation in easy-to-fly Safe Aircraft.

For a time the airline would go through corporate and name changes as it was absorbed into a giant consortium, for Keys would soon sell Pitcairn Aviation to North American Aviation, one of the four super holding companies then dominating civil commercial aviation in the United States. For a few months the line continued to operate as Pitcairn Aviation, Inc.; then early in 1930, the name was changed to Eastern Air Transport, Inc. In 1934 its name would be changed again and it would become the last of what were to be referred to in the Civil Aeronautics Board, the government's economic regulatory body for air transportation, as the "Big Four" in the U.S. air carrier industry—the first three being American Airlines, Trans World Airlines, and United Airlines. Harold F. Pitcairn was out of the airline business, but what he had started on a cow pasture of his family's estate in Bryn Athyn, would one day be known as Eastern Airlines, which, by odd coincidence, would, half a century later, use the motto, "The Wings of Man."

# Rotary-Wing Success

Selling the airline was not easy for Pitcairn; only a handful of the top executives and engineers would remain with the Pitcairn-Cierva Autogiro Company and Pitcairn Aircraft, to pursue rotary-wing development. All other employees, many of whom were his personal friends, would float with the airline into the Keys orbit. He had insisted that their jobs be protected in the transition and wrote each a personal letter to explain that the operation of the line by Keys's large, well-funded organization would be for their ultimate benefit and that the airline would go on to greater things. And so it did: most of his line pilots advanced with the growth of the carrier, progressing through each new generation of aircraft that came into air-carrier use, the Curtiss Condors, the DC-2s and DC-3s. Many of them moved to new air carriers such as Paul R. Braniff, Inc., Interstate Air Lines, Boeing Division of United Aircraft & Transport Corporation, and Southern Airways. Some percolated to top management positions as corporate executives. Others, who were in their twenties when the line was sold and were then flying 110-mph, fabric-covered, open-cockpit Mailwings, would some day fly four-engine jets for major U.S. air carriers.

One of the most outstanding careers among former Pitcairn Aviation air-mail pilots was that of Henry R. Merrill, the same "Dick" Merrill who would always claim kinship with the squirrel population of northeast Georgia. He remained with the airline through its several changes of name, ownership, and development. As Eastern Airlines's senior pilot, he was to be selected as the personal pilot of the President of the United States and to fly the most famous people in the world, including many crowned heads of Europe, on their travels across America and the oceans of the earth. Dick Merrill continued to set flying records well into the 1970s and at the age of eighty-four, with more than forty-seven thousand hours logged in large aircraft (he stopped logging hours he flew in small air-

Pitcairn's first successful Autogiro, the PCA-1 prototype. Compare the size of this with the Cierva C–8 and C–19; it was a large aircraft. The shock-absorbing landing gear structure is notable, as is the dual rudder empennage design, carried over from the C–19 design, and the little wings with the turned-up tips. The basic fuselage is Mailwing, and the windshields are strictly Mailwing types.

craft by 1939), still held every pilot rating issuable by the Federal Aviation Administration, including the authority to issue pilot type-rating certificates for every airplane manufactured in the United States, even for all of the wide-body, so-called "jumbo" jet airliners.

Sterling Smith, who as a youngster had acted as "groom" for Harold Pitcairn's Farman Sport in 1923, and who then had been hired as Pitcairn Aviation's first employee to perform the same function—now called "line service"—would remain an Eastern employee for many years, and on the occasion of the airline's fiftieth anniversary in 1979 was acclaimed as number one on its seniority list.

The sale of the airline had pumped new financial strength into Pitcairn's companies, enabling them to plunge into a variety of aeronautical activities: Agnew Larsen was directed to explore the possibility of further enlarging the Mailwing because of the immediate prospect of increasing airline sales and was further directed to organize an experimental division for rotary-wing development. The Autogiro venture was rapidly gathering momentum because of increasing public interest, stimulated by the almost daily flights of the C-8 over the suburbs of Philadelphia. Writers tried to outdo each other in describing the whirling-wing aircraft as everyone's "dream plane," trumpeting it, with typical press hyperbole, as the perfect machine for personal travel, fast enough to fly a hundred miles an hour, or from Philadelphia to Boston in less time than it took to drive a car from Philadelphia to New York. Yet it was capable of slowing virtually to a walk, so that it could land, with no fear of stalling and spinning, in backyards, on tennis courts, golf courses, beaches ... almost anywhere.

Pitcairn was pushing hard day and night to produce his own entries for the Guggenheim Safe Airplane Competition scheduled for the fall of 1929, for he believed that the Autogiro would win the competition hands down, which would do the same thing for his rotary-wing business that winning the 1926 Sesqui-Centennial Race had done for his earlier ventures in fixed wings.

The prototype model produced by the Pitcairn-Cierva Autogiro Company, called the PCA-1, was larger than any Autogiro constructed up to that time, a three-place, open-cockpit fuselage constructed on the famous Pitcairn chrome-molybdenum, square-section steel tubing, faired into sweeping lines by wooden formers, then covered with doped linen, hand-rubbed to a glossy finish.

The project turned out to be more difficult than Pitcairn's group had imagined, for increasing the scale of the basic Cierva design created a multitude of new problems in aerodynamics and stress analysis. Soon Cierva's wooden rotor blade format had been completely rejected and replaced with blades using a steel spar as their main strength member, with wooden ribs sheathed in plywood to form the airfoil. A tiltable horizontal tailplane system was incorporated to deflect propeller blast upward to prespin the rotor. This would reduce pretakeoff taxiing requirements, a major drawback of the earlier Cierva versions. However, Cierva's systems for supporting the long rotor blades by cables, to keep them from drooping excessively

Close-up view of the propeller-blast-deflecting empennage on the prototype PCA-1.

when at rest and also to maintain approximate 90-degree spacing between the blades in flight, were retained and incorporated in the initial PCA-1, in the interest of producing and testing the machine for the Safe Airplane Competition. On paper it was a good design, but during its initial flight-test program, Pitcairn soon realized that he was again to suffer a great disappointment with his first attempt on a prototype aircraft.

From the earliest ground checks under power, the whirling rotor blades developed peculiar and violent vibrations, indicating dangerous dynamic imbalances. Pitcairn and his engineers went back to their drafting boards to grapple with principles still dimly understood, in an effort to solve the exasperating problem in time for the Guggenheim event. It was like a bad dream: the dynamic and aerodynamic complexities of the rotor system made it difficult to identify the sources of the perplexing vibration problems and then to solve them, for as one problem seemed cured, another showed up, having been blanketed by the first.

Then a new impediment surfaced. In the fine print of the rules of the Guggenheim contest was a requirement, easily overlooked: in order to qualify for the contest, an entry must have a flat, eight-to-one angle of glide. *Must.*

Obviously the specifications, addressed to fixed-wing aircraft, were written before anyone on the committee had ever heard of rotary-wing aircraft, which could descend almost vertically and stop in a few feet. Pitcairn attempted to have the contest committee amend or at least waive the glide angle rule, in recognition of the exceptional capabilities of the Autogiro. The committee adamantly refused to make any changes.

Nevertheless, Pitcairn proposed to fly the route of the Guggenheim program in the PCA-1 as an observer—in reality as a nonparticipant being observed—but that plan was also thwarted; as the date of the competition approached with no solutions to the persistent rotor vibration problems being found, Pitcairn reluctantly notified the Guggenheims that the Pitcairn-Cierva Autogiro Company of America would not participate.

For months Pitcairn worked shoulder-to-shoulder with his engineering staff to solve the perplexing operational and technical problems and mysterious aerodynamics of the rotary wing.* It was a relentless, frequently unproductive effort. But little by little they solved baffling puzzles and worked through a maze of totally new stumbling blocks. They solved some problems by changing blades and blade angles, airfoil designs, stressing, and construction. They added and relocated weights to change blade balances and experimented with different blade lengths. Up to that time, Pitcairn's engineers had relied completely on Cierva's mathematical analyses and designs as source materials, but in the course of their labors they eventually formulated their own rotor design criteria. A new blade form was Larsen's contribution: somewhat simplified from Cierva's double tapered planform, it incorporated chord (blade width) and airfoil contour changes and introduced new snubbing and shock-absorbing devices within the interblade cable system. Feelings of frustration disappeared as the vibration problem reduced with every change modification; the Pitcairn group was slowly but perceptibly solving the enigma.

While the PCA-1 experiments continued, Cierva came to the Unit-

---

* Although not a trained engineer, Pitcairn had developed an almost intuitive grasp of mechanics and aerodynamics, in addition to an innate gift of imagination when confronted with esoteric problems in either discipline. It must not be forgotten that he was awarded twenty-four patents, only three of which were shared inventions.

Cierva makes a no-rollout landing in the C-19. The approach to the landing was only one degree out of vertical. Note that he is flying from the rear seat and that the wingtips are turned up for in-flight stability.

Juan de la Cierva, inventor of the Autogiro.

Juan de la Cierva prepares to demonstrate his C-19 at Pitcairn Field, Willow Grove in September 1929, prior to showing it at the Cleveland Air Races. G-AAKY was a small aircraft. Its dual rudder system was rigged to pre-spin the rotor blades and reduce the extensive taxiing to get them up to speed. This was Cierva's first visit to the United States.

The PCA-1A with its redesigned landing gear and rotor system but retaining the Cierva-designed blast-deflecting empennage. The new Willow Grove factory is in the background.

ed States to demonstrate one of his own Autogiros at the Cleveland air races in the fall of 1929. Immensely disappointed by not being able to fly the first American Autogiro before the foremost aviation leaders of the nation, Pitcairn, who had worked so long and so hard, watched and cheered while his friend electrified the massed spectators with the unique performance characteristics of the C-19, which bore the *British* registration G-AAKY. Pitcairn steadfastly believed that he would have his own Autogiro at the next year's meeting.

He was not the only American who felt a twinge when G-AAKY stole the show at Cleveland. For months the army and the navy had been anxious to obtain Autogiros for evaluation, having seen the C-8 in action many months before, but the still-baffling problems of the PCA-1 precluded its demonstration to anyone. Yet by the middle of October, redesigns of the rotor, thoroughly tested in numerous wind tunnel experiments, were bearing fruit. The propwash-deflecting tail was replaced by one of more conventional design and the short stub wings, required for the installation

of ailerons to provide lateral control, now sported upturned tips for stability. At last, they were making some real progress.

Pitcairn was not satisfied with the propeller blast deflector to prespin the blades of the rotor system. After they had begun their slow rotation, the craft still had to be taxied about for several minutes to bring them up to flying-rotational speed before taking off. As in the fixed-wing airplanes he had built, the Autogiro had a set of wires to support the lifting surfaces when the ships were at rest—"ground wires," which prevented them from drooping to the ground. Unlike the "flying wires" which held the wings of fixed-wing designs in place, the Autogiro's blades were held in their flying position, called "the disc," by the centrifugal force of the mass of the blades themselves—*if* they were spinning fast enough. If the pilot attempted to take off before the required rotation speed had been

The PCA-1B was almost entirely an all-Pitcairn design. The blast-deflecting empennage had been eliminated and the vertical fin extended to the pilot's headrest. It was the first successful American designed and built rotary wing aircraft. As an experimental aircraft, it did not require an approved type certificate, but in its various versions, it logged hundreds of hours.

achieved, the blades, not having developed the requisite centrifugal force, would flex upward under the weight of the aircraft, a condition known as "coning," since the blade movement described an inverted cone shape.

Pitcairn directed his engineering staff to explore a method of gearing the conventional engine/propeller mounted on the front of the fuselage to the rotor system, so that the blades could be spun up while the ship was standing still. If takeoff rpms could be thus achieved, the Autogiro might be able to take off with no taxi time; just spin-up, open the throttle all the way, and fly. He suggested that it might be a good item to put in the next model that they were already working on to follow the PCA-1.

Pitcairn was basking in good news from every direction. The PA-7 Super Mailwing, with completely redesigned wings and a larger fuselage, had been purchased off the drafting board by several air-mail lines who had reserved delivery positions by cash advances. Now, a letter from Washington advised that the newest of the Mailwing line had received its Approved Type Certificate from the Department of Commerce—seven of them, almost completed, were even then on the assembly line in the Bryn Athyn factory; and the new Autogiro factory was almost completed at Willow Grove, so that rotary-wing production could soon begin—when the bugs were ironed out of the PCA-1 prototype. Life indeed looked rosy.

Not for long, though: on October 29, 1929, a day that would be forever known in the annals of American finance as "Black Friday," the bottom fell out of the stock market. Then, two weeks later, the Bryn Athyn factory was gutted by a fire which destroyed all seven PA-7s on the line. Fortunately, the entire engineering department had been moved to the spanking new Willow

The first PA-7 Super Mailwing. It began as PA-6 No. 50 on the production line, but was extensively modified in response to the recommendations of line pilots. This one, wearing the livery of Colonial Air Lines (AM 1), shows the new, rounded rudder and wingtips and the forward fuselage profile change that created greater in-flight stability and speed.

Grove factory, a huge brick, concrete, and steel building with eighty thousand square feet of floor space, so that precious engineering data and drawings escaped destruction. But all of the equipment, supplies, jigs, and construction materials at the Bryn Athyn factory, as well as the charred, twisted skeletons of what had been a string of almost-finished airplanes, were total losses.

It was a disastrous episode, but Pitcairn was able to pull everything together so he could continue his aircraft operations at the new plant facility. Against the background of calamity there was a bright hope for the future: at the tail end of December 1929, after a succession of failures, the PCA-1 solutions finally came together. The first Autogiro designed and built entirely in the United States was flying successful-ly. It was an extraordinary achievement.

For several months thereafter the PCA-1 flew as a purely experimental aircraft for the Pitcairn-Cierva Company's own test program use, not for commercial sale; hence it did not require an Approved Type Certificate from the government. Over many weeks of test-flying, minor shortcomings, reported by Pitcairn's test pilots, principally Jim Ray, Jim Faulkner, and Pitcairn himself, led

The PCA-2, a giant step forward. Harold Pitcairn is here tracking the rotor blades as they are pre-spun by the unique clutch/gear train system, a Pitcairn innovation that would lead to true vertical flight. The rotor drive shaft is shown ahead of the tripod rotor mount. Jim Ray is the pilot.

to improvements and recommendations, all of which were promptly incorporated in the commercial prototype then being constructed, the PCA-2. When the new Autogiro was rolled out of the Willow Grove factory in the spring of 1930, it was a striking example of American ingenuity and inventiveness; except for the generic name, Autogiro, it was a far different aircraft from that with which Cierva had bowled over the Cleveland aviation meeting. For the first few days after it was rolled out of the factory door, test pilot Ray,

by then one of the most experienced rotary-wing pilots in the world, did little more than run up the engine and try out the newfangled prespin rotor drive arrangement which was to prove to be one of the most significant advances in the newly emerging technology. Then, on a clear, still morning, Ray announced to the boss that he was going to take off in the much-modified machine.

Pitcairn had a great deal riding on that prototype, for it was the one he proposed to sell to the public as his long-dreamed-of Safe Aircraft. Standing on the tarmac out front of the factory with everyone else who had waited so long for this day, he saw the metal propeller spin into invisibility as Ray hit the built-in starter that eliminated hand-propping. Then, after a few seconds, the four twenty-two-foot-long rotor blades, which had been drooping from their restraining cables, began to move as Ray engaged the prespin drive clutch.

The blades moved slowly at first, but within thirty seconds were whirling fast enough to become a blur. Then Ray's sure hands opened the throttle of the 300-hp Wright R-975 engine. The Autogiro moved forward perhaps two or three times its own length and took off into an easy climb-out.

Immediately after returning to earth, Ray reported that from the beginning the PCA-2 had performed smoothly, without any of the vibrations he had anticipated, which indicated that everything had been harmonized in the rotor system. It flew so sedately, Ray said, that he was confident he could transition any fixed-wing pilot into it in less than an hour, and he further believed that nonpilots could be taught to fly it in half the time required to learn the rudiments in as docile a training plane as the Orowing.

At long last, it seemed to Pitcairn that he was on the verge of making a safe-flight aircraft available to the average citizen.

A new and unexpected snag developed: federal aviation authorities had no precedents whatsoever for certification of rotary-wing aircraft and would have to develop the indispensible specifications and performance characteristics for that purpose from scratch. They had to build their entire rule book from actual experience with the Pitcairn machine. Pitcairn was told that issu-ing the Approved Type Certificate required for commercial sales of any aircraft would involve a series of proving flights that would eat up a whole year.

Throughout the end of 1930 and well into 1931, the unusual-looking "windmill planes," as they had been dubbed by the press, were seen and heard thrumming over Willow Grove, Trenton, Philadelphia, and even New York City. In all kinds of weather they flew, sometimes singly, sometimes in a pair, for the experimental PCA-1 was frequently used as a chase plane for the PCA-2 during the latter's certification program. Both aircraft were flying faultlessly, week in and week out, as the performance figures were noted in the records of the Department of Commerce. Things were progressing well.

The highest point in the flight-test program came early on. Both Cierva and Pitcairn were invited again to display Autogiros at the Chicago air races in the summer of 1930. This time, Pitcairn was ready, willing, and able to do so. Cierva notified Pitcairn and the race officials that he would be there, too.

A rare shot of the PCA-2 (foreground) flying over the Cunard and French Line wharves on the Hudson River, with Manhattan as a backdrop. The still-experimental PCA-1 is flying as chase plane.

(*inset*) Jim Ray is stopping traffic on Manhattan in this 1930 passage overhead. The rotary wing era was dawning.

Heading for home. The PCA-1 flies wing on the PCA-2 as they pay their respects to the Statue of Liberty. The East River shows lower Manhattan on the left and Brooklyn on the right. Jim Faulkner is in the PCA-1B and Jim Ray is in the about-to-be-certified PCA-2.

The Cierva C-19, which had stolen the 1929 Cleveland air show, was physically unable to fly the 750-mile trip across the Alleghenies from Willow Grove to Chicago and had to be disassembled and trucked to the meet. But both the PCA-1 and the PCA-2 were flown both ways by Jim Ray and Jim Faulkner.

The long, all-day cross-country flights by the brace of Autogiros were not stunts; they were legitimate test flights to determine the nature of actual operational problems that would confront individual owner-users in the field, and the results were carefully noted in their logbooks. When Pitcairn joined his

pilots in Illinois, he was immensely pleased to learn that no serious problems had developed on the arduous jaunt over the region which had been known as "the Hell Stretch" by air-mail pilots. The sole incident was that the rotor blade support cables had shown a tendency to stretch slightly after a few off-airport landings, when they had stopped for fuel en route, and had

had to be replaced when they arrived at the air race location. That was all.

Pitcairn's massive Autogiros performed flawlessly and repeatedly before hundreds of thousands of aviation enthusiasts, all of whom were astonished by the sensational performances of the aircrafts' routine operations. Periodically, they left the restricted area of the air race field and flew over the city of Chicago, stopping traffic every time. The Pitcairn Autogiro demonstrations took the spotlight from those of Cierva's smaller Autogiro, which flew only in the immediate vicinity of the airfield.

For Pitcairn, the public reaction to the exposure of his two Autogiros seemed an unqualified vindication of his decision. The public clamored for Autogiros. The mass market was there.

As time dragged on in the official certification process, Pitcairn was nettled by the delays, which were costing him money, reminiscent of the early part of his air-mail line's nonoperations. His hopes were buoyed by the sheer volume of mail coming into his office in downtown Philadelphia. They ranged from requests for personal interviews from journalists to the usual run of inquiries about future availablility, generated by the enormous press and newsreel coverage of the Chicago trip. But many letters were accompanied by checks to assure early delivery positions when the Approved Type Certificate was issued. The applicants for future consignments were willing to wait.

Pitcairn's cash-flow situation remained strong from the fixed-wing production of the Willow Grove factory, with some twenty-five thousand dollars a month coming from the delivery of the new, larger PA-7 Super Mailwings that had made such a hit with all of the air-mail carriers. He also had high hopes for the still-larger PA-8 version, slated to be the greatest Mailwing of them all. When it was certificated in September 1930, it was a classic of classics, powered by the Wright Whirlwind J-6-9 (nine-cylinder) 300-hp engine, capable of hauling a half-ton of mail for six hundred miles at two miles a minute.

It was, by any current measure, a guaranteed winner, worthy of Pitcairn's highest hopes for a brilliant and lucrative future. But it was not to be. Despite Pitcairn's projected sales for it, the PA-8 was fated to be the last of the Mailwings. Eastern Air Transport, Pitcairn Aircraft's sole custmer, would buy only six, for a total cost of seventy-five thousand dollars. Airlines were moving gradually into larger equipment for carrying passengers. The McNary–Watres Act, signed into law by President Hoover in April 1930, had sounded taps on the airmail-only lines. Although many of the older Mailwings would continue to carry mail for some of the major airlines— American Airlines, for example, used them on several routes until 1938—the era of the single-engine,

(*top*) A PA-8 Mailwing in winter flight. Flying an open cockpit airplane in such weather is an incredibly painful experience.

The only surviving airworthy PA-8, the largest Mailwing to be built. This airplane was restored by Jack Rose of Seattle and was sold to the late Steve McQueen, of Hollywood. In this model the designers had returned to the long strut.
Photo by Ted J. Koston, Oak Park, Ill.

Pitcairn's attempt to cope with adverse climate is shown in this prototype PA-8 undergoing tests at the Willow Grove factory. The cockpit had side windows and a raised turtleback, as well as a heater. But the era of the open-cockpit, single-engine, mail-only, commercial-airline airplane was coming to an end by the time the Big Mailwing came along.

Thomas A. Edison visited the not-yet-certified PCA-2 at a Newark Airport demonstration and told pilot Jim Ray and a group of newspapermen, "That's the answer to safe flying." The front cockpit here is covered and the windshield has been stowed. Note that the rudder still carries the "X" prefix for "experimental."

open-cockpit, mail-only airplane was almost over.

In compensation for that loss, the era of the Autogiro was just beginning, materially assisted by the adulating press. Anything relating to Autogiros rated front-page treatment. When the dean of American inventors, Thomas A. Edison, saw the Autogiro fly and said, "This is the answer to safe flight," the statement was carried by newspapers in every major city. In November 1930, when Juan de la Cierva, the Autogiro's thirty-six-year-old inventor, had arrived in New York Harbor on the S.S. *Bremen*, he was met by a flotilla of four Autogiros which flew over in formation as the liner was anchored at quarantine. Newsreel photographers vied with press photographers for volume of coverage. A few weeks later the already famous aviatrix, Amelia Earhart, after taking instruction at Willow Grove from Skip Lukens, became the first woman to solo an Autogiro, generating more publicity for the company and its product and further whetting the public's appetite.

Test flights ranged farther and farther afield. Early in January, Jim Ray flew the PCA-2 on a round trip from Willow Grove to Miami, landing on many small and unprepared fields during the twenty-five-hundred-mile journey, which was carried out in all kinds of weather. Ray encountered snowfalls, fog, gusty winds, dust storms, and heavy rains. Whenever visibility became restricted, he slowed his groundspeed to as little as ten miles an hour and sometimes followed railroad tracks or roads at altitudes as low as a hundred feet. If the weather worsened, he would simply pull back to zero forward speed and land in an open field. It was a sensational exhibition of the versatility and speed range of the new flying machine. His arrival

Another rare photograph. Amelia Earhart sitting on the rim of the company's PCA-2, in which she set an official altitude record of 18,415 feet.

Jim Ray flew the PCA-2 from Willow Grove to Miami, Florida to demonstrate the cross-country ability of the Autogiro. When he landed in a public park, the chief of police issued a parking ticket, unwittingly helping to generate publicity. Jim is wearing his sealskin flying helmet in this posed gag shot.

at the improvised landing spot in Bay Front Park, Miami, was witnessed by thousands of people, including many local and state dignitaries and, fully covered by the national press, he was issued a "parking ticket" by the Miami chief of police for illegally parking an aircraft on public property. Then Ray flew the chief of police to the All American Air Races, held in conjunction with the dedication ceremonies of Miami's Navy Field, where once again the 'giro was the object of all eyes.

The Autogiro stimulated wanderlust as no other flying machine ever had, and Ray's jaunt to Florida and back demonstrated to the public that the rotary-wing aircraft was here to stay as a practical and reliable means of personal transportation.

Pitcairn Field, Willow Grove, had truly become a mecca for people interested in private flying as well as for famous pilots and leading avi-

ation figures who flocked there to see what the Autogiro was all about. More orders for Autogiros arrived with every mail delivery; in February 1931, the New York publisher, George Palmer Putnam, inquired about purchasing a PCA-2 for his wife of less than a week, Amelia Earhart.

At Pitcairn headquarters the mood was ebullient as the government certification program was finally coming to a successful conclusion. The plant was reorganized to meet the expected challenge and Walter C. Clayton was named as chief engineer of Pitcairn Aircraft, which would produce the commercial versions. In January 1931, Pitcairn-Cierva Autogiro Company of America changed its name to Autogiro Company of America; Agnew

Hollywood took advantage of the Auto-giro's publicity, too. This PCA-2 was used in a motion picture, *Misleading Lady*, starring Claudette Colbert and Edmund Lowe. Jim Ray was the pilot.

Racing pilot Frank Hawks (right) was another famous pilot who checked out in the PCA-2 and marvelled at its performance. Jim Ray is on the left.

Larsen was named as its chief engineer and long-range plans were being formulated to develop a series of Autogiros covering the entire market spectrum, from small two-seaters for private and sportsman-pilots to large commercial craft. Cabin models were already on the drafting tables.

The U.S. rights to Cierva's inventions and patents, which Pitcairn Aeronautics, Inc., had acquired in 1929, as well as the Pitcairn et al. patents pertaining to rotary-wing aircraft, were now vested in the Autogiro Company of America (ACA), which would issue all future licenses for the manufacture, use, and sale of rotary-wing aircraft in the United States under those patents. The first license which ACA issued was to the Buhl Aircraft Company, of Detroit in March 1931, and modified licenses were also granted to Kellett Aircraft* and to Pitcairn Aircraft in 1931. This was the "industry."

The Approved Type Certificate was issued to the PCA-2 by the Department of Commerce on April 2, 1931, and Pitcairn Aircraft proudly announced that it was accepting orders for the three-place utility model. The door to the future had swung open; the Safe Aircraft dream had come true at last.

---

* Formed by W. Wallace Kellett and C. Townsend Ludington and their brothers, Rodney Kellett and Nicholas Ludington. W. W. Kellett and C. T. Ludington had been located at Pine Valley Airport in 1923 with aircraft dealerships.

The reorganization of Pitcairn's aviation interests, particularly of the engineering departments, with Clayton named as chief engineer of Pitcairn Aircraft, succeeding Larsen, had been a tremendous blow to the professional pride of W. Lawrence LePage, whose duties had become ever more administrative in nature and less in his professional specialty, aeronautical engineering. LePage, rankled by the slight, left the Pitcairn organization and joined the staff of *Aviation*, the most prominent journal of the day, writing on rotary-wing design and operations.

Within a few months his name graced the roster of engineering talent assembled by Kellett Aircraft, founded by Harold Pitcairn's old friends W. Wallace Kellett, C. Townsend Ludington, and Rodney

The end of PCA-2, Serial No. 1. A fuel surge just at touchdown caused a torque problem, with this result. Pilot Jim Ray walked away unhurt.

Edwin T. Asplundh, who joined Pitcairn in 1929 and took charge of the manufacturing division of Pitcairn's aviation companies.

G. Kellett, all prominent in Philadelphia aviation since the early 1920s. By January 1931, LePage would be Kellett's chief engineer, heading a staff which included such aeronautical luminaries as Eliott Daland, formerly of Huff-Daland and the Keystone Aircraft Corp.; Ralph H. McClarren, of New York University, and A. D. Kligman, formerly of the Naval Aircraft Factory. Production of a two-place side-by-side Autogiro was forecast for the early spring of 1931.

One persistent black cloud continued to linger ominously on the horizon: the October 1929 panic in the stock market had been followed by a national financial recession. Most government and industry economists claimed that it was, at most, a temporary situation, a resettling of the world's booming, almost run-away postwar economies, and that the stock market would soon exhibit an upward trend on a more solid economic footing. On the expectancy of an improved economy, many businessmen plunged boldly ahead. Harold Pitcairn was one of them.

Rotary-wing flight came of age in 1931. The PCA-2 really was the ice-breaker. As big as it was, the PCA-2 could fly as fast as 120 mph or amble along at 25 mph in still air. Although it was not a true helicopter, Pitcairn's experienced company Autogiro pilots demonstrated regularly that it could land easily out of

The PCA-2 received its Approved Type Certificate (ATC #410) April 2, 1931. Its first purchaser was the *Detroit News,* which owned radio station WWJ. William E. Scripps, an aviation enthusiast, had already bought a fixed-wing airplane, hence the "No. 2" on the side of the cockpit. This aircraft is now displayed in the Henry Ford Museum at Dearborn, Michigan.

The Coca-Cola Company operated a PCA-2. The pilot was William Campbell.

The Champion Spark Plug Company PCA-2 was flown by Capt. Lewis A. Yancey to all parts of the North American continent.

The Silverbrook Coal Company pilot, Slim Soule, operated this PCA-2 in some of the most rugged terrain in the east for several years, without any problems.

almost vertical descents, and in a stiff breeze could hover over a point on the ground indefinitely, which seemingly made the Autogiro a perfect vehicle for observation and aerial photography. Cross-country flying was greatly simplified. If a pilot became lost, or was caught in adverse weather conditions, he only had to call it a day, land almost anywhere and ask for directions, or wait for the situation to improve. No wonder press and magazine writers made so much of it.

Recognizing the tremendous publicity value inherent in operating an aircraft that garnered front-page coverage and photographs wherever it flew, the first batch of orders had come from air-minded (and promotion-minded) corporations that could make use of the phenomenal machines. The first delivery was to the Detroit News Company, which under Bill Scripps had long been a vociferous advocate for aviation. Then followed Silverbrook Coal; Socony Vacuum Oil (Standard Oil of New York); Champion Spark Plug, Standard Oil of Ohio; Coca-Cola; Sealed Power Piston Rings; and

Beech-Nut. The federal government ordered several, including one for NACA testing and evaluation at Langley Field and three that went to the U.S. Navy, designated as the XOP-1—"Experimental Observation, Pitcairn." Production lines in the factory were soon chock-a-block with aircraft and scores of assembly-men were bustling about Autogiros and PA-7s and PA-8s in various stages of construction.

A week after the type certificate was received, Amelia Earhart returned to Willow Grove to be checked out in the PCA-2, determined to set some records in the Autogiro. First, she proposed to fly one as high as it would go, then to fly from coast to coast and back, a six-thousand-mile round trip to demonstrate the tremendous travel possibilities of the Autogiro over all sorts of terrain, including the jagged Rocky Mountains. Up to that time, most Autogiro flying had been over relatively flat land, except for the crossings of the Alleghenies by Ray and Faulkner in their flight to and from the 1930 Chicago air races.

On April 8, seeking the altitude record, she took off early in the morning but returned within an hour; the aircraft had operated perfectly, but she had become so chilled during the ascent that she returned for warmer clothes. At noon, she took off again, climbing until she disappeared. For almost three hours Pitcairn and National Aeronautic Association officials paced the tarmac and scanned the sky. Then someone pointed to the northwest and shouted, "There she is!" At first only a pinpoint which occasionally flashed as its whirling blades caught the sun, the PCA-2 grew in size, circled the field twice, and landed easily a hundred feet in front of the hangar area. When the NAA official barograph was examined, it showed

that she had established an Autogiro altitude record of 18,415 feet. More publicity. More pictures in the press. The Beech-Nut Company told Amelia that she could cancel her own order for an Autogiro; the chewing gum manufacturer would sponsor her transcontinental round-trip flight and assign her the Auto-giro it had ordered, number 13 on the line and already under construc-

Johnny Miller, a professional pilot, ordered a PCA-2 to use for flying exhibitions at country fairs. When he learned that Earhart had been advanced ahead of him on the production and delivery line, he took off for the West Coast without fanfare and beat her by two weeks. This is the PCA-2 he looped repeatedly in his flight exhibitions. At age 80, Miller was still flying high-performance single- and multi-engine aircraft as a flight instructor.

Amelia Earhart, America's most famous woman pilot, was subsidized by the Beech-Nut Company to fly this PCA-2 during 1931. Her original objective was to be the first to fly an Autogiro from coast to coast.

tion. It would be a sure-fire combination, an advertising coup. The investment of time and money, the irritations of delay and engineering frustration, were forgotten by Pitcairn and his crew. The future had arrived.

Early in April 1931, Harold Pitcairn received a letter from former U.S. Senator Hiram Bingham, then president of the National Aeronautic Association, and who had been the sponsor of the Air Commerce Act of 1925 that imposed government regulation on the helter-skelter disorganization of flying in the barnstorming era. Since Senator Bingham's letter had arrived together with a sizable bundle of congratulatory letters, telegrams, cables, and personal notes, Pitcairn had opened it expecting nothing more than felicitations from an old friend. It was much more than that.

Dear Mr. Pitcairn:

I am pleased to advise you that upon the unanimous report of the Collier Trophy Committee of the National Aeronautic Association, the Collier Trophy award for 1930 is made to "Harold F. Pitcairn and his associates for their development and application of the Autogiro and the demonstration of its possibilities with a view to its use for safe aerial transport."

Two paragraphs followed, but Pitcairn was too overcome with emotion to read on. He was flabbergasted. Twenty years earlier, the Collier Trophy had been awarded to Glenn H. Curtiss. On the base of the imposing trophy were inscribed the names of Orville Wright, Elmer A. Sperry, Grover C. Loening, and others famous in aviation. Some years the award had gone to groups: the Personnel and Pilots of the U.S. Air Mail Service, the U.S. Army

When Slim Soule resigned from flying the Silverbrook PCA-2, he used one for aerial application and found it much superior to any fixed-wing airplane of that time.

'Round-the-World fliers, the Aeronautics Branch of the Department of Commerce. Now he and his little band of associates, working from private capital on his small airport in the suburbs of Philadelphia, had been accorded this signal honor.

Pitcairn communicated immediately to Senator Bingham the hope that the presentation could be scheduled to allow Juan de la Cierva to attend, for he should also be recognized. It would take time to arrange for Cierva's visit because of political problems in Spain; King Alfonso had been exiled and a new regime under the dictator de Rivera was falling. Riots in the streets and church burnings in Madrid had required Cierva to return there to see to the safety of his wife and six children. Bingham responded that it would be impossible to delay the ceremony, for the Collier Award

One of the classic Autogiro pictures: Jim Ray landing on the South Lawn of the White House, April 22, 1931. It was a skillful maneuver. Compare the next photo.

presentation was to be made by the President of the United States at the only time convenient to him. Accordingly the award had been scheduled for April 22 at a White House ceremony. It could not be changed.

President Herbert Clark Hoover had been Secretary of Commerce under President Coolidge. In his official capacity as the top administrator of that department, which included the Aeronautics Branch, he had participated in many meetings with Harold Pitcairn, who had assisted in the drafting of aeronautical safety regulations for the federal and state governments. Nevertheless, it came as another great surprise when Pitcairn received a personal invitation from the President to land an Autogiro on the south lawn of the White House so that, rather than holding the ceremony indoors with heavy-handed formality, the presentation could be made out-of-doors with the award-winning aircraft and its creators framed against an imposing and un-

This picture follows the last by only a few seconds (compare the position of the men on top of the White House) and demonstrates the tremendous short-landing capability of the Autogiro. It rolled no more than ten feet after touching down.

forgettable backdrop of the White House itself.

While preparations were being made for the occasion, Pitcairn Aircraft dispatched a contingent to the National Air Show in Detroit and once again stole the show. Not only did they have three Autogiros on the floor of the exhibit hall, they also had a skeletonized display to show the internal details of the aircraft's construction, plus two additional Autogiros that flew demonstrations during the week-long meeting. In addition to the large PCA-1 and PCA-2 ships, Pitcairn unveiled a new, smaller model, the PAA-1,* a smaller, two-place

Autogiro directed at the private-owner market. Orders flooded in as a result of the exhibition, which was seen by thousands of attendees, including a youthful U.S. Army second lieutenant named H. F. (for Franklin) Gregory, a freshly minted observation pilot of the Army Air Corps.

On April 21, 1931, Ray flew the prototype PCA-2, in which he had by then logged several hundred hours, from Willow Grove to College Park, Maryland, a few miles northeast of Washington, D.C., and had the aircraft washed and put away for the night. The next morning the attention of a large array of dignitaries waiting on the south lawn of the President's residence, as well as that of hundreds of spectators who lined the fence of the south

* The model designators were changed from time to time: The first two models, PCA-1 and PCA-2 reflected the name, Pitcairn

Cierva Autogiro Company of America; thereafter, the PAA-1 and PAA-2 stood for 'Pitcairn Aircraft Company Autogiro.' When the manufacturing company name was changed in 1933 from Pitcairn Aircraft to Pitcairn Autogiro Co., Inc., the designators reverted to "PA."

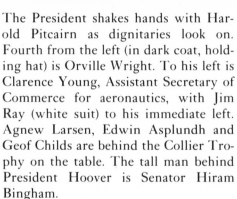

The President shakes hands with Harold Pitcairn as dignitaries look on. Fourth from the left (in dark coat, holding hat) is Orville Wright. To his left is Clarence Young, Assistant Secretary of Commerce for aeronautics, with Jim Ray (white suit) to his immediate left. Agnew Larsen, Edwin Asplundh and Geof Childs are behind the Collier Trophy on the table. The tall man behind President Hoover is Senator Hiram Bingham.

Immediately after the Collier Trophy ceremony. Orville Wright, President Hoover, Jim Ray, Assistant Secretary Clarence Young, Senator Hiram Bingham, Harold F. Pitcairn.

lawn toward the Ellipse, was drawn to the unforgettable sound of an approaching Autogiro. As the slow turning of the then-unusual rotor blades elicited oohs and aahs from the assembly, Ray dropped the PCA-2 down to three hundred feet to eye wind-generated movements of the flags atop the Executive Mansion, then swung in directly over the building and eased back on the throttle and control stick.

With newsreel cameras grinding away and press cameras clicking like a field of crickets, Ray with consummate skill landed almost exactly on the spot that had been selected and rolled no more than a few feet to a stop. It was a sensational demonstration, later brought home to millions in movie houses all over the country. If anything could prove the safety of the Autogiro, it would be motion pictures of the aircraft lightly landing within a few feet of the President and many members of his cabinet.

The presentation ceremony, attended by Orville Wright, Senator Bingham, Colonel Clarence M. Young—then secretary of commerce for air— and many other dignitaries, was impressive. The Autogiro Company of America was represented by Harold Pitcairn, Agnew Larsen, Geof Childs, Edwin Asplundh, and Jim Ray. As President Hoover shook hands with him after reading the award citation, Pitcairn's eyes momentarily locked

Jim Ray's hurried departure from the South Lawn, showing the dust raised by propeller blast. The takeoff run was less than 150 feet and the climb out was steep—but safe. The Autogiro would not stall its wing.

with Larsen's. Just fifteen years ago they had been youthful dreamers at the Curtiss school in Newport News, planning someday to build the Safe Aircraft. The two men exchanged little smiles. "Someday" was here.

From still photographs, it appears to have been a quiet, staid, dignified, unhurried ceremony. However, Ray was becoming more concerned by the minute. Before taking off from College Park that morning, he had checked the weather and learned that a severe weather front would be moving through the Washington area by early afternoon, accompanied by a squall line with violent winds. While the festivities dragged on, Ray grew uneasy about getting out before the weather pinned him down, for the award ceremony would not be a complete success until he had taken off as easily as he had arrived. An aside to Pitcairn accelerated the proceedings. Just as the treetops began to sway before the approaching storm, Ray received the consent to go.

Climbing into the cockpit, he fired up the big radial engine, engaged the rotor drive, and within forty-five seconds waved back to the cheering crowd and fed in the throttle. After a run of about thirty feet, he climbed steeply into darkening skies, wheeled to the left, and headed northeast. Looking back over his shoulder, he could see the squall line lashing the Potomac River to a froth, less than a mile away.

One month later Amelia Earhart began her much heralded coast-to-coast pilgrimage in the Beech-Nut PCA-2. Starting from Newark Airport on May 29, she arrived in Los Angeles on June 7, only to find that a relative unknown, Johnny Miller, a twenty-five-year-old pilot from Poughkeepsie, New York, had made the same trip in the Silverbrook Coal PCA-2 the week before. A week later a new Autogiro owner—a new private pilot!—Walter Hoffman took his bride on a whirlwind honeymoon from Nantucket to Santa Barbara, California.

The U.S. Navy bought off-the-shelf PCA-2s, designated them XOP-1s (Experimental Observation, Pitcairn, model 1) and commenced testing them for naval applications.

In September 1931, the XOP-1 earned its Navy wings. Lt. A.M. Pride, USN made three successful landings and takeoffs from the U.S.S. *Langley*, America's first aircraft carrier. Here, Lt. Pride circles back after taking off. Harold Pitcairn was an observer on board the *Langley* for the trials.

Apparently intent on attaining a round-trip record, Earhart quickly set off, eastbound. On her return voyage, while taking off from Abilene, Kansas, the Beech-Nut 'giro was suddenly engulfed by a small tornado-like windstorm, known locally as a "dust devil;" as a result, while hundreds of onlookers recoiled in horror, the craft went totally out of control, as any aircraft would have under the same circumstances, and crashed violently into the middle of an automobile parking lot, showering the area with shards of shattered rotor blades. The strength and durability of the Pitcairn fuselage design again proved itself: Earhart emerged a bit shaken but uninjured. Unfortunately, she had to complete her transcontinental trip by rail—but she was by no means through with flying. As soon as it could be arranged, she obtained another PCA-2, which she flew as Beech-Nut's rotary-wing ambassadress for several years.

Things had never looked brighter to Pitcairn. The Navy's XOP-1, an off-the-shelf PCA-2, had won its

The U.S. Marines also procured PCA-2s for service testing. This one was used to help quell the Nicaraguan insurrection in 1933.

Navy wings by making qualifying landings on the U.S.S. *Langley*, the fleet's first (and at that time only) aircraft carrier. Kellett Aircraft Company, Autogiro Company of America's second licensee, had received its Type Certificate on a two-place side-by-side 'giro which was selling well, and the Buhl Aircraft Company of Detroit, the first licensee, was well under way with the design of a "pusher" version, with the engine and propeller located behind the cockpit. The day of the Autogiro was at hand. Aviation historians were beginning to take note of it.

In the summer of 1931, Pitcairn received a discreet letter of inquiry from Paul Edward Garber, recently named curator of aviation artifacts for the Smithsonian Institution, in Washington, D.C. Garber had convinced the secretary of the institution that the first Autogiro in America should be enshrined along with the historic Langley Aerodrome, *The Spirit of St. Louis*, and the NC-4.* Pleased that his C-8 would be permanently exhibited with such eminent aircraft, Pitcairn promptly donated the C-8 to the Smithsonian Institution. On July 22, 1931, Jim Ray flew the much-traveled three-year-old "antique" 130 miles from Willow Grove to the broad grassy Mall, which dominates Washington's center, landing literally at the Smithsonian's front door. Perhaps, retrospectively in light of what had happened in the past three years, Pitcairn's overoptimism may be excused, but he erred in degree rather than in substance when in his presentation speech he said: "The time

* The Wright Brothers' first man-carrying powered airplane, now prominently displayed in the Smithsonian's National Air and Space Museum, was at that time on exhibition in the Science Museum in South Kensington (London), England as the result of the bitter controversy between the Smithsonian and Orville Wright concerning who had truly pioneered manned, powered flight. Wilbur Wright had died in 1912.

Another landing in downtown Washington, D.C. Jim Ray delivers the Cierva C-8 to the Smithsonian Institution's front door by landing on the Mall. It was the last flight of the first rotary wing aircraft in America. July 22, 1931.

is fast approaching when the air will hold a vast number of similar but more perfected machines, all engaged in the everyday social and commercial activities of our people." Then, with characteristic humility, he added, "But all through the passing years this oldest Auto-

giro in the United States—flown here on its last flight—will remain as a silent reminder of the genius of its inventor."

Throughout 1931 it was almost impossible to pick up a magazine or newspaper that did not carry some story about Autogiros. They were

Dr. Charles Abbott, Secretary of the Smithsonian Institution, shakes hands with Jim Ray as Harold Pitcairn grins his approval. To Ray's left stand Geof Childs, Clarence Young, William P. McCracken and George Lewis, all of the Department of Air Command (forerunner of the FAA). This aircraft is now on exhibit at the Smithsonian's Silver Hill facility.

Jim Ray takes off from the parking lot on the east side of the Capitol, to carry Senator Hiram Bingham to the Burning Tree Country Club. He had to climb out over the Senate Office Building to make the ten-minute trip, one that would take an hour by automobile.

photographed landing or taking off from downtown locations, parks, wharves, lawns in front of private homes, and flying over cities, rivers, mountains, and down inside Niagara's gorge. Ray landed a PCA-2 on a parking lot at the east face of the U. S. Capitol, took Senator Bingham on board, and whisked him off to the door of the clubhouse of the Burning Tree Country Club. What was almost a two-hour trip by automobile took twelve minutes in the Autogiro. Such convenience appealed to the golfing crowd and other sportsmen. Ensuing publicity issuing from Pitcairn featured people mounting privately owned Autogiros at the front doors of their estates and heading off for happy hunting or fishing grounds two or three hundred miles away, flying far

The PAA-1, scaled down from the PCA-2 and created especially for private pilot ownership. Almost two dozen were built and sold in the depths of the Depression (1931).

above the automobile traffic clotting the narrow roads. Imaginative drawings in Pitcairn's advertising placed Autogiros at fox hunts, ranch sites, and cabins in remote woods. Many of the accompanying photographs featured Autogiros on the front lawn of Pitcairn's home, Cairncrest. The flexibility of personal travel was the main thrust of the sales campaign. Pitcairn was selling dreams, not hardware.

To allay the doubts of those who wondered if the frail-looking rotary-wing craft could stand up under hard usage, the strength and agility of the Autogiro were proved when Canadian pilot Godfrey L. Dean looped the loop—twice!—in a PCA-2, saying later that he just wanted to see if he could do it. Johnny Miller outdid Dean. As a professional exhi-

bition and air-show pilot, Miller looped the PCA-2 *repeatedly* before huge crowds all over the United States, frequently four or five times in a single performance. The press ate it up.

Pitcairn's PAA-1, which had been unveiled at the Detroit air show, was certificated by the Department of Air Commerce in July 1931 and met with immediate, almost overwhelming success. A scaled-down version of the PCA-2, the PAA-1 had been developed specifically to fit the requirements of the user Harold Pitcairn had always had his sights pointed for, the limitless market known as the private owner. Powered by the 125-hp Kinner radial engine, the tandem open-cockpit two-seater could fly cross-country at a leisurely 76 mph for 250 miles and permit its pilot to drop in to places unavailable to fixed-wing pilots. It was economical to fly and to maintain, yet offered the Autogiro's kind of flight flexibility to people who flew just for fun, as well as those

The PAA-1 was just the right size and several were purchased by the state of New Jersey for forest fire patrol over the pinelands.

Harold Pitcairn's personal Autogiro was a PAA-1, used to commute regularly from his home in Bryn Athyn to Ocean City, N.J., 70 miles away, an all-day trip by car. In his PAA-1, it was a 45-minute hop. Here, he is pulling over the prop of the Autogiro on the beach in front of his seashore home.

Win some, lose some. This is the PAA-2, a PAA-1 modified to use an inverted Chevrolet auto engine, with special landing gear ("training wheels") to compensate for the forward center of gravity. Only one was built.

who wanted a more economical ship for aerial photography, fire spotting, and short-range business transportation. This, thought Pitcairn, when he had first seen the drawings, was the Safe Aircraft for Everyman that he had been seeking so long. When Notre Dame Coach Knute Rockne was killed in an airline crash, the public became even more receptive to the concept of a truly safe and reliable craft.

Each technological advance led to new problems never before encountered in aeronautical engineering, requiring expansion of research programs into many other scientific disciplines, including hydrodynamics, ballistics, harmonic analysis, machine design, and structural engineering.

All the while, Pitcairn and Cierva kept up a lively correspondence concerning their mutual successes in solving the practical problems of rotary-wing operation. Cierva's British-made Autogiros were still

Jim Ray arrives at Pier 38, New York, to pick up Juan de la Cierva; a thoroughly photographed event.

smaller than Pitcairn's and the time had come for constant personal discussions. Pitcairn invited his friend to come to America for a working vacation in a fresh new environment. He also wanted the Spanish inventor to meet the Pitcairn-Cierva Autogiro engineering group, which had grown in the last year.

Cierva returned for his third visit to the United States on the S.S. *Aquitania* at the end of 1931 and was met in a spectacular manner at dockside—with the pre-alerted newsreel and press photographer corps in full attendance.

While the *Aquitania*'s huge bulk was being warped into the dockside position, Jim Ray hovered about the area in a PCA-2, dawdling along as no other aircraft of the heavier-than-air category could do. Then, when the plume of steam from the huge whistle indicated that the unloading process was about to begin, Ray eased around and made a landing on Pier 34, next to the ship. The unprecedented accomplishment held the observers spellbound, including the hardheaded newsmen who viewed most affairs they covered as boring. If the arrival of the Autogiro was extraordinary, the departure was breathtaking. As soon as he was specially cleared by Customs and Immigration, Cierva strode down the gangplank and climbed into the front cockpit of the PCA-2, as Ray loaded his luggage in beside him. Then Cierva waved cheerfully as Ray started the engine, engaged the rotor prespinning mechanism, and fed in the throttle. As the cameras of the phalanx of photographers clicked away, the Autogiro took off and climbed away steeply from the ridiculously small space on the end of the dock. After circling the scene once, Ray flew to the lawn of Pitcairn's home. Cierva was enjoying a glass of wine with his host in Bryn Athyn less than forty-five minutes after stepping from the gangplank in New York.

Ray takes off again. Half an hour later he delivered Cierva to the lawn of Harold Pitcairn's home.

Until then the relationship between Pitcairn and Cierva had been conducted in an affable but somewhat formal manner. Their few encounters in Europe, were hardly conducive to socializing in a feet-up-on-the-table manner. Then, at the second visit, the rotor prespin system, which had been invented in the United States, had slightly chilled the atmosphere, for Cierva may have wondered what kind of a genie he had let out of the bottle. The American with whom he was now associated was clearly no dabbler, no rich-kid hobbyist, as the Spaniard may have been told.

Cierva had arrived at Cairncrest at the beginning of the festive season of Christmas, but for him it was a depressing time. Harold and Clara Pitcairn were sensitive to their guest's feelings. Cierva was separated from his wife and children by thousands of miles, and he knew that Spain might erupt into a violent social revolution at any time. In the child-filled Pitcairn home, Juan de la Cierva was embraced as a member of the family. He was included in all of the Pitcairns' activities and for five days never had an opportunity to speak a word having to do with business, technology, or politics. This was a complete change of pace for him. From that week on, Pitcairn and Cierva were friends.

Four days after Christmas, the mad whirl of social and business engagements caught up with them. Cierva flew the Pitcairn and Kellett Autogiros and journeyed with Pitcairn to Saint Clair, Michigan,

The one and only Buhl Autogiro, built under a license from the Autogiro Company of America. This arrangement with a pusher propeller had certain advantages for aerial photography, but the Depression had dried up the market and Buhl Aircraft closed down after this aircraft flew successfully. Buhl's chief engineer, Etienne Dormay, stands in front of the machine, with test pilot James Johnson in the cockpit.

where he flew the new pusher-style Autogiro of the Autogiro Company's third licensee, Buhl Aircraft. Cierva and Pitcairn were entertained in Grosse Point by Henry Ford, General William D. Mitchell, and Lawrence D. Buhl. They then returned to Philadelphia, where they were presented jointly with the highly esteemed John Scott Award, to Cierva (for inventing) and to Pit-

cairn (for developing) the Autogiro. President Hoover invited them to meet with him at the White House, to discuss aviation in general and the Autogiro in particular.

On the last day of 1931, Pitcairn held a dinner party at Cairncrest to honor Cierva, to celebrate the past and salute the future with the select group who were leaders in the emerging rotary-wing industry. W. Wallace Kellett and C. Townsend Ludington joined the coterie of engineers and licensees who had participated in the momentous advances of the year.

It was a festive occasion. The group clinking glasses in Cairncrest's great hall believed they held the future in their grasp. If they could just hold on until the pesky Depression went away, their skies had no limit.

# The Technology Improves

When the long-post-poned award presentations and all the other extraneous matters had been put behind them, Pitcairn and Cierva got down to business. The first item on the agenda was for the visitor to meet some of the new members of the Pitcairn engineering team: the brilliant Harris S. Campbell, Walter C. Clayton, Carl B. Chupp, Paul H. Stanley, Agnew Larsen, and Julian P. Perry. All were invited by Pitcairn to gather in the Stone Room in Cairncrest.

Cierva's presentation, couched in mild, almost bland tones, had a stunning effect as he proceeded with a novel theory that he had developed in England. He had not yet worked out the mathematics of the system, he explained, but fundamentally it had to do with a revolutionary change in the entire application of rotary-wing flight. As he proceeded in an almost pedantic manner, the enormous significance of his thinking overwhelmed his audience.

Until that time every Autogiro's whirling blades had spun about a fixed, or rigid, spindle mounted atop the fuselage-supported pylon so that the lift vector, or upward force, thereby produced was somewhat comparable with that of a large circular wing the same size as the rotor disc. It was, in effect, a high-lift device. Lateral control for banking and turning, and longitudinal control for up-and-down changes of pitch, were provided by conventional aircraft controls, including long-used fixed-wing control surfaces: ailerons, elevators, and aerodynamic rudder. To change the attitude of the rotor disc (and the lift vector), it was necessary to maneuver the entire aircraft, hence the requirement for ailerons attached to stubby fixed wings, as well as the conventional empennage controls: rudder and elevators.

The fundamental advantage of the free-swinging, aerodynamically rotated blade system was that, even at slow flight speeds of the aircraft, the rotating blades—the primary lifting surfaces of the craft—continued to develop lift, eliminating the slow-speed stall characteristics of fixed-wing aircraft. However, to be effective, the conventional fixed-wing ailerons and elevators of the Autogiro still required a flow of air over their surfaces; without forward speed through the air, the controls could be moved with little effect. The spinning rotor blades would of course continue to develop lift and make possible virtually zero-speed landings so that experienced Autogiro pilots could land after almost vertical descents. Unfortunately, what they made look so easy led to problems when essayed by novice pilots. When landing in gusty wind conditions, neophytes would sometimes allow the descending 'giro to drift sideways or backward just at touchdown, resulting in occasional tip-overs. Although no one was ever seriously injured in such relatively slow-motion episodes, it was an expensive experience for the pilot, and resulting press coverage usually gave the entire Autogiro business a black eye.

For many months Cierva had been pondering ways to eliminate wind-drift landing incidents and some means of providing effective control in zero-speed flight conditions, as when landing straight down. What was needed was a completely new approach, perhaps to replace the classic control system completely, which would obviate any need for the stub wings. This would be a tremendous advance.

The solution had come to Cierva in a flash of insight while attending the opera one rainy night in London. As he had approached the opera house, a long line of umbrellas had bobbed along ahead, glistening with rain in the light of the marquee. An hour or so later, as the music flowed over him, he visualized a raised umbrella as a rotor disc, with the protruding tip representing the axis of the rotor's lifting force. Suddenly, Cierva saw that if the umbrella handle were tipped to and fro, it would tilt the umbrella's angle—the "disc"—and with it, the direction of lift. Suppose, he thought, the whirling blades of an Autogiro rotor were mounted, not on the conventional fixed spindle, but on a tiltable or swiveling spindle, so that the pilot could control the direction of the rotor's thrust. The answer would be to effect such *direct control* by an upside-down or hanging control stick, just like the handle of a raised umbrella. He couldn't wait until the opera was over; then and there he gathered his belongings and rushed to his home. Before the night was over, he had sketched out a universal-joint mounting for the pylon spindle and its inverted control stick. He was certain now that a flexible-control system would provide full directional control, whether or not the aircraft itself had any forward airspeed; he had devised a means for varying the pitch of the lift thrust or lifting force directly, without changing the attitude of the entire aircraft. He had invented "cyclic pitch" for rotary-wing flight. With direct control in the rotor, ailerons and wings to carry them could be eliminated.

As so often happens in the inventive process, once the primary concept evolves, ideas for further improvement began to pour out in a flood. From the very beginning, the principal shortcoming of the conventional fixed-spindle Autogiros had been that their ability to land within confined spaces was not matched by a comparable takeoff capability: Autogiros could land in many places from which they could not take off under their own power, simply because they needed a takeoff run to become airborne. Cierva had agreed with his friend Pitcairn that the full value of rotary-wing flight could only be realized when it would be possible to make takeoffs with no ground run, that is direct-lift takeoffs, straight up—followed by translating into forward flight.

Conceiving the swiveling rotor spindle also opened to Cierva the broader concept of controllable rather than fixed-pitch settings of the rotor blades. By providing for a selective changing of the pitch angle of the rotating blades, he expected to achieve the direct liftoff objective. This is where Pitcairn had come in, with the rotor prespin device which had been incorporated in the PCA-2 and all subsequent Pitcairn designs and had made possible the extremely short takeoff characteristics demonstrated most prominently in the White House and Pier 34 takeoffs. This, said Cierva later, had led to his next logical step.

Cierva had calculated that if a set of rotor blades could be created with precisely the correct amount of weight and strength, and the multiple blades could be moved simulta-neously to a zero-lift condition, they could be accelerated to 125 percent of the normal lift-off rotational velocity, a condition he called "over-spinning." This excess rotational speed would generate kinetic energy, which, under the basic laws of physics, would be stored in the rotating mass of the blades themselves. If somehow the spinning blades could be instantly, simultaneously— that is, "collectively"—moved to lift-generating angles of attack, while disengaging the rotor drive system so that the engine's power could be transmitted to the conventional propeller to provide forward thrust, the stored kinetic energy would be expended to generate a burst of lift which would cause the aircraft to rise vertically. Before the energy decayed, the Autogiro would be able to fly away in a normal climb-out.

The dual concepts of "cyclic" and "collective" controls, so quietly but intensely explained by the Spanish inventor, electrified the Autogiro Company's engineers, particularly if the two systems could be integrated. Either cyclic or collective control presented substantial engineering problems; to incorporate both systems and to provide for both to operate conjointly and also independently seemed impossible. But if they could make the theory work in practice, it would be as great an advance in aeronautical technology as the Autogiro itself had been.

For a month the Stone Room hideaway was the scene of endless conferences and think sessions usually lasting far into the night. Everyone worked at a fever pitch while wrestling with the problems of transforming imaginative concepts into practical mechanical devices.

Pitcairn was deeply enthusiastic, for he could see that the development of these ideas could lead to the helicopter devices he and Larsen had been working on for years. But he was also a practical man of business, and he could see the potential financial impact, too. During 1931, he had produced and delivered twenty-four PCA-2s and seventeen PAA-1s, even though the former had not received its Approved Type Certificate until April and the latter not until July. Just as he was beginning to realize some return on his investment, he was working on a project that would have tremendous implications for his business. Within a few years every Autogiro design on which Approved Type Certificates had been so laboriously—and expensively—obtained would be obsolete. When the new direct-control design on which he was working became perfected enough for government certification, the public would no longer be interested in the older models, with the fixed spindle. He was concerned that even the public disclosure of such a possible development might kill the present market. Pitcairn had reason to be concerned; in five years he had spent well over a million dollars on rotary-wing research and development and was just beginning to see light at the end of the tunnel.

On the other hand, public accep-

tance of the PCA-2 and the PAA-1 had portended greater things to come, which indicated that there would be wider acceptance of a vastly improved version with even more sensational performance.

Business was good, both for his own Pitcairn Aircraft Company, which was producing the commercially available Autogiros for sale to the public, and for his friends, Kellett and Ludington, whose Kellett Aircraft Company was doing business at a plant near Philadelphia Municipal Airport.

Both the army and the navy were evaluating Autogiros for possible military applications, and while the theoreticians were working the slide rules in the Stone Room, Pitcairn Aviation had produced the prototype of another Autogiro of the old time-tested style: the PA-18.* It was another winner in the marketplace, just the right machine for the right time, so Pitcairn believed.

He had observed that the somewhat large PCA-2 was too much for the individual owner and that the PAA-1 was too small. His new PA-18 venture was a compromise, with slightly greater size but with a 165-hp engine (40 horses more than the PAA-1 had) which gave it sizzling performance and greater all-around utility. It was priced right—$6,750, including flight instruction—and surely would be the Autogiro to induce the private-pilot owner to move into rotary-wing aircraft.

He had another project in the works as a possible hedge against the deepening Depression. He real-

The PA-18 was a slightly larger version of the PAA-1 and was another immediate success. A total of 19 were built and sold. This one is taxiing at Wings Field, near Ambler, Pa.

ized that the market for private Autogiros (and airplanes of any category) would be limited. On the other hand, he had watched carefully the development of scheduled airline service, both mail and passenger, noting that growing numbers of people were flying on the commercial lines for business and for pleasure. He had planned to enter the business of common carriers by air (air carriers) with a specially designed Autogiro that would dwarf any Autogiro ever made. He had already designated it as the PA-19.

The PA-19 was by no means as large as the Ford Tri-Motors, Curtiss Condors, or Lockheed 10s that were in widespread air-carrier use, but it offered transportation that the larger planes could not approach. Pitcairn's intuition was that a cabin model that could carry four passengers in plush comfort would provide fast, convenient air transportation for communities not served by the major air carriers and that could never afford to build airport facilities required for airline service with large airplanes.

Flying his own PAA-1 back and forth from Bryn Athyn to his summer home in Ocean City, New Jersey, he had detoured several times to fly over the sprawling naval base at Lakehurst, where the naval lighter-than-air dirigibles were hangared and which was used by the German leviathan of the sky, the *Graf Zeppelin,* as the terminus of its regular transatlantic crossings. By surface transportation—automobile or railroad—passengers connecting from Philadelphia and New York faced a fatiguing journey of an hour and a

A symbol of success: completed Autogiros lined up for delivery in the Pitcairn Willow Grove factory. Every one had been paid for, right in the middle of the Depression!

half, perhaps two hours, if the ferries were crowded. In a cabin Autogiro, the hop from Lakehurst to downtown Manhattan or Philadelphia would take no more than half an hour. To Pitcairn, Autogiro air-taxi and intercity feeder service made good sense and the sheer convenience of such convenient transportation could create a substantial commercial market for the PA-19 he had in mind.

As he studied the problems of an entirely new control system for rotary-wing aircraft, he was nagged by the thought that he might be making a mistake to keep pushing on the two new designs, the PA-18 and the PA-19.

After studying the pros and cons

in the quiet of his private study at Cairncrest, the room in which he could have the absolute isolation required for concentrating on solutions, he made the decision to go ahead with both Autogiros.

After more than a month of wrestling with the problems of cyclic and collective pitch controls, he had come to the conclusion that transforming the inventions into practical, reliable hardware for highly demanding aviation applications could take as long as five years and that in the meantime the factory could be kept busy. In any event, if and when the new all-inclusive control systems were perfected, they could be built into future production models and retrofitted to those already in service.

After almost five weeks of intensive scientific analysis, Cierva sailed for England on February 14, 1932, with the complicated problems of aerodynamics and mechanics still unsolved. It had been an enjoyable experience for everyone concerned, a seemingly impossible challenge such as all engineers relish.

Having made up his mind to press on with the PA-18 and the PA-19, Pitcairn went outside of his own organization and persuaded the well-known, highly respected Robert B. C. Noorduyn to put his touches of grace on the Cabin Model. It was a felicitous move; Noorduyn had worked with Anthony Fokker and with Guiseppe Bellanca in the development of their cabin model passenger planes and would one day design the classic "Norseman," which to this day is widely used all over Canada as a bush plane.

Perhaps it should have been expected that Cierva would have disclosed his extraordinary invention to his British associates before leaving England for what promised to be a lengthy stay in the United States and that the London group would have been addressing them-

selves to the problems at least a month before their American counterparts were exposed to them. In all of their time together, Cierva had not communicated that information to Pitcairn, who had not raised the question with his house guest. In any event, it came as a distinct shock to Pitcairn when he received a cable from Cierva Company, London, that it had produced a prototype of the swivable-spindle, cyclic pitch control 'giro and that its first tests had been entirely satisfactory. Pitcairn openly wondered to Edwin Asplundh, one of the few truly close friends he had, what to make of it. His major suspicion was that there was some sort of breach between Cierva and his own group. A small red flag went up in the back of Pitcairn's head. Perhaps he and they were competitors, not collaborators, no matter what Cierva's relationship with him might be. For some reason he no longer felt as comfortable as before.

# The Biggest Autogiro

On March 1, 1932, the first PA-18 rolled out of the hangar, to begin the flight tests leading to its type certification. It should have been an eminently newsworthy occurrence, but no paper covered the story; every journalist in the country had zeroed in on the little town of Hopewell, New Jersey, where, the night before, the infant son of Charles and Anne Lindbergh had been kidnapped. Pressures to cover every angle of the story soon had press photographers beseiging Pitcairn to rent them Autogiros from which they could take aerial photographs at low level of the isolated Lindbergh home, but the company president adamantly refused to participate in any intrusion on the privacy of the Lindbergh family. Charles Lindbergh was his friend.

The kidnapping hit Pitcairn especially hard. Although he had always lived a low-key existence, never flaunting his wealth or social position, he was aware that Cairncrest was isolated, far from police protection, and vulnerable to the same kind of lunacy. It would not be hard for anyone to subject Cairncrest to a similar trespass. To secure his home and family, he had installed extra locks on the doors and windows accessible from ground level, all of which he would check assiduously every night before retiring. He also purchased a compact Savage .32-caliber semi-automatic pistol.

The PA-18 was an aeronautical gem from the first turn of its rotor blades, exceeding most of its engineering and theoretical performance projections. Probably the most beautifully proportioned Autogiro ever to fly, it received its Approved Type Certificate from the Department of Commerce in the phenomenally short time of five weeks and was released for sale to the public. Pitcairn's assessment of the market had been correct: within a year and a half more than nineteen PA-18s were produced and sold, vindicating his decision to proceed with the basic machine while experimenting with the direct-control system.

Toward the end of March 1932, an inconspicuous news item reported that Juan de la Cierva had flown "the first wingless airplane." Few readers were interested in the foreigner's feat, but Pitcairn engineers realized that Cierva had flown a direct-control Autogiro, while they had just begun to work on design drawings and were nowhere near to cutting metal to fabricate an actual test machine.

In January 1933, Harold Pitcairn and his attorneys changed the corporate name of the operating manufacturing company from Pitcairn Aircraft Company to Pitcairn Autogiro Company, Inc. This would indicate the total transition from fixed wing to rotary wing.

Against the background of the international collapse of finance and with banks failing at every turn, aviation was nevertheless growing. No less than twenty-one airlines were functioning in the U.S. and mail routes were coming up for rebidding.

As usual, Pitcairn was actively engaged in several projects at the same time. For many months he had been conferring with officials of the Commonwealth of Pennsylvania and the federal government to coordinate and synchronize aviation regulations, for many of the states had decided to create their own rules of aircraft operation to fill in what they considered voids in the Department of Commerce regulations. On his trips to Washington, Pitcairn was also trying to obtain some sort of assistance from federal authorities to aid in Autogiro research and development. He actively solicited orders from government agencies for Autogiros; he believed the Department of Commerce should have some, as well as the Department of the Interior, the Bureau of Mines, the Department of Agriculture, and that the army and navy should certainly evaluate the newest models.

To his consternation, Pitcairn found that Autogiros were being maligned and undercut by an invidious whispering campaign. Some competitors in the fixed-wing industry had begun to charge that rotary-wing aircraft were unsafe, expensive, and highly specialized and that the public would be well advised not to travel in such craft.

Pitcairn took every opportunity to set the matter straight in speeches, public appearances, and articles. He recounted how for several years

* This tends to lead to a certain amount of confusion. The Pitcairn-Cierva Autogiro Company of America (PCA) had been changed to the new and simpler name of Autogiro Company of America (ACA), which remained as before, the patent-repository holding company which engaged in basic research and theoretical engineering. The Pitcairn Autogiro Company (PA) was the licensed manufacturer of aircraft to be produced for public sales, i.e., the operating company. The interlocking nature of the principal (Harold Pitcairn) and the closeness of his engineering group, which cut at times across the corporate distinctions, and the close friendship between Pitcairn and Cierva undoubtedly was the reason for the friction that would develop between Pitcairn Autogiro and the other licensee of ACA, Kellett Aircraft Company, as shall be seen.

he had flown his personal Autogiros from the lawn of his home to places all over the East Coast. These flights were not stunts, but normal trips. He detailed how he commuted regularly from Bryn Athyn to his summer home adjacent to the beach at Ocean City, New Jersey. This was a seventy-mile trip which took several hours by automobile. He made the flight in forty-five minutes, or less, landing on the beach at his own front door. The focus of his presentations was always on cross-country *safety* rather than speed or travel flexibility, which he pointed out as additional factors. As for reliability, he pointed out Ray's flights to Florida and back, and the transcontinental flights of Autogiros, some flown

by new private pilots. He showed newsreels of Lew Yancey flying the Champion Spark Plug Autogiro all over the North American continent, over locales ranging from Yosemite National Park to the heavy jungle of the Yucatán Peninsula, where Yancey landed in clearings next to Mayan ruins. He showed how Autogiros operated in areas inaccessible to automobiles, yet did not need an airport or landing field at either end of the trip, only a small cleared area. After a lifetime of self-effacement and avoidance of personal publicity, Pitcairn became the

Lew Yancey and the Champion PCA-2 operating in Yosemite National Park, surrounded by the Rocky Mountains.

Yancey and the PCA-2 operating out of a remote jungle strip in the Yucatán Peninsula of Mexico: Chichen Itza. No other aircraft was capable of landing in that area.

leading spokesman for the infant industry, in every level of American society. It was a labor of love.

Withal, there was always a nagging question in his mind: What was transpiring at Cierva Ltd. across the ocean? When he could not stand being uninformed any longer, he sailed to England with Ray and Larsen to investigate personally. The trip removed all illusions.

The British group had modified an early Cierva C-19 Autogiro to provide for direct rotor control by tilting the spindle (and the rotor disc) for both lateral and longitudinal control, using the upside-down, or hanging, control stick. The ship

had risen only a few feet and had not flown cross-country. Both Pitcairn and Ray took turns in the experimental vehicle and agreed that it was still a long way from being a reliable direct-control machine. It vibrated furiously, and the upside-down control stick had to be held with both hands by the pilot. Despite press reports, the Cierva 'giro was a long way from perfection.

Back in Bryn Athyn, armed with the knowledge that their progress was almost equal to that of the British engineers, Pitcairn's team continued to nail down, one by one, the solutions to problems that developed in models and wind tunnel tests. Synnestvedt & Lechner, as patent counsel, were kept busy processing drawings and diagrams, applying for patents on each new invention as it developed, averaging more than one a month. It was slow, tedious work, but progress was being made. The experimental tilting-hub, direct-control ship had already been assigned a number: PA-22.

In the face of the worsening Depression, the factory was humming with activity. Its production lines were filled with PAA-1s and PA-18s; the first production model of the PA-19 Cabin Model was in the paint shop, almost ready for the installation of its interior appointments.

The Queen of the Fleet: the PA-19, sometimes referred to as the "Cabin Job." It was the largest Autogiro ever built and performed beautifully. Note the downward-viewing windows low on each side of the cabin, ahead of the wing. Even in soft snow, the PA-19 was able to take off with a full load.

In the engineering research department, the fuselage of the experimental direct-control PA-22 was taking shape and machinists were fitting the tiltable rotor system for initial stress testing. When each of the major components had met specifications, the fuselage and rotor mechanism would be mated so that ground testing could begin.

The PA-19 Cabin Model was introduced on October 19, 1932, and created a sensation. No longer was an Autogiro to be regarded only as a Spartan, open-cockpit craft, difficult for a woman to enter while wearing skirts, or for older passengers to board. Instead, the PA-19 rivaled the luxurious comfort of fine automobiles. One entered its cabin through a wide door, after having mounted a few retractable steps that

The sheer size of the two-ton PA-19 is apparent in this photo. It would transport five people at more than 120 miles an hour with its 420-hp engine. The boarding ladder was quickly removable and stowable.

reached to the ground. Its interior was beautifully appointed and tastefully upholstered with fine whipcord and broadcloth and a plush carpet. In flight, the cabin ship was even more impressive; being thoroughly soundproofed by layers of insulation built into the structure, it was quiet enough to carry on a conversation while the pneumatic bumps of flight, objectionable to passengers of fixed-wing aircraft, were virtually eliminated by the flexing rotor blades. And it was *big!* With a gross weight of more than two tons, it was the largest Autogiro ever built.

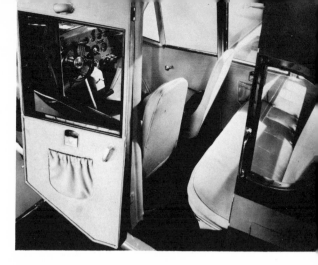

Step right in and feel at home: The PA-19 was both roomy and plush and far ahead of its time. Both front windows could be lowered, as in the case of contemporary automobiles. (Note the right front window crank.)

The front office of the PA-19 showing the throw-over control wheel, flight instruments (and instrument lights for night flying) and location of the low, downward-vision windows.

Most important to Pitcairn was that by the time the Cabin Model was completed, his design team had solved enough of the problems of the tiltable disc that they replaced the fixed spindle, which had been planned for the PA-19, with a fore-and-aft tilting spindle, providing "partial direct control." It was not a true direct control, for tilting was effected by turning a hand crank rather than by a control stick and was actually a device for trimming the ship for improved takeoff, cruising, and for approaches to landings. But it demonstrated that the inventions flowing from the Autogiro

A PA-19 over Manhattan in a Pitcairn promotion picture. It was an eye-catching aircraft. The then-new Empire State Building is at the right; the Chrysler Building, at the left, is partially obscured by the art work.

Company of America's engineers to the Patent Office were solid in actual practice. It was a memorable accomplishment, for the Cabin Model was flying long before the British Cierva group completed testing their own direct-control machine.

For the next few weeks the Cabin Model flew up and down the East Coast between Cape May and Montauk Point, landing many times, not only on airports, but in public parks, on beaches, and on private estates, performing perfectly and gar-

nering favorable publicity. Pitcairn was so pleased that he ordered five to be manufactured and set the price at $14,500 each. He was certain that its luxury, outstanding utility, and ability to operate from almost anywhere would find wide favor and generate a volume of orders. In normal times he would have been correct, but those were not normal times. The Depression had grown progressively worse. Banks were closing, brokerage firms were going into bankruptcy. No one felt secure.

The bottom had dropped out of the national economy.

Orders for the PAA-1 and PA-18 suddenly tailed off, leaving Pitcairn with an excess inventory of all production models.

Against this dismal background, the first experimental PA-22 direct-control Pitcairn Autogiro had been completed and was being readied for preliminary testing. It was tiny compared with the PA-19, but like its large predecessor it had a cabin instead of the open-cockpit format. Strictly an experimental ship, the first test version had a decidedly unorthodox appearance. Its landing gear consisted of a single "bull" wheel located in the fuselage about at the center of gravity; this wheel carried the main load. A pair of small wheels, castored to turn freely, were mounted on two struts extending from the front of the fuselage. For the first time, a Pitcairn Autogiro would have no stubby wings, no ailerons, no elevators, just a rudder. All pitch and roll control would be provided by the

The PA-22 was the first Pitcairn direct-control Autogiro, with all lateral and attitude control incorporated in the rotor system. The stub wings bearing the ailerons have been eliminated. This first version in 1932 did not have the jump-takeoff feature. This "bull wheel" design intimated a roadability philosophy which was quickly bypassed in the test vehicle. This was the watershed development that spelled the end of the fixed-spindle Autogiro.

"orientable hub," a swivelling spindle controlled by an upside-down stick hanging from the cabin ceiling.

The first test of the rotor, which was not yet equipped with prespinning mechanism, was a disaster. No sooner had the blades begun to pick up speed than an out-of-balance oscillation set up, making the diminutive ship and occupant bounce wildly until the throttle was retracted. Obviously, considerable redesign was going to be required.

The economic future looked bleak indeed, but perhaps there was room for some hope. The former governor of New York, Franklin D. Roosevelt, had been elected President in the November 1932 elections and would take office on March 4, 1933. Roosevelt had charisma; his promise that he would lead the nation back to prosperity inspired confidence.

When things were looking their worst, another break came for Pitcairn: in January 1933, he received a personal invitation from Henry L. Doherty, a prominent financier and promoter who was making great strides developing vacation resorts in southern Florida, to come to Miami to enjoy the surf and sun and,

most important, to discuss the possible uses of Cabin Model Autogiros in Doherty's far-flung operations. Pitcairn was already waiting for the next southbound train when he saw a headline in the *Evening Bulletin:* an assassin had fired several shots into the open limousine carrying the president-elect through the streets of Miami. Roosevelt had been hit, but was miraculously unhurt; Mayor Anton Cermak, of Chicago, on the rear seat with Roosevelt, had been mortally wounded. Seated between them—unhit—had been Henry L. Doherty.

The extent of Doherty's interests in south Florida impressed the visitor from Bryn Athyn. In a few years the entrepreneur had acquired the ultra-plush Roney Plaza Hotel in Miami Beach, the equally posh Miami Biltmore, across Biscayne Bay, and had created the magnificent Anglers Club on Key Largo, some

The upside-down, or "hanging" control stick of the PA-22, which tilted the entire disc of the rotor blades, took some getting used to, because control movements were reversed from normal airplane control movements. This was the first step from the fixed-spindle design and eventually led to the development of helicopter concepts.

Five PA-19s were made. Two were sold in the United States, two in Europe and one was held for factory testing and later destroyed. This one was purchased by Florida Year-Round Clubs to transport clients between the Roney Beach Hotel, the Miami Biltmore and the Anglers Club on Key Largo, 30 miles south of Miami. It was in regular use until 1935.

fifty miles across open water to the south. During their conversations, Doherty revealed plans to establish additional hunting and fishing preserves in the Everglades and farther down the chain of Florida Keys. For some time he had shuttled guests between his hotels, country clubs, beach clubs, and fishing clubs by fleets of automobiles and speedboats, but surface travel was time-consuming and uncomfortable, sometimes taking almost all day to cover circuitous overland routes to places only a few miles away. How much time, he asked his visiting aviator, would it take to make such trips by Autogiro?

Pitcairn could have answered the question off the top of his head, but having seen the sizable array of Doherty's automobiles and speedboats, he recognized that his host could

easily afford to buy all five Cabin Models—or a dozen of them—which would certainly help alleviate the cash-flow situation at Pitcairn Autogiro. Why not, he responded quickly, fly one down from Willow Grove and find out? It was agreed.

Pitcairn called the factory and ordered "Florida Year Round Clubs" lettered on the sides of a PA-19, then told Jim Ray to fly it to Miami as soon as the paint was dry. It was a well-calculated move. Merely flying the large Cabin Model twelve hundred miles and having one on the scene where nationally known business leaders in the club's well-to-do membership gathered would create just the kind of exposure the Autogiro now needed most. Advertising and publicity could never replace the experience of seeing, feeling, and *flying in* the real article.

The other U.S. PA-19 was purchased by Col. R.L. Montgomery of Villa Nova to commute between his front lawn and his home in Georgetown, South Carolina: four hours by Autogiro, 12 hours by train.

Ray followed the old air-mail route that he had once pioneered, stopping at Richmond, Raleigh, Greensboro, Spartanburg, Atlanta, Jacksonville, and Palm Beach. At each waypoint festive receptions featured prominent local politicians and officials. It was a triumphal tour, and Pitcairn took every advantage of it.

Public response to the flight was even more than he had hoped for and the landing Ray made on the front lawn of the Roney Plaza was photographed and subsequently reproduced in newspapers all over the country. For several years that Autogiro was the promotional darling of Miami's publicity department, particularly when chilly weather began to edge into the northeastern states. Photographic layouts featuring the big 'giro transporting sportsmen to remote islands were big factors in inducing the annual trek of wealthy northerners to the sun-drenched Southland. Unfortunately, Doherty only used that one Autogiro, but the publicity from Florida paid off: the Guinness Brewing Company, of the United Kingdom, eventually purchased two PA-19s; another PA-19 was sold to a wealthy Philadelphia sportsman-pilot, Colonel Robert L. Montgomery, who flew it regularly from the lawn of his Main Line estate, commuting to his home in Georgetown, South Carolina, an easy six-hour Autogiro trip, rather than a two-day trip by railroad or by automobile. The fifth PA-19 was retained by Pitcairn Aviation as its demonstrator.

Technologically, operationally, and practically, the PA-19 Cabin Model was a complete success and under normal circumstances Pitcairn should have sold hundreds of them, but the Depression had taken its toll. No more would be made.

# The Depression Strikes

By early spring 1933, the experimental PA-22 direct-control ship had been redesigned, had undergone successful ground testing for vibration problems, and then had been pronounced ready for taxi tests. As the Autogiro Company's engineers watched expectantly, test pilot Ray slid into the left seat of the little cabin and started the Pobjoy engine. After warming it up for a few minutes, he began to taxi it slowly across the grass runway to spin the rotor blades, since no rotor drive had as yet been incorporated in the test ship. It wound up smoothly with no vibrations or imbalances. Repeatedly, Ray taxied up and down the runway, each time a little faster so that the rotor blades increased their rpms almost to lift-off speed, as planned. Unexpectedly, the PA-22 rose a few feet into the air, although actual flight had not been scheduled for that day. As the ship rose, it wobbled violently from side to side, darted to an altitude of twenty-five feet, fell off to the right, then recovered close to the ground. Suddenly it zoomed up to fifty feet, fell off steeply to the right, turned on its side, and hit the ground with a resounding crash. The aircraft was a washout. Ray escaped with only minor injuries; after seeing the wreckage from the outside, he considered himself very lucky.

For several days Pitcairn, Ray, and the engineers studied drawings and pre-test reports, trying to ascertain what had gone wrong and how Ray, one of the most experienced Autogiro pilots in the world, had so completely lost control. When Jim pointed to the absence of wings on the craft and observed that notwithstanding their absence, it felt as if nonexistent ailerons had been rigged in reverse, no one smiled. Undoubtedly he had found the answer: the loss of control stemmed from the fact that the control system involving the upside-down stick *did* operate in reverse. Movements of the hanging stick had exactly the opposite results of similar movements of standard aircraft or Autogiro controls: to roll the direct-control ship to the left, the stick had to be moved to the right; to put the nose down,

217

The PA-22 was designed with foldable rotor blades, to make highway use feasible. The original "bull wheel" was an engineering concept for ground propulsion, but after it was eliminated, the rotor system was retained.

the pilot had to pull the stick back, completely contrary to all of the reflexive control movements ingrained by hours of practice in fixed-wing and fixed-spindle Autogiro aircraft.

Complicating the problem, Ray added, was the fact that as soon as the ship lifted off the ground, the stick had become a live thing in his hands, indicating excessive feedback from the rotor. The aircraft would have to be rebuilt, almost from scratch, just when the company's affairs were again stretching tightly.

In spite of the heady press releases about appointments of new sales outlets and dealerships and widespread press coverage of famous people being transported in Pitcairn Autogiros, sales were scarce and sporadic. Dropping the price of the PA-18 one-third, to $4,940, did not help. Since sales to the federal government seemed to be the best objective, the special performance of the PA-22 might make it the company's salvation.

The rotary-wing industry, never large, was shrinking. By 1933 the Buhl Aircraft Company was out of it, bankrupt, another victim of the Depression, having produced a single pusher-type Autogiro. This left the Pitcairn and Kellett Autogiro companies as the Autogiro Company of America's only licensees. And new frictions were developing between the formerly friendly principals of those companies.

Under the terms of the licensing agreement with Cierva, the Autogiro Company of America was obliged to exchange developmental information with the British parent company. In turn, both U.S. licensees of the Autogiro Company of America, Pitcairn Autogiro and Kellett Aircraft, were to forward immediately detailed information of any new evolutions to the Autogiro Company, which was contractually designated as the repository for all rotary-wing patents, the purpose being to avoid the duplication of expensive research and development programs.

Initially, the Kellett organization cooperated fully in accordance with the terms of the contract, for to do so made good business sense. This was a friendly, nascent industry: former Autogiro Company and Pitcairn Aircraft engineers were on Kellett's engineering staff and the success of the Kellett Autogiro was proudly disseminated in the Autogiro Company of America's widely read newsletter, *Autogiro News*.

But once the technique was understood, Cierva's formerly secret invention was like the "Egg of Columbus," as Thomas A. Edison once described it: other inventive minds would find ways and means of improving on it. While the Autogiro Company of America's and Pitcairn Autogiro's engineers were working on problems of direct control, Kellett's engineers, including LePage and Richard H. Prewitt, were too. Independently of Cierva—although later in time—Prewitt, Kellett's chief engineer, had hit upon the tiltable spindle to provide for direct control, and Kellett was, without telling Pitcairn's Autogiro Company of America, proceeding to adapt a Kellett K-2 with that type of control. Thus, contrary to the terms and spirit of their original agreements, Cierva, Pitcairn, and Kellett were all fumbling around for solutions to identical control problems, all with limited success, creating exactly the situation the licensing agreements were designed to avoid. Unhappily, the contractual boat which they were supposedly rowing in the same direction was springing leaks. Communications between Kellett Aircraft and the Autogiro Company of America dwindled off to nothing. Worse than that, in a formal response to a letter from the Autogiro Company, inquiring directly about what was transpiring in their developmental work, Kellett responded in somewhat starchy language that they were not required under the terms of the agreement to disclose any of their experimental activities on devices not yet perfected, whereupon communications between longtime friends took on increasing layers of frost. Soon all exchanges were reduced to writing and were filtered through counsel.

Within weeks of its crash, the Pitcairn Autogiro PA-22 experimental direct-control machine had been rebuilt completely. Although it continued to carry the PA-22 designation, its "bull" wheel had been replaced by a more conventional tail-wheel configuration, but it still used the inverted control stick, and nagging vibration problems persisted. Ray would not be deterred by the operational problems; literally teaching himself to fly the new system, he flew at every opportunity, although he cautiously confined himself to flights within the boundaries of the field.

Pitcairn's insistent requests for Cierva's personal assistance in straightening out their business relationship concerning cross-information had their effect when the latter agreed to return to the United States for a month or so in the springtime. Besides, he hinted, he had a new invention that he wanted the Autogiro Company's engineers to know about.

Cierva arrived on May 16, 1933, aboard the S.S. *Paris*. He was met by Pitcairn and Ray at Newark Airport with the impressive Cabin Model PA-19 and was flown directly to Cairncrest. Pitcairn had hoped to have Cierva's undivided attention on the problems at hand but found that it was impossible to sequester him in the Stone Room with his

slide rule and blackboard. As soon as the visit was made known, America's scientific community wanted to lionize the celebrated inventor.

The day after Cierva's arrival, the Franklin Institute awarded him the Elliott Cresson Medal for "the original conceptions and inventive ability which have resulted in the creation and development of the Autogiro." On the same occasion, medals were presented to Orville Wright and Igor Sikorsky. It was an historic occasion: for the first time, Wright, Sikorsky, Cierva, and Pitcairn were together at one place.

Three weeks later Cierva and Pitcairn were awarded honorary degrees of doctor of engineering by Stevens Institute of Technology.

Between awards, Cierva worked intensively with his friends on the control and stability problems of the PA-22. After examining the ship and watching it in operation, he made a number of recommendations about rigging and adjusting its blades. Then, he asked Pitcairn to assemble the engineers for a disser-

Top: Cierva (left) and Pitcairn contemplating the PA-22's direct-control vibration problems with the jump-takeoff rotor system.
Middle: Joined by plant manager Haberle, with the unfinished Willow Grove factory in the background. Obviously no solution at hand.
Bottom: Geof Childs discusses the problems after Cierva himself took the PA-22 for a test flight. This was during Cierva's 1932 visit. The jump-takeoff feature was added in late 1932.

Solving one problem of the jump-take-off PA-22 rotor system usually disclosed another. The Pitcairn Autogiro team reflects the tensions of the testing program. Seated on the running board of the vintage Packard are Harold Pitcairn, Childs, Asplundh and pilot Jim Faulkner. Oil-spattered test pilot Ray watches the adjustments being made, while engineer Paul Stanley is at the extreme right. The new factory building has been completed and the company name painted on the facade.

tation on some new concepts he had developed.

No one in the group, by now highly experienced in rotary-wing engineering, was prepared for what Cierva disclosed in his quiet, methodical manner. As he proceeded with his explanation, they realized that he had conceived a completely new control system for rotary-wing aircraft that was far superior to anything then in existence.

Up to then, direct control had relied on the physical tilting of the rotor spindle, which resulted in cyclically changing the angle of attack of the rotor blades and their flying to a controlled tilted plane of rotation. A jump-takeoff capability would be provided by a two-stage "collective" pitch system which involved setting a zero-thrust pitch angle of the rotor blades for rev-up, followed by a simultaneous (collective) pitch change of all blades to high-lift angles to produce rotor thrust for immediate lift-off. However, neither of the systems had yet been perfected to the point of government certification.

Now Cierva had conceived a control system for cyclically changing the pitch of the rotor blades relative to a fixed or nontilting spindle. Under the new creation, movements of the pilot's controls would physically change the blade pitch angles at precise azimuths in their plane of rotation as they whirled around the fixed spindle, thereby varying the direction of aerodynamic thrust. The collective, or jump-takeoff system of simultaneously changing all blade angles, would also be incorporated into the single rotor head. The consequences were staggering.

The Stone Room hideaway at Cairncrest was the setting for engineering meetings that lasted for days—and frequently nights—as Cierva developed for Pitcairn, Larsen, Campbell, and Stanley the complex mathematics of his new control concepts. Paul H. Stanley, a mathematician in his own right, was Cierva's most apt pupil, but the others struggled valiantly to understand the formulas and diagrams, which soon filled several portable blackboards. They were encouraged by the fact that the PA-22 was flying successfully after the master's recommendations had been followed, for the tilting-disc cyclic system had been proven experimentally. But they perceived that the movable spindle technique would soon be superseded by the selective individual-blade cyclic-pitch control invention.

In view of the enormity of the prospective change, the Autogiro Company of America's corporate (i.e. Harold Pitcairn's) decision was that it should not change the entire course of its experimental development, which meant that they would not drop the tilting-hub system. Instead, it was agreed that Cierva's British company should proceed

with the development of the new device and that Pitcairn's engineers would engage only in continued experimentation which would lead to the commerical certification of the tilting-disc and two-stage selective jump-takeoff control systems. In the interim, Cierva's newest invention, already protected by European patents, would be further protected by U.S. patents as well.

Before these things could happen, however, Cierva had to take time from his busy schedule to receive yet another aviation award. Political turmoil in his homeland had precluded Cierva's presence in the United States to accept the 1932 Guggenheim Medal for "the World's Most Notable Achievement in Aviation," but the Guggenheim Foundation had informed him that it would be pleased to make the presentation in conjunction with Engineers' Day at the 1933 Chicago World's Fair, the Century of Progress Exposition.

As a refreshing change from the usual grandiloquence of such ceremonies, which normally involved a banquet, speeches, and formal attire, it had been suggested that it would be more appropriate to make the presentation in the huge sports arena known as Soldiers Field adjacent to the man-made island on which the exposition was located—now the site of Meigs Field, an important general aviation airport. The plan was to have Cierva arrive in an Autogiro and land on the football field, where the awards dais would be erected.

The PA-19, with Jim Ray flying, delivers Juan de la Cierva and Harold Pitcairn to Soldiers Field, Chicago, for the award of the Guggenheim Medal in 1933. The Chicago World's Fair was being held on an adjacent manmade island, now the site of Meigs Field.

On June 28, as thousands watched, the PA-19 Cabin Model, piloted all the way from Bryn Athyn by Jim Ray with Cierva and Pitcairn on board, circled the huge stadium and exposition area several times. Heads turned and necks craned as the slow-turning rotor blades flashed and glinted in the sun; then the handsome Autogiro turned in toward the football field, landed lightly, and rolled to a stop within ten feet of its touchdown spot. The unique arrival brought the crowd to its feet, as press and newsreel photographers recorded the stirring event. For several days Pitcairn's name was again on the front pages of the world press.

After six weeks of intense activities in America, Cierva was looking forward to returning to the Continent. Not only was he itching to get back to his engineering studies, he was constantly concerned about the safety of his family in Madrid, for news services reported increasing tensions between Spain's political factions.

Cierva had planned to spend his final day at Bryn Athyn conferring with the Autogiro Company of America's patent counsel, Raymond Synnestvedt, and had arranged his drawings and technical descriptions so that the new invention could be explained in a few hours for the U.S. patent application. Then his host would fly him to Newark Airport in time to board the S.S. *Paris* for a midnight departure. Enjoying a quiet breakfast with Harold and Clara in Cairncrest's sunshine-flooded dining room overlooking the green hills of eastern Pennsylvania, Cierva was thoroughly relaxed. His trip to America had been rewarding, and a number of vexing problems had been resolved.

From time to time the Pitcairn children would come in to say goodbye to "Uncle Juan," who was as much at ease with them as he was with their elders. While they were on their second cup of coffee, Raymond Synnestvedt arrived and joined them in social conversation within the family group. Leafing through the pages of *The New York Times*, Clara Pitcairn's eye caught the list of ship sailings from the Port of New York. She looked twice at the schedules, then asked her guest what time his ship sailed. Casually, he pulled the ticket from a coat pocket, then saw with a start that he had misread the schedule: the *Paris* was sailing at noon, not at midnight! Surely he would miss it.

Pitcairn proved equal to the occasion. He told Cierva to finish packing, then called Jim Ray at the airfield and requested him to bring the Cabin Model, a PCA-2, and a

PA-18 to Cairncrest immediately, fueled to fly to Newark. Within the hour the inventor's luggage, including a large steamer trunk, had been loaded into the aircraft and the flight was on its way. Cierva, Synnestvedt, and Pitcairn were in the big cabin ship so that, en route, the inventor could explain for patent purposes the concepts and mechanics of the new control system. Synnestvedt's eyes widened as he perceived the impact of the basic sketches and descriptions, for he recognized instantly that this could be the most important invention since the original solution to rotary-wing flight. Little did he know at the time that the papers he reviewed during that hectic flight to Newark would be the keystone for the future of the entire vertical-lift industry or that they would have a critical impact on the fortunes of Harold Pitcairn.

The mad dash was successful; Cierva boarded his ship with moments to spare. Clutching his briefcase, he waved gaily to his friends on the dock, just as the ship's lines were being loosened.

Progress on the direct-control experimental 'giros was being made on both sides of the Atlantic. Ray was flying the revamped PA-22 regularly, having mastered the upsidedown control stick at last, and was making vertical descents under full control in all sorts of wind conditions, but the vertical-takeoff mechanism had not been incorporated because it had not been solved to Pitcairn's satisfaction. In England, a Cierva C-30 had been modified to incorporate both tilting cyclic control and the two-stage collective system. Cierva invited Pitcairn to come to the British Isles to see for himself, but Pitcairn believed that Ray could make a better evaluation of the British company's progress, so he sent Jim abroad instead of going himself.

In the late summer of 1933, after making several flights in the C-30 tilting spindle, Ray advised his boss that he should come over with Larsen and Stanley.

The American contingent soon concluded that the C-30 direct-control experimental ship was working acceptably for its prototype status but was not yet commercially feasible and was not, in fact, superior in any way to their own PA-22. However, the visitors saw the advance test model of the C-30 Mark III perform jump-takeoffs, using Cierva's two-stage collective-pitch system. Since the jump-offs were measured in feet rather than in yards, the Pitcairn team agreed that their English friends were not making much greater progress than the Willow Grove engineers. The basic C-30 tilting cyclic control exhibited bouncing problems similar to their own PA-22: it was unstable in all flight regimes, tended to roll one way or another with any changes in power settings, and exhibited serious ground resonance problems. Both pilots, Ray and Pitcairn, agreed that extended flights would be mentally and physically exhausting. The plain fact was that the PA-22 was as good as the C-30 and was in many ways better.

To Pitcairn's great disappointment, his group's visit to Cierva Autogiro Company was reaching the point of diminishing returns and was becoming almost an expensive waste of time: Cierva was seldom available for consultations and when he was absent, his British colleagues were reserved, almost distant, resentful of questions about techniques. When Cierva told Pitcairn that vital personal business in Spain required his extended absence, Pitcairn believed that there was little reason for all of the Americans to linger, so he returned home with Larsen and Stanley, leaving Ray to stay and learn more about both the direct-control and jump-takeoff testing. At least the Britishers had respect for Ray's ability as a test pilot, even though they were openly hostile to engineers who probed into their mechanical developments.

While the president had been out of the country, the Willow Grove factory, under the administration of Geof Childs and Edwin Asplundh, had felt the vicious bite of the Depression, which had killed Autogiro sales. Pitcairn returned to find that Pitcairn Autogiro had a full complement of workers on the production lines but no orders, nor any outstanding prospects for future sales. Only one decision was possible: Harold reluctantly ordered the Willow Grove factory to be closed and all commercial operations suspended; flight operations were terminated for the winter and the work force laid off. Executive offices were moved into a lean-to alongside the main hangar for following up experimental work.

Sadly, Harold wrote to his friend Cierva that he was retaining Jim Ray, Agnew Larsen, Paul Stanley, and Harris Campbell, plus a bookkeeper, a telephone operator who doubled as a secretary, and two Autogiro mechanics, who would maintain aircraft operated by customers in the field.

On the very eve of Christmas, on what should be the happiest season of the year, it was Harold Pitcairn's sad responsibility to inform all of his other employees that, as of the first day of January 1934, they would be out of work. Even Geof Childs and Edwin Asplundh would have to go.

# Air Transportation Upheaval

While beset with the immediate problems of Autogiro development, which continued to drain him financially and physically, Harold Pitcairn persevered in his abiding interest in the developments of air-carrier aviation.

For several years he had solicited advice and counsel from his old friend Lester D. Seymour, who was known to his intimates as Bing. During the early struggles of Pitcairn Aviation's air-mail line, Bing Seymour was general manager and chief engineer of National Air Transport. At the instance of Colonel Paul Henderson, Seymour was of enormous assistance, feeding Pitcairn information about airplanes which NAT had deemed suitable or unsuitable, and greatly affecting the decision to begin producing the PA-5 Mailwing. In seven years Bing had moved upward in the air-carrier industry, eventually becoming president of American Airways, Inc. In 1933 he had run afoul of a political vendetta between Senator Hugo L. Black—who was subsequently appointed by President Roosevelt to the Supreme Court—and former Postmaster General Walter Brown.

Against the tide of the ever-worsening national Depression, the airlines had continued to grow, mostly because of the federal subsidization created by the Amended Air Mail Act. Pitcairn's former organization, by then renamed Eastern Air Transport, had added several branches and had established a direct route from Richmond to Jacksonville, via Raleigh, Florence, Charleston, and Savannah, supplementing the Richmond–Atlanta–Jacksonville line that Pitcairn Aviation had pioneered. The line had spurs to Augusta and to Tampa/St. Petersburg.

Other, so-called "feeder" lines had sprung up: there were more than a dozen, all eyeing the rebidding dates for air-mail contracts. Most of them operated without air-mail subsidies, but instead established route networks so that they could bid against the huge incumbent mail/passenger lines that had been approved by the Postmaster General. Aviation was by then a big business and the game was hardball.

As Pitcairn had predicted, three major consortia had consolidated their positions by gathering in almost all of the small, independent carriers and had developed huge, sprawling routes from coast to coast and from New York to Miami. There were somewhat justifiable complaints that their success had been rigged and in certain quarters there were rumors of skulduggery.

The fact was that in May 1930, President Hoover's Postmaster General, Walter F. Brown, in an effort to create long-range continuity and stability of air-mail service, had effected a change in the basic law regulating the assignment of routes: he gave himself (and subsequent postmasters general) total authority to select carriers not only on the basis of low bids, but also considering the adequacy of the service they had rendered and the reasonableness of their request for compensation. He was, in effect, commercial aviation's czar.

With this announcement he had awarded four major "trunk" routes: the northern tier east-west route went to the de facto incumbent carrier, United Airlines; the central route went to Transcontinental Air Transport (TAT)–Maddux (put together by C. M. Keys), and the southern tier was given to American Airways. The north-south East Coast route went to Eastern Air Transport (also a Keysian creation).

The first result of the industry conference called by Brown (which was subsequently to be called the "Spoils Conference" by the press) was to squeeze the independent Western Air Express, which had been created by Harris M. "Pop" Hanshue, into a merger with the Keys conglomerate, thus forming Transcontinental and Western Air (T&WA), a wound Hanshue would never forget. The word was out: independent airlines might just as well forget about bidding against the big lines that had been blessed by Postmaster General Brown.

Walter Folger Brown's motives were honest and truly in the national interest; he was determined to create the strongest, most efficient air-transportation system possible. But his methods were justifiably deemed as high-handed by Hanshue and others who had been frozen out, and they promptly took the matter to their representatives in Congress. Theirs was a wasted effort; during the Hoover administration some minor congressional inquiries were held, but nothing ever came of them. The President backed up his cabinet member's exercise of discretion and the majority of Congress was loyal to the chief executive. So there the matter rested, simmering.

What brought it to full boil was the cavalier treatment given an East Coast independent, Ludington Airlines, created and operated by the same C. Townsend Ludington from whom Harold Pitcairn had bought his Farman Sport at the Pine Valley Field and who also had a hand in the Kellett Aircraft Company.

Ludington Airlines, known to everyone as the "New York–Philadelphia–Washington Airline" (motto: "Every Hour on the Hour") was a short line, operating on a shoestring, using Stinson tri-motors, but making a profit without any government subsidy. When Eastern Air Transport's four-year route authority (which dated from Pitcairn Aviation's first carrying of the mail) came up for rebidding, Townsend Ludington dropped his low bid into the mail. The rejection of the Post Office Department came in an unseemly short period of time and Ludington was squeezed into "merging" with Keys, i.e., Eastern Air Transport. Ludington saw the odds against him and let the matter drop. He had too many things to do to frazzle himself with a losing cause. Fate stepped in.

One of Ludington's former employees, then working in Washington, D.C., had lunch with a friend named Fulton J. Lewis, a young cub reporter for the Hearst chain of newspapers. In casual conversation it came out that the Ludington bid of twenty-five cents a mile had not been enough to win the eastern route. For some reason that figure stuck in Lewis's head. A week later, making the rounds in the capital, he picked up a news release from Eastern Air Transport saying that the line had won the route again on a bid of eighty-nine cents a mile. Lewis's news instincts, which would within a few years propel him into international prominence, took him into the public records, for he smelled a rat. When his editorial superiors would not allow him to break the story in their newspaper, he turned to Congress.

The election of Franklin D. Roosevelt and the appointment of FDR's political quarterback, James J. Farley, to Postmaster General had changed everything, particularly since Roosevelt had won in a landslide. The reversal of attitudes was personified in Alabama's Senator Hugo L. Black, who was then looking for a political "cause." Blocked by his own employers, Lewis took the facts he had assembled to Senator Black. The result of the disclosure of the "Air Mail Scandal," as it came to be called, was a full-blown Senate inquiry, with Black as chairman. The 1930 Brown–airline meeting was promptly dubbed the "Spoils Conference" and for months witnesses were paraded before the senatorial inquisition.

This culminated in the national crucifixion of the former Postmaster General, who had been made to appear as a dictator at best, or a thieving political hack at worst. Pitcairn knew that Brown was neither; as one of the early air-mail operators, he knew Brown personally and held him in high esteem. Pitcairn immediately injected himself into the fray, fearing that if Brown's philosophy were upended, chaos would result in America's delicately balanced aviation industry. His voice was lost in the torrent of abuse heaped on the former Postmaster General.

On February 9, 1933, President Roosevelt invited the commanding general of the United States Army Air Service, Benjamin D. Foulois, to the White House and asked him directly if the army could carry the air-mail. When Foulois declared that it could, Roosevelt directed Farley to cancel all existing air-mail contracts forthwith. Air mail, he said jauntily would henceforth be transported by military pilots flying military aircraft, and that was that.

The presidential decision caused a triple calamity. Military appropriations, especially funding for aviation, had been drastically reduced as a result of the Depression. With training missions radically cut back, army pilots were not technically competent to operate on schedule in adverse weather, as airline pilots did routinely. Military aircraft assigned to the task were obsolete or obsolescent, poorly instrumented, unfit for the demands of mail service. Mail pouches had to be crammed into open cockpits and sometimes were banked around the pilots themselves. Soon, almost daily banner headlines were reporting crashes resulting in the deaths of young army pilots assigned to fly the mail. Within a few weeks Roosevelt's impetuous, politically oriented decision became a political albatross.

It was also a calamity for the airlines. They depended on federal mail subsidies to operate, since the volume of passengers traveling by air did not generate enough income alone to pay the basic operating costs. Furthermore, all air carriers were involved in upgrading and re-equipping with a new generation of airliners, including the Boeing 247 and the Douglas DC-2 and DC-3,

which replaced the Curtiss Condor, Ford Tri-Motor, Boeing's twenty-passenger Model 80, and all single-engine airliners. No banks or financial houses would consider loans to them without a reasonable expectation of being repaid, with interest. Cut off at the pockets, the airlines neared financial disaster. If they were to go under, God only knew how the complex passenger airline system would be reestablished.

The entire nation was affected by the precipitous fiat, for the country's total economy depended on the rapid delivery of business correspondence, negotiable instruments, and bank clearances upon which major business operations had come to depend. At a time when bolstering the sagging economy was the primary concern, the route structure flown by the army was so restricted, because of the limited fleet available, that many cities were arbitrarily eliminated from the service pattern.

For weeks Pitcairn took time from his own pressing business problems to become deeply involved in the political battle to save the airline industry. Again resisting his passion for avoiding personal publicity, he wrote and spoke out forcefully for a reconsideration of the President's decree and called on the public to press Congress for a reversal of it.

It took six months of cajoling, importuning, and pressuring on the local level before the Air Mail Act of 1934 was created. Even then this legislation was shot through with face-saving political gestures. Eventually it had been shown that the "scandal" witch hunt had been unfounded and that Walter F. Brown had done nothing illegal or improper. Certainly, he had had no personal financial interest in the decision, as the Senate committee had tried to claim. Under the terms of the new act, all bids were thrown open, with two major prerequisites. First, each of the bidders—including all of the pre-existing operators, at whom the restrictions were obviously directed—had to divest itself of any manufacturing and equipment companies; a second and blatantly unfair requirement was that no person who had occupied a top-echelon position in the affairs or organization of any carrier holding permanent air-mail authority under the former Postmaster General's decision could hold an executive position in any of the reorganized airlines.

With the air thus cleared—according to the administration's specifications—the air-mail routes were reopened for bids. No one was surprised when the four major companies that had been in the eye of the political hurricane rebid and won their old routes back, having gone through the legal legerdemain of re-incorporating and restructuring to meet the technical requirements of the new act.*

* Thus, American Airways became American Airlines; Eastern Air Transport was renamed Eastern Air Lines, and Transcontinental and Western Air became TWA, Inc. United Airlines retained its name but was separated from United Aircraft & Transport Corporation.

One of the major executives whose heads rolled under the congressional ax was Lester D. Seymour, president of American Airways. However, Seymour was still one of the most able marketing executives in the country. Harold Pitcairn promptly utilized his old friend Bing Seymour's expertise by requesting him to make a survey of sales potential and recommendations of sales-development policies regarding a projected direct-control, jump-takeoff, "roadable" Autogiro for the civilian market. Once again, Pitcairn sensed that he was on the verge of accomplishing his longtime ambition to make the Safe Aircraft for everyone a reality.

Pitcairn was hopeful that the economy might turn the corner within the year. The Roosevelt administration had created numerous federal agencies, bureaus, and authorities to bring the country to a recovery, and the mood everywhere was one of guarded optimism. Aviation was once again surging ahead.

With the turmoil and uncertainties of the air-mail dispute behind them, the major trunk air carriers began to expand in route structures and in the size and types of their fleets. New small air carriers had begun to spring up as feeder lines, using smaller single-engine and twin-engine aircraft. Lockheed had brought out its Vega, Orion, and Sirius; Jerry Vultee had a high-performance ten-place, single-engine passenger ship on the drawing board, and Eddie Stinson had his Reliant single operating for several small lines. Both Lockheed and Stinson were also preparing to introduce multi-engine airplanes for such purposes: Lockheed's Model 12 and Stinson's improved tri-motor. Pitcairn's hopes for the possibilities of the Cabin Model PA-19 Autogiro lifted as the situation improved.

A new market was developing. Businessmen were finally beginning to notice the competitive advantages that private aircraft provided, especially with the advent of Walter Beech's Staggerwing, Spartan's Executive, and Waco's new S-6 cabin biplane. Private fliers were beginning to buy enclosed-cabin airplanes: the new Taylor Cub, the Luscombe all-metal Phantom (although it had fabric-covered wings), and the Fairchild 24.

From the beginning Pitcairn had believed that a small two- or three-place direct-control Autogiro—especially equipped with jump-takeoff capability—would be salable to a large segment of the private-flying public, because it would put personal air transportation literally into everyone's backyard. He also believed more than ever that larger Autogiros would provide exceptional air service to hundreds of small communities simply because they offered the convenience of downtown-to-downtown air transportation. He asked Paul Stanley to explore the possibilities of ten- to eighteen-passenger 'giros. When the time was propitious, Pitcairn was going to be ready for the market.

Meanwhile, the direct-control, jump-takeoff experimental program

The Pobjoy-powered PA-22 in its final form warms up prior to a successful flight test. The ship now carries the name "Autogiro Company of America."

The PA-24 was not a new design, but a modified version of the successful PAA-1 two-place Autogiro, retrofitted with a 160-hp Kinner engine and a sliding canopy. It is a handsome aircraft, even by today's standards.

continued at the Willow Grove field. The PA-22, now rebuilt to a more conventional appearance, was flying nicely—most of the time. The direct-control theory had proved to be sound, although in practice the system was sometimes erratic, seemingly susceptible to the handiwork of gremlins. From time to time, after a series of successful flights, its blades would untrack, setting up violent vibrations and requiring great physical strength on the part of the pilot, usually Jim Ray, to keep the upside-down stick from beating a tatoo on his skull. Whenever an undesirable characteristic would de-

velop, Pitcairn and his engineering colleagues would work until they solved it. Synnestvedt and his associates were busy with the Autogiro patent applications. In 1934, twenty-six patents were issued to Pitcairn's group, including four to Harold Pitcairn himself, with dozens of others still pending at the Patent Office.

# Castastrophe at Croydon

Strong super-nationalistic trends were beginning to surface all over the world, and with them a perceptible drift toward militarism. Japan, flaunting its Parity Treaty with England and the United States, was openly building a vast naval force. As the political star of Adolf Hitler rose, Germany's flag-carrier aircraft were beginning to look ominously warlike. It did not require much imagination to see how easily Lufthansa's slim airliners could be converted to bombers.

The majority of Americans believed that they were isolated by the breadth of the Atlantic Ocean from military threats, but aviation people knew better. Germany's huge new dirigible, the *Hindenburg,* was in regular transatlantic passenger service, and rumors abounded that every leisurely trip it made at low altitude across the United Kingdom and the United States generated reams of high-resolution photographs for the Nazi War Ministry. The aviation press carried stories and photographs from normally secretive Russia that a long-winged, single-engine airplane, the AN-25, designed by someone named Antonev, had flown non-stop for almost six *thousand* miles! The Russians were bragging that all of Europe and most of the United States was within range of their aircraft. Most people in the United States ignored the flight as a "stunt," disregarding the epic flights of Lindbergh and others of less than a decade before, but the level of concern in some official quarters was clearly indicated when the British Home Office requested the equivalent of $4.5 *million* for gas masks to be distributed to England's civilian population.

To Harold Pitcairn the time seemed ripe to raise the profile of the Autogiro before military purchase commissions. Army and navy planners had already taken notice of the older stub-winged versions, but had never realized the improvement of operating characteristics afforded by the direct-control system, which made the machine more attractive to them.

Others were thinking along exactly the same lines. The *Illustrated*

In 1935 Pitcairn constructed two military direct-control Autogiros, the PA-33. The Army designation for this one was YG-2; the same craft tested by the Navy was called the XOP-2. Here the two-ton, 150-mph YG-2 observation/liaison version is being run up at Pitcairn Field prior to a flight test. This was the prototype, with no engine cowling and the original empennage.

The PA-33/YG-2 as submitted for Army service testing. An engine cowling and fairings on the pylon and rotor head have been installed and a vertical fin and military-striped rudder added.

*London News,* one of the most respected journals in the world, published a spread featuring artists' conceptions of possible military applications for rotary-wing aircraft: reconnaissance, liaison, ambulance service, and quick transportation of high-ranking officers. The graphic presentation turned out to be amazingly accurate, but almost forty years ahead of its time.

Whether it was due to the *News's* articles or not is hard to tell, but the United States Government was beginning to take rotary-wing flight seriously. Early on, the navy had procured some almost off-the-shelf PCA-2s, redesignating them as XOP-1s, but the army's interest had been nil. In 1934, both services took a new look; requests for bids were

The PA-33/YG-2 opened up in the modification shop. The PA-22 type of overhead control stick has been replaced by a conventional style set into the cockpit floor. The rear cockpit's control lock and instrument panels are typical of the 1935 era.

advertised and responded to by both Pitcairn and Kellett.

Pitcairn's group had been working on numerous design studies and modifications—including Autogiro ambulances—based on the Cabin Model and enlarged versions of the Cabin Model for feeder-line operations. The PAA-1 had been redesigned with a larger power plant and redesignated (and certificated) as the PA-24. Now a new design, the PA-33, was submitted as Pitcairn's bid for army utility. It was a two-place, open-cockpit, direct-control Autogiro weighing thirty-three hundred pounds—three times the size of the PA-22's eleven hundred pounds. By this time the experimental PA-22 was flying well, with its direct-control problems virtually

Wearing its Army livery, the YG-2 crosses the wind-streaked Delaware River. It was turned over to the National Advisory Committee for Aeronautics (NACA) at Langley Field for service testing. In March 1936, it was destroyed in an accident. No more were ever built.

solved, but with the PA-33's increase in size, scale effect again became a factor. Tremors that had been either undetectable or unobjectionable in the smaller machine became *very* objectionable in the PA-33, which was renamed the YG-2 by the army, and in a slightly different version, the PA-34, renamed as the XOP-2 by the navy.*

Preparatory to engaging in the acceptance flight-test program then being organized, the army had posted an army observation pilot, H. Franklin Gregory, from Fort Sill, Oklahoma, to the experimental flight center operated by the National Advisory Committee for Aeronautics (NACA), at Langley Field, Virginia, to evaluate rotary-wing operations. The youthful first lieutenant considered it as no more than a routine change of assignment at the time, but it would ultimately lead to his being the top figure in U.S. Army rotary-wing aviation, with the rank of brigadier general. Until he arrived at Langley Field, his sole exposure to the unusual aircraft had been as a spectator at the Cleveland air races several years before.

As airplanes of every size appeared in the fleets of the air carriers, corporate operators, and private fliers, more and more airports appeared near towns and cities to accomodate them. The American public began to forget about the "windmill planes," except as curiosities. In spite of Pitcairn's relentless efforts to fan the almost dead ember of interest into some sort of flame, it was not hard to forget them. Only a handful—not more than a hun-

dred—had been sold in the entire country, so that, except in Philadelphia and at Langley Field, their flights were seldom seen anymore. It was a perfect example of out of sight, out of mind.

From time to time occasions arose where 'giros proved newsworthy. In May 1935, the U.S. Post Office Department dedicated a huge new post office at Thirtieth Street, sixteen blocks from downtown Philadelphia. When plans had originally been considered some prescient official of high standing had required that the roof be stressed and kept clear of obstacles, so that Autogiros could use it regularly as a landing place to expedite the transportation of mail from the airport that served Philadelphia—the Camden Airport, across the Delaware River—to the region's main post office and distribution center.

When the post office was dedicated, ordinarily an event duly reported on an inside page of the newspapers, it had been announced that Autogiro operations would begin immediately. This drew a huge crowd of curious onlookers. While newsreel cameras ground away and still photographers clicked plate after plate into their Graflexes, Autogiros took off, flew to Camden's air-carrier airport and returned, all in a matter of minutes, as compared with a traffic-bucking hour or more required by mail truck. Again, as they fluttered slowly onto the block-square rooftop, their story landed on the front page of every newspaper in the country.

* In army usage, "X" indicates "experimental;" "Y" denotes an existing model undergoing field testing. "G" was the army's designator for Autogiros ('giro), since "A" had been assigned to attack planes. "XOP" is of course navy for "Experimental Observation, Pitcairn."

The successful PA-22 makes a 1933 landing on the roof of Philadelphia's 30th Street Post Office, only a few blocks from City Hall.

The PA-22 settling in for a landing on the Post Office building. The load of mail it carried to the Camden Central Airport shortly thereafter was the first air mail to be flown from a Post Office rooftop.

Editorial writers extolled the potential of rotary-wing flight and the possibilities of downtown landing sites to allow commuters to travel to and from work, far above the traffic jams on the crowded highways.

The Department of Commerce, which then regulated aviation safety, perked up some of the slackening public interest in personal Autogiro flying by offering a competition for a rotary-wing craft that would fly one hundred miles in an hour, be able to land on and, furthermore, take off from a 30-foot-square space, and then be able to fold its wings and be converted into a highway vehicle. It was a big order for anyone to fill, but no less than seven companies bid on it. Using the basic design of the experimetal PA-22 as a starter, Pitcarin and his engineers came up with the winning design.

Because Pitcairn Autogiro Company had (temporarily, it was hoped) shut down its production lines, the "roadable" was to be produced as a handmade experimental ship by the Autogiro Company of America; hence the model was designated as the AC-35. In preliminary design studies it shaped up as a two-place, side-by-side cabin ship with direct control, including the hanging stick, like the PA-22. Rather than mount the engine in the conventional manner at the front of the aircraft, the AC-35 designers proposed to bury it inside the fuselage aft of the cabin. A selectable driveshaft system would enable the pilot/driver to transfer engine power either to a front-mounted propeller connected to the engine via an extended propeller shaft passing between the cabin's two seats or to a single tail wheel at the aft end. To overcome torque problems, Pitcairn recommended incorporating dual contra-rotating propellers on the same concentric center, a new arrangement for the engineers to wrestle with. Overall, it was a fascinating project and was enthusiastically confronted.

While the AC-35 was gestating, news around the world was becoming worrisome. In 1935, Italy invaded Ethopia. In 1936, Hitler and Mussolini formed an alliance for mutual military aid, the Rome-Berlin Axis. Inexorably, they were preparing for war, building battleships, submarines, and air forces of unprecedented size. As with the Ethopian crisis, the League of Nations did nothing. No one wanted to ruffle the surface further.

In America and in England, vertical-lift takeoff developments had become most encouraging. Cierva's C-30 Mk III, equipped with the tilting-rotor cyclic/collective systems, had jumped fifteen feet on many occasions and the re-revamped PA-22 had been hopping more than ten feet straight up and flying off with only a slight amount of settling back in the transition from vertical to horizontal flight. Success was at hand, but Pitcairn believed that the PA-22 still required too much flying expertise to risk offering it as a vehicle for amateur pilots; he adamantly refused to submit it for an Approved Type Certificate until it met

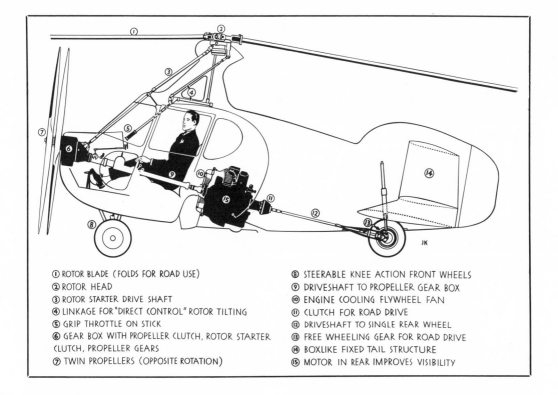

① ROTOR BLADE (FOLDS FOR ROAD USE)
② ROTOR HEAD
③ ROTOR STARTER DRIVE SHAFT
④ LINKAGE FOR "DIRECT CONTROL" ROTOR TILTING
⑤ GRIP THROTTLE ON STICK
⑥ GEAR BOX WITH PROPELLER CLUTCH, ROTOR STARTER CLUTCH, PROPELLER GEARS
⑦ TWIN PROPELLERS (OPPOSITE ROTATION)

⑧ STEERABLE KNEE ACTION FRONT WHEELS
⑨ DRIVESHAFT TO PROPELLER GEAR BOX
⑩ ENGINE COOLING FLYWHEEL FAN
⑪ CLUTCH FOR ROAD DRIVE
⑫ DRIVESHAFT TO SINGLE REAR WHEEL
⑬ FREE WHEELING GEAR FOR ROAD DRIVE
⑭ BOXLIKE FIXED TAIL STRUCTURE
⑮ MOTOR IN REAR IMPROVES VISIBILITY

The presentation schematic drawing for the proposed roadable Autogiro designed for the U.S. Department of Commerce. The AC-35 (for Autogiro Company) did not have the jump-take-off rotor system, but was an interim design. It introduced the contra-rotating propeller arrangement to eliminate torque problems. The overhead stick is revived.

his own high performance standards. Above all, he wanted any aircraft bearing his name to be *safe*.

Communications from England created the impression that Cierva Autogiro had conquered the aerodynamic problems of rotor control and that their machine was flying impeccably every time, making Pitcairn and his colleagues feel that they had somehow fallen behind. To determine how wide the technological gap actually was, Pitcairn again sent Ray, who was by then totally proficient in direct-control jump-off

flying, to London, to evaluate the C-30 Mk III.

It was of some relief to receive a coded cable—relationships had reached that stage by then—from Ray, who after several flights in the Mark III reported that it was no better than and possibly not as good as the latest version of PA-22. Ray was ordered to return home.

Soon afterward Cierva himself cabled Pitcairn, requesting that he send Larsen to England for three or four weeks, saying that "his collaboration at this time would be invaluable." Deeply enmeshed in the AC-35 project, Pitcairn did not believe that he could do without Larsen at that time, unless the C-30 Mk III had made great advances since Ray's recent visit, so once again, he dispatched his chief pilot to London to assess the value of Larsen's attendance. Ray grumbled that of late he was spending more time at sea than in the air, but he repacked his bags, kissed his wife good-bye again, and went.

This time his reaction was far different. After a few tests flights in the rerigged Mark III, Ray enthusiastically cabled that he had flown jumps of up to thirty feet and that British Autogiro pilots had jumped even higher. He agreed with Cierva that the entire "Autogiro family" should assemble in London to compare notes and prepare for a new commercial Autogiro design.

Pitcairn and Larsen sailed within the week but were soon to be gravely disappointed, for Cierva was not available for the consultations they had traveled so far to have with him. He was occupied with other things; no one seemed to know quite what. The Cierva company officials knew only that Cierva himself had been distraught and worried for several days and had left, pleading urgent personal business. Feeling that they had been left hanging out to dry, Pitcairn and Larsen, somewhat irked, sailed for home. They had no idea of what Cierva was going through. Before leaving, Pitcairn directed Ray to stay in England and keep him advised.

No one in either the Cierva Company nor the Pitcairn group had ever realized the extent to which Juan de la Cierva was involved in Spanish politics, for it was a subject he had never discussed. By birth, he was a Monarchist. When the king had been exiled, Monarchists had joined together and then had affiliated with leaders of the Church, the Clericals, to form the Nationalist Front. Against their political force, Liberals, Socialists, and Communists (who had earlier thrown in with the Anarchists) united in a confederacy of convenience to form the Popular Front, calling themselves "Republicans." In the national elections of February 1936, the Popular Front had won.

Up to that time internal stability in Spain had been maintained by the army, led by General Francisco Franco, a leader highly popular with his troops. This situation was recognized by the leaders of the newly elected government, who promptly and discreetly banished Franco by assigning him as governor general of the Canary Islands.

The Anarchists/Communists then showed their hand. During March and April of 1936, many wealthy landowners were dispossessed by mobs and their estates were plundered. In major cities murder was almost commonplace. Churches were burned; labor strikes crippled the economy. Public buildings were bombed and newspaper offices were burned out. When National Front leaders uncovered a detailed Communist plot to shuck any veneer of cooperation with the Liberals and Socialists and to take over the country themselves by force and violence sometime in July, some dramatic countermeasure was needed.

Under strict secrecy, a complicated plan was made to procure a twin-engine airplane in England, using the cover of a vacation trip for a retired British Army officer, his daughter, and her young girl friend to Casablanca. The DeHavilland Rapide, flown by a Captain Bebb, made the trip—with a minor change: the vacationers disembarked at Casablanca and returned to the United Kingdom by ship; Captain Bebb continued with a single passenger, named Luis Bolen, to Las Palmas, picked up Francisco Franco, and flew him to Tetounan, in Spanish Morocco. He then made the eighty-mile hop northward over the Mediterranean Sea to Spain. That day, Franco assumed command of the Spanish Army, which was still loyal to him, announcing that he proposed to fight the "Communist threat." On July 17, 1936, Franco led the army in revolt against the Communist-dominated government and asked military assistance from Mussolini and Hitler in a "Crusade against Communism." It was the beginning of the Spanish Civil War.

Not for years was it known that the historic air journey was organized and engineered by Juan de la Cierva. Many of Cierva's relatives, including his wife and children, still lived in Madrid, an area held by the Communists, and were in constant fear of losing their property and possibly their lives. He had joined them there.

Jim Ray stayed on in London for several months, reporting that with Cierva away, not much went on, either in test-flying or in basic engineering. Not until September was their friend able to spirit his endangered wife and children into France and ultimately to England. Ray cabled:

REGRET CIERVA STILL DISTRESSED BY THE POLITICAL SITUATION BUT I HOLD HIS PROMISE TO WITHDRAW FROM PARTICIPATION SHORTLY.

By that time Pitcairn needed Ray

The experimental AC-35 in the Pitcairn factory prior to the installation of the rotor sytem and without its fabric covering. Although the general form of the PA-22 is obvious, the engine had been buried in the fuselage and geared to the rear wheel and the dual propellers, and was selectable by the pilot.

The AC-35 roll-out in its original configuration. Note the steerable landing wheels for highway use, the contra-rotating propellers and the cellular empennage.

more at Willow Grove than in London; the AC-35 was almost ready for its initial test flights, and Ray was the one he wanted to conduct them. He told Jim to come home. They would consult with Cierva when the political situation settled down.

The Department of Commerce ship, after a spate of normal teething problems, was a good flying machine almost from the day the paint dried on its squat fuselage. Most of all, once it passed the initial taxi and short-hop phases, it displayed such novel attributes that test-flying it was more fun than any other aircraft Ray had ever flown.

He would take off from Pitcairn Field, Willow Grove, skim at low altitude to some outlying community, land, fold the rotor blades, and drive around town, stopping traffic dead every time. Then, followed by everyone who had wheels, he would drive to the outskirts, manually extend the rotor blades, shift the power from the tail wheel to the propeller up front, and take off from the roadway, leaving a goggle-eyed throng behind.

As was to be expected, the test-flying program disclosed certain problems that had to be solved before the machine could be turned over to the Department of Commerce: the contra-rotating propellers produced an irritating noise level for the occupants and for people on the ground and did not seem to offer any distinct advantages over a standard installation, so that was changed. If highway operations

Jim Ray prepares to take the AC-35 for its first test flight before the engineering group on the factory ramp.

The first modification of the AC-35 during its initial flight test program. The contra-rotating propellers have been eliminated and torque problems met by creating fixed vanes on the ship's nose. The cellular empennage has been replaced with a more conventional system.

were extended too long, or if the roadable had to drive slowly in traffic, the oil overheated and frothed; new oil radiators and fans solved that. When he finally informed his boss that the AC-35 was operating like a charm, arrangements were made to deliver it to the government. The only question was, where?

When Pitcairn called Eugene L. Vidal, director of Air Commerce (the equivalent of today's FAA) and asked him where the AC-35 was to be delivered, Vidal harpooned his longtime friend with a tone of mock horror.

"Where are you supposed to deliver it?" he responded as if in disbelief. "It's a 'roadable,' isn't it? We expect you to deliver it to the front

The completely successful "roadable" AC-35 as it was delivered to the Department of Commerce Building. It can be seen now, virtually unchanged, in the National Air and Space Museum.

door of the Department of Commerce Building on Fourteenth Street, Washington, D.C."

Pitcairn motioned to Ray sitting across the desk from him, to pick up the extension telephone and listen in.

"Now, Gene," he said slowly to his fellow Pennsylvanian, "do you really want us to deliver it to your door?" Ray had by this time caught the drift of the conversation and was nodding his head enthusiastically, his sharp-featured face split in a grin.

"What's the matter? Can't you do it?" needled Vidal.

"Sure," said Pitcairn, reassured by Ray's tacit response. "Just close off Pennsylvania Avenue between Thirteenth and Fifteenth on next Monday morning at ten o'clock and keep the street open."

On October 26, 1936, Jim Ray delivered the AC-35 to the U.S. Government in a manner that put him on the front pages again. When he landed in front of the Occidental Restaurant and the Willard Hotel, less than two blocks from the White House, every news service and newsreel company in the national capital was there. (Visitors to the National Air and Space Museum can see motion pictures of the landing displayed every ten minutes in the vertical-lift exhibition.)

After the formal transfer of ownership, Ray checked out a Division of Air Commerce pilot, Walter Brownell, in the techniques of flying with the upside-down hanging stick. For a few weeks it was like the old days, flying for several hours every day, bouncing around, free as a bird, loving every moment of it. Together, like a couple of kids, the veteran pilots played with the fascinating new toy, practicing operations from all types of terrain, sometimes flying, sometime driving.

Brownell proved to be an apt pupil; after Ray had signed him off—reluctantly, because he hated to see the idyll end—the government pilot covered the East Coast with the one-of-a-kind Autogiro that could drive as well as fly. In eight months he put thirty-five hours of flying time on it, and drove some seventy-five miles on the highway. He flew one trip from Washington to Charleston, South Carolina, when no one else could, because of ground fog. His report to the department was that it was the first time he had ever flown in such conditions without apprehension; at one point he landed, for the fog had become so thick that automobiles ran with their headlights on; he slowed to an almost complete stop, let down to a gentle bump alongside the highway, folded the rotor blades, and completed his trip to the Charleston airport by highway. He said that the expressions on the faces of the department of Air Commerce people who were waiting for him was a study as he drove up and parked next to their car.

On another trip he developed a crack in the exhaust collector ring while traversing rugged terrain. This would have been very serious in a fixed-wing airplane. All he did was to land on a field next to the road, drive to the nearest town, and pull into a welding shop, where repairs were quickly made. He also noted that everywhere he went, someone took his picture and sold it to the local newspaper editor for a few dollars. He had clippings from large cities and small towns, to prove his point.

Everyone concerned with the effort was pleased that the AC-35, as small as it was, could be considered a smashing success. It did everything asked of it and operated safely in all kinds of weather; when things got to be too much for the pilot, he could elect to use his other option. As a pioneering venture in its own special category, the AC-35 was spared the ignominy of falling prey to the acetylene torch: when its useful days at the Department of Commerce were over, it was enshrined in the Smithsonian Institution, where it can be seen today—no more than 150 feet from the Pitcairn PA-5 Mailwing—the third major historical artifact of aviation in the Smithsonian directly attributable to Harold F. Pitcairn.

The success of the AC-35 project had lifted everyone's spirits. Immediately, Pitcairn directed Larsen and Stanley to commence design studies to retrofit earlier commercial models, the PAA-1 and PA-18, most of which were still flying, with the improved direct-control system and to bring them up to date with other current Autogiro developments.

He was also entertaining a new idea: if a larger, more comfortable version of the AC-35 could be produced, perhaps the civilian and military markets would open up. A cabin type should be more attractive to serious all-weather operators than the ancient open-cockpit versions, particularly in rain or during the cold seasons of the year. It was worth taking a hard look.

Just when Pitcairn's mood was rising, word came in the aviation press that in France the Bréguet Aircraft Company had developed and patented a vertical-lift aircraft, a true helicopter. This development required further examination, since details were not yet available. Was it possible that Pitcairn and Cierva had lost the initiative?

Pitcairn decided that his design team, now that they had the AC-35 under their belts and the PA-22 was flying consistently well, should have a joint session, or series of sessions, with Cierva and the British engineers to harmonize all technical developments and proceed with their commercial endeavors. He made arrangements for Ray, Larsen, and Stanley to move with their wives and families to London and stay until the job was completed, if it took as long as a year. Once all of the technical problems were overcome, they would be able to begin to manufacture the new generation of Autogiros for the public and military markets. Cierva communicated that he was completely in agreement: the Cierva group was just about ready to break the technological log jam and move into production again.

Within a few weeks after the Pitcairn delegation arrived in England, communications from Larsen indicated that the momentous move might be another exercise in futility; toward the end of November 1936, he wrote, Cierva, notwithstanding his promise to Ray several months before, continued to be absent from the Autogiro plant, as had been the case before. Larsen's tone was sympathetic: "One of Juan's brothers in Spain has been arrested by 'government troops' and Juan is very worried." But then the letter's mood grew bitter: "The lack of cooperation of the British group is appalling . . . [the Spanish Revolution] continues to rob us of Juan's presence, which is a disaster, as far as we are concerned."

The transplanted Americans were discouraged, disheartened, and homesick, but they lived with the hope that the situation would soon change for the better. Perhaps Juan would break out of the mire of Spanish politics and come back to the fold. They waited and waited, in vain.

In a late-night telephone call, Cierva told Larsen that it would not be long; he had a few things to do, then he would be able to devote his full time to the newest Autogiro concepts. Larsen said, somewhat curtly, that the sooner the better; he and his associates were spending a great deal of money and, so far, had nothing to show for it. "One more trip," promised Juan.

Early in December 1936, Cierva boarded a KLM (Royal Dutch) DC-2 airliner at Croydon Aerodrome, London, bound for Amsterdam, Holland. Flight 518, scheduled for a ten o'clock takeoff, was delayed by heavy morning ground fog. By ten-thirty, when the forward visibility had risen to sixty feet, Captain Hautmeyer taxied the silvery Douglas out to the grass field, positioned it on a broad white line marked on the turf as a guideline for the direction of instrument takeoffs over flat land in poor visibility, and slowly opened the two throttles. Carrying thirteen passengers and a crew of four, the plane surged forward and gathered speed. For some reason— perhaps an unlocked tail wheel, or a momentary surge of asymmetrical thrust—the DC-2 swerved slightly to the left and the pilot lost sight of the twenty-one-hundred-foot-long guideline stretching into the haze. Instead of cutting the power and aborting the takeoff, the pilot elected to continue on solid instruments. When the airspeed indicator reached its takeoff speed, Hautmeyer gently tugged the yoke and rose from the ground in a normal climbing attitude as he had done hundreds of times before. He did not realize that his swing to the left had pointed him directly at a rise a mile from the airport, on which lay the quiet little town of Purley. Intent on his flight instruments, he probably never saw the tiled roofs he hit. The airliner ripped the roofs from two homes, lurched sideways acorss a crowded street, sheared off a large tree, and blew up. Fourteen people perished in the worst airline accident England had ever experienced. One of them was the thirty-nine-year-old inventor of the Autogiro, Juan de la Cierva.

# The Dorsey Bill

Juan de la Cierva's death was for Harold Pitcairn a shattering personal tragedy from which he never fully recovered. During their eight years of close association, he and Cierva had worked closely to perfect the Autogiro, and what had begun as an arms-length business association had ripened into a close personal relationship. Between 1928 and 1936, Pitcairn had made some fifteen trips to Europe to confer with the inventor, and Cierva had visited the United States four times. Then, when they were on the brink of success with the single-hub cyclic/collective pitch control system, disaster had struck. Only after Cierva's demise did the Philadelphian learn that his friend's estates and funds were seriously depleted by the turn of events in Spain and that Juan's wife and children, then living in London, were virtually destitute. For many years Pitcairn quietly and without public knowledge contributed substantially to the financial support of the bereaved family.

Because of his personal involvement and material commitment to the development and improvement of Autogiro technology, Pitcairn had been elected to the board of directors of the Cierva Autogiro Company and had participated in company affairs with his British associates on a proper, if not totally amicable, basis. The invitation to Autogiro Company of America's top engineering staff to coordinate all activities in London had been agreeable to the entire Cierva company's board and its engineering force; however, since the Croydon catastrophe a coolness transcending typical British formality had developed between the Englishmen and their American colleagues. Larsen and Stanley particularly recognized the thinly disguised resentment of their continued presence and that the mood soon was reflecting outright hostility. Dr. Bennett, who was appointed successor to Cierva in the important position of technical director, was openly jealous of his own province, and extremely possesive of all mechanical research projects under his direction. He bluntly rebuffed all efforts to communicate on technical matters. Not only were overtures to discuss direct-control methods abruptly shunted aside— the reason given being that Pitcairn's people were entitled to no information until the devices in work had been perfected—but Bennett adamantly declined to meet with Larsen and Stanley to explain the last mathematical computations Cierva had been working on concerning the fixed-spindle full-control cyclic/collective pitch rotor head. With each passing day, as the personal situation became increasingly strained, it became clearer that fruitful collaboration on experimental programs was a thing of the past.

From time to time Reginald Brie, Cierva's premier test pilot, would invite Jim Ray to fly the C-30 Mk III to obtain his analysis of its operational performance; to be cooperative, Ray almost always made recommendations about rigging, control harmony, and handling properties after each flight, all of which were presumably passed on by Brie in his routine flight-test reports to Bennett's engineering group. But the flow of helpful information went only one way.

The opportunities to fly the latest equipment had some worthwhile aspects: from actual experience, Ray was able to inform Larsen and Stanley that although the ship would jump straight up, sometimes as high as thirty feet, and would fly away without excessive settling back, it was still erratic in straight-and-level flight. Its controls were heavy and still snatched and jerked, frequently requiring the pilot to use both hands, and the aircraft was unstable in all azimuths. When revving up the rotor blades prior to takeoff or when touching down to a landing, the C-30 Mk III continued to exhibit ground resonance tendencies that had already been overcome by the Autogiro Company of America in its experimental vehicles. His ultimate conclusions were that the Mark III was every bit as bad as it had been when he had flown it the previous June and that little if any progress was being made with it.

While in England, Larsen also communicated information to Pitcairn as soon as it came to hand, not that there was much to report. In one personal letter he confided his suspicion that the real reason for the persistent refusals of the Cierva engineers to discuss solutions to technical problems was simply that they were hiding their lack of advancement behind a facade of simulated activity, while in reality nothing was going on.

After six weeks of irritating noncooperation, Pitcairn had had enough; in February, he concluded that his key people were wasting time and money by being in Europe, particularly when he needed their expertise, for he had conceived an entire line of jump-takeoff Autogiros, ranging from a two-place personal model to large passenger-carrying versions for commercial operations, including airline use. Because he was anxious to have these aircraft thoroughly engineered, he cabled Larson and Stanley to return to Willow Grove, but requested Ray to remain in England. In a personal letter he explained his reasoning to Jim: first of all, it seemed that he was the only member of the American contingent who had maintained any sort of personal relationship with the Englishmen, so he could keep an eye on rotary-wing developments both in London and elsewhere on the Continent, where the Cierva Autogiro Company, Ltd., had licensed a number of firms to build Autogiros. Second, in light of the wall of animosity that had developed, Pitcairn was slightly concerned by rumors then being circulated in the small world of aviation affairs that Louis Bréguet in France and both Anton Flettner and Dr. Heinrich Focke in Germany—all of whom were Cierva licensees—were using some of the latest Cierva inventions in helicopter research. Ray was to be Pitcairn's eyes and ears for a few months and keep him up to date on what was happening overseas.

Ray's first few communications seemed to confirm the suspicions that Larsen had advanced; the moment the U.S. engineers had departed, the activities at Cierva had dwindled, almost as if the London group had been putting on an act to impress the visiting Americans with how busy they were. Otherwise, Ray had nothing much to report, except that he was bored, lonely, and unhappy so far from home and asked to be allowed to return. Pitcairn, however, insisted that he stay for a while longer to chase down rumors that were growing in number about the helicopter programs in France and Germany and asked his European observer to travel to those countries to ascertain exactly what was going on, especially with Flettner and Focke.

Within a few weeks Ray transmitted the information that he had pinned down the Flettner rotary-wing development, which used a single-rotor system for lift plus a pair of laterally displaced airplane propellers for thrust to pull the aircraft horizontally. However, the Flettner machine did have the ability to rise and descend vertically and was able also, by the pilot's reversing the pitch of the outrigger-mounted propellers, to fly both forward and backward. Pitcairn read the report with a great deal of interest, for what had been described was one cut above the jump-takeoff Autogiro; the craft seemed to possess hovering capability, which indicated to him that a variably selective collective-pitch system was incorporated and that Flettner was using a fixed spindle with the full-control hub system. It would not take long for him to advance to the next step and create a true helicopter from the hybrid machine. Pitcairn was also glad to learn that the experimental craft was tiny, with no payload capacity, except for its pilot. As yet, Ray had not been able to find out any specifics on Focke's development.

In 1937, the U.S. Army had procured seven Autogiros of Kellett manufacture to be used for qualifying additional rotary-wing pilots for field testing and had deployed them first to the newly formed Autogiro School at Patterson Field, near Dayton, Ohio. In charge of the training and evaluation program was First Lieutenant H. F. Gregory, by that time the army's senior Autogiro pilot. The machines to be operated under simulated combat conditions were a great advance over the original fixed-spindle Autogiros; with the new tiltable-spindle direct-control system, they were, operationally speaking, a second generation of the Autogiro type, far different from the versions used in the NACA experiments, but they did not represent the latest state of the art: the jump-takeoff feature pioneered in the PA-22. As a result, preliminary findings and conclusions under Gregory's carefully structured military-use evaluation program were that a rotary-wing system was in reality little more than a high-lift device on a conventional airplane and that, even with the additional performance feature of direct control which permitted nearly vertical approaches and landings in restricted spaces, Autogiros still required a takeoff run, however short. It was his opinion that the Autogiro offered no more—and in many cases less—performance than the performance of many ultra-light fixed-wing aircraft also being evaluated for similar uses: artillery spotting, photo-reconnaissance, liaison, transportation of command-level officers, air ambulance, or general ob-

servation duties. Moreover, little "grasshopper" planes could be obtained for considerably less cost than the Autogiros under test.

Pitcairn was well aware of the conclusions of the military program, but had faith that the advent of the jump-takeoff Autogiro would put an end to the controversy about the comparative virtues of fixed and rotary wing. Once the ability to land and to take off from small, unprepared areas was demonstrated, there would be no room for any further argument. His thinking, however, went far beyond the immediate needs of the military establishment; he was looking ahead to an eventual mass civilian market for both personal and commercial flying, unfettered by the need to use specially prepared airports.

He thoroughly believed that ordinary citizens, including many who were afraid of airplanes, would flock to buy the versatile Safe Aircraft that had been his dream since he could remember; sales could amount to hundreds, perhaps thousands—perhaps hundreds of thousands—simply because Autogiros would be so safe and easy to fly. He also had high hopes that the larger Autogiro designs, to which he had assigned Paul Stanley, would produce an equally broad commercial market, so that he felt assured of achieving his lifetime ambition of making flying available to everyone. While the world news swirled with momentous developments that seemed now to be leading directly to war, U.S. Autogiro evaluation testing continued at a number of selected military installations about the country. Contrary to Pitcairn's comfortable outlook on the future of the Autogiro, Lieutenant Gregory's confidential reports to his superiors continued to reflect his sentiment that rotary-wing aircraft still promised more than they actually delivered, particularly since he was receiving intelligence information from inside Germany that the Focke helicopter, first flown by Edwald Rohlfs in June of 1936, had flown higher than eight thousand feet and at speeds of 120 mph. Gregory, and military planners everywhere, were pondering the implications of an aircraft with full hovering capability.

After spending several weeks in Bremen, Jim Ray had confirmed that Focke-Achgelis & Company had indeed been flying a rotary-wing ship and that he had seen it from a distance. No one was permitted to to view it close up, until, in the fall of 1937, Charles A. Lindbergh visited Germany at the invitation of Hermann Goering to observe the vast strides that had been made in aircraft design and production. Everywhere, for Lindbergh, the red carpet was rolled out. The factories of Dornier, Junkers, Messerschmitt, and Focke-Wulf, all of which were pumping hundreds of new combat aircraft into the Luftwaffe, were open to his inspection. Then Lindbergh was taken to the little Focke-Achgelis company and shown the Fa-61.

As he watched the demonstration involving vertical, hovering, and maneuvering flight, the machine at first seemed to be an Autogiro with two lifting rotors laterally disposed, since it had a conventional aircraft engine and propeller mounted on the front of the fuselage. When the engine was shut down, however, he saw that the "propeller" was only a stub-bladed cooling fan for the engine; all lifting, control, and propulsion functions were effected solely by means of the rotating blades. It was a true helicopter.

Because of his reputation, Lindbergh's subsequent reports of what he had seen abroad were assayed by aviation people as pure gold. Harold Pitcairn avidly read Lindy's observations about the Fa-61, including the remark that it was clearly a prototype test machine, having room for only one pilot and no other payload. He also recognized that Dr. Focke had used some of Cierva's closely guarded patents to achieve fully selective collective pitch for his vertical movements, although he, a director of Cierva Autogiro, had not been so informed. As soon as passage could be arranged, Pitcairn sailed for England to meet with his British associates to clarify unequivocally the state of their present and future relationships.

In the meetings he was told forthrightly that Dr. Focke had indeed built his helicopter under license from Cierva Autogiro Co., Ltd., which for a fee had divulged the fully controllable cyclic/collective pitch hub system. Furthermore, as part of the arrangement, Cierva Autogiro had received a cross-li-

The first true, operating helicopter, the Focke-Achgelis Fa-61, publicly unveiled in Berlin in 1938, wearing the Nazi swastika. The conventionally mounted engine on the nose creates the appearance of an Autogiro, but when the ship was at rest, the "propeller" was merely a stub-bladed cooling fan for the air-cooled radial engine. All lift, thrust and maneuverability came entirely from the two laterally displaced rotor systems. With this, the Autogiro became a military dead issue.

cense agreements to build Focke-Achgelis helicopters—which seemed to Pitcairn to explain the cessation of the C-30 MK III jump-takeoff program so soon after Cierva's death.It had been dickering with Focke-Achgelis and the Bréguet Company of France about forming a consortium specifically to build helicopter derivatives of the Fa-61. Ray's observation had been accurate: everyone on the Continent was bypassing Autogiros and pushing hard on helicopters.

Pitcairn returned to the United States undiscouraged by the European trend toward helicopters, for he was no novice in the "new" de-velopment; as far back as 1916, a dozen years prior to his acquaintanceship with Cierva, he had been working on helicopter designs, including small-scale flying models fabricated from Larsen's precise engineering drawings that had been made from Pitcairn's rough sketches. In 1923, he had made his first application for a patent on a helicopter device, on which letters patent had been granted in 1927. Ten years later he personally held more than two dozen patents on helicopter and Autogiro devices and had recently conceived a new helicopter design incorporating advanced techniques that he had developed over years of experience in building actual rotary-wing aircraft. He refused to be stampeded by the European developments, for he believed that the Autogiro offered more than the helicopter did for most purposes: it could carry a greater payload, it was faster in cross-country flight, its production cost—and therefore its retail price—and maintenance costs would be substantially less, because of the simplicity of the structure. Whereas a helicopter required entirely new piloting techniques, any fixed-wing pilot could transition easily and quickly into an Autogiro, which used conventional aircraft controls. What was more, the Autogiro was proven, whereas the helicopter was still in its earliest experimental flight stage; it would be years before the helicopter would develop to be as useful as the Autogiro already was. Besides, Autogiro technology would not stand still; advances would come methodically as a gradual evolution, to meet the needs of users.

In the machinery of international politics, wheels were rolling within wheels. Hitler had already seized the Rhineland and Austria and was openly eyeing Czechoslovakia and Poland, while the great Free World powers—England, France, and the United States—had allowed their military power to deteriorate to the point of ineffectiveness and were impotent to stop him or Mussolini. Both Italy and Germany had contributed military aid to Franco in Spain—American newspapers carried stories of trainloads of German "tourists" en route to war-torn Spain, and communiqués from the front had told of sleek monoplane fighters bearing the name Messerschmitt appearing in great numbers as part of the Condor Legion.

At last England and France were beginning to re-arm and re-equip with modern weapons: the Royal Air Force had just assigned the first few Hurricanes and Spitfires to fighter squadrons to replace old biplane types. In the United States, Congress was beginning to loosen the budget strings of the War and Navy departments. Contracts had been let for experimental high-performance fighters, and two- and four-engine bombers, as well as for other arms and tools of war. The emphasis was on combat aircraft, which caught the public eye, for few people considered the military applications of low-and-slow aircraft, especially those unusual machines with the windmill wings. If rotary-wing aviation was to receive any consideration from the government, strong measures had to be taken to attract attention.

Since America's rotary-wing industry, consisting of those companies operated by Pitcairn and Kellett, were both near Philadelphia, it was politically logical to approach a member of Pennsylvania's congressional delegation, Frank J. G. Dorsey, soliciting him to sponsor legislation for funding experimental programs in the national interest for military versions of the Autogiro. Congressman Dorsey, one of the few members of Congress who understood aviation, agreed to do so as soon as the proposed legislation could be drafted in appropriate language.

Again, the Stone Room at Cairncrest was the setting for a series of planning sessions involving Pitcairn and his associates as they formulated a philosophy for an advanced Autogiro that could demonstrate its value to the military services. His final decision was to develop a larger version of the PA-22 jump-takeoff ship, which would include some of the features of the AC-35, such as folding rotor blades and roadability. The new 'giro, to be known as the PA-36, would have a two-place cabin with an all-metal fuselage, be able to operate at air speeds of 100 mph, and be flown by the average army-trained pilot. Pitcairn assertively stressed his paramount objective: he wanted to have the PA-36 built, flight-tested, and ready for demonstrations to the Congress in time for the public hearings of the not-yet-introduced legislation. His goal was that the demonstrations would take place on the Mall, right in front of the Capitol, for that would ensure national and even international press coverage. The top military brass in Washington would surely see the demonstrations as well as the news reports, photographs, and editorial comments in the capital's newspapers.

Pitcairn's group was so busy with his pet project that they barely noticed reports that King Edward VIII, who had abdicated the throne of England for the sake of the woman he loved, was succeeded by his brother, who was crowned in May 1937 as King George VI, within a few days of the spectacular explosion and fiery destruction of the giant German dirigible *Hindenburg*.

Normally, Pitcairn retained full administrative authority over all projects of the Autogiro Company of America, but because he had again stretched himself too thin by engaging in a multitude of endeavors, he was receptive to a suggestion from Agnew Larsen. In view of the company's overall financial situation—its operational budget was eight thousand dollars a month, with no offsetting income—and the enormous costs anticipated for tooling up for fabricating the PA-36, Larsen proposed that rather than having the ship built entirely in-house, he could arrange to have the all-metal fuselage and other components subcontracted to the Luscombe Aircraft Company based in Trenton, only a few miles away. The rotor control system would be designed, assembled, and tested by the Autogiro Company's engineers. His calculations had shown that in this manner the PA-36 prototype could be produced for fifty thousand dollars, almost half of the original cost estimate. Then, Larsen added that he wanted overall control of the program, obviously to demonstrate to his associate of more than twenty years that he, too, had executive and administrative abilities.

After reviewing the proposal at length, Pitcairn accepted it, again emphasizing the importance of meeting the deadline he had established. Without hesitation, Larsen said that he would have the aircraft flying within six months.

Early in 1937 Congressman Dorsey dropped a bill into the legislative hopper of the House of Representatives, "To Authorize the Sum of $2,000,000 for the Purpose of Autogiro Research, Development and Procurement for Experimental Purposes." The bill was assigned its chronological number, H.R. 8143, and was referred to the Committee on Military Affairs.

Few people outside of—or in—the aviation industry paid much heed to the Dorsey bill's introduction; the amount requested for Autogiro research and development was insignificant, compared with other legislative actions which provided for many millions of dollars for military contracts to acquire aircraft from major companies such as Boeing, Brewster, Curtiss, Consolidated, Douglas, Grumman, Lockheed, North American, Republic, and others. Fighters and bombers were priority items in the national military buildup; liaison aircraft were far down the congressional shopping list.

As paltry as $2 million may have seemed against the funding provisions for combat airplanes, it was a huge sum as far as the poverty pockets of rotary-wing aviation were concerned. It quickly generated vigorous competition between the Pitcairn and Kellett organizations, with new engineering companies developing to enter the picture.

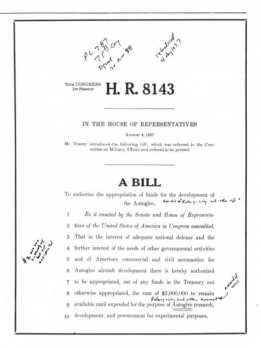

The August 1937 Dorsey Bill (H.R. 8143) provided $2,000,000 for Autogiro research and development. The Bill was amended to reduce the amount of the appropriation and to include the words "rotary wing and other aircraft." In 1938, that meant helicopters.

Relationships between the Kelletts and Pitcairn had become increasingly strained during the past few years of their business association, partly because of Pitcairn's personal intimacy with Cierva. This had created the conjecture by the Kelletts that when Cierva had worked in Pitcairn's home while ensconced as a guest, they had been excluded from developmental discussions in which Kellett Aircraft had a right to participate under the licensing agreements with the Autogiro Company of America.

Kellett Autogiros, built under license from the Autogiro Company of America, also had single-control rotor systems. This KD-1B single-seater was flown by John Miller for Eastern Air Lines on a special air mail contract from the roof of the 30th Street Post Office, Philadelphia, to Central Airport, Camden, in 1938 and 1939. Kellett Autogiros were service-tested by the Army, but the Fa-61 development in Europe turned military thinking to the helicopter.

Furthermore, the Kelletts apparently felt, with some reason, that they had been placed at a serious competitive disadvantage; new, independent rotary-wing research engineering groups, not being bound by any contractual requirements to share technical information prior to receiving patent protection (or to respect the Autogiro Company of America as *the* repository for U.S. rotary-wing patents) could operate in complete secrecy and could possibly steal a march on the pre-existing companies.

Other irritations had also abraded the relationship. While Pitcairn Autogiro was shut down and out of production of commercial aircraft and the Autogiro Company of America was struggling with the intricate technical problems of direct control and vertical lift-off, Kellett had continued to produce aircraft and had won a military contract to supply seven KD-1 Autogiros, for the field-testing program directed by Lieutenant Gregory. This had chafed Pitcairn, who did not believe that the KD-1 was an appropriate level of the Autogiro art to be so evaluated. In addition, Kellett had sold direct-control Autogiros to domestic and foreign customers, including foreign governments, in spite of the Autogiro Company's assertions that overseas sales violated the basic licensing agreement with Cierva Autogiro. In any event, by 1937, Pitcairn and the Kellett brothers had become seriously alienated.

Pitcairn was biding his time, relying on perfecting the proposed PA-36 prototype with all of the special performance capabilities that would move the Autogiro into its "third generation," operationally a completely different aircraft from any bearing the name "Autogiro" that had preceded it. He felt in his bones that the PA-36 would generate public recognition of its utility, but he was also realistically sensitive to the fact that he would soon have competition in jump-takeoff design; he had heard that Kellett engineers, led by Dick Prewitt, were also working on a collective-pitch system for jump-takeoffs, and there was some talk in the industry of other ventures in rotary-wing experimentation.

The situation had become ripe for what is currently known as "industrial espionage," since everyone had a deep interest in what everyone else was doing behind closed doors in guarded areas. Before leaving their worktables, engineers and draftsmen locked their drawings in safes and destroyed each day's work papers by burning them.

Pitcairn, who was ordinarily open and straightforward, was advised by his lawyers that he must vigilantly protect his patent position on any and all new developments and that any public disclosure of any new idea or mechanical device by writings, drawings, photographs, or any form of illustrations, or by the spoken word, could compromise future patent protection.

Pitcairn intended to continue his indefatigable campaign to promote public and political interest in the commercial, military, and personal-use features of the Autogiro, by contributing to magazines, making speeches and personal appearances, and granting interviews, but under the constraints imposed by his legal advisers he was no longer speaking out as freely as he had in the past. Every public statement was pre-reviewed by counsel and was then presented verbatim without editorial changes.

All Autogiro Company personnel were strictly enjoined not to talk shop outside of the company's gates, even within their own family groups or with each other. Secrecy was the order of the day.

For months Ray continued to fret regularly about his assignment in faraway London, increasingly uncomfortable because the Cierva company's engineers had become openly antagonistic whenever he appeared on the scene. Pitcairn had asked him to try to sell the entire AC-35 roadable Autogiro program to the British company for possible relicense to European manufacturers in their licensing organization, but Ray had been told bluntly that Cierva had no interest in any Pitcairn Autogiro design, roadable or not, because they had decided to change the character of Cierva's research activities. Of course, no one would tell him what direction those activities might take. All he could learn during a conversation over lunch with Alan Marsh, one of the test pilots, was that the Cierva was going to close down its commercial manufacturing line.

The information raised Pitcairn's eyebrows, for Cierva controlled all the European patents most vital to rotary-wing design. Now what would the British company do with those patents? Would they license the cyclic/collective pitch control head to anyone? As a director of Cieva Autogiro, he should have been fully apprised of and consulted with on any and all policy changes contemplated by the company, but his information was sketchy, even though he carried on a regular correspondence with Jim Weir, who was now president of Cierva Autogiro. Just what was going on?

Again he resisted Ray's insistent pleas to be allowed to return to Bryn Athyn; more than ever his test pilot was needed right where he was, for word had leaked out of Germany that Focke's man-carrying helicopter had been seen flying at many different locations, indicating that it was engaging in cross-country operations, and that a larger version of Flettner's hybrid design had also flown successfully. Pitcairn was sympathetic to his friend's dreadful homesickness but remained firm. In a personal handwritten letter he said, "It must be trying for you.... However, there is no flight test work here for you and I would like you to remain in England for two or three more months so as to keep us informed as to what is going on

The nascent PA-36 Whirlwing. The all-metal fuselage, minus its rotor system, shows the original two-bladed propeller and the steerable main landing gear, indicating that roadability was still a consideration.

there. In the meantime, take a vacation trip for a while and get away from the atmosphere...."

For the dislocated, unhappy American, the message may have been lost concerning the lack of flight-test work and the implication that the only place he could be productive for the company was in the United Kingdom. The Autogiro Company of America was, and would be for many months to come, purely a research engineering operation involved with plans, designs, engineering, and model testing but not engaged in any flight activities.

The schedule provided that in a few months the PA-36 would be ready for flight testing in preparation for the Dorsey bill demonstrations, which would, Picairn hoped, lead to a substantial award of federal research and development funding, which might in turn lead to a sizable military order.

Unexpectedly, an entirely new problem presented itself for Pitcairn's determination: the Brewster Aircraft Company had recently received a large government order for single-engine fighter planes and needed a factory adjacent to open ground on which a flight-test center could be created. Having noted that Pitcairn Field, only a few miles from Philadelphia, was practically unused and that the Autogiro business was reportedly moribund, Brewster initiated negotiations to purchase the entire tract, including all improvements, for an offered amount of slightly more than a half-million dollars.

From the first, it appeared to Pitcairn that the Brewster officials expected to obtain the facilities of Pitcairn Field easily, since the hard-cash tender was a sure thing. But completely convinced that the superiority of the PA-36 would be recognized as soon as its demonstration flights began, he had projected orders for the ship that could run into millions of dollars. As soon as people actually saw an easy-to-fly aircraft that could operate from spaces as small as tennis courts and back-yards without the need for prepared landing facilities and would permit a pilot to land almost anywhere when the weather deteriorated, fold the rotor blades, and motor on the public highways, the rush for the PA-36 Autogiro would begin. From his viewpoint refusing the offer of a mere half-million dollars was logical and made good business sense.

As the announced date for public hearings on H.R. 8143 approached, the War Department instituted a minor reorganization, designating the Procurement Section of the army's Materiel Division as the issuing agency for all rotary-wing military contracts and reassigning First Lieutenant H. F. Gregory from his duties as assistant commandant of the Air Corps Field Autogiro School to the post of project officer of the Procurement Section, at Wright Field. The routine reassignment of personnel and the newly issued orders scarcely ruffled the surface of the flood of army reforms, but would eventually have a tremendous effect on the future of America's rotary-wing industry.

So did another aviation occurrence over which Pitcairn had no control: in February 1938, the Nazis removed all restrictions from the Focke helicopter and during a week-long industry exposition in Berlin, encouraged press and newsreel photographers from all over the world to record Hanna Reitsch, Germany's premier aviatrix, making repeated public demonstrations of the Fa-61 inside the cavernous *Deutschlandhalle*. The Fa-61 rose straight up from the floor, pivoted in complete turns to the left, then to the right, flying forward, backward, and sideways, hovering all the while. Few American newspapers failed to carry photographs of the continuing feat, and motion-picture theater patrons marveled as they saw the swastika-marked helicopter gently maneuvering as if suspended from an invisible cable.

Attention to the now-publicized features of the amazing characteristics of the newest whirling-wing aircraft ran a great deal higher in aeronautical engineering circles than in the minds of the general public, which viewed the development with only a transitory interest—to them it was just another "windmill plane." But rotary-wing experimenters from all over the world were soon beating a path to the door of Focke-Achgelis. Two American engineers, among the first to arrive in Bremen, were already experienced in rotary wing: Havilland H. Platt, mechanical engineer who had been quietly working on vertical-lift devices of original design, traveled to the new shrine of aviation in company with W. Lawrence LePage, a seasoned Autogiro expert who had worked with Pitcairn Aviation and the Autogiro Company of America, and had then moved over to become chief engineer for Kellett Aircraft, participating in its commercial and military programs. LePage immediately hit it off with Dr. Focke, for not only were they consumed with the same nonpolitical interest in rotary-wing technology—Dr. Focke had been eased out of the Focke-Wulf Company because of his political differences with the Nazi Party—they were both cognizant of the engineering problems of rotary-wing flight. Besides, to LePage's astonishment, Dr. Focke was still a comparatively young man; for all of his accomplishments, he was only forty-five years old. Not only did the designer talk freely about his helicopter, he gave the Philadelphian a fine set of motion pictures, including close-ups in slow motion, of the machine's rotor heads in various flight regimes.

On April 26, 1938, the Committee on Military Affairs convened in public meeting for two days of hearings on the Dorsey bill, with twenty-five witnesses scheduled. In spite of all the assurances that the PA-36 would be flying so that it could be demonstrated to the committee, the schedule had slipped badly; at the time of the hearings not even a mockup was available. Nevertheless, going into the committee chamber, Pitcairn's mood was optimistic. He had prepared meticulously an illustrated slick-paper booklet for each committee member, a dignified factual presentation of the history and background of the Autogiro and the great advances that had been made with it since 1928, right up to the jump-takeoff developments, including artists' renderings of the versatile PA-36. Copies had been circulated to the committee members well in advance.

Moreover, the witness list was studded with famous civilian authorities on the subject of rotary-wing flight and high-ranking military leaders, most of whom Pitcairn knew personally to be pro-Autogiro so that the weight of the testimony would have to impress the committee into passing the bill as written, for the purpose of funding "Autogiro research, development, and procurement." In retrospect, there was one conspicuous absence in the roster of witnesses: Lieutenant H. Franklin Gregory was not included.

Assistant Secretary of the Navy Charles Edison, called upon as the first witness by Chairman Andrew J. May, put a slight damper on the proceedings by testifying that the navy did not have a major interest in rotary-wing aircraft, but that it might have—if they had hovering capability. He also volunteered that, in his opinion, it would take more than $2 million before the Autogiro would be fully developed.

The second witness, Professor Alexander Klemin, dean of the Guggenheim School of Aeronautical Engineering of New York University, was more favorable toward the Autogiro and endorsed the proposed funding, then added the thought that the word Autogiro in the purpose clause "might be implicitly taken to mean 'aircraft of rotary-wing type'" and suggested that it might be rewritten to state clearly that it would include all types of rotary-wing activities. He also dwelt at length on the feats of Hanna Reitsch and the Focke-Achgelis helicopter. As the string of witnesses took the witness chair to tell of how valuable a tool rotary-wing aircraft were for various purposes, one could sense the repolarization of the committee's thinking. By the time Pitcairn testified, toward the end of the second day, the recurrent theme had taken full effect: the remaining committee members still on the rostrum had obviously heard more about rotary-wing flight than they really wanted to know and the chairman was cutting witnesses off in an open effort to wind things up that day so that he and his group could turn to other matters. Pitcairn submitted his testimony in print by putting his prepared booklet into the record, then submitted himself to questions from the congressmen. In answer to a direct query, he acknowledged that the PA-36 was not yet in being as he had promised; his subsequent statement that he had spent three and a quarter million dollars out of his own funds in the last decade of Autogiro pioneering elicited no comments; no one cared.

It took only a ten-minute post-hearing meeting of the committee to agree unanimously that the purpose clause of the bill to be submitted to the full House of Representatives should be amended by striking out the word Autogiro and substituting therefore, "Rotary Wing and Other Aircraft." That was the way the bill read when it passed the House, then the Senate (where it was sponsored by Senator Logan) and was signed into law by the President on August 1, 1938, as the Dorsey–Logan Act.

The tempo of rotary-wing research activity began to pick up almost immediately, for government financing would put money where none had ever been before, and new business alliances developed. Under the circumstances, there was no longer any reason to keep Ray in London as Pitcairn's European observer, so he cabled Jim the welcome news that he should pack up his family and come home.

Ray arrived at the Port of New York of October 26, 1938, accompanying, by sheer coincidence, an English helicopter inventor named Raoul Hafner, who was on his way to Philadelphia to attend the meeting on rotary-wing aircraft sponsored by the Philadelphia chapter of the Institute of Aeronautical Sciences at the Franklin Institute. The convocation, arranged by Ralph H. McClarren, himself an eminent rotary-wing engineer, and E. Burke Wilford, of Gyroplane fame, was slated to be a major gathering of experts in the narrowly defined discipline. Professor Focke and Louis Bréguet had been invited, but had declined for personal reasons, sending papers to be read at the meeting by their friend Hafner. All of America's leaders in the new science appeared, except Harold Pitcairn, who was confined to bed by illness, and heard presentations by such outstanding practioners of rotary wing as Richard H. Prewitt, Gerard P. Herrick, Havilland Platt, W. Lawrence LePage, and Wilford. Speeches were made by Congressman Dorsey and Lieutenant Franklin Gregory; Jim Ray reported on

his recent experiences in Europe in an impromptu, completely extemporaneous speech, and introductions were acknowledged by Grover Loening, W. Wallace Kellett, and several army officers in the Wright Field program. Pitcairn was well represented by Agnew Larsen and Paul Stanley. Another extremely interested spectator was Michael Gluhareff, an engineer long associated with Igor I. Sikorsky.

During luncheon, Gluhareff, seated next to Gregory, informed him that Sikorsky had recently turned his full attention to the technical problems of hovering flight and control systems involved with it and invited Gregory to visit United Aircraft's Vought-Sikorsky laboratory in Stafford, Connecticut. Having already visited the Pitcairn and Kellett organizations while he was in Philadelphia, Gregory said that he would detour to Stafford on his way back to Wright Field. It was an invitation that he could not refuse.

Igor I. Sikorsky, a major aviation pioneer, had been a force in the industry since the early 1900s. Before the 1914–1918 War, when Tony Fokker, T.O.M. Sopwith, Harry Hawker, the Farman Brothers, and Glenn Curtiss were still involved with small one- and two-place, single-engine airplanes, Sikorsky had designed and built a huge four-engine, plushly outfitted cabin aircraft for the Czarist government. After the Russian Revolution, he had immigrated to the United States, where for more than twenty years he had produced a stream of aircraft

Because the Whirlwing's production was so delayed, Pitcairn Aviation submitted this PA-38 design concept with its bid for the Rotary Wing Aircraft Competition in conjunction with the Dorsey Bill authorization. The award went to Platt-LePage for its XR-1 helicopter.

and flying boats of all sizes, more than 160 of which were then being used by one airline—Pan American—to transport passengers from the U.S. to points all over Central and South America and as far as the Philippines and the Far East. In the mid-thirties, the Chance Vought Division of United Aircraft Corporation had created for the great inventor's use an experimental center and had encouraged him to engage in any aeronautical activities that interested him. With his displaced compatriot, Gluhareff—a distinguished engineer in his own right—Sikorsky began to re-examine one of his first aeronautical concepts, the helicopter, with which he had unsuccessfully experimented in Russia prior to the Great War.

Although Sikorsky was not present at the time of his visit, Gregory was escorted through the Stafford center and was elated to find that basic progress was being made with several crude mechanical devices representing various facets of vertical-lift development. He continued to believe that Autogiros as a class lacked the kind of performance required by the military establishment and was totally fascinated by the possibility of developing in the United States a true helicopter which could rise and descend vertically—and be able to hover over one spot. Now he knew that someone of proven inventive ability was zeroing in on the problem.

# The Choice

Within a few weeks of the Franklin Institute symposium on rotary-wing flight, Harold Pitcairn was back on his feet and able to hold a somewhat belated welcome-home party for Jim Ray in the secluded Stone Room, the scene of so many technical sessions. There, he and his associates could relax in a convivial, social atmosphere.

While bringing Ray up to date with recent developments involving the Autogiro Company, the status of the PA-36 program was laid out in detail, including the optimistic outlook they all held for the military and commercial futures of the jump-takeoff cabin ship and its successors. Somewhat to everyone's surprise, having heard them out, Ray took an antithetical and unpopular position. He said quietly that, in his opinion, they were all following a cold trail and making a serious mistake by putting so much reliance on the PA-36, and indeed on the Autogiro itself. His own analysis was that the strong public reaction to the success of the Focke-Achgelis and Flettner machines presaged a demand for an aircraft with *hovering* capability, whether it was really needed or not, and that there lay the direction of rotary wing's future. As Pitcairn, Larsen, and Stanley sat astounded, Ray continued that while he had followed developments of many of the aircraft companies licensed by Cierva Autogiro everywhere, Autogiro people were buzzing about the long shadow that the successful Fa-61 would cast on the future of rotary-wing flight and they had unanimously concluded that their future efforts should be concentrated on the development of aircraft that could hover. His strong impression was that any rotary-wing aircraft without that specific ability was a dead issue for military use—which was the only source of profitable orders under the circumstances of the worldwide Depression. Then he recommended that the PA-36 program be scrapped and be completely replaced by a helicopter development program.

His strongly stated position and suggestion precipitated a heated discussion which turned into an argument of increasing passion, with Ray on one side, Larsen vigorously defending the other, and Pitcairn sitting off to the side, listening intently. On many of the points made, he could agree with Ray, but on the whole he had to go along with Larsen: the Autogiro would do everything that the helicopter could do, except hover. He was aware that Cierva–Focke-Achgelis cross-licensing agreements had been made within the complex framework of the Cierva-created European Autogiro industry, but he had spent so much time and money on Autogiro research and development which had resulted in successful commercial applications of the ships, that he still had confidence in their outlook. In addition, he had made the decision to trust the future of his company to the advanced technology of the PA-36 in a maximum effort that was already well under way and did not believe that it was technologically, financially, or politically feasible to switch courses in midstream. If the Autogiro Company were awarded substantial federal R&D funding, some of it could be channeled into helicopter research, but under the circumstances there was simply no way he could terminate the program that embodied all of the experience accumulated over the last ten years and start again from scratch.

Pitcairn also faced another acute problem which could be solved only by him. For many months he had been told by his accountants that the two-thousand-dollar-a-week drain on his resources would lead to serious consequences if he did not do something to stem the flow. He was paying top salaries to Larsen, Stanley, several draftsmen and machinists, and to Jim Ray. While Ray was in Europe, the company could somewhat justify his retention on the payroll, but now that he was back, the total lack of any flying activities simply did not justify paying his high salary to have him sit around doing nothing. A dreadfully painful decision had to be made—a particularly distressing one in the light of the disagreement between his two close friends with whom he had begun his aviation enterprises so long ago on the cow pasture in Bryn Athyn. When all the scales were balanced, they weighed heavily in favor of retaining Larsen, who was fully committed to administering the production program of the PA-36 prototype, already well under way, although he had missed the deadline for demonstrating it at the congressional hearings. Pitcairn had already forgone any salary from the company so that only one last personnel cut was possible. It fell on Harold Pitcairn's reluctant shoulders to tell Jim that he was going to have to find other employment.

Awash in the aftershock of his decision—for Ray had attributed his termination to this disagreement concerning the continuation of the Autogiro program—Pitcairn was only mildly cheered by a report from Bing Seymour that his nationwide marketing survey had disclosed great public interest in the proposed vertical-takeoff Autogiro with roadability features, if it could be sold for a reasonable price. The results of the appraisal fell completely in line with Pitcairn's own conclusion that cost would be an important aspect to the creation of a mass sales operation, and he knew from his extensive experience that he could produce a successful commercial PA-36-type Autogiro for considerably less outlay than anyone could manufacture a helicopter having anywhere near the same performance. After days and nights of wrestling it around in his own mind, particularly since the Ray–Larsen set-to in the Stone Room, he continued to believe that the lack of hovering capability would not deter sales, as long as users could operate safely and conveniently from their own off-airport landing places. Notwithstanding the developments of France's Bréguet and of Germany's Flettner and Focke—and soon, others—he was supremely confident that the jump-takeoff type of direct-control Autogiro would be just the design to fulfill his high hopes of producing Everyman's Safe Aircraft that he, with Larsen's help, had started to work on in the summer of 1916. Therefore, even after the amendment of the purpose clause in the Dorsey bill, which most observers considered a setback—if not the death knell—to Autogiro development, Harold Pitcairn kept plugging away on the PA-36, still convinced that if the ship had been demonstrated as planned, the amendment would never have been made by the congressional committee.

Not until October 1938, more than six months after the deadline, was the PA-36 prototype rotor system being readied for ground testing, and it did not seem realistically possible that a flying version would be available for public exposure for another six or possibly nine months. But things were moving ahead, however slowly: Larsen had arranged to hire a test pilot with extensive Autogiro flight experience in both fixed-spindle and swiveling-spindle, direct-control types to participate in the initial rotor testing and taxi runs, and then to become the flight-test pilot. Lou Leavitt, who had been Kellett's number one test pilot for several years, seemed to be just the man to jockey the PA-36 into shape.

A week before Christmas 1938, James Weir, president of Cierva Autogiro, advised Pitcairn by letter that the executive committee had decided to abandon the Autogiro business in order to direct its efforts at perfecting helicopters, beginning with a small single-place model patterned after the Fa-61, to be called the W-5 ("W" for "Weir"), followed by a two-place W-6 already on the drafting tables. With this notice of the change in policy and direction of the British company of which he was a director, Harold felt that it was imperative for him once more to travel to England and reach some firm understanding about the future alliance, if any, between Cierva Autogiro Co., Ltd., and his Autogiro Company of America. As a result, he missed a gathering of rotary-

The much-modified Whirlwing of 1939. A four-blade propeller has been installed and the rotor system includes the jump-takeoff feature. The tailwheel drive system has been eliminated, as it was considered unnecessary.

·

wing specialists which turned out to be the first face-to-face meeting of Igor I. Sikorsky and Captain H. Franklin Gregory, who was by then clearly and undeniably emerging as the most powerful and influential person in the U.S. government in matters having to do with rotary-wing flight. During an almost desultory conversation, Sikorsky told Gregory that his crude helicopter device had hovered several times, then invited him to return to Stafford in a few months to see for himself what kind of progress was being made.

By the time Pitcairn returned from England, depressed by the schism that was widening between him and his Cierva associates, and the obviously strenuous rearmament efforts of the United Kingdom in every phase of military equipment, he was pleased to find that the PA-36 was undergoing preliminary rotor tests under its own power, including high-speed taxi tests just short of actual lift-offs. The first flight was scheduled for the near future, as soon as everyone concerned agreed that the blades were all perfectly balanced and rigged and that the machine was ready.

For several weeks the snarling Warner Scarab engine and its four-bladed propeller could be heard as the silvery machine sped back and forth on the runway, its rotor blades whirling in autorotation. After each series of runs, Leavitt would taxi to the ramp to report his performance evaluations at that particular testing level. Engineers and mechanics would crawl over the ship from top to bottom, making inspections and minor adjustments. By early spring of 1939, everything was pronounced ready and all hands emerged from the company's shops and drafting rooms into the bright sunshine to see the PA-36's maiden flight.

Rather than essay a direct jump-takeoff for his first actual flight, Leavitt elected to begin with the technique he knew best, the ordinary rolling takeoff, so he taxied to the north end of the grass runway, turned the ship into the light breeze, engaged the rotor drive until the blades were up to speed, then released the clutch and began to roll. The diminutive aircraft moved only a few feet before becoming airborne, then climbed in a gentle left turn, swung around the field, and came in for a smooth landing. Now jump-takeoff testing could begin.

For several weeks every scheduled test hop was terminated prior to taking off. Time and again, Leavitt returned to the ramp, claiming that the engine was running rough or that he was sensing excessive ground resonance or that the blades were not tracking correctly, yet each time a thorough examination by Larsen's group was unable to confirm the problems claimed by the pilot. The matter came violently to a head when Pitcairn called Leavitt and Larsen into his office and demanded to know just what was causing the delay. Leavitt said the ship was not ready yet for jump-takeoffs; Larsen said it was. People in adjacent offices could hear the growing noise level and increasingly strident tones, then Leavitt burst

out of the door, his face beet red, and stormed out of the building, leaving Pitcairn and Larsen open-mouthed—and without a capable test pilot.

Leavitt's precipitous departure at an extremely critical stage of the proceedings required an immediate replacement if the PA-36 was to be demonstrated properly to the military selection committees for the purpose of winning the company a contract. Soliciting Jim Ray to return to the fold and help brought an immediate refusal; Ray replied that he had recently become involved in an airline operation on the West Coast and was disinclined to quit his new job to return to Willow Grove; the icy tone of the rejection distressed Pitcairn greatly.

A series of cables from Pitcairn to Alan Marsh, who as one of Cierva's test pilots had had a great deal of experience in jump-takeoff techniques, induced the British expert to come to the United States and join the effort to perfect the PA-36. Marsh arrived as banner headlines in American newspapers proclaimed that Hitler and Stalin, always considered implacable enemies, had entered into a mutual nonagression pact, a move which had world capitals exchanging diplomatic messages, horrified by the implications of the move: with Germany's flank thus protected, Hitler could now move militarily along his eastern border toward Poland. All of Europe realized it was suddenly teetering on the brink of war.

Recognizing that a war in Europe would require Marsh to return to England on the first available ship, Pitcairn immediately began to look around for a backup pilot to fill up the potential void and found just the man he needed working for the Department of Agriculture in Bloomfield, New Jersey. Fred W. Soule, then engaged in aerial applications for the treatment of Dutch elm disease, had been a former fixed-wing aircraft test pilot who had been hired by the Horizon Company, of Wilkes-Barre, Pennsylvania, producers of Silverbrook Coal, to fly their PCA-2 Autogiro, one of the first to be sold commercially in 1931. Since learning to fly Autogiros under the instruction of Jim Ray and Jim Faulkner, Soule had, in almost ten years, accumulated thousands of hours in Autogiros of every type, including direct control, in passenger hopping, special air-show demonstrations, and agricultural flying. Nicknamed Slim because of his uncanny resemblance to Charles A. Lindbergh, Soule agreed to leave his Department of Agriculture position to join in the PA-36 program.

With the pilot situation in hand, things began once again to move ahead; it would not be too long before full demonstrations could be made to the military, after which federal orders should be expected to follow from the Dorsey–Logan Act authorization. Then another blow fell: while most factions of the aviation industry were receiving enormous, almost unlimited federal

funding, the House Appropriations Committee arbitrarily reduced the Dorsey bill contribution to a mere $300,000, simultaneously designating the army as the sole government agency to administer the entire rotary-wing program. This meant that the future policy position of the United States government concerning that aspect of aviation would be molded by one man: Captain H. F. Gregory, of Wright Field.

After many months of intensively testing direct-control Autogiros in the field—but without the jump-takeoff feature—Captain Gregory had made the judgment that rotary-wing technology for military purposes would have to take a quantum jump forward and again recommended to his superiors that future emphasis—and the allocation of funds to be provided pursuant to Dorsey bill allowances—be devoted to helicopter development. He was authorized to draft a Circular Proposal, the first step required under the law to issue contracts on the basis of bids submitted, including therein criteria for aircraft to be supplied for army testing.

To obtain the concurrence of all government aircraft users, a hush-hush meeting was called at the War Department in Washington, attended by policy-level officials of the Department of Agriculture; the Biological Survey; the Coast and Geodetic Survey; the newly formed Civil Aeronautics Authority; the Department of the Interior; the National Advisory Committee for

The Pitcairn Whirlwing, last of the line. This was the design concept on which Harold Pitcairn pinned his hopes. It was easier to fly than a helicopter, less expensive to buy and to maintain and it could do everything a helicopter could do, except hover. When the Navy Department took over Pitcairn Field and Pitcairn closed down his own operations, this aircraft was cut apart and the pieces donated to the World War II aluminum drive.

Aeronautics; the navy's Bureau of Aeronautics; and the army's Field Artillery, Coast Artillery, Infantry, and Air Corps, with Captain Gregory as the principal briefer because of his acknowledged expertise in rotary wing. After technical presentations and analyses, followed by hours of discussions, arguments, and counterarguments, it was the unanimous decision of the group that all research and development funding under the Dorsey–Logan Act should center on aircraft that would meet, among others, the criterion that they must be able "to take off over a 50 foot obstacle placed zero feet ahead"—i.e., vertically.

At the time the requirements of the proposed Circular Proposal were approved, no aircraft in existence, with the possible exception of the Fa-61, could meet them; clearly, it was the government's policy to eliminate research funding for Autogiros under the very act that had been solicited originally by the leaders of that tiny industry. It was tantamount to the Autogiro's death sentence, for without federal aid Autogiro research and development programs would suffer from financial malnutrition until they expired. At no time during the discussions had the potential of the PA-36 been considered.

By the end of the summer of 1939, both Marsh and Soule had flown the PA-36 after rolling takeoffs, and had returned to report that they would soon be making the vertical jump-takeoffs for which it was designed. For several weeks Marsh had been explaining to the keen-eyed Soule the theory and practice of jump-takeoffs, but it was clear that Slim's only dual instruction would be obtained by standing on the ramp and watching proceedings carefully, for the little aircraft, built by Luscombe to somewhat higher specifications

than supplied by Larsen, seemed too heavy to jump with both pilots on board at the same time. Excitement grew as the big day neared for the machine's real test.

For months the busy Pitcairn group had been aware of the war clouds gathering over Europe; nevertheless, it came as a shock to them, as it did to all Americans, when the sonorous voice of Edward R. Murrow announced over a crackling radio broadcast from London, that early on the morning of September 1, 1939, Nazi panzer armies, without provocation, had smashed their way into Poland and that England and France, which had guaranteed the independence of Poland by treaties, had promptly declared war on Germany and had mobilized their armed forces. The world would never be the same again. World War II had begun.

# The Whirlwing

With the declaration of war in Europe, it was indeed necessary for test pilot Alan Marsh to return to his homeland for military service, leaving Pitcairn without an experienced jump-takeoff Autogiro pilot, for in the PA-36's initial ground- and flight-test program all flights had been made with the conventional rolling takeoff and had not yet progressed to the straight-up phase. The president took backup pilot Soule off to one side and asked him for suggestions and recommendations about proceeding with the flight operations on the one-and-only PA-36.

Slim had quickly taken to the little 'giro, although it was still heavier than it should have been. The old upside-down control stick had been replaced in the new design by a conventional control-wheel arrangement as used in both fixed-wing and fixed-spindle Autogiros, in which he had flown extensively. The only new thing for him to learn was the somewhat touchy technique of vertical takeoff, which had plagued the Cierva Company pilots, including Marsh, for many months and had taken Jim Ray some time to learn in the PA-22.

"Mr. Pitcairn," Slim said, "I believe that I can teach myself to make jump-takeoffs, but you are going to have to give me a little time to feel my way into them, so the program will be delayed. If you want to take another crack at Jim Ray, you might be able to get things moving faster with him doing the testing."

Pitcairn reached up to put his hand on the shoulder of the tall, lanky pilot with the sharp features and clear eyes and said, "No, Slim. You are my man. If you will do the job, take all the time you want."

That afternoon, when the wind had died down, Soule taxied the PA-36 out to the runway in front of the hangar and as the entire engineering department and Pitcairn himself watched, tried out the as-yet untested jump-takeoff mechanism, for neither Lou Leavitt nor Alan Marsh had ever proceeded to that stage.

Wiggling in the seat to get comfortable, he slowly advanced the

Test pilot Frederick W. "Slim" Soule at the controls of the Whirlwing. He literally taught himself to make jump-take-offs and demonstrated the PA-36 successfully to military authorities on many tours around the U.S. The instrument panel layout, the arrangement of the flight controls and the modern appearance of the cabin were pure Pitcairn. The overhead "hanging" control stick had been eliminated in the refined Autogiro.

throttle to 1800 rpm on the engine tachometer and engaged the rotor starter clutch, which simultaneously moved the rotor blades to zero angle of pitch. Slowly at first, then faster and faster, the blades revolved until they passed the normal flight-lift speed by two or three percent, at which point Soule opened the throttle all the way, thereby automatically declutching the rotor drive, accelerating the engine and propeller, and simultaneously snapping the overspinning rotor blades into lift-off angles of attack. However, instead of leaving the throttle in the wide-open position, he immediately retracted it in a rapid push-pull movement so that the little aluminum two-placer 'giro's rotor blades expended their kinetic energy in only a foot or two into the air, straight up and straight down. But gently. Surprisingly gently. Thankfully, gently.

It took the better part of ten days

And it took off straight up! The Whirlwing is shown in a 1941 demonstration at the peak of its jump, about to translate into forward flight over a 20-foot-high barrier. Soule frequently jumped the PA-36 over 30-foot-high barriers and achieved translational flight with no loss of altitude.

for Soule to develop the feel for the jump-takeoff control pressures and movements; as he increased the zero-thrust overspin, each jump became slightly higher, with forward movement included, so that the PA-36 began to take short hops, like a rabbit. Hop a few feet up and for-

ward, settle down, rev up the engine again, ease the rotor tilt forward a bit, pop the throttle/declutch system forward and back, each time for a fraction of a second longer, so that the hops got higher and longer, increasing from a couple of feet to a few yards, to 120 feet at a bound, which led Soule to declare cheerfully, "Well, we've caught up to the Wright brothers' first flight!"

As his confidence in the machine grew and the technique of both taking off and flying away became ingrained in Soule's motor-reflex system, he told Pitcairn, Larsen, and

Stanley that he proposed to make a complete test-flight circuit of the field, from jump-takeoff to full autorotative landing the next morning.

The next morning's flight may not have been spectacular to casual observers, but as the silvery Autogiro lifted straight up from the tarmac for a few feet, then sailed off with no settling back, completed a circuit of the field, and then returned to land gently on the small spot from which it had departed only a few moments before, it was to Pitcairn, sheer beauty. The PA-36 had finally performed exactly as planned and designed. That afternoon, it was named the Whirlwing.

One of the aerodynamic peculiarities of the freewheeling Autogiro rotor-blade system is that it automatically increases its rotative speed—and thereby produces more lift—as the load is increased. In addition, the rotational speed increases with horizontal or cross-country airspeed. In the past, engineers in the Pitcairn fraternity had wrestled with and overcome these problems, as well as the special and somewhat esoteric problems of "scale effect" which arise when the size of an aircraft is increased. Using the precious PA-36 as their test bed, Pitcairn and his engineers set up a flight-test syllabus to obtain performance information in various flight regimes, especially under increased payloads and high speeds.

It was during the speed testing that the first accident occurred. Slim had been making runs up and down the Pitcairn Field runway at low altitude, each run progressively faster, accurately timed with stopwatches. As power settings, rotor speeds, and fuel-consumption curves were plotted against actual airspeeds, he would roar down the field no more than ten feet off the ground, then throttle back slightly, pull up into a chandelle to reverse his course, and howl back over the route with added power. On the fourth or fifth pass, just before he was going to pull up for his turnaround, the control stick began to jump around wildly in his hand and an enormous shudder shook the aircraft as if it were a rag in the mouth of a giant dog.

Reacting instantaneously, Soule pulled the throttle back against the stop, and began to look for a place to set down, for he was no more than thirty feet in the air and still had a pretty good head of steam from his speed run. Trying to keep the aircraft under control, he headed for an open spot just off the airport boundary, believing at first, in those adrenaline-packed moments when everything goes into slow motion, that he had thrown a rotor blade in the high-spinning speed tests. He almost got out of the episode cleanly, but at the last moment the rotor smashed into a roadside telephone pole and destroyed itself, letting the fuselage drop into a cushioning patch of undergrowth, so that neither it nor the pilot was any more than scratched.

If all of the rotor blades had been smashed into splinters against the telephone pole, it might have taken Pitcairn and his engineers many months to ascertain the cause of the accident, but fortunately one blade was spared—the one that had failed in flight. When they saw its condition, the reason was obvious. In the interest of lightness of construction, the rotor blades were hollow, as is an aircraft wing. Unlike an aircraft wing, however, rotor blades whirl around so that the air mass contained within the hollow structure becomes subject to the phenomenon of centrifugal force. With relatively slow-moving rotor blades, this does not create a serious problem, but in the high-speed tests of the PA-36 the column of air had been whirled forcefully outward through the blades toward the tips, building up such internal pressures that the tip of one blade had literally exploded, as the tattered fabric of the sole remaining airfoil showed. The solution was to put air vents at the blade tips while the almost undamaged fuselage was being refurbished.

The unfortunate accident came just at a time when Captain H. F. Gregory, in the capacity of the army's selection and evaluation officer, was in the process of drafting the solicitation for industry bids on rotary-wing aircraft for military applications—the winning bidder to be the prime recipient of Dorsey–Logan Act funds.

The normal glacial pace of democratic bureaucracy had been somewhat accelerated by the onset of war three thousand miles to the east and especially by the manner in which the Nazi hordes had overwhelmed and totally crushed Poland. Military leaders and top officials and officers of the U.S. Government were suddenly dreadfully aware of the unpreparedness of their nation to take military action; the Germans had massed sixty infantry divisions, fourteen mechanized and motorized divisions, three mountain divisions, more than four thousand airplanes, and thousands of tanks and armored cars and had destroyed the defense forces.

At the time, the *total* army enlisted strength of the United States was less than 130,000 men, including three organized and six partially organized infantry divisions and two horse-mounted cavalry divisions—but no mechanized, motorized, or tank divisions, although there were some 1,500 men assigned to widely scattered tank units. The entire U.S. Army Air Corps had only 1,175 obsolescent combat aircraft and 17,000 men.

The situation had galvanized the normally sluggish government into action on all matters involving military preparedness. For several years the Army Air Corps had been evaluating what were then huge four-engine bombers built by Boeing, Consolidated-Vultee (destined to be renamed Convair), and soliciting bids from other aircraft manufacturers for twin-engine attack bombers and single-engine and twin-engine fighter planes. By the end of 1939, the production dynamo of the United States was beginning to creak into action.

The early success of the PA-36 had been encouraging, for its performance had indicated the correctness of Pitcairn's analysis that an Autogiro could do everything that a helicopter could do—except hover—and that hovering was not a total prerequisite for military or civilian use, but a specialized capability that would cost a great deal more to purchase and to operate. Unknown to Pitcairn, Igor I. Sikorsky's experimental single-blade test stand was just beginning to lift a few inches off the hangar floor at a time when the PA-36 was flying successfully. The first man-carrying Sikorsky VS-300 was making only tethered flights when the PA-36 was performing jump-takeoffs and fly-aways. Pitcairn's enthusiasm with the PA-36's performance, however, was somewhat modified when he read the end-of-the-year statement from his auditors: the PA-36 budget of $50,000 had ballooned to $200,799.11—some 300 percent greater than he had authorized, and the flight-test program was still more than a year behind schedule.

Equipped with a new set of blades, properly vented, the PA-36 was soon ready for further testing involving progressively higher jumps. This would be the most crucial part of the program, for probing the full extent of the Autogiro's ability to climb straight up and fly away without settling back during the transition would mean operating right to the limit of the ship's and pilot's capabilities.

The key word used by the engineers was *decay;* they had learned from the PA-22 developmental program that the kinetic energy stored in the physical mass of the rotating blades in overspeed condition would, as predicted, develop lifting force when the blades flipped from zero-lift to a positive angle of attack. However, they also found that once the rotation power from the craft's engine had been disengaged, the aerodynamic drag of the rotating blades slowed them down quickly so that the burst of lift soon evaporated, or decayed, which would result in the aircraft's losing altitude, i.e., settling back, until the forward thrust of the propeller was able to create the aerodynamic forces that would maintain the lift-generating rotation of the rotor blade. The problems increased as the height of the jumps increased, because of the time factor involved: it took longer to reach thirty feet, say, than five or ten feet, hence there was a greater potential for decay in the lifting force and a real possibility of settling back to the ground from the height of a three-story building if lift was lost.

Up to then, Soule's fly-aways had come after low jumps, not more than four or five feet, which was all that was necessary for the usual Autogiro flight from unprepared sites. His technique, self-taught, was to ram the throttle forward, simultaneously disengaging the rotor drive, then tilting the rotor disc forward, so that the jump was forward, rather than straight up, and the aircraft arched ahead as it translated into a climb-out. Now, however, he was entering into a completely new realm of flight.

Beginning with jumps of five and six feet, he made progressively higher and higher jumps, many of which were photographed by Pitcairn's motion-picture camera for later analysis in slow motion. Unfortunately, the camera was not grinding when the PA-36 had its worst accident, for it was spectacular.

Up to that time, the engine-coupled rotor drive declutching system had worked perfectly for dozens of test hops; as Soule would shove the throttle all the way forward, the mechanism of the rotor-drive system normally would declutch so that the rotor would run free and the blades would flip to lift-off position, all in an instant. Because there was no power to the blades, there was no torque effect, which Pitcairn knew from his extensive helicopter experimentation was a major problem in helicopter design. As a result, the PA-36 could jump off and fly away under control. However, on this particular flight the system came afoul of Murphy's Law: the engine ran up normally and the rotor soon reached its proper overspin lift-off speed, but when Soule shoved the throttle into the full-on position, the PA-36 performed a wild gyration, rocked back and forth, then banged down hard enough to warp the entire frame. The result was that the starter gear on the wide-open Warner engine (buried in the fuselage just behind the cockpit) impinged on the air-cooling vanes mounted on the propeller shaft, which was whirling around twenty-four hundred times a minute, causing the vanes to shatter like shrapnel, and cut the PA-36 in half just a few inches aft of Soule's pilot seat. It would take months to repair the damage, but everyone knew immediately what had happened: the declutching mechanism had hung up so that the engine was still delivering power to the rotor when it went into the takeoff mode, thereby imparting the twisting moment that was the bane of helicopter design. What had caused the accident was known, so the system could be corrected the next time around.

Early in 1940, there was a lull in the hostilities while the Nazis regrouped the three-dimensional assault forces that had completely destroyed Poland almost overnight in what the German leaders called their blitzkrieg, or lightning war. For almost a year, the western front was inactive, and life in England, France, and especially the United States seemed to be normal. Some U.S. war correspondents in England flippantly referred to the situation as the "sitzkrieg."

While the press and the general public were most interested in high-altitude bombers and high-speed fighters (in the United States they were still referred to as "pursuit" ships), military observers had noted the German technique of vertical envelopment and the closely coordinated efforts of the infantry, artillery, armored forces, and the

Luftwaffe, including the wide use of parachute troops to seize areas lightly defended behind the main lines of defense. Suddenly the rotary-wing aircraft's ability to get combat troops into and *out of* an area, which parachutists could not do, took on a new—and classified—interest, not only for assault purposes. Rotary-wing ships could be used for liaison, command officer transport, ambulance, rescue, artillery spotting, reconnaissance. The military potential of rotary wing had been recognized at last.

In accordance with the law regulating the allotments of federal funds, the army issued Circular 40-260, soliciting bids for the design of rotary-wing aircraft for special military uses, specifying the fifty-foot vertical takeoff requirement. Obviously, everyone anticipated that bids would come in from Pitcairn and Kellett, the only two aircraft companies in the country with actual rotary-wing manufacturing experience, in spite of the intricately drawn performance specifications which were heavily loaded in favor of helicopter development. The army also had reason to believe that bids would be received from at least one other rotary-wing company that had recently come into being.

After a thorough analysis, which led to the unanimous conclusion that no aircraft in America could meet the fifty-foot standard, since the PA-36 was still being rebuilt after the accident, Pitcairn submitted plans for a new model, a design study called the PA-38, an open-

cockpit, direct-control Autogiro with the jump-takeoff feature and a swiveling machine gun in the rear cockpit. Kellett submitted plans for two somewhat similar machines, but without the jump-takeoff feature, which it had not yet perfected. This led to some restrained jubilation in the Pitcairn group, who assessed their own submission as being so far superior to the Kelletts' that they would surely win the Dorsey bill funding award. They had no doubt that the fifty-foot vertical takeoff requirement was so unrealistic that it would be waived, simply because no bidder in the U.S. could comply with it.

However, there were two other bidders. United Aircraft Corporation submitted a bid on a design study prepared by their Vought-Sikorsky Division, based on a model known as the VS-300, the original model of which had been wrecked in a flight test. Their submission was theoretical, for they had no solid design on paper at that time. The fourth bidder was a brand new company called the Platt-LePage Helicopter Company.

Wynn Lawrence LePage, the youthful aerodynamicist loaned by the British National Physical Laboratory in 1925 to assist in wind tunnel testing at the Massachusetts Institute of Technology and the technician who had worked with Pitcairn and Larsen on the PA-1 Fleetwing—"the Hop-Ship"—had finally come of age in the science of rotary-wing flight. LePage had been hired by Geof Childs as his front-office assistant and technical adviser. He had been increasingly burdened with administrative details while assigned to fewer engineering duties. Shortly after Pitcairn's sale of his airline and the refocusing of attention on rotary-wing aircraft research and development, LePage had resigned and supported himself as a journalist. A few months later he had joined Kellett Aircraft Company, first as assistant chief engineer, then as chief engineer. In 1931 he had participated in the design of all Kellett Autogiros, from the earliest fixed-spindle versions to direct-control arrangements, and in the preliminary experiments with their jump-takeoff prototypes. In 1937, when the Great Depression had virtually destroyed all aircraft sales, LePage had returned to journalism as his primary source of income, while continuing to engage in rotary-wing research on his own time, and had collaborated with other "independent consulting engineers," as they designated themselves, to explore new avenues of aerodynamic theory.

In his investigations and analyses, LePage had struck a friendship and formed a partnership-alliance with Havilland D. Platt, a superlative mechanical engineer who had been working, without any conspicuous success, on helicopter design. Shortly after the public demonstrations of the Focke-Achgelis Fa-61 by Hanna Reitsch in Berlin, LePage had journeyed without delay to Bremen to see the machine for himself and had become friendly with the distin-

W. Lawrence LePage, principal designer and aerodynamicist of the Platt-Le-Page Helicopter Company. LePage had begun his rotary wing career with Pitcairn Aircraft, then had moved to Kellett Autogiro and became chief engineer. He then formed his own company which won the Dorsey Bill award.

guished German pioneer-inventor. When war had been declared, all exchanges of technical information had stopped, but LePage had seen enough in the Focke design to begin working on a similar design for a pure helicopter. Although the first two Platt-LePage helicopter ventures were failures, they were able to achieve some measure of success on their third version in a working model. When the military rotary-wing competition was announced, notwithstanding the fact that their design had never flown as a man-carrying machine, they had scaled-

The Platt-LePage XR-1 in hovering flight. Jim Ray was test pilot on some phases of its development.

up their drawings and submitted them with their bid in the 40-260 competition.

When the bids were opened on April 15, 1940, the contract and the award of the Dorsey–Logan Act funds were bestowed on the Platt-LePage company, specifying that, in accordance with the terms of their bid, they would deliver a full-size, flyable helicopter for army acceptance testing by January 1, 1941. In accordance with army customs, the first experimental rotary-wing aircraft selected for funding was designated XR-1. All other bidders were eliminated from the competition.

Pitcairn was momentarily set back by the way things had gone,

for he felt in his bones that the PA-36 was far superior to any other rotary-wing aircraft in the U.S. and that it would become better after it had passed through its inevitable teething stage. Already, Paul Stanley had drawings in the works for multipassenger Autogiros, larger than any that had been built, with all sorts of new power arrangements and engines, and the disappointed Pitcairn was not particularly surprised when he was told on a confidential basis that his group's submission was the best engineered of any proposal submitted, but that the air corps had made up its mind that it wanted a helicopter. His confidant told him that the army had gone through the formality of a bid procedure only because it was required by law before the contract could be issued and that the entire

Dorsey–Logan Act funding would probably be awarded to the sole helicopter entry.

Because of the rapidly escalating pressures to bring America's armed forces up to strength, Congress was beginning to act swiftly in the way it knew best: by opening the purse strings and passing legislation enabling the President to act to meet the national emergency. Only a year before, less than a week after war had been declared abroad, Congress had proclaimed that the United States would remain strictly neutral, but in the meantime the Nazis had systematically subjugated Poland, the Netherlands, and Belgium, and occupied most of France. In May 1940 Winston S. Churchill had been named Prime Minister of England, just in time to oversee the evacuation of 338,000 men—the tattered remnants of the British Expeditionary Force—taken off the shell-torn beaches of Dunkirk. In the summer of 1940, England stood alone against the Nazi onslaught.

To prepare for any eventualities, the Congress allocated supplemental funds for military acquisitions: $1.8 million to the army and $1.5 million to the navy, some of which filtered down to the Procurement Section of the army's Materiel Division at Wright Field. Captain H. Franklin Gregory was well aware that the award of the Dorsey bill funds to the unknown helicopter company, Platt-LePage, which had not yet produced a flying model, had left him leaning on a slender reed. From all appearances, it would be some time before the XR-1 would be available for evaluation. However, he had an ace up his sleeve: with the money made available by Congress he issued a special contract to the Kellett Aircraft Company to retrofit a pair of their YG-1Bs with tilting rotors (without jump-takeoff) and redesignated them as XR-2 and XR-3; since the aircraft were already in the military inventory, he did not have to go through another bid proceeding. Pitcairn was aware of the army's continued interest in the jump-takeoff Autogiro, but his PA-36 was not ready for evaluation as yet, and he held back on any proffers to the government until it would be. Nevertheless, he doggedly continued to pin his hopes on the design.

By July 1940, while newspapers were reporting tremendous air battles over England in an obvious prelude to invasion, the PA-36 had been completely rebuilt and greatly lightened by removing the roadability feature, which was not required for military use. After spending an hour or so in its cockpit to knock some of the rust off his technique by making a few conservative rolling takeoffs and circuits of Pitcairn Field, Slim Soule made three consecutive successful jump-takeoffs and fly-aways, returning exhilarated by the 'giro's performance, which was better than ever. Pitcairn smiled his quiet smile. The Autogiro Company was back in the running.

After two weeks of flawless performances by the rejuvenated PA-36, Pitcairn personally invited

Captain Gregory to come to Willow Grove so that he could see the actual performance of the third-generation Autogiro. Not a design study or a reduced-size test version, but a two-place, flyable, usable, existing aircraft which, right off the shelf, could meet all of the requirements of the military, except one: it could not hover. This was a shortcoming Pitcairn assessed as minor. When Gregory accepted the invitation, his host also invited the press.

The demonstration flights of the Whirlwing were sensational. Pilot Soule repeatedly performed jump-takeoffs for press and newsreel cameras, popping straight up and flying away over an eighteen-foot high barrier set five feet in front of the rotor disc, then came back to make soft landings after nearly vertical zero-speed approaches. Within days motion-picture theaters all over the country showed audiences better than any still cameras or printed words the incredible, dramatic flight characteristics of the newest of the Pitcairn "wing" line. The day of the backyard aircraft seemed at hand. Gregory was much impressed, but remained noncommittal as to whether the Autogiro would fill the high performance requirements established by the military.

The publicity, however, had made such an impression on civilians that Pitcairn quickly received an invitation from officials of the New York World's Fair to demonstrate the Whirlwing as part of the aircraft display pavilion, which led Soule to make a captivating suggestion. Since

the fair's theme was a tall slim pyramidal structure called the Trylon, and a small domed building called the Perisphere, why not perform jump-takeoffs at the base of the Trylon, spiral steeply up its length, then come back to the takeoff spot in a vertical descent? There was no doubt that such maneuvering would glean extensive additional publicity which would reach the eyes of congressmen and high-ranking military and naval officials in Washington, so Pitcairn agreed to the spectacular exhibition, provided that the authorities of the World's Fair would permit such operations over the grounds. He knew a good idea when he saw one.

Somewhat to his surprise, the dignitaries, who were also seeking ways to publicize the fair, were receptive to the proposal, although somewhat guarded in their tendency to agree with it. In a letter clearly constructed with the aid of legal talent, they said that, first, they had to be shown that the feat was not only possible, but safe; they suggested that the Autogiro be flown to New York's recently dedicated LaGuardia Field for a special demonstration.

The next morning Soule flew the PA-36 Whirlwing from Willow Grove to Manhattan, then dropped low to cruise up the East River and landed at LaGuardia Field directly in front of the little knot of officials out on the end of Runway 31, far from public view. Then he proceeded to put on a show of the ship's unique gyrations that the observers had heard about but had never seen.

After Soule showed how he proposed to spiral up the Trylon, by actually doing it several times over their heads about an imaginary structure, it did not take long for the officials, and their insurance and legal advisers, who were also in the group, to agree that the demonstration should be allowed to go on. They climbed into their automobiles and headed for the fairgrounds to see the show themselves. Unfortunately, they did not see it and no photographs were ever taken of the feat. While taking off to meet them, Soule experienced a repetition of his earlier accident when the rotor-drive clutch did not disengage as the throttle was opened all the way. As he reported to Pitcairn on the telephone, "Things happened so fast, I haven't caught up with the ship yet!" Again, the ship had reared up and rolled over, smashing its rotor blades. The pilot was not hurt, the Luscombe-built fuselage—"built like a bridge," Soule said—was only scratched, and the rotors could be replaced as soon as the ship was trucked back to Willow Grove. Fortunately, no newspapermen were there to cover the story. All the World's Fair people were told was that the demonstration had to be canceled because the aircraft was needed back at Willow Grove and that time constraints precluded another such effort.

Within a few weeks the little demonstrator had been repaired and was flying successfully again. In October 1941, Soule flew to the civil airport at College Park, Maryland, where he made ten perfect jump-takeoffs for observers from the Departments of Commerce and the Interior, then hopped off, following the Anacostia River to its confluence with the Potomac, where at Bolling Field he demonstrated the extraordinary flight characteristics of the Autogiro to the U.S. Army Air Corps' top brass, including General H.H. Arnold. As part of the demonstration, Slim had requested that automobiles be parked to form a square within ten feet of the PA-36, then to and from that vividly restricted space made takeoffs and landings again and again as the U.S. Army Air Corps' officers marveled at the performance.

Harold Pitcairn, who had attended all of the sensationally successful demonstrations, was understandably exalted by the enthusiastic reception of his pride and joy. He was certain that his tenacity in staying with the vastly improved Autogiro design would pay off in immediate recognition by all military authorities of its superior operational qualities. "The demonstrations couldn't have been better," he chortled in a letter to Bing Seymour. Then he added slyly that he had inferred, during the luncheon conversation with General Arnold's staff members, that "Apparently there is some dissatisfaction with the Dorsey bill award." Clearly, he anticipated an improvement in the military's attitude toward his rotary-wing contributions to America's combat preparedness. At the very least, Captain Gregory surely would receive word from the highest echelons in Washington to return to Willow Grove and take another hard look at the PA-36.

Captain Gregory did indeed receive such a direction and observed one of Soule's more scintillating Whirlwing demonstration schedules, involving jump-takeoffs, fast and almost-standstill slow-flight, and vertical landing approaches. The entire program was tremen-

dously impressive, for it constituted clear proof that the Pitcairn Autogiro was capable of doing everything that had been set up in the rotary-wing criteria following the Dorsey bill appropriation.

When Harold Pitcairn went to bed that night, he anticipated a letter from the army within the week authorizing him to go ahead with production. He slept on success.

# PART FOUR

# The Helicopter

# World War II

The expected letter of authorization never came. Captain Gregory had indeed been very impressed by what he had seen during his Willow Grove revisit, for the Whirlwing was manifestly a far different aircraft from any Autogiros he had known in the past and certainly did have a lot going for it. However, his reversed, favorable evaluation had been modified as he headed back for Wright Field, by exposure to another technological development.

Instead of proceeding almost due west to Ohio, Gregory had again detoured to the northeast and visited the Vought-Sikorsky facility in Stafford. After a bit of chitchat and preliminary socializing with the courtly Sikorsky, Gregory went right to the point: What was the status of the Russian inventor's rotary-wing experimentation? With typical self-effacement, Sikorsky humbly apologized that the test vehicle, the revamped VS-300* was not really perfected yet, but, while crude and undeveloped, had been flying well enough for a couple of months for the fifty-nine-year-old inventor to haul it out to the little field adjacent to the experimental laboratory and fly it for his visitor. It was an inelegant, angular flight-test device, a spidery framework of welded steel tubing, on top of which were mounted four rotors, powered by a single 75-hp Lycoming engine. Its large lifting rotor had been set amidships; two smaller rotors, laterally disposed, were mounted on outriggers toward the rear of the skeletonized craft, to provide pitching-and-rolling control forces. A small rotor mounted vertically at the very rear of the ship blasted air sideways for the purpose of counteracting torque. The pilot sat completely in the open, secured by a

---

* The VS-300, being an engineering-test article, retained its design number through no less than eighteen modifications, most of which were of major changes involving the number and disposition of rotors, blades power plants, and fuselage structure. The original VS-300 was a tiny test stand with no payload. The version Gregory saw here was the fourth version of the series of VS-300s.

safety belt, grasping a pair of vertical levers, with his feet on airplane-like rudder pedals. For perhaps ten minutes Sikorsky put the machine through its paces as Gregory watched in fascination; he hovered, maneuvered in all directions—forward, backward, sideways—pivoted end for end and moved straight up and straight down. When Sikorsky asked Gregory if he would like to try it himself, he was almost knocked down in the young officer's rush toward the pilot's seat.

Once at the controls, Gregory recognized that the system that had been developed on the teeter-totter he had seen the year before had been transferred somehow to the VS-300, but was completely unlike any he had ever used; hence it bucked and wavered, swayed and darted like a fractious horse and he was happy to get it back on the ground without any damage to the machine or to himself. He sat back as the rotor blades overhead slowed to a stop and looked at the older man grinning at him across the ramp. Gregory was in a peculiar situation. He had seen the Dorsey bill funding of the XR-1—"which will serve to furnish information as to the feasibility of the helicopter"—pour out for a machine that was still undelivered, and had spent more funds to re-examine some older army Autogiros. In a few days' span he had seen Pitcairn's PA-36 fly again and again—and now he had seen America's first actual helicopter, and had flown it, more or less.

Gregory and Sikorsky sat in the latter's automobile on the Stafford Plant's parking lot and discussed what the army needed in the way of a helicopter: it had to have an enclosed cabin and be able to carry two people. Then Gregory added that it must have a single-rotor control system with both cyclic and collective pitch in a single main lifting rotor. Sikorsky would have to eliminate the two horizontal outrigger rotors at the rear of the helicopter before it would be acceptable to the army.

Sikorsky reported that he had started off with a single-rotor concept but that his first man-carrying test vehicle had undergone a roll-over in tethered flight. The version he had just flown was Sikorsky's trial horse to find alternative ways to obtain roll and pitch control. His next version, Sikorsky said, would have two overhead rotors, one for lifting and lateral control and a second one, mounted at the rear of the test ship, to provide pitch control. Gregory insisted vehemently that he must have all flight controls in a single rotor, which made the older man snap, "One thing at a time. I will do it my way!" Then he reiterated that he was not so sure that a single rotor could contain lifting and maneuvering control mechanisms. The ball was in Frank Gregory's court.

And, indirectly, in Pitcairn's. Igor Sikorsky was aware of the details of two patents held under the Autogiro Company of America. By that time these patents were known to all aeronautical scientists simply as "580" and "582."* The Russian expatriate was aware of Pitcairn's (ACA's) firm grip on the single-rotor, cyclic/collective mechanism under the patents.** In retrospect, he may have been playing some of his high hole cards face-down when he reiterated stubbornly, "I'll do it *my* way!" The fact was that he had already asked United Aircraft's legal department to look into the possibility of some sort of accommodation with the Autogiro Company of America on the matter of a license

---

* In patent law circles, the trio of suffix numbers is used for convenience. The patents referred to were 2,380,580, already issued on the tilting-rotor disc cyclic control and the three-position jump-takeoff collective pitch (neutral, no-lift; steep pitch jump-takeoff; flat pitch fly-away), and the contemporaneously filed 2,380,582, the miraculous single-hub invented by Cierva in which the spindle was fixed and all cyclic and collective pitch functions were performed by turning the individual blades in their pitch angles while they were rotating at high speed. The Cierva invention, which Pitcairn was then independently experimenting on with hand-crafted models of hubs, was originally for Autogiro application where the rotor blades rotated automatically without engine power, hence the two terms *autogiration* and *autorotation*. The latter term has continued to be currently in use in rotating-wing parlance.

** The complexity of 582 was to make for legal history. Synnestvedt & Lechner filed the detailed application on November 16, 1933, but the actual Letters Patent were not issued until July 31, 1945—twelve years later. Thus, at the time of the Gregory-Sikorsky meeting, 582 was a "patent applied for."

for its critical patent position. His multiple-rotor investigations were probably carried out for several reasons. First, he was learning more and more about the aerodynamic problems and solving them in his own painstaking way. Second, he was creating a patent position of his own. And third, he was aware that sooner or later everyone in the tiny rotary-wing industry would have to work out some sort of cross-licensing of patents which were going to be developed outside of the realm of the Autogiro Company of America's closely guarded vault of rotary-wing patents.

At this crucial point word was received that Platt-LePage's company test pilot had taken off in their one-and-only, handmade, experimental XR-1, despite clear orders on the flight bulletin board and placards on the instrument panel not to do so. The multiple-rotor system was undergoing some extensive changes. The pilot had disregarded the orders and attempted a takeoff, with disastrous results. The XR-1 was almost totally wrecked.

This put the Dorsey bill funding winners back on the starting line, a serious blow for them, but possibly offering a glimmer of hope for financial subsidy from the government for further improvement of Pitcairn's jump-takeoff Autogiro. Harold Pitcairn was not privy to the Gregory-Sikorsky dialogue. He did not know that Gregory had informed his superiors in the War Department of his belief that future rotary-wing funding should go to Vought-Sikorsky, in view of the failure of the XR-1 to be delivered, and that he had been authorized to proceed in accordance with his own estimate of the situation.

Pitcairn typically had several projects going at one time. While he spent hours on end experimenting with rotary-wing full-control hubs,* he was also energetically engaged in the military PA-36 project for which he continued to have high hopes and extended himself into other endeavors related to the war in Europe and the preparedness for war in the United States.

American newspapers reported that London was taking nightly pastings from Nazi bombers and that huge convoys steaming from U.S. ports to the United Kingdom across the North Atlantic were being decimated by interdicting gauntlets of German U-boats, the infamous "wolf packs" lurking beneath the surface of the sea. The ponderous fleets of merchantmen, forced to steam at the speed of the slowest ship of the group, were sitting ducks for the hidden enemy, which exacted a frightful toll.

Within two hundred miles of the coast of the United States, convoy-protecting blimps kept the submarines well below periscope depth, for the shape of the predators, invisible from the crow's nest of a

ship, was clearly outlined from aloft. But once beyond the range of land-based aircraft, the Nazis had an open season.

The Royal Navy could not afford to assign aircraft carriers to every convoy laden with war materiel from the "Arsenal of Democracy," but a high-ranking officer of the Royal Air Force had a suggestion: the Autogiro, equipped with the jump-takeoff feature and direct control, could take off and land upon restricted areas, including the decks of aircraft carriers. Why not use them to operate from platforms set upon merchantmen in convoy as mobile eyes-in-the-sky for antisubmarine defense? Grasping at any suggestions to reduce the dreadful attrition rate, the Admiralty included the RAF officer in the British Purchasing Commission sent to the United States. The officer was Wing Commander Reginald A. C. Brie, former test pilot for the now-idle Cierva Autogiro Company.

In late 1940, Brie presented himself to his old friend Pitcairn to procure Autogiros for actual in-service testing under war conditions, conceding that the Admiralty was not wildly enthusiastic about the idea. Although Pitcairn Autogiro was also not producing any aircraft, the idea was attractive to the company's president. He agreed to fill Brie's order for a short run of seven Autogiros having the direct-control and jump-takeoff features, although such a short production run would obviously not be profitable. Pitcairn believed that the success of the

---

* In 1938-39, Harold Pitcairn was awarded six patents on rotors and rotor-blade combinations and had three patent applications pending.

Harold Pitcairn and Agnew Larsen in 1941, at the formation of the Pitcairn-Larsen Autogiro Company, created to produce convoy protection Autogiros (PA-39s) for the Royal Navy. A photo of the PCA-2 in flight hangs behind Pitcairn.

proposed operation at sea would be noted by the U.S. Navy and would change its somewhat negative position toward the Autogiro.

Since Pitcairn Autogiro was not in business, Larsen proposed a new arrangement: if Pitcairn would lend his name to it, Larsen would create a new corporation, to be called the Pitcairn-Larsen Company. For the purpose of fulfilling the British contract, the company would reacquire seven old PA-18, two-place, open-cockpit Autogiros, many of which were still being used regularly, although most were by then ten years old. He would then retrofit the original fixed-spindle hubs with direct-control, jump-takeoff rotor systems. The new model would be designated the PA-39. After giving the matter some thought, Pitcairn agreed with this plan.

He also had another very active iron in the fire.

As the tempo of the war in Europe had increased and America's

The PA-39 Autogiro was a PA-18 airframe retrofitted with the direct-control, jump-takeoff rotor system, for the British Air Purchasing Commission. Only seven were built. This PA-39, the sole survivor of the group, has been rebuilt and reconditioned to flying status by Stephen Pitcairn.

preparedness program moved into high gear, Congress had expanded funding for the civilian pilot training program (CPTP) and advanced flight training of pilots for the Army Air Corps and naval aviation. The first stage of instruction was undertaken at civilian contract flight schools which provided ultralight aircraft: Piper and Taylor Cubs, Stinsons, Luscombes, Aeroncas. Then flight students moved up into larger open-cockpit biplanes for aerobatics and formation flying. The navy used N3Ns built at the Philadelphia Naval Aircraft Factory and the army was using Boeing/Stearman trainers and some Ryans.

However, newspapers said that flight programs were being held back because of a shortage of such advanced training planes. For a while Pitcairn considered purchasing the rights to Reuben Fleet's little biplane trainer, but the new owner of the design—Brewster Aircraft—stiffly refused to deal with him, although Pitcairn obviously was both set up and qualified to build high-quality, fabric-covered airplanes in his almost unused Willow Grove factory. Philosophically, Pitcairn surmised that the rejection stemmed from his refusal to sell them the factory and airfield.

Instead of being bowed by the rejection, Pitcairn dusted off the PA-7 Super Mailwing designs and ran his practiced eye over them to see if it could be modified into a two-place intermediate training plane. The airplane's proven stability, enormous structural strength and relatively slow landing speeds would make it an ideal aerobatic trainer. He designated it the PA-40, had the blueprints redrawn in the new configuration, and, with high hopes, began to make the rounds in

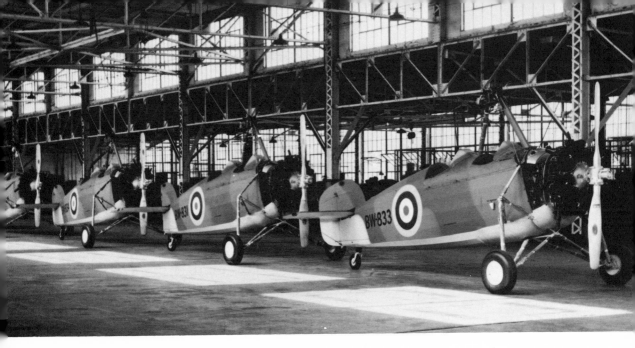

Six of the seven PA-39s lined up for delivery in the Pitcairn Autogiro factory at Willow Grove. One was retained by Pitcairn-Larsen for further testing; one was retained by the Royal Navy for tactical planning in the United States. Three were lost in shipment to Europe. The size of the factory is evident.

Washington. For reasons he never understood, and which were never explained, military authorities did not take advantage of his production ability, although the need was clear and the equipment eminently suitable. The PA-40 program was quietly shelved.

Pitcairn returned to give his full time to the rotary-wing hub experimentation and to the PA-36, while Larsen was put totally in charge of the PA-39 program.* More and

* The apparently missing PA-37 and PA-38 were engineering design studies of two special-use Pitcairn Autogiros incorporating the direct-control, jump-takeoff features. Although the working drawings were designated as being in the "PA" series for internal uses, they never carried into actual aircraft.

more it seemed that the future of his company depended on the jump-takeoff Autogiro, both the experimental PA-36 and the PA-39 for the British navy's use.

By this time Pitcairn's engineers and production staff were able to produce the seven PA-39s within a few weeks after the well-used PA-18 machines had been bought back from their civilian owners. As each totally rebuilt Autogiro was shoved out the factory door, it was flight-tested by Slim Soule and turned over to Wing Commander Brie for final acceptance. One was retained for Pitcairn-Larsen for continued flight testing to improve performance for future reorders. Six were delivered to the English group, one of which was retained for service testing from escort vessels at Newport News, Virginia, by Brie. The other five were dismantled, carefully packed, and shipped to the United Kingdom. For the first time the magnitude of the submarine-inflicted toll was brought home to Pitcairn and his associates: only two PA-39s arrived in England. The other three, together with all spares for the entire group, were lost in transit, victims of the very submarine action they were designed to combat.

Preparing a demonstration itinerary for the PA-36 to army bases all over the country, Pitcairn heard from his military contacts that the XR-1 project funded by Dorsey money had fallen behind: the Platt-LePage helicopter had not been ready on January 1, 1941, and probably would not be ready until spring. He was cheered by the fact that many military commanders training in the field had indicated to Washington that they wanted to see the Pitcairn Autogiro—the PA-36—in action.

Early in February 1941, Slim Soule tossed a small suitcase in the PA-36 and took off from Willow Grove, headed for Washington, D.C. and its contiguous military fields on the west bank of the Potomac—Bolling (army) and Anacostia (navy). After his two-hour flight he landed, refueled, and performed fifteen jump-takeoffs for a crowd of government officials, including the entire congressional Appropriations Committee for Naval Affairs and a large array of newspaper and newsreel cameramen. As thousands of civilians watched from across the Potomac or from small boats on the river, the shiny bright PA-36 jumped, swung around, made steep turns, and returned to land lightly,

looking for all the world like a chromed hummingbird. It was a highly successful beginning of what was an ambitious program to demonstrate to everyone that the Autogiro now could do everything that the military needed and to make the lack of a practical helicopter clear. The theme of the trip was, "Here it is, *now!* You can use it, *now!* Why wait any longer? Buy it *now!*"

From Washington, Soule flew the little PA-36 three hundred miles at its 95-mph cruising speed directly to Fort Bragg, North Carolina, where he made a dozen jump-takeoffs—he exuberantly reported to Pitcairn that it was a "Great demo! We had a whole division out to see it!" Then he flew three hundred miles to Fort Benning, Georgia, where he performed the feat nine times. At Fort Knox, Kentucky, he made seven jumps, then returned to Willow Grove to have the control system examined after its vigorous workouts. Everything was functioning perfectly, although the latter part of the trip was made in sub-zero conditions and Soule had to take to his bed for a week because of a severe head cold that developed into a strep throat. As soon as he was back on his feet, he climbed back into what he had affectionately began to call *his* "Whirlwing" and headed halfway across the United States from Willow Grove to Fort Sill, Oklahoma, a thousand miles away on a direct line, almost twice that distance by the route he took: Washington, D.C., then Richmond, Greensboro, Greenville, Atlanta, Birmingham,

Meridian, Jackson, Monroe, and Dallas. He experienced only one problem en route: approaching Meridian, Mississippi, he blew an internal cooling fan in the engine buried in the fuselage behind him, but made an uneventful precautionary landing, had the fan repaired, and went on his way. It was, by any measure, a superlative "proving flight."

For a week he participated in field maneuvers at Fort Sill under simulated combat conditions, which involved the firing of live ammunition by both infantry and artillery. This gave him a chance to demonstrate the exceptional ability of the ship for forward observation duties. He would consult with the gunners on the ground, then jump into the aircraft, hop off the rough, unprepared terrain, climb to altitude over the target, and observe the impact of the high-explosive shells. Then he would return quickly to the firing line and show the marked map of the target area. Time after time, he was able to direct shells on the target within three rounds.

The Autogiro was pressed into all sorts of duty, from carrying messages to moving officer personnel into critical areas. Everyone was greatly impressed.

Soule returned to Pitcairn Field clutching a handful of kudos from military field commanders—but he returned by surface, not by air. As he was departing Indianapolis two days before, a high-pressure oil line had let go and sprayed the cockpit and the pilot with a haze of hot oil,

which required that the PA-36 be returned to its nest by truck. Nevertheless, everyone agreed that the extensive flight had proved the Autogiro to be a valuable military tool: a report came from Wright Field saying that "out of the tests of various aircraft by the different Branches have come certain recommendations, the *gist* of which is that, to date, they are fairly well satisfied with the characteristics of the O-49 [an army observation aircraft] but due to the jump-takeoff and vertical landing characteristics of the Pitcairn demonstrator [the PA-36], practically all branches have come in with requests for the procurement of a number of these for service test, in connection with their desires for a vehicle for Command and Liaison work . . ." Surely, when the word filtered back to Washington, orders would be forthcoming.

Months came and went, but no military order materialized. It was baffling. Pitcairn knew that the Platt-LePage XR-1 had not flown until June of 1941 and that Sikorsky's VS-300 with the outrigger twin rotors had been modified to a two-rotor configuration that was still unsatisfactory to Major H. F. Gregory, who insisted on a single rotor with both cyclic and collective pitch controls. What he did not know was that in a classified report, Gregory had recommended that the air corps Materiel Division explore the further development of the Sikorsky aircraft in a larger version to be called the VS-316 in-house and designated as the XR-4 by the army.* Gregory's memorandum contained the information that "There are sufficient funds yet unobligated from Special Appropriation by Act, Public No. 61—76th Congress to cover the cost ..." The last of the Dorsey bill funding would go to Vought-Sikorsky. On this commitment, he had received assurances from Igor Sikorsky that a VS-300 with a single rotor was flying at Stafford and that he would be able to have the larger, two-place helicopter, the VS-316, engineered and capable of flying before the year was out.

As the summer wore on, Pitcairn felt a twinge when he learned that Jim Ray had become the test pilot for Platt-LePage. He missed the companionship of his old friend but read with some interest that the XR-1, upon which the Dorsey-Logan Act largesse had been spent, was flying only within a confined space, rising no higher than a few feet, and for only a few seconds at a time. It made him wonder anew at the complete indifference at high policy levels for the frequently demonstrated capabilities of the Autogiro to do everything a helicopter could do, except hover. And as Slim Soule's demonstration trip had shown, for most purposes that was unimportant. No matter which way he looked at the situation, Pitcairn

came out to the same conclusion: the Autogiro had it all over the helicopter as far as training, transition from fixed wing, load-carrying capacity, initial cost, operational costs, simplicity of operation, and safety. All the bad qualities had been worked out of it over a period of evolution and refinement.

Perhaps unfortunately, while in this introspective mood, he learned that the PA-39 program was a dead issue since the British Purchasing Commission had not extended the contract for further antisubmarine Autogiros, as had been anticipated. Furthermore, the entire project had resulted in a substantial financial loss, rather than almost breaking even, as had been the original plan. In a rare outburst, undoubtedly induced by the piling up of frustrations, disappointments, and endless pressure over an extended period, Pitcairn exploded.

Calling Larsen into his office, Pitcairn told his loyal old friend of almost a quarter of a century that he had absolutely no conception of cost control, was completely devoid of any administrative ability, and that, while he had engineering ability, he was totally unfit to run a company on his own. It was a furious tongue-lashing, uncharacteristic of the usually mild and tactful Pitcairn, and it came just at the wrong time.

In twenty-four years of close association, never had a bitter or angry word been exchanged by the two men, although Larsen's subordinates had sometimes felt the sharp edge of his tongue and Pitcairn had

* The XR-2 and XR-3 in the military chronology were two early Kellett Autogiro direct-control models, but without the jump-takeoff feature. X: Experimental; R: Rotary Wing.

seen at first hand his chief engineer's temper in disputes with both Ray and Leavitt. Now he was to feel it himself. Larsen, quaking with rage at what he considered an unfair, unjustified attack, rejoined with an equally impassioned display of vocal fireworks, including some remarks of a somewhat personal nature. It was a harangue from which there was no retreating.

Pitcairn, instantly regretting that he had expressed his sentiments so bluntly, sat and listened, waiting for the storm of words to subside. He believed that both outbursts had been triggered by the same set of background factors that had spring-loaded their tempers to the snapping point. He hoped that as soon as they were both through yelling, it would all blow over.

Instead of popping off his psychological pressure valve and returning to normal, Larsen grew more irate as he went along, until he terminated on a note of bitter finality and resigned from all positions in the Pitcairn organization. The friendship and professional relationship that had spanned the years and had so enriched the science and technology of aviation and contributed to much to its early history was broken off as sharply as the stem of a goblet. Larsen, still fuming, stomped out of Pitcairn's private office and down the hall to his own, where he began to clean out his desk.

Pitcairn was deeply hurt. He had lost Ray, then Larsen. The triumverate that had begun on the Bryn Athyn pasture to build the airline and the foundations of the rotary-wing industry was broken up.

Things were moving too fast to give much time to reflecting or philosophizing. An entrepreneur approached Pitcairn, seeking to lease the factory building in which the Mailwings and Autogiros had been built, but which was now almost empty. The new product would be aircraft, of a sort. The company was called AGA (for Autogiros, Gliders & Airplanes), since the proposed tenant was confident he could obtain government orders. Retaining fifteen hundred square feet for his own engineering research, Pitcairn entered into the lease.

The occupant of the other part of the vast floor space was as good as his word, partly. No airplanes or Autogiros were ordered, but within weeks the factory had been tooled up to produce boxy assault gliders, designed to be towed behind transport airplanes, a military tactic that had been pioneered successfully by the Wehrmacht. Every day, as he saw the squared-off ugly ducklings coming off the line, so unlike the sleek, beautiful Mailwings and Autogiros that had preceded them, Pitcairn shook his head sadly.

He was affected not merely by the total disparity of appearance, but because no one in the military hierarchy seemed to recognize that Autogiros could not only take people into combat areas, but could take them out again.

Almost nightly he read newspaper articles about the new darlings of the journalists: little airplanes that had been dubbed The Grasshopper Fleet. Piper Cubs, Stinsons, Aeroncas ... the news was full of them acting in military maneuvers all over the United States as "aerial motorcycles" and liaison vehicles, since they could land on roads, open fields, and small prepared airstrips near the front lines and command centers. Clara sometimes looked at him strangely when he threw down the paper and clenched his fists in helpless bafflement. When, he wondered, would these people ever learn that the PA-36 Autogiro could operate without roads, or big open fields, or landing strips? Part of the problem, he knew, was that the selection of rotary-wing aircraft came under a different military authority now than did the selection of small fixed-wing airplanes.

Pitcairn's hopes were also pinned on the public's acceptance of the PA-36 type of Autogiro. He already had his preeminent rotary-wing engineers Paul Stanley and Harris Campbell hard at work preparing drawings of the civilian version of the much plushed-up Whirlwing. At his behest they had also drawn larger Autogiros, four- and six-place models, and Stanley had one in the works for thirty passengers or more. After looking at the assault gliders on the other side of the factory wall, he had prepared preliminary figures and calculations on an Autogiro which would jump-takeoff with forty combat-ready soldiers on board.

Sitting in the living room in Cairncrest with the brilliant Sunday morning sunlight flooding across the carpet, Pitcairn leaned over from the newspapers on his lap to tune in some restful music on the radio. There was no music. An obviously shaken announcer was reading a news item just torn from the wire service teletype: Pearl Harbor, America's military outpost in the Pacific Ocean, had been attacked by a large fleet of Japanese aircraft and it appeared that the Pacific Fleet berthed or anchored in the harbor had been virtually wiped out. Thousands of people, military and civilian, had been killed or wounded. The army air base had been destroyed. With the Hawaiian Islands defenseless, an invasion was expected at any moment.

# Pitcairn's Helicopter

On Monday morning, December 8, 1941, an ungainly contraption of fabric-covered aluminum and steel tubing was wheeled out of the Stafford, Connecticut, Vought-Sikorsky building into the bright sunshine and chill breezes of the flight-test area, as a small group of onlookers watched with interest and high hopes. This was the first version of the—still experimental—VS-316, the two-place offspring of the final successful test model of the VS-300. Configured similarly to the last VS-300, a single-rotor pylon was mounted over the fuselage in the conventional style of Autogiros, with a smaller antitorque propeller mounted in a vertical plane on the left side of the rear fuselage. There were no other propellers or rotors. Painted silver, as all of Sikorsky's test articles were, the ship vibrated slightly when the inventor himself started the engine, then engaged the rotor drive. As the overhead blades increased their rotational speed, the aircraft pulsated on its landing gear, then rose several feet into the air, settled back gently to the concrete surface, rose again, and again settled back. The third time it lifted off, the aircraft turned slowly within its own length in hovering flight, then moved forward and backward a few feet, slid to the right and to the left, then returned to its original position over the landing pad and settled down lightly. As the test pilot—the great inventor himself—cut the engine switch, the onlookers, including Major H. Franklin Gregory and other army officers, threw their caps into the air, hugged each other, and cheered wildly. They had just seen the first flight of the first practical helicopter in America.* Although it would carry only two people in its boxy cabin, the witnesses harbored no doubts that this prototype would soon be

---

\* Major Gregory personally distinguished the Sikorsky helicopter from the Platt-LePage product on this criterion: in his estimation, a single-place helicopter, including the Flettner and Focke-Achgelis, was not "practical" for military usage, since it would not lift a payload.

developed into a line of even larger helicopters. Major Gregory without delay set the military/political machinery into motion to include the newly designated XR-4 into the Wright Field flight test and evaluation program to divert federal funds to the Sikorsky laboratory. The first step was to work the bugs out of the machine at Stafford.

War had been declared on Japan on the very day of the Sikorsky flight; three days later Germany and Italy declared war on the United States, plunging the nation into a two-front campaign. The first theater of action was in the Pacific, where, during the first half of 1942, Americans were subjected to a series of military disasters for which they were totally unprepared.

Believing that the Hawaiian Islands would surely be invaded by overwhelming Japanese forces, the federal government replaced all of the island territory's paper money with a special series overprinted "HAWAII" so that it could not be seized by the invaders and be used to fund operations in the continental United States. In February 1942, Singapore fell. With their flank thus protected, the Japanese invaded the Philippines, then pressed on to New Guinea and the Solomon Islands, targeting on Australia and New Zealand. The Japanese juggernaut seemed unstoppable; within weeks all serious defenses had crumbled in the Philippines, except for isolated pockets named Bataan and Corregidor, which continued to fight to the end for several months without seri-

The two-place Sikorsky V-316 helicopter, which was designated the XR-4 by the Army for research and testing. As the R-4, it was the first practical, payload-carrying helicopter in America. It was built under licenses from the Autogiro Company of America.

ously impeding the enemy advance. When Bataan fell, General MacArthur was ordered to proceed to Australia to oversee the defense of that continent and to prepare to mount a counteroffensive. Japanese marines took possession of American territory in the Aleutian Islands, and the West Coast of the U.S. was placed on full military alert. There was a bright moment when Jimmy Doolittle, one of America's real aviation heroes, led a bombing raid from some unidentified takeoff point (it proved to be the U.S.S. *Hornet*) and struck the Japanese cities of Tokyo, Osaka, Kobe, and Yokahama.

Early in 1942, the Firestone Tire and Rubber Company acquired AGA Corporation (the successor to the Pitcairn-Larsen Company), renamed it G&A Aircraft and took over the lease of the Pitcairn Aircraft factory at Willow Grove. G&A continued to work day and night producing assault gliders for the future invasion of enemy-held territory. War communiqués reported tremendous air and sea battles being

An inflatable-float equipped XR-4 landing on the deck of a ship under way, a year after the PA-39 demonstrated the same capability.

waged in faraway places in the Coral Sea and near a fly-speck-sized island known as Midway. The enemy thrusts were being contained.

Few people, except for a handful of army personnel and some very surprised observers-by-accident, knew that the Sikorsky VS-316/XR-4 was flown from Stafford to Dayton in the middle of May 1942. Test pilot Charles L. (Les) Morris, with Igor I. Sikorsky as co-pilot for the last leg of the trip, took off on May 13 and flew a circuitous route to Wright Field, covering 761 airline miles in sixteen hours of flying time and making sixteen stops along the way over a five-day period; then he delivered it officially to Lieutenant Colonel H. F. Gregory on May 18. Newspapers paid scant attention to the XR-4 and its feat; that summer, U.S. marine landings on Guadalcanal Island, in the heart of the Solomon Islands, dominated the headlines. The flow of battle was slowly but perceptibly reversing.

Once it had become clear that the army and all other branches of government had embraced the XR-4 and that substantial orders were surely forthcoming for the unique flying machine, the dimensions of the patent royalty payments came into sharp focus.

United Aircraft's (the parent company of Vought-Sikorsky) patent counsel had made a detailed investigation of the patent position of the Autogiro Company of America and had come to the conclusion that it was practically all-encompassing and legally impregnable. Many of the patents derived over the years of rotary-wing experimentation came at the very beginning of the special science and hence qualified as "pioneer" patents. The key patent was 582 (2,380,582, footnoted above, page 293), which covered the aerodynamic, fixed-spindle cyclic and collective pitch conjoint-systems in one rotor hub. Sikorsky's VS-300, flown in the bucking dance by youthful Frank Gregory, had a multiple rotor system, which was Sikorsky's way of getting around 582, but Gregory's insistence on a single rotor (and hub) had forced him to use a system that infringed Pitcairn's (ACA's) 582, among others.

As long as Vought-Sikorsky was using the patent-protected mechanisms experimentally (i.e., in-house, not for sale to anyone), no patent royalties were due. But as soon as it began selling patent-involved helicopters to anyone for a profit, the royalties became due and payable. The law was clear, precise, and indubitable, although the facts might be tried in a court of law.

Sikorsky's position was that the royalties should be paid, and let's get on with it. Earnest negotiations began forthwith between United Aircraft's legal department and Synnestvedt & Lechner and Pitcairn.

Under the law, Pitcairn had every right to demand that the Autogiro Company of America receive the full license fee or royalty provided by the law, roughly 5 percent of the selling price of each aircraft utilizing his patents.

However, in a burst of patriotism,

Pitcairn agreed to license United Aircraft and its subsidiaries, Vought-Sikorsky and Nash Kelvinator (a manufacturing subcontractor) to manufacture helicopters for the government for a negligible royalty. It was, Pitcairn believed, the greatest contribution he could make to the rotary-wing phase of the war effort. On July 22, 1943, he wrote to the commanding general, Army Air Forces Materiel Command, Wright Field:

> For some time we have been giving a lot of thought to what contribution the Autogiro Company of America might make to the country in this time of conflict, beyond the engineering assistance which we have made available to our licensees. For the good of the war effort and to conserve public funds, we have decided to reduce to a nominal rate the royalty charged for the fruits of our fifteen years of invention, development, and experience in rotary-wing aircraft. Therefore, on machines and equipment supplied to the United States Government by our licensees, we will reduce our royalty from 5% on the basis of fully-equipped machines to eighty-five one-hundredths of one per cent (.85%) of the [government] contract price, to be effective for the duration of hostilities with Germany, Japan, and Italy ...

He was practically giving away all of his rotary-wing expertise.

Pitcairn's astonishing offer was given top priority by the Wartime Royalty Adjustment Board, which quickly accepted it, adding to the duration of the reduced-royalty pe-riod, "the end of all present hostilities, plus six months," whereupon the original royalty rate would be automatically reinstituted. Since the U.S. government was the sole purchaser of helicopters at the time, the savings to the taxpayers—and the corresponding loss to Pitcairn's Autogiro Company of America—would be in excess of $5 million under then-existing contracts. Pitcairn had made more than a mere gesture.

When the war had engulfed the United States, Harold Pitcairn *personally* held nineteen patents on rotary-wing devices, including helicopters, out of the 164 patents held by the Autogiro Company of America, and he continued to use his inventive powers throughout the war years. Usually he was energetically engaged in several projects at once: early in his experimentation with Larsen, he had conceived the idea that rotary-wing torque problems could be eliminated by providing jet propulsion at the blade tips. Originally they used a pressure vessel, wound with heavy wire to contain any explosion, with the compressed air which was vented through the hollow lifting rotor blades to nozzles pointed tangentially to the disc of the rotor.

In the intervening years the new science of rocketry and jet propulsion technology had developed, and a new company, calling itself Aerojet, Inc., invited Pitcairn to Pasadena, California, to discuss a proposal to design and build a reaction-engine powered helicopter. Pitcairn crossed the continent many times on the overcrowded railroads until the character of his and Aerojet's experimentation became known to high-ranking officials who reviewed classified projects. The navy solicited Pitcairn to transfer his efforts to the Dahlgren Jet Laboratory at Annapolis, to pursue the same objective. Within days, the navy had included another new company, Reaction Motors, Inc., upon Pitcairn's recommendation, and experiments were initiated on tip-mounted propulsion units. At least Annapolis was closer to Bryn Athyn than Pasadena, so work progressed faster. For months the experimenters worked with liquid oxygen and alcohol to develop fuel mixtures for the rockets mounted on the rotor system affixed to an old PA-18 hub and pylon.

The Rand Company, also located in California, contracted with Pit-

cairn to produce subassemblies to be incorporated in a new secret weapon called a "guided missile," which required him to travel coast to coast again several times on jam-packed railroads which were transporting military personnel to and from training bases and ports of embarkation. The secrecy of the mission on which he was working required constant trips to Washington, D.C., to obtain approvals from the War Pro-

The Firestone OX-61 direct-control, jump-takeoff pusher Autogiro with enclosed "greenhouse" type canopy, later used on Sikorsky helicopters. Only one was built, with the help of Autogiro Company of America engineers. The cancellation of the contract by the government led to the subsequent design of the XR-9 helicopter by Pitcairn's engineers.

duction Board for the procurement of critical materials. Many times, as he stood in the aisles of the trains clickety-clacking along the rails, Pitcairn thought how much easier and more convenient it would be to fly a lightplane or an Autogiro, but the government had arbitrarily grounded all nonmilitary or noncommercial flying for the duration. Special dispensation was required to board the overcrowded airliners.

Pitcairn also kept in close touch with the operators of his factory building, G&A Aircraft, Inc., and from time to time assigned Stanley and Campbell to help them on special engineering problems. One of Firestone's first efforts was a rather awkward-looking pusher-type Autogiro produced for the army in its broad feasibility-testing program. Using the jump-takeoff system with a pusher engine mounted aft like the Buhl Autogiro, the G&A Autogiro had a glass-enclosed nose section for an observer and the pilot, who sat behind him, a new idea in rotary-wing aircraft. It came along just a bit too late, for by then the XR-4 helicopter had captivated the military selection board. Only one G&A Autogiro was made and the army canceled the contract.

One day soon after the cancellation order had been received, Pitcairn was at lunch with some of the Firestone and G&A executives, more or less rehashing their unsuccessful joint effort, for Pitcairn, Campbell, and Harris had contributed all of their expertise to the project, although the ship was actually built by G&A. In a casual way, one of the Firestone officials raised the issue which no one had ever mentioned subsequent to the fiery episode in the Stone Room between Ray and Larsen five years before. Not realizing that he might be treading on thin ice, the executive asked Pitcairn why, since he controlled so many rotary-wing patents, had he not developed a helicopter of his own? It was evident, he pressed on, that for the forseeable future the biggest customer—indeed the *only* customer—for rotary-wing aircraft would be the federal government, which clearly favored helicopters, because of their ability to hover. Some others at the table, knowing of the background, held their breaths, sensing that the pin had just been pulled on a long-dormant emotional grenade.

Instead, the question had provided Pitcairn with the opportunity to explain to someone who had no personal involvement and no ax to grind the chain of logic which had resulted in his single-minded approach to rotary-wing flight and its future. Slowly, methodically, Pitcairn laid out his analysis of the issues and the reasons for his conclusion that in the long run the Autogiro had more to offer for the *average flying citizen* than did the helicopter. He reviewed the ease of maintenance, alluding to the experience that he and other Autogiro users had so clearly proven. Since there was no need for the Autogiro rotor to provide both lift and thrust, there were fewer operational prob-

The XR-9 helicopter on the ramp in front of the Pitcairn hangar at Willow Grove. The single-place XR-9 was demolished at the hands of a military test pilot. The wreck was rebuilt, stretched 18 inches and made into a two-placer, as shown here. The rock-steady flying characteristics of this ship were praised by every pilot who flew it. Designed by Autogiro Company of America engineers, it was built by G&A Aircraft Company, a subsidiary of Firestone.

lems; where helicopters were requiring many hours of maintenance on the ground for each hour of flight time, Autogiros could be flown for hundreds of hours with only routine periodic maintenance, such as engine oil changes and lubrication of hub mechanisms. It was easier to fly, simple for a fixed-wing pilot to transition to, could do everything a helicopter could do, except hover in still air, and people really did not need that, except in special cases.

As he spoke, he flushed out all the pros and cons he had reviewed in his own mind so many times as he had reassessed his position. When he concluded, the Firestone official was impressed with his logic as it might apply to a purely civilian market where costs of purchasing, operating, and maintaining a flying machine might be of great importance in the decision whether or not to buy. But, he pointed out, with the government, price is no object, once the decision—whether good or bad—is made to go in a particular direction. Then he raised a pointed, very direct question: Could Pitcairn and his small engineering team work with the G&A manufacturing people to create a flyable helicopter?

Pitcairn made a tent of his fingers over his chest while he leaned back in his chair and stared at his thumbnails for several seconds. Perhaps he had been too stubborn in his position about sticking to the Autogiro. Perhaps Jim Ray had been right that night in the Stone Room. Then he looked up, took a little breath, said that of course they could design and assist Firestone in building it, and agreed to dedicate his group to that task at the Willow Grove plant.

For several months Pitcairn, Stanley, and Campbell worked on the preliminary designs of a single-place helicopter that could easily be enlarged to a two-placer. While the Autogiro Company engineers were working on the basic engineering problems, G&A applied for and received army approval to proceed with the project under the designation of XR-9.

The new design took shape slowly. Test and demonstration pilot Slim Soule worked with a mockup of the control system, including the separate collective and cyclic pitch levers, the throttle and engine controls, trying to develop a feel for the machine that was so completely foreign to any he had ever flown. Believing that the physical control system was so unlike anything with which he was familiar and not wanting to go through another episode of flying self-taught as he had in the PA-36, Slim made arrangements for helicopter instruction in some of the R-4s (the "X" designator had been removed once

the ships were accepted for service use) that had begun to appear at military airfields. It was to be a most interesting experience.

The R-4's controls, he found, were a double handful. The collective pitch control, situated by the pilot's knee, high to the left, required the constant firm grip of one hand, and the cyclic pitch control, located in the position of a conventional airplane control stick, required a similarly firm grip with the other hand. Since both levers developed substantial control feedback, they had to be grasped at all times when the machine was flying, which made for hard work aloft.

Moreover, he learned that the craft was thoroughly unstable in all axes and required constant concentration by the pilot in every flight regime. In the early models he was exposed to, Slim soon discovered that performance was marginal. One hot summer morning, when the air was dead calm, an R-4 thrashed the air in vain, attempting to take off with Slim and his instructor on board. In time, he learned the technique.

When he returned to Willow Grove, Soule was pleased to find that the XR-9 was ready for its first test flights since preparatory ground run-ups had been successfully concluded. He climbed into the clear-view cabin, started the engine, and ran it up for a while, then engaged the collective pitch as he had learned to do in the XR-4. As the overhead blades whirled around, he felt completely different sensations from those he had developed in the R-4

types. There was smoothness and a lack of vibration and absolutely no feedback on the controls. Gingerly, he increased the throttle and eased upward on the collective pitch lever, causing the helicopter to rise from the ground for perhaps eighteen inches, where it hung in full hovering flight, as steady as a rock on a string. Instead of having to grasp the controls in viselike grips, he could move them easily with the pressure of a thumb and two fingers. By the end of the week he was flying the XR-9 with the aplomb of a veteran. From the very beginning it was a beautiful flying machine and in less than a month of flight testing was converted to its two-place version, the XR-9B, in the configuration required by

Maj. Keith Wilson, U.S. Army, hovering the XR-9B at Willow Grove. He reported that it could be flown hands-off for minutes at a time, an impossibility with other helicopters he had flown. But it was born too late. By 1945 the end of the war was in sight, so there were no military orders for it.

the army. An invitation was tendered to Colonel Gregory for flight demonstrations. Pitcairn was once more elated by the latest development. Perhaps there would be a Pitcairn-designed aircraft in the war yet, even if built by another company.

Frank Gregory's introduction to the XR-9B took place at Pitcairn Field, where Slim Soule demonstrated the light control forces and easy handling characteristics of the graceful machine, rising slowly, pirouetting in hovers, climbs, and descents, moving precisely, as an ice skater might perform school figures. Then Soule stepped out and waved Gregory toward the pilot's seat.

The only flight instruction given was Slim's caution that all one needed was a light touch on the controls, totally unlike the grip-of-death required on the helicopters he had flown before. Standing only a few feet in front of the helicopter as the rotor blades began to spin up, Soule could see the momentary whitening of Colonel Gregory's knuckles as he grasped the two control columns, and Soule made hand signals for Gregory to loosen up. Then the XR-9B rose and flew under the masterful hand of the youthful colonel.

The demonstration was impressive. Gregory arranged for an early appraisal by one of the top test pilots assigned to the Wright Field evaluation group, whenever orders could be issued for his temporary transfer to Willow Grove. Since the XR-9B flew as well as, perhaps better than, its single-seat predecessor, the entire Pitcairn-Firestone team looked forward to the arrival of the acceptance test pilot, confident that their helicopter would immediately be included in the Army Air Force's evaluation program.

The much-heralded army pilot arrived a few weeks later. After he had been properly greeted and housed, he was immediately taken to Pitcairn Field and introduced to the aircraft.

After a short demonstration flight by Soule to show how sprightly its performance was, and the lightness of controls, stressing the small, delicate movements of both its cyclic and collective levers, the guest was invited to try it himself. As Gregory had done, the test pilot gripped the sticks too hard. Unlike Gregory, he ignored Slim's anxious gestures from a few feet alongside the helicopter, telling him to relax his hold. The sole example of the XR-9B rose slowly from the tarmac, then Soule saw the army pilot suddenly push the cyclic stick all the way forward, instantly standing the ship on its nose, totally destroying the blades, power train, and engine. Many observers attributed the incident to ham-handed flying, but while Slim surveyed the wreckage of the machine, which he knew was easier to fly than the R-4, he shook with anger. He believed then—and would believe forever—that the little aircraft had for some reason been deliberately wrecked.

Having proved that his engineering group was fully capable of producing a helicopter with superior performance for either military or civilian use, it might have been supposed that Pitcairn would have followed the strong trend toward that design. But his personal belief never slackened that a substantial postwar market would develop for civilian personal-use Autogiros that did not require large airfields for their operation. Many straws were flying in the wind that indicated such a development: personal-use aircraft for the civilian market after victory had been achieved were already being widely advertised in the aviation press, then dominated by military developments against the background of total global war. Pitcairn had eyed with interest the advertisements about peacetime models that would be offered by all of the lightplane manufacturers, Piper, Beech, Cessna, Aeronca, Ercoupe—even North American and Grumman were preparing to enter the market in the coming "Air Age." He decided to advertise Pitcairn Aviation's intention to provide Autogiros for the anticipated boom market. He was aware that helicopters would also be offered to the public, but was absolutely certain that they would be so expensive to purchase—and especially to maintain—and so difficult for the average person to learn to fly, that he planned to stay with the easy-to-fly rotary-wing craft called Autogiros. His market analysis still was that Autogiros were so comparatively economical that cost-sensitive individual customers would select them in large numbers for operations from small open areas near their homes, golf clubs, and resort areas. He ordered Luscombe to make a second, improved Whirlwing. His dream of producing a Safe Aircraft for the average citizen never flagged. Unfortunately, his beautiful dream was to become another casualty of the war.

Soon after the United States became embroiled in the war, the U.S. Navy had been reorganized into a number of new naval districts, each of which had its own training, operational, and administrative func-

Then . . . Aerial photo of Pitcairn Field, Hallowell/Willow Grove, as it appeared in 1929. The white circle is in the center of the field's landing area. The new Pitcairn Aircraft factory lies alongside the highway at the right. An airplane is parked in front of the hangar nearest to the camera. The second large hangar can be seen just behind the grove of trees.

tions. The aviation department of the Fourth Naval District, headquartered at Philadelphia's Navy Yard—by then known as the Naval Base—had quickly outgrown the facilities of its own Mustin Field close by the rapidly expanding Philadelphia Airport (now Philadelphia International Airport), which was then being heavily used by the Army Air Forces for training operations. The Navy began looking for possible close-in sites on which its own training and operational functions could be carried out. It did not take long to decide that the then almost unused Pitcairn Field was conveniently located, being no more than ten miles away and in wide-open farm country. In 1942 the government notified Pitcairn of its intention to acquire the airport, giving him two choices: either he could sell the field to the Navy Department for its appraised value, to be established by competent real es-

. . . and now. The United States Naval Air Station, Willow Grove, from virtually the same position. The Pitcairn Aircraft factory building is at center right, close to the highway.

tate experts; or the government would institute condemnation proceedings under its right of eminent domain, and take it. Rather than go through the protracted court proceedings involved in a condemnation suit, Pitcairn reluctantly agreed to sell it on the appraisal basis. Since it lay in the middle of a farming area, the value was set on the basis of open land. It was appraised and sold for less than one-third of what Brewster Aircraft had offered three years before. By 1943, when the XR-9B program was on the rocks, Pitcairn Field was being transformed into the Willow Grove Naval Air Station, which it remains to this day.

The government's taking of the airfield, together with all of its hangars, ramps, run-up areas, runways, and associated facilities, had excluded the large factory building which had produced in turn Mailwings, Autogiros, assault gliders, and the XR-9 helicopters. But without access to the field itself for experimental and production flight testing, the factory was of scant value as an aviation establishment, which dealt a bitter blow to Pitcairn's long-range plans. With great sadness, he ordered the beautiful little PA-36 Whirlwing and its partially finished sister ship to be cut into pieces and the aluminum shards donated to the national scrap drive. It was a black day for Harold F. Pitcairn.

Notwithstanding the emotional and financial setback, Pitcairn continued to delve into possible advances in the science of aviation technology. He requested Paul Stan-

ley to produce a compendium of all rotary-wing knowledge that had accured to the Autogiro Company of America to enable the emerging new crop of aeronautical engineers to use the accumulated information as source material.

The war was progressing favorably for the United States. Allied forces in North Africa had met to drive Rommel's Nazi legions across the Mediterranean Sea. By the summer of 1943, Allied forces had occupied Sicily and by November had invaded Italy, only a month after Mussolini had been ousted as the head of state. During 1943, Germany was being hammered day and night by heavy bombers based in the British Isles. Britain was laden with combat troops and war materiel being assembled in preparation for the Allied invasion of Europe. Across the Pacific, Allied forces were systematically taking Japanese-held islands, from tiny atolls to the huge and mountainous New Guinea. Newspapers and popular magazines—and letters from servicemen—told about the appearance of the highly unconventional aircraft called "helicopter" in all theaters of the war. In a few months, there were highly speculative and imaginative articles in the Sunday supplements about the bright future of rotary-wing aircraft. Helicopters would be as commonplace as automobiles, they predicted.

In June 1944 the long-awaited cross-channel invasion succeeded under the command of Dwight D. Eisenhower. Three months later,

Allied armies were nearing the Rhine River, as Nazi defense lines established during the occupation of France collapsed. By early fall the Nazis had their backs to the wall and their cities were being reduced to rubble. A violent counterthrust into the center of the Allied line at a place called Bastogne was the final lunge of a defeated enemy. Inexorably, the vise closed on the Third Reich. On May 5, 1945, less than a year after the invasion began, the war in Europe was over.

In the United States, government restrictions on private flying were lifted as the nation turned its full attention to the war in the Pacific.

Sikorsky helicopters of improved design were showing up at more and more military outposts, landing in open spaces in jungles and in native villages as the waves of invasion washed over Biak and the Philippine Islands and Okinawa and Iwo Jima. The helicopter was being tested under actual combat conditions, although it was not yet developed as an offensive weapon. It was a liaison ship, and sometimes a spotting craft; that was all. But it won its first reputation under fire. Most people anticipated that a long, bitter struggle confronted them against implacable enemies. During the island campaigns advancing toward the Japanese homeland, the lesson had been learned that the Japanese resisted to the last man. To the surprise of all but a handful of top administration leaders and nuclear scientists, the war against Japan ended with dramatic suddenness after American bombing planes dropped atomic weapons on the major Japanese cities of Hiroshima and Nagasaki. By the end of the year, the battered world was at peace.

With the unconditional surrenders of the Axis powers, the U.S. economy underwent an upheaval. Military contracts for armaments were canceled wholesale, causing the closing down of many aircraft factories as well as shipyards, steel mills, and gun factories. One of the victims was the Platt-LePage Company; the XR-1 contract was canceled in April. The time had come to convert from the production of war materiel to peacetime civilian goods, and the lightplane aviation industry was girding to meet an anticipated challenge to produce 100,000 lightplanes for the mass market of ex-military pilots and returning veterans that everyone agreed had been developed by aviation's great advances, spurred on by the war. A general mood of optimism pervaded the executive suites of all the aviation companies that within a few years private flying would be as natural, normal, and commonplace a form of transportation as automobiles. After a couple of false starts the Air Age had arrived at last.

# Changing the Rules

Firestone's G&A executives had also caught the postwar flying fever. They called upon Pitcairn's little group of rotary-wing engineering experts to rework the XR-9B helicopter into what would be renamed the GA-45 and directed at the specialized short-haul business market: construction companies, ranchers, earth-resource prospectors, and similar rough-terrain outfits. The refined, richly appointed GA-45 was soon being demonstrated to corporate and private prospective owners.

The GA-45 was not alone in the rotary-wing marketplace. Bell Aircraft, which had produced thousands of fighter planes during the war, had planned well for the postwar changeover. Arthur Young, a helicopter researcher and designer in the Philadelphia suburb of Paoli, had designed a helicopter of his own in 1941. With the imminent ending of the war, his product had been bought by Bell and redesignated as the Bell-47. When it was produced by the New York company for civilian sales, in March 1946, the Bell 47 was the first helicopter in history to receive an Approved Type Certificate.

Frank N. Piasecki, who had once been a draftsman for Kellett Autogiro and had also worked for Platt-LePage after completing engineering school, had formed a group called the P-V Engineering Forum. In 1943, P-V had developed and flown its own experimental helicopter (and Piasecki himself, the machine's test-pilot as well as its principal designer, had received the nation's first helicopter pilot's license from the Civil

The GA-45 was the commercial version of the XR-9B for the postwar civilian market. In this photo, Slim Soule is delivering a G&A in 1946.

The GA-45, with Slim Soule as its pilot, was demonstrated all over the east. Here he approaches to land at the front door of the still-new LaGuardia Field terminal building. When no orders for it materialized, Firestone shut down G&A Aviation and retired from the aircraft manufacturing business.

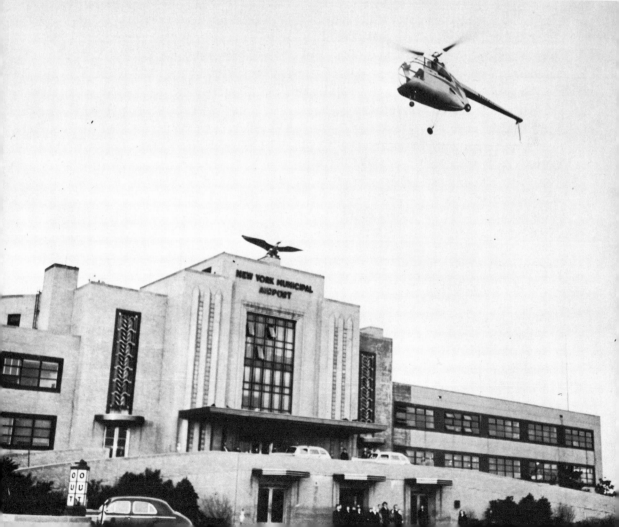

Aeronautics Administration after demonstrating his one-man prototype). Charles Kaman and Stanley Hiller were shown in newspapers and newsreels flying their own helicopter designs. Clearly, all of these developments raised questions of possible patent infringements. But before patent protection proceedings could be initiated, the issue became dormant. The peacetime aviation business, for which everyone had had such high hopes, simply collapsed.

It had looked good for a while. During 1946, the first full year of peace, at a time when the pre-existing civil aviation fleet—including all types of aircraft, from airliners to private planes—totaled less than 38,000 units, U.S. manufacturers rolled 33,254 new airplanes out of their factories, and more than 31,000 war-surplus aircraft, including light and heavy bombers, fighters, primary and advanced trainers, and cargo/troop carrying transports (mostly C-46 and C-47 types, the latter being the military designation of the classic DC-3) were sold to civilian purchasers by the Reconstruction Finance Corporation. This influx of airplanes nearly tripled the size of America's civil aviation fleet in eighteen months and saturated the market. In 1947 civil light (i.e., personally flown) aircraft sales dropped from more than 33,000 to less than 16,000 units and the following year saw the sales plummet to 7,302. Many aircraft manufacturers turned belly-up and went out of production. The civilian helicopter buyers also melted away.

Pitcairn was notified that the Firestone Tire and Rubber Company was going to terminate the lease on his factory and go back to what it did best. The GA-45 Approved Type Certificate application was withdrawn and the factory was left empty and unused, adjacent to an inaccessible airfield which was (and is) still occupied by the navy as U.S. Naval Air Station, Willow Grove.

By then Harold Pitcairn was fifty-one years old and had assumed many other business obligations which kept him increasingly occupied in nonaviation matters. His beloved Clara was not well and it became vitally important for him to be with her as frequently as possible, particularly since their children were growing up and leaving home; of their eight, only four were still at Cairncrest and he wanted to share time with them rather than spending long hours in aviation business affairs.

In the summer of 1933 he had purchased a summer home on the shore of Lake George, in upper New York State, where it was cool in the evening and he could engage on the weekends in his new hobby of sailing. For several summers he had commuted from Bryn Athyn to Lake George by Autogiro, until private flying was terminated during the war. Now he could stay there for days at a time, sailing with his family and friends, and racing nearly every weekend. Even while vacationing, he was too energetic to sit back and relax; an avid competitor, he soon organized a group of sailing enthusiasts to form a racing association which held competitions several times a week. Eventually, as the contests became formalized, Pitcairn assisted in rewriting the New York Yacht Association rules, which govern all sailboat competition in the United States.

From early youth he had been raised in an environment of religion as well as the work ethic. He had attended theological school for a time and although he subsequently elected to follow a career in business rather than the clergy, he continued to have a deep interest in matters of faith and religion. Over the course of many years, including the airmail and Autogiro eras, he participated in doctrinal classes in his church and at his home and continued to work on a compilation of selected subjects from the theological writings of Swedenborg, of whom he and his brothers, Raymond and Theodore, were devout students. He had almost put his efforts in Autogiro invention and experimentation behind him, although he kept the Autogiro Company of America active and retained Paul Stanley to continue design studies of helicopters and Autogiros. While engaged in many other business activities, Pitcairn still saw a need for less-expensive and easier-to-operate Autogiros as urban growth problems were certain to overwhelm private airports and drive them out of existence and perhaps cut down on the number of communities being served by airlines. Stanley was designing jet-engine propelled Autogiros capable of carrying up to four hundred passengers for short-range

intercity service, particularly those with small airport facilities. Cost-analysis figures projected that such equipment could produce more profit for air-carrier operators than could helicopters, but that the time to move into the market was not yet ripe, so Pitcairn decided to stay out of it for a while longer.

It was a solid, but cautious, judgment. No one was selling enough rotary-wing aircraft to make re-entering the business worthwhile: in 1946, Bell Aircraft sold a total of three and in 1947 sold only twenty-five, while Piasecki's company sold seven. On such small volume, an infringement suit would hardly be merited.

As the war had ended, so had the doors to the U.S. Treasury for military equipment purchases. Americans at every level of society were beginning to relax, trying to regain their prewar way of life, but it was not to be. America's former ally, Russia, in a test of strength of America's character and resolution, made the first move in what was soon to become known as the Cold War by blockading all surface transportation routes to and from West Berlin, which is located deep inside the Russian-controlled zone of East Germany. The United States, France, and England, as co-occupiers of West Berlin, mounted an airlift to supply the blockaded city with food, medical supplies, and coal, supplies necessary for life, to save their protectees. When the United States Air Force pulled every available transport airplane into the specially organized airlift, the full attention of its leaders, and every ordinary citizen, turned to the very real and frightening possibility of another war with a major power, this time with the atom bomb as a factor.

Military planners in the Pentagon were aware of the depth of the communist/capitalist confrontation, of which Berlin was only a part. Long-range projections indicated that if they could not make the Allies back down over Berlin, the Russians would incite other confrontations at far-flung locations all over the world, keeping Uncle Sam, the Peacemaker, on the run. Fighting such "brushfire wars," as they were called, would require a whole new arsenal of weapons to give compact fighting groups great firepower and mobility over all sorts of terrain. The equipment was at hand. What was needed were congressional appropriations to acquire it.

Although the R-4 Sikorsky helicopters had really come into service too late to have any serious impact on the outcome of the worldwide conflict, the limited use they had seen had opened the eyes of military tacticians to their potential. Frank Gregory's assertion that "anything a horse can do, a helicopter can do better," which had once been scoffed at as the overenthusiastic hyperbole of a young officer, had been shown to be accurate. Reports and recommendations of assault commanders reiterated that helicopters should be assigned to all combat operations. With the Cold War heating up, queries began to issue from the

Pentagon to Sikorsky, Bell, Piasecki, Kaman, and Hiller concerning their design and production status for military-use helicopters. The interest was not one-sided. Manufacturers were more than happy to receive such questions from the government, because there was no other market. For Harold Pitcairn, who was out of the manufacturing business, but who continued with his Autogiro Company of America to be the holder of hundreds of key rotary-wing patents, a new problem arose.

Under the terms of his World War II agreement with the United States of America, Pitcairn's patriotic waiver of virtually all of his patent royalties on helicopters during World War II had expired on March 2, 1946. Subsequent to that date he was entitled to the standard rate royalty of approximately 5 percent of the retail sales price of the complete aircraft. Reverting to this level would make a substantial difference in the amount of the income to the Autogiro Company—and to the government's cost of each helicopter. For example, at the reduced payment level, during 1944–1947, United Aircraft had paid the Autogiro Company $79,000, averaging $19,750 a year. For 1948, United Aircraft's accounting department projected that, on the basis of new government orders then on the books, whereas under the wartime fee schedule they would pay $39,000, under the newly revived normal rate, the royalties due to the Autogiro Company would jump to

$235,000. The issue was resolved by Sikorsky's renewing its lump-sum licensing agreement, but it did not take long for the entrepreneurs of all the new helicopter manufacturing companies to realize how the Autogiro Company's formidable patent position would affect their own operations, particularly if they began to receive heavy orders from the military.

Orders for helicopters were already being issued as the Congress reacted to the Berlin situation, and the amounts—especially against the paltry $300,000 of the Dorsey bill funding only a decade before—were staggering. In 1947, Kaman Helicopter, which up to then had produced less than a dozen helicopters all told, was concluding negotiations with the navy on a contract for $26 *million!* Bell, Piasecki, and Hiller were closeted with government negotiators. And, of course, Sikorsky was sitting on the top of a pile of orders and paying the Autogiro Company royalties on a specially negotiated contract.

Everyone in the industry had to bargain with the government while speculating what Pitcairn's patent royalty position would be in the future, since it was common knowledge that the Autogiro Company of America held key patents needed to produce helicopters—memoranda that circulated within the newer companies indicated that they had examined and evaluated the situation very thoroughly. Piasecki's patent counsel advised forthrightly, "We find that we apparently infringe ten patents held by the Autogiro Company of America," then continued: "The validity of these patents cannot easily be questioned as they appear to be very well drawn up by counsel not only skilled in patent practice but very familiar with the rotary-wing art."

Then it was recommended that, first, Piasecki should find what other manufacturers' attitudes were toward Autogiro Company patents and also should ascertain from Pitcairn how much a license from Autogiro Company would cost.

For months, as industry-government negotiations continued, no one else seriously discussed licensing with the Autogiro Company. To bring matters to a head, after consultation with his own patent attorneys, Pitcairn decided to obtain a Bell helicopter—since the Bell-47 had been type-certificated and was being sold commercially without paying Autogiro Company any royalties—to ascertain whether there were any infringements and to be able to make an informed judgment as to their next step. Slim Soule, then engaged in aerial application of cranberry bogs in New England, was using two Bells in his operation and agreed to fly one to the lawn at Cairncrest, where he had landed so many times before in Autogiros, for a close examination by the patent lawyers, engineers, and technical experts of the Autogiro Company.

Their examination was thorough, to the point of disassembling some parts, then taking photographs and making drawings. When the investi-

gation was over, Pitcairn's group had compiled a long list of patent infringements in the Bell machine. Now the issue could be framed, but the decision of whether or not to proceed would have to be that of Harold Pitcairn. Clearly, at least one helicopter manufacturer, Bell, had elected to go ahead without obtaining a license, although some of the others were engaging in discussions short of actual negotiations with his patent firm, Synnestvedt & Lechner. If any one manufacturer went into commercial or military production without such a license, Pitcairn had only two alternatives: he could let the matter go without prosecuting his patent-protected position, or he could stand up and fight. It was not a decision to be lightly entered into, for at least four new helicopter firms were then in existence with the possibility of others coming into being at any time, which could lead to a multiplicity of lawsuits in different courts, in dif-

Council of war. When Harold Pitcairn made the decision to sue the United States of America to protect his patent position, these were the men upon whom he depended to help prepare the case. A key participant, in left foreground, is Raymond Synnestvedt, who had advised Pitcairn in 1924 to protect his helicopter inventions by patenting them. To his right is Kenneth Synnestvedt, his brother and professional associate. At the right rear, with the moustache and wearing the dark suit, is chief engineer Paul H. Stanley.

ferent parts of the country, at great and duplicated expense to the Autogiro Company. On the other hand, as a tactical stroke he could hit Bell Aircraft with a suit to show his intention to assert his rights, which might have the effect of pulling them all into line, thereby ending the controversy.

For several evenings Pitcairn sat alone in his Cairncrest study, wrestling with the decision. Over a span of twenty years he had spent almost $4 million of his private funds on rotary-wing research and development in his single-minded objective of producing the Safe Aircraft for the common man. Under the law of the land, the patents which he had accumulated were entitled to the same protection as the products of any other inventors: not to be used by manufacturers who took advantage of their inventions, unless they were compensated for such use. He decided to sue.

With the decision made, he stood up and stretched. Then, as he had done almost every evening since 1932, he slid open the right-hand desk drawer, picked up his Savage .32 automatic pistol, and made the rounds of the lower floors of his stately home, assuring himself that all windows and doors were secure against prowlers.

Suit was begun in 1948 in the Federal District Court for the Northern District of New York against the Bell Helicopter Corporation with appropriate publicity so that all other infringers would be sure to know about it. However, the institution of the action was also noted in other quarters: the principal government procurement officer for helicopters had for some time been opposed to the suppliers paying royalties to the Autogiro Company and had in fact advised them not to do so. It was an incredibly high-handed position for the government lawyer to take.

The intent of the Congress in such matters had been clearly stated in the language of the act of 1910 creating the United States Court of Claims [28 U.S.C. Sec. 1498] which provided as follows:

> Whenever an invention described in and covered by a patent of the United States is used or manufactured by or for the United States without license of the owner thereof or lawful right to use or manufacture the same, *the owner's remedy shall be by action against the United States*, in the Court of Claims for the recovery of his reasonable and entire compensation for such use and manufacture. [Emphasis added.]

As a result of this clear, precise, and unambiguous language, for more than forty-five years all government contracts for materiel or equipment had included a clause to protect the government from such patent-claim lawsuits by specifying that the contractor/supplier was legally bound to indemnify (i.e., insure) the government/purchaser against any such infringement claims and judgments. That provision placed the onus on manufacturers to make certain that no patent-protected devices would be incorporated in machinery provided to the government under the procurement contract, unless the manufacturer held a license to do so. Two methods were available for manufacturers to avoid liability: first, each manufacturer could negotiate a license agreement with the patent holder on which an agreed-upon royalty would be paid, usually at a lower rate than the statutory amount—as United Aircraft (Vought-Sikorsky) had done with the Autogiro Company of America—or, second, the government itself could obtain a blanket license for all patent-protected equipment procured by it and pay the royalty fees directly to the patent holder.

Since there was no question about the validity and protection of the Autogiro Company's array of patents, one would suppose that the action against Bell would have had a catalytic effect on the industry, prompting an across-the-board group of applications, particularly as United Aircraft's negotiated contract for Sikorsky helicopters had obviously not done their program any harm. But it didn't happen. Instead, everyone sat back to see what was going to develop as far as his competitors were involved. Pitcairn's legal advisers indicated that, as they had feared, he might be involved in a long-term war of attrition, taking opponents on one at a time in the abnormally drawn-out proceedings of a patent prosecution. On advice of counsel, Pitcairn agreed to withdraw the claim in *Autogiro Company of America, Inc.* vs. *Bell Helicopter Corp.* without prejudice (which means in legal language that he could re-institute the case again, if he should want to) and then reviewed the situation.

The first indication that the ice was cracking was an invitation from the Navy Department patent lawyer charged with military helicopter procurement to discuss the possibilities of a government blanket license.

Apparently this invitation was relayed to all manufacturers who were still hanging on the issue of obtaining licenses. Then Synnestvedt & Lechner heard a disturbing rumor that the navy lawyer with whom they were presumably negotiating was engineering a change in the law. Nevertheless, negotiations continued between Raymond Synnestvedt and Harold Pitcairn on one side and the Navy Department procurement lawyers on the other. Then the bomb went off.

Meeting in the naval headquarters building in Washington, Pitcairn and his attorney were abruptly informed that the standard military procurement contract had been rewritten to reverse unilaterally the long-standing government policy. Simply by eliminating the contract indemnity clause, instead of the suppliers being responsible for patent infringement damages created by Congress, the government of the United States would save the suppliers harmless; it, the United States government, would indemnify *them*. The navy lawyer had already told at least one of the suppliers* that the navy would "take care of everything."

Pitcairn and Synnestvedt were thunderstruck. This meant that to recover its legally protected patent royalties, the Autogiro Company of America would have to bring suit against the United States of Amer-

---

* Frank N. Piasecki, who would so testify under oath.

ica in the Court of Claims. The navy lawyer acknowledged that fact. Furthermore, he made it painfully clear that if the Autogiro Company did sue the government, he would exert every effort to have the full weight of the government's legal departments thrown against any such ac-

tion and that the prosecution of such a lawsuit could take as long as fifteen years, by which time all of the old Autogiro patents would have run out and the plaintiff company would end up recovering nothing.

With that, he coldly ushered his visitors to the door.

# The Lawsuit

The Korean War was "the Helicopter War." Rotary-wing aircraft were used for transportation, gunnery, ambulance service, and assault landings. Military leaders were calling for more helicopters. The pioneer's dream had come true, but for Pitcairn, all the work and accomplishment seemed lost. By an arbitrary change in the fine print of military contracts, Pitcairn's Autogiro Company of America was excluded from the patent protection it *deserved* under the law. Involved were millions of dollars.

Harold Pitcairn returned to Bryn Athyn almost in a state of shock. As a staunch patriot and believer in the American way of life, he had been stunned, for he could not conceive that such a thing could come about in a country founded on the premise that what was right, was right. He had once voluntarily almost *given* his legal rights away in the service of his country, but he would not allow them to be *taken* from him, unfairly, by a bully. His ordinarily calm face darkened with rage as the unfairness of the situation sank in.

For hours he sat in his little study, collecting his thoughts.

"Very well," he said in deceptively soft tones to the four walls of the little room, "we will sue the government." It had become, to him, a matter of principle. Justice would prevail, eventually.

The lawsuit, officially captioned *Autogiro Company of America* vs. *The United States of America* commenced after long months of preparation, on September 21, 1951. This was the first of a two-part trial, the form of which is peculiar to patent infringement cases. The first trial was based upon the primary issue of the government's liability for its alleged infringements of the Autogiro Company's many patents. Only after that had been tried, a decision been made by the court, an appeal taken to a higher court, and the liability issue settled at law, could the second trial on the issue of damages—the plaintiff's "reasonable and entire compensation"—begin. It was going to take a long time to get that far.

True to his word, the government's patent lawyer aided his trial

Honorable Donald E. Lane, who heard and decided the epic patent case.

Ralph H. McClarren, one of America's first rotary wing engineers and a principal witness during the patent litigation.

counsel in drawing out the proceedings interminably. Objections were interposed at every turn, from the very beginning of the earliest phase of the case, known as "discovery process." Four long years were consumed in the drudgery of pretrial proceedings, interrogatories, depositions, and in examining files, page by page. The legal convolutions involved overtaxed the manpower facilities of Synnestvedt & Lechner, so they induced J. Edward Shinn, a prominent trial lawyer with whom they had been associated in the original suit against Bell Helicopter in New York, to join their firm. Shinn was tough, dogged, and thorough, never losing sight of his objective or becoming discouraged by the innumerable twists and turns of the

path toward the facts. Every time Shinn filed a motion to produce information, the government objected, which meant that every point had to be argued before proceeding further. It took fifteen hundred days of constant battling to assemble the material required to prepare for trial on the merits of the case.

The actual trial before the trial commissioner appointed by the court began on May 18, 1958, not quite seven years from the date the action was instituted, with Shinn still carrying the load, ably assisted by Kenneth and Raymond Synnestvedt—the same Raymond Synnestvedt who had set Harold Pitcairn on the course of patenting his inventions thirty-four years before.

The self-satisfied smugness of the

government's lawyers dwindled as it became evident that Shinn had marshaled a powerful host of witnesses to present the facts of his case: Harold Pitcairn, the Synnestvedt brothers, James H. Ray, Brigadier General H. Franklin Gregory, Ralph H. McClarren, and Frank N. Piasecki, who told the whole sordid story of the government procurement officer's course of action to circumvent the royalty payments rightfully due Pitcairn's Autogiro Company of America. Shinn had a motion picture prepared by Carl Gunther, Pitcairn's historian and archivist, to show the pioneer rotary-wing developments of Pitcairn and his engineers.

It was a dramatic piece of proof when the flickering screen in the darkened courtroom showed the PCA-1 and the PCA-2 flying in formation over Manhattan Island; the PA-19 Cabin Ship landing in Soldiers' Field; Jim Ray landing on the White House lawn and his AC-35 delivery on a grass plot in downtown Washington. The early expertise in vertical lift and descent was proved beyond any question when the screen showed Slim Soule climb into the PA-36, make a twenty-foot-high jump-takeoff, and fly away. Shinn smiled grimly as he meticulously laid one small legal and factual brick after another to create a legal edifice which would be not only imposing, but impregnable.

Harold Pitcairn was then fifty-nine years old, almost completely withdrawn from aviation, so that he could devote more of his time to nu-

merous business and philanthropic interests. His brother Raymond, then seventy-three, had relinquished many posts and Harold, as executive vice-president of Pitcairn Incorporated, the holding company for the family interests, was deeply involved with its multifaceted activities, as well as serving on boards of directors of many other large corporations. It was not generally known that he continued to retain Paul Stanley on the payroll of the Autogiro Company to design advanced versions of Autogiros for personal and feeder-line transportation. Stanley was one of the last of the group Pitcairn had pulled together to make aviation and Autogiro history; Geof Childs had passed on to his reward, and seldom did Harold see either Edwin Asplundh or Bing Seymour, both of whom lived in western Pennsylvania. He had made up with Agnew Larsen and Jim Ray, though he had had no contact with either for several years, until Ray showed up as one of his key witnesses.

Although the court proceedings were going well, according to Shinn, Pitcairn was concerned about the effect the trial was having on his old friends and contemporaries who were carrying the testimonial load, including the Synnestvedts and McClarren, who was on the witness stand for both direct and cross-examination for 108 trial days. Presenting evidence covering both the details of construction and the chronology of rotary-wing developments and inventions required relentless, time-consuming, mind-bending con-

Photo in Court Room, Court of Claims, Washington, D.C. Left to right: Donald E. Lane, Commissioner, Court of Claims; Donald Johnson, Court Reporter; Ralph H. McClarren, Expert Witness for Plaintiff; James G. Ray, Expert Witness for Plaintiff; Raymond H. Synnestvedt, Counsel for Plaintiff; Kenneth P. Synnestvedt, Technical Patent Advisor; Esther J. Freeh, Assistant to Counsel for Plaintiff; J. Edward Shinn, Chief Trial Counsel for Plaintiff; Betty Greeley, Kenneth P. Synnestvedt's Secretary; Foreground, left to right: Francis H. Fassett, Government Trial Counsel; Carl B. Harper, Technical Consultant for Defendant; W.B. Schmidt, Assistant to Trial Counsel for Defendant.

centration, without respite, day and night, month after month, year after year, and Pitcairn was concerned about the toll it might be taking. Fatigue had etched new lines in their faces and shadows had developed under their eyes. Pitcairn hoped that the coming of spring would rejuvenate all their spirits and that soon the travail would end.

Spring was coming, indeed. The hours of sunshine were appreciably longer each day and Cairncrest's broad lawns, where Autogiros used to land, were greening. Brightly colored flowers were beginning to bloom and trees were budding out with new mantles of leaves as the entire Clan Pitcairn looked forward to a festive occasion: on April 23, 1960, Raymond Pitcairn's seventy-fifth birthday party would bring many old friends and family members together for the large party that had been arranged in Bryn Athyn's

Assembly Hall. For a few hours it would be like old times. Ed Asplundh, recently elected chairman of the board of Pittsburgh Plate Glass Company, and his wife had accepted Clara's invitation to stay at Cairncrest; as did Bishop and Mrs. DeCharms, who had traveled with the Pitcairns to observe airline developments in Europe in 1924. Son John would be under their roof for a night or two—Clara could still hear in memory the sounds of their childrens' footsteps pounding up and down the circular stairway and halls of the homestead in which they had been raised. She had missed those sounds of activity. Sometimes, to her the big home seemed depressingly empty, even with Harold at her side.

A few days before the party Shinn received a telephone call from Pitcairn, expressing his personal concern with the cumulative effects of the constant strain on his friends Raymond and Ralph and asking how much longer the situation would continue. Shinn cheerfully calmed his client's fears. The case was progressing favorably on all points, he said, although it was slow going because of the nature of technically oriented adversary proceedings. Both of the older men working with him were sound mentally and physically. Furthermore, he would soon be moving on to other witnesses, so the older men were almost finished with their stints on the witness stand. Pitcairn expressed his gratefulness to Shinn for putting his mind at ease and said that he was looking forward to the next trial session.

Raymond Pitcairn's birthday party was a resounding success, attended by more than 450 guests, who enjoyed the festivity and fun. Harold, as master of ceremonies, although normally quiet, diffident, and reserved, was almost ebullient and made humorous remarks, frequently bringing down the house as he introduced attendees who in turn toasted the guest of honor. He read congratulatory letters and telegrams from high government officials, including President Eisenhower and Vice President Nixon, as well as notes from workmen and artisans who had toiled years before under Raymond's direction during the construction of what had become the world-famous Bryn Athyn Cathedral. Social, industrial, and political leaders from all over the world felicited Raymond. It was one of those heartwarming occasions that linger in memory long after the crowds of guests have disappeared.

As the party broke up with people waving and calling good-byes, the Pitcairns, their son John, and house guests the Asplundhs gathered their possessions and returned by automobile to nearby Cairncrest, reminiscing about the exhilarating evening. As they filed through the great oaken front door and strolled down the hallway toward the grand staircase, their host excused himself for a moment, allowing the others to precede him upstairs to their sleeping quarters. He stepped into the wood-paneled study just off to the right of the hallway, waved a cheery good-night, and said he would be up in a minute.

Clara recognized her husband's normal routine of going about the house's ground floor to secure all windows and doors, usually a ten-minute undertaking, and was preparing for bed when the stillness of the night was shattered by a gunshot.

Clara, whose bedroom was closest to the stairway, rushed pell-mell down the steps and found her husband alone in his study, slumped over his desk, his small Savage automatic pistol at his side. Harold Frederick Pitcairn was dead.

# Final Decision

Harold Pitcairn's death posed an enigma that was complicated by the fact that the event was misreported in the press and without all of the evidence having been made public. The night reporter who had telephoned the wire services of several major newspapers omitted the most important word in the coroner's report—*accidental*—so that the next morning's headlines reported Pitcairn's death merely as a suicide. Yet there was no note, no indication of depression or unhappiness. In addition, the police investigation disclosed that two shots had been fired; one had penetrated the ceiling directly over the desk in the first-floor study, another had struck Pitcairn in the eye. The next morning it was discovered that the semi-automatic pistol was defective: when cocked, it had a supersensitive "hair trigger," and it had a faulty disconnector so that it would fire more than one shot at a time, a condition known as "doubling." None of this information ever came out. Mrs. Pitcairn declared that she never wanted to hear another word about the tragedy.

The court case proceeded. The sheer enormity of the case beggars description: in the forty-six months of the trial on the merits, there were 186 trial sessions. Fourteen witnesses testified, some for as long as three months at a time. Over 1,000 exhibits were presented and 14,766 pages of testimony were transcripted. Documentary evidence bulged the examiner's files. And at the end of the case the parties requested findings of fact and conclusions of law in briefs that ran to 4,000 pages.

Four more years were consumed while the trial commissioner studied the voluminous record and the requests; not until March 5, 1966, were his findings printed in a 232-page document. He found that the patents held by the Autogiro Company of America were valid and had been infringed, and that the United States government was liable. The underlying conclusion was that Harold Pitcairn had been the key person in the development of the rotary-wing industry in the United

States, a true pioneer.

The law's delay took a bite out of the following year before the motions for a new trial filed by the government were briefed, argued, and disposed of, followed in due course by an appeal to the United States Supreme Court, when the trial commissioner's findings were sustained. Not until July 9, 1973, did the second-phase trial (on the issue of compensatory damages) begin. This legal marathon took another year, 8,700 pages of testimony, and 790 exhibits, with the government fighting at every turn.

Again the trial commissioner found in favor of the Autogiro Company. Again the government filed appeals and motions for a new trial, all of which had to be argued. The full Court of Claims took the case under advisement.

On July 12, 1977, the seven-judge court awarded the plaintiff $31.4 million dollars in damages—$14.4 million in actual royalties, plus another $17 million in "delay compensation," a penalty assessed against the government for putting the private company to trial of a case to recover royalties which should have been rightly paid to it in the first place.

On July 23, 1977, the U.S. Supreme Court declared the matter ended after twenty-six years of litigation. The award of an additional $600,000 in delay compensation brought the total to $32,048,738 and a draft on the Treasury of the United States was forwarded to plaintiff's counsel.

The highest court in the land had declared, as a matter of fact and law, that Harold F. Pitcairn, who had founded Eastern Airlines, had also founded America's rotary-wing industry. At last, justice had prevailed.

# Appendix

## EARLY PITCAIRN BIPLANE SERIES

| | PA-1 Fleetwing | PA-2 OX-5 Sesquiwing | PA-2 C6A Sesquiwing | PA-3 Orowing | PA-4 Fleetwing II |
|---|---|---|---|---|---|
| Wing Span Upper | 38' | 32' | 32' | 36' | 33' |
| Wing Span Lower | 33' 1" | 24' 8½" | 24' 8½" | 35' 11¾" | 30' |
| O.A.L. | 25' 11" | 22' 10⅛" | 22' 6¼" | 26' 2" | 22' 1¾" |
| O.A.H. | 9' 11¼" | 8' 4¼" | 8' 4¼" | 9' 2" | 8' 11" |
| Wing Area Sq. Ft. | 350.67 | 219.8 | 219.80 | 338.37 | 252 |
| Gap at Fuselage | 6' | 5' 1¼" | 5' 1¼" | 64⅞" | 62" |
| Stagger | 25" | 19¹⁵⁄₁₆" | 19¹⁵⁄₁₆" | 14¾" | 18" |
| Weight Empty | 1802 | 1369.6 | 1488.4 | 1345 | 1165 |
| Total Weight | 2879 | 2091.6 | 2218.4 | 2100 | 1950 |
| Useful Load | 1077 | 722.0 | 730 | 755 | 785 |
| Wing Loading, Lbs./Sq. Ft. | 8.24 | 9.5 | 10.1 | 6.2 | 7.7 |
| Power Loading, Lbs./H.P. | 18.0 | 17.4 | 12.45 | 23.35 | 21.7 |
| Fuel Capacity | 38 | 30 | 30 | 30 | 38 |
| Max. Speed | 106.2 | 120 | 145 | 90 | 102 |
| Cruise Speed | 80 | 96 | 116 | 80 | 87 |
| Stall Speed | 48 | 64.5 | 66 | 46 | 45 |
| Rate of Climb Full Gross FPM | N/A | 600 | 950 | N/A | 600 |
| Payload | 800 | N/A | N/A | 300 | 340 |
| Engine | Curtiss C-6 | OX-5 | C-6 | OX-5 | OX-5 |
| H.P. | 160 at 1750 | 90 | 160 | 90 at 1400 RPM | 90 |
| Cargo Space | 4 Pass. | Racer | Racer | 2 Pass. | 2 Pass. |
| Approximate Price | 4,500 | N/A | 5,000 | 1,850 | 2,850 |
| Date Manufactured | 1925 | 1926 | 1926 | 1926 | 1927 |

# PITCAIRN MAILWING SERIES

| | PA-5 Mailwing | PA-5 Sport Mailwing | PA-6 Super Mailwing | PA-6 Sport Mailwing | PA-6B* Sport Mailwing | PA-7M Mailwing | PA-7 Sport Mailwing | PA-8M Super Mailwing |
|---|---|---|---|---|---|---|---|---|
| Wing Span Upper | 33' | 33' | 33' | 33' | 33' | 33' | 33' | 35' |
| Wing Span Lower | 30' | 30' | 30' | 30' | 30' | 30' 3½" | 30' 3½" | 32' |
| O.A.L. | 21' 10½" | 21' 10½" | 22' 10½" | 22' 10½" | 22' 10½" | 23' 9" | 23' 9" | 24' 10" |
| O.A.H. | 9' | 9' | 9' 3" | 9' 3" | 9' 3" | 9' 6½" | 9' 6½" | 9' 9" |
| Wing Area Sq. Ft. | 252 | 252 | 252 | 252 | 252 | 243½ | 243½ | 278 |
| Gap at Fuselage | 62" | 62" | 63" | 62" | 62" | 62" | 62" | 63" |
| Stagger | 22" | 22" | 22" | 22" | 22" | 22" | 22" | 22" |
| Weight Empty | 1612 | 1612 | 1840 | 1892 | 1892 | 1820 | 1820 | 2294 |
| Gross Weight | 2620 | 2620 | 3000 | 3050 | 3050 | 3050 | 2950 | 4000 |
| Useful Load | 1008 | 1008 | 1295 | 1295 | 1295 | 1229 | 1129 | 1706 |
| Wing Loading | 10.4 | 10.4 | 11.5 | 12.1 | 12.1 | 12.5 | 12.1 | 14.4 |
| Power Loading | 11.9 | 11.9 | 13.6 | 13.8 | 13.8 | 12.7 | 12.3 | 13.3 |
| Gas Tank | 56.5 | 56.5 | 63 | 63 | 63 | 63 | 70 | 80 |
| Oil Tank | 6 | 10 | 6 | 6 | 6 | 6 | 6 | 8 |
| High Speed | 131 | 131 | 128 | 128 | 144 | 145 | 145 | 150 |
| Cruise Speed | 112 | 112 | 110 | 110 | 120 | 120 | 120 | 122 |
| Stall Speed | 45 | 45 | 45 | 45 | 45 | 45 | 45 | 50 |
| Rate of Climb Full Gross | 100 Ft/Min | 1100 Ft/Min | 900 Ft/Min | 900 Ft/Min | 900 Ft/Min | 900 Ft/Min | 900 Ft/Min | 1100 Ft/Min |
| Payload | 500 | 500–600 | 500–600 | 500–600 | 500–600 | 636 | 636 | 1000 |
| Engine | Wright J5-9 | Wright J5-9 | Wright J5-9 | Wright J5-9 | Wright J5-9 | Wright J6-7 | Wright J6-7 | Wright J6-9 P&W Wasp, Jr. |
| H.P. | 220 | 220 | 220 | 220 | 220 | 240 | 240 | 300 |
| Cargo Space | 22 cu.ft. | 2 Pass. | 40 cu.ft. | 2 Pass. | 2 Pass. | 42 cu.ft. | 2 Pass. | 55 cu.ft. |
| Approximate Price | 9,850 | 10,000 | 11,500 | 11,000 | 11,500 | 8,550 | 8,000 | 12,500 |
| Date Manufactured | 1927–1928 | 1927–1928 | 1928–1929 | 1928–1929 | 1928–1929 | 1929–1930 | 1929–1930 | 1931 |

*N.A.C.A.—Low Drag Engine Cowling

# PITCAIRN AUTOGIROS

| | PCA-1-2 | PCA-3[1] | PA-1-1 | PA-18 | PA-19 | PA-20[2] | PA-21[1] | PA-22 | PA-24[2] | PA-33 (YG-2) | PA-34 (XOP-2) | PA-36 | PA-39 | AC-35 |
|---|---|---|---|---|---|---|---|---|---|---|---|---|---|---|
| Rotor Diameter | 45' | 45' | 37' | 40' | 50' 7½" | 37' | 45' | 32' | 40' | 50' | 50' | 40' | 42' 3" | 34' 3½" |
| No. of Blades | 4 | 4 | 4 | 4 | 4 | 4 | 4 | 3 | 4 | 3 | 3 | 3 | 3 | 3 |
| Fixed Wing Span | 30' 0" | 30' | 22' 9" | 21' 3" | 30' 8" | 22' 9" | 30' 8" | None | 22' 9" | None | None | None | None | None |
| O.A.L. | 23' 1" | 23' 1" | 18' 7" | 19' 5" | 25' 9" | 18' 7" | 23' 1" | 20' 10½" | 18' 7" | 22' 8" | 22' 8" | 20' 5" | 20' 4¾" | 22' |
| O.A.H. | 13' | 13' 4" | 11' 10" | 11' 4" | 13' 9½" | 11' 10" | 13' 4" | 8' 3½" | 11' 10" | 11' 6" | 11' 6" | 10' 3½" | 9' 11½" | 8' 2" |
| Rotor Blade Chord | 22" | 22" | 18.6" | 18.6" | 22" | 18.6" | 22" | 15" | 18.6" | 18½" | 18½" | 17.7"–10.5" Tapered | None | 12" |
| Wing Chord at Root | 52" | 52" | 30" | 36" | 60" | 30" | 52" | None | 30" | None | None | None | None | None |
| Wing Chord at Tip | 30" | 30" | 30" | 36" | 24" | 30" | 30" | None | 30" | None | None | None | None | None |
| Fixed Wing Area Sq. Ft. | 88 | 88 | 51.6 | 55.0 | 95.5 | 51.6 | 88 | None | 51.6 | None | None | None | None | None |
| Weight Empty | 2093 | 2121 | 1178 | 1344 | 2681 | 1198 | 2029 | 600 | 1257 | 2453 | 2429 | 961 | 1340 | 828 |
| Gross Weight | 3000 | 3063 | 1750 | 1900 | 4041 | 1770 | 3000 | 1140 | 1800 | 3300 | 3302 | 1541 | 1946 | 1300 |
| Useful Load | 907 | 942 | 572 | 556 | 1360 | 572 | 971 | 460 | 543 | 747 | 873 | 580 | 606 | 472 |
| Payload | 375 | 408 | 214 | 180 | 590 | 214 | N/A | 170 | 183 | 281 | 307 | 290 | | 208 |
| Max. Speed | 118 | 120 | 120 | 100 | 130 | 88 | N/A | 105 | 100 | 150 | 150 | 120 | 117 | 115 |
| Cruise Speed MPH | 98 | 100 | 75 | 85 | 100 | 79 | N/A | 90 | 87 | 125 | 125. | 105 | 98 | 100 |
| Slow Flight MPH | 20–25 | 20–25 | 20–25 | 20–25 | 20–25 | 20–25 | 20–25 | 17 | 20–25 | 20–30 | 20–30 | 15 | 22.1 | 20–25 |
| Rate of Climb FPM | 800 | 800 | 550 | 700 | 850 | 550 | N/A | N/A | 750 | 870 | 870 | N/A | 933 | 720 |
| Direct Control | No | No | No | No | No | No | No | Yes | No | Yes | Yes | Yes | Yes | Yes |
| Jump Take-Off | No | No | No | No | No | No | No | Yes | No | No | No | Yes | Yes | No |
| Jump-Off Height | No | No | No | No | No | No | No | 3'-4' | No | No | No | 35' | 25' | No |
| Roadable | No | No | No | No | No | No | No | By Prop. Only | No | No | No | Yes, 35 MPH | No | Yes, 30 MPH |
| Service Ceiling | 15,000 | 1,500 | 10,000 | 12,000 | 12,500 | 7,150 | N/A | N/A | 12,000 | 13,700 | 13,700 | N/A | 14,500 | 12,900 |
| Fuel Capacity | 52 | 52 | 27 | 30 | 90 | 27 | 52 | 17 | 27 | 66 | 66 | N/A | 20.4 | 18 |
| Engine | Wright R975 | P&W Wasp, Jr. R985 | Kinner B5 | Kinner R5 | Wright R975-E2 | Kinner B5 | Wright R975-E2 | Pobjoy "R" Niagra | Kinner R5 | Wright R975-E2 | Wright R975-E2 | Warner Super Scarab SS-598-E | Warner 165D | Pobjoy Cascade |
| H.P. | 300 | 300 | 125 | 160 | 420 | 125 | 420 | 84 | 160 | 420 | 420 | 165 | 175 | 90 |
| Price | 15,000 | 15,000 | 6,750 | 4,940 | 14,950 | 3,900 | 15,750 | Experimental | Modification of PAA-1 | N/A | N/A | Experimental | N/A | Experimental |
| Date Manufactured | 1930–1932 | 1931 | 1931–1932 | 1932–1933 | 1933–1934 | 1933 | 1931 | 1933 | 1933 | 1935 | 1935 | 1939 | 1940 | 1935 |

[1]Same as PCA-2 except for engine
[2]Modified PAA-1

## PITCAIRN AUTOGIROS
## S.G.T.A. DESIGN CONCEPT
### SUBMERGED GAS TURBINE AUTOGIRO

| Model | Gross Weight | No. of Engines | H.P. | Seats | Top Speed* MPH | Min. Speed | Rate of Climb* | Vertical Climb* |
|---|---|---|---|---|---|---|---|---|
| SGTA-1 | 3000 | 2 | 500 | 4 | 173 | 6.8 | 3475 | |
| SGTA-2 | 13,399 | 1 | 2200 | 23 | 242.5 | 25.5 | 3860 | |
| SGTA-2A | 12,269 | 2 | 2500 | 17 | 260.5 | 20.5 | 4550 | |
| SGTA-2B | 15,988 | 2 | 2500 | 22 | 260 | 25 | 4025 | |
| SGTA-2C | 20,000 | 2 | 4400 | 27 | 276 | 24 | 4285 | |
| SGTA-3 | 33,316 | 2 | 5300 | 45 | 280 | 27.2 | 3425 | |
| SGTA-4A | 4940 | 2 | 950 | 6 | 216 | 20 | 3225 | |
| SGTA-5 | 12,500 | 2 | 2500 | 2 | 277 | 18.5 | 4490 | |
| SGTA-5B | 12,500 | 2 | 2500 | 2 | 364.5 | 0 | 8700 | 1500 |
| SGTA-6 | 64,000 | 2 | 9320 | 84 | 356 | 16.5 | 5310 | |
| SGTA-7 | 320,000 | 8 | 39,280 | 400 | 402 | 42 | 4250 | |

*In gyrodyne configuration. Bleed jet exhaust gas through blade tip during take-off, landing, climb and hover.

## C.F.A. DESIGN CONCEPT
### CRUISE FAN AUTOGIRO

| Model | Gross Weight | No. of Engines | Thrust | Seats | Top Speed MPH | Min. Speed | Rate of Climb* | Vertical Climb** |
|---|---|---|---|---|---|---|---|---|
| CFA-1 | 293,047 | 4 | 44,800 | 400 | 400 | 24 | 6000 | |
| CFA-2 | 68,241 | 4 | 10,040 | 100 | 406 | 18 | 6000 | |
| CFA-3 | 18,871 | 2 | 8250 | 20 | 357 | 0 | 9110 | 1970 |
| CFA-4 | 75,760 | 2 | 8250 | 100 | 400 | 0 | 6090 | 243 |
| CFA-5 | 300,000 | 4 | 44,800 | 400 | 400 | 0 | 6090 | |
| CFA-6 | 3929 | 2 | 1192 | 5 | 220 | 0 | 5300 | 262 |
| CFA-7 | 12,029 | 2 | 4400 | 15 | 377 | 0 | 12,070 | 3180 |

*Bleed exhaust gas through blade tips or use separate turbine to give blade tip jet propulsion. Used only to hover, climb, land and take-off.

**Cruise fan jet pods tilted down 45° for take-off and climb.

## *EARLY PITCAIRN BIPLANE SERIES*

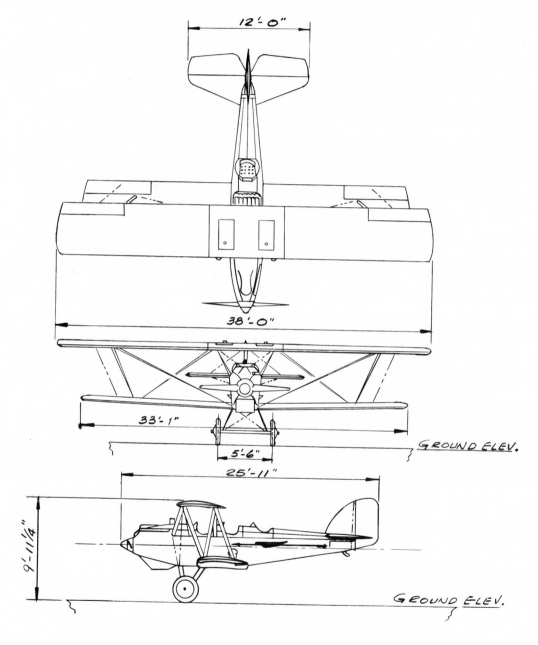

PITCAIRN AVIATION, INC.
PHILA., PA.
"FLEETWING"   PA-1
ENGINE - CURTISS C-6

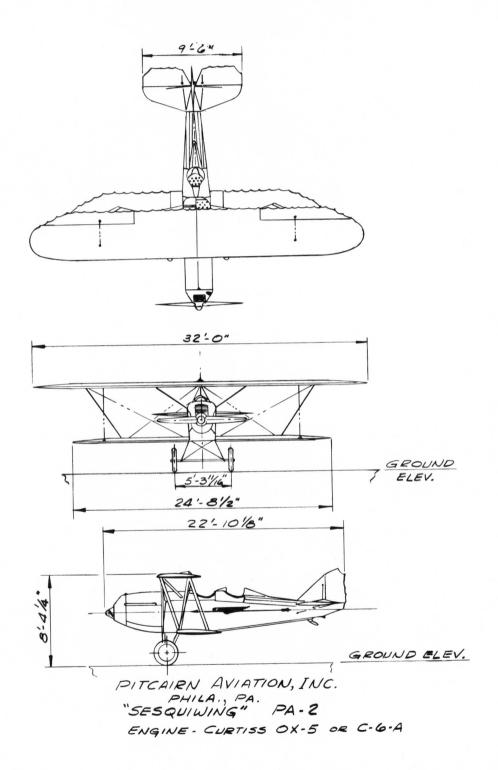

9'-6"

32'-0"

5'-3 11/16"

24'-8 1/2"

22'-10 1/8"

8'-4 1/4"

GROUND ELEV.

GROUND ELEV.

PITCAIRN AVIATION, INC.
PHILA., PA.
"SESQUIWING"  PA-2
ENGINE - CURTISS OX-5 OR C-6-A

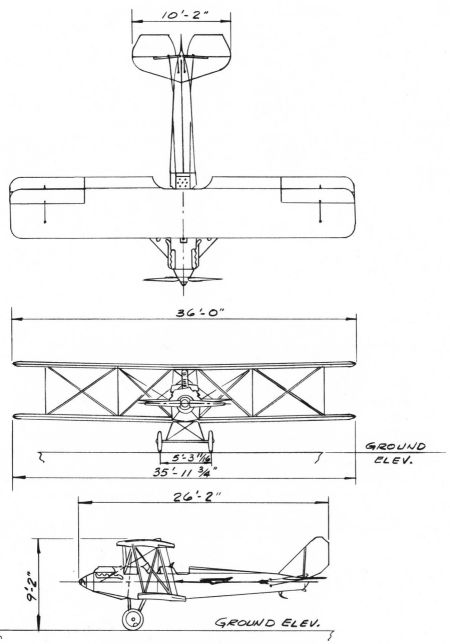

10'-2"

36'-0"

GROUND
ELEV.

5'-3"11/16
35'-11 3/4"

26'-2"

9'-2"

GROUND ELEV.

PITCAIRN AVIATION, INC.
PHILA., PA
"OROWING"    PA-3
ENGINE - CURTIS OX-5

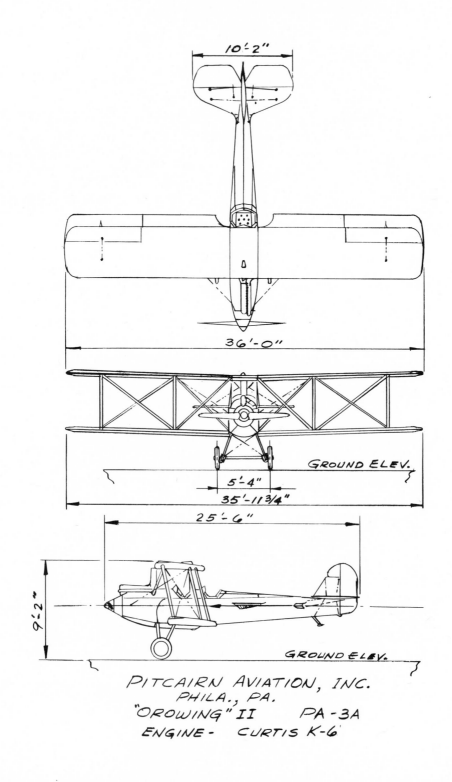

PITCAIRN AVIATION, INC.
PHILA., PA.
"OROWING" II    PA-3A
ENGINE - CURTIS K-6

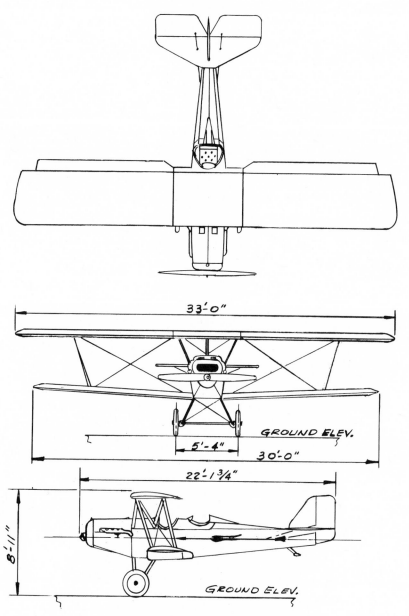

33'-0"

GROUND ELEV.

5'-4"

30'-0"

22'-1¾"

8'-11"

GROUND ELEV.

PITCAIRN AIRCRAFT, INC.
PHILA., PA.
"FLEETWING" II    PA-4
ENGINE - CURTIS OX-5

## PITCAIRN MAILWING SERIES

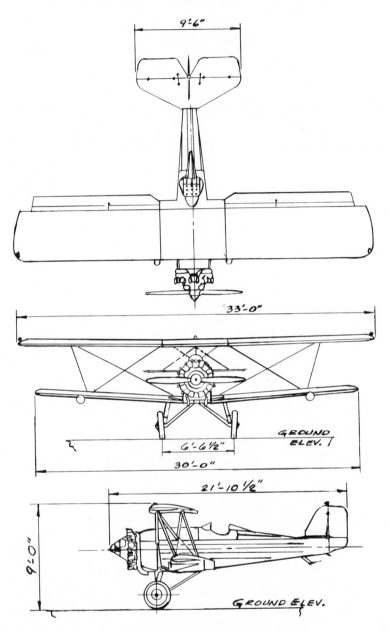

9'-6"

33'-0"

GROUND
ELEV. 1

6'-6½"

30'-0"

21'-10½"

9'-0"

GROUND ELEV.

PITCAIRN AVIATION, INC.
PHILA., PA.
"MAILWING"       PA-5
ENGINE-  WRIGHT "WHIRLWIND" J-5

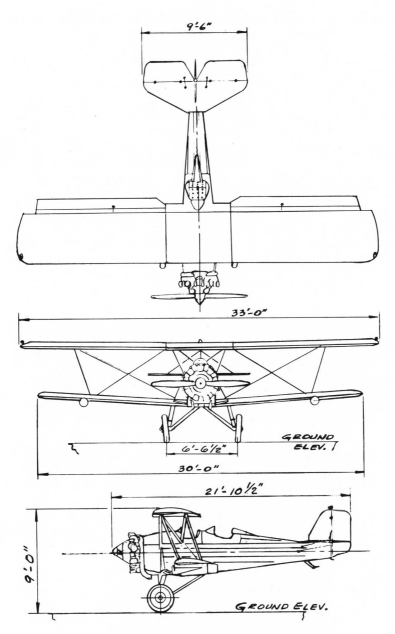

9'-6"

33'-0"

6'-6½"

GROUND
ELEV.

30'-0"

21'-10½"

9'-0"

GROUND ELEV.

PITCAIRN AVIATION, INC.
PHILA., PA.
"SPORT MAILWING"    PA-5A
ENGINE - WRIGHT "WHIRLWIND" J-5

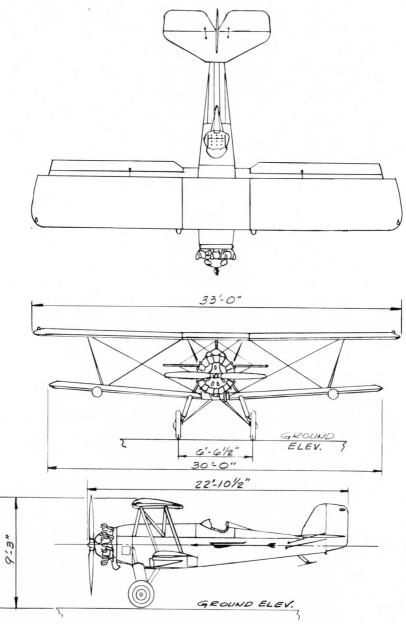

33'-0"

GROUND
ELEV.

6'-6½"

30'-0"

22'-10½"

9'-3"

GROUND ELEV.

PITCAIRN AIRCRAFT INC.
PHILA., PA.
"SUPER MAILWING" PA-6
ENGINE - WRIGHT J-5

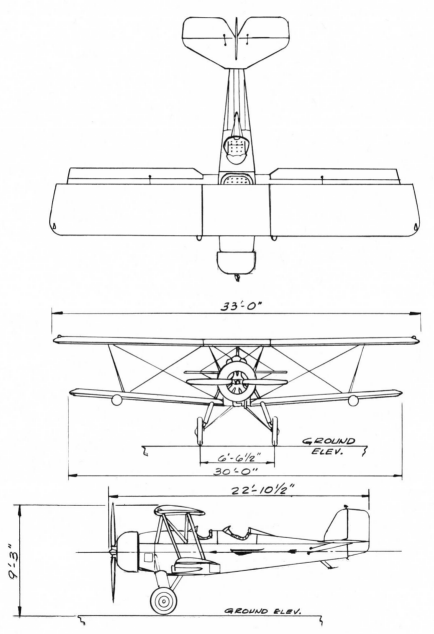

33'-0"

GROUND
ELEV.

6'-6½"

30'-0"

22'-10½"

9'-3"

GROUND ELEV.

PITCAIRN AIRCRAFT INC.
PHILA., PA.
"SPORT MAILWING"  PA-6A
ENGINE - WRIGHT WHIRLWIND J-5-C

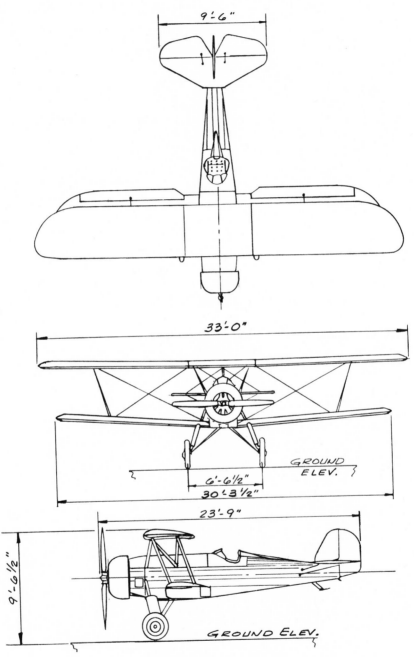

9'-6"

33'-0"

GROUND
ELEV.

6'-6½"
30'-3½"

23'-9"

9'-6½"

GROUND ELEV.

PITCAIRN AIRCRAFT INC.
PHILA., PA.
"SUPER MAIL WING" PA-7
ENGINE - WRIGHT J-6

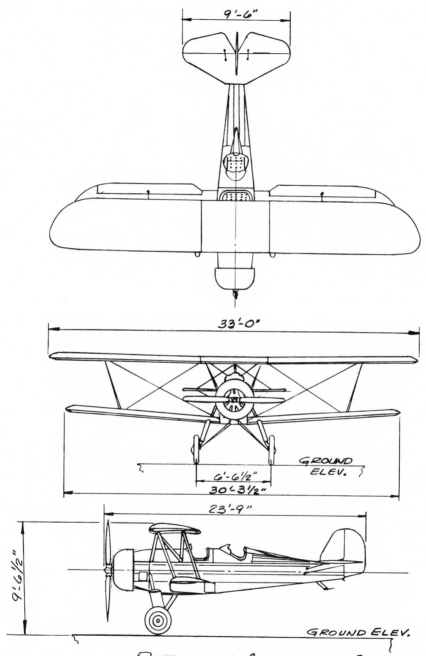

9'-6"

33'-0"

GROUND
ELEV.

6'-6½"

30'-3½"

23'-9"

9'-6½"

GROUND ELEV.

PITCAIRN AIRCRAFT INC.
PHILA., PA.
"SPORT MAILWING"      PA-7A
ENGINE -      WRIGHT J-6

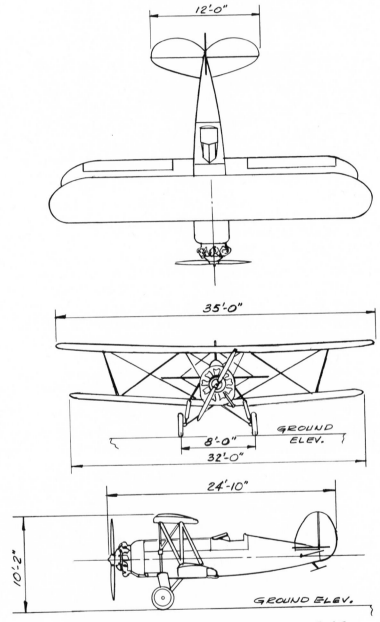

12'-0"

35'-0"

GROUND ELEV.

8'-0"

32'-0"

24'-10"

10'-2"

GROUND ELEV.

PITCAIRN AIRCRAFT INC.
PHILA., PA.
"SUPER MAILWING"     PA-8
ENGINE-. WRIGHT WHIRLWIND 300

## PITCAIRN AUTOGIROS

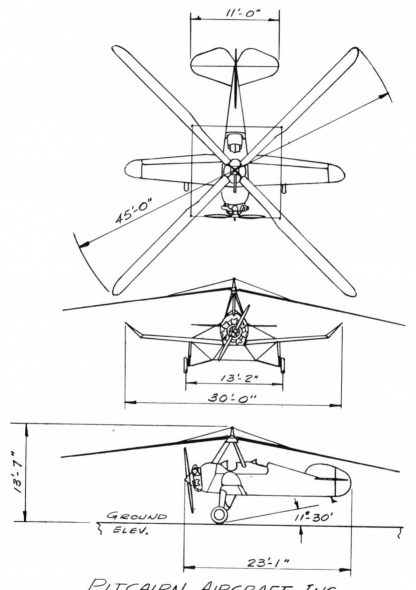

PITCAIRN AIRCRAFT, INC.
PHILA., PA.
AUTOGIRO          PCA-2 (3-PLACE)
ENGINE- WRIGHT WHIRLWIND 300

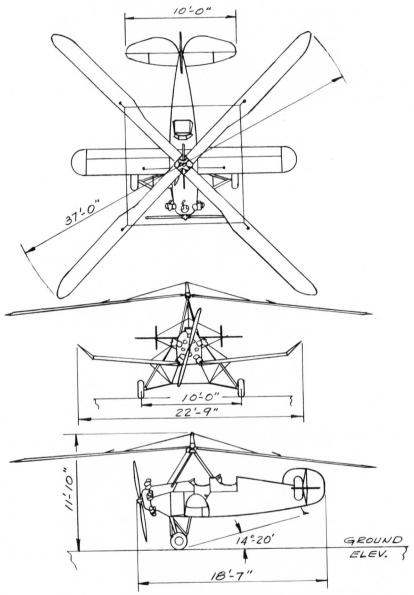

10'-0"

37'-0"

10'-0"

22'-9"

11'-10"

14°-20'

GROUND
ELEV.

18'-7"

PITCAIRN AIRCRAFT, INC.
PHILA., PA.
AUTOGIRO     PAA-1  (2-PLACE)
ENGINE-   KINNER B-5

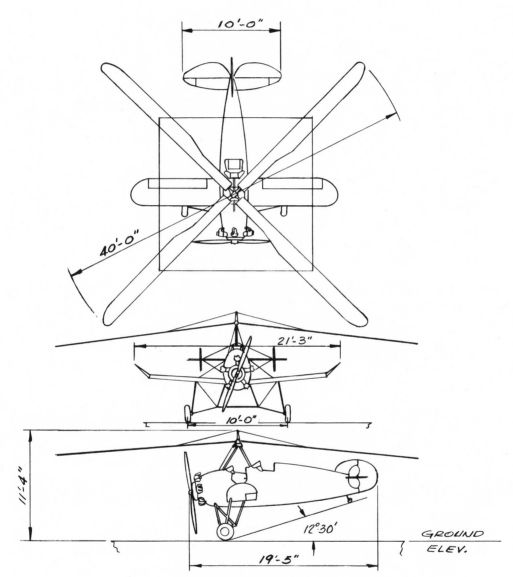

10'-0"

40'-0"

21'-3"

10'-0"

11'-4"

12°30'

19'-5"

GROUND ELEV.

PITCAIRN AIRCRAFT, INC.
PHILA., PA.
AUTOGIRO        PA-18 (2-PLACE)
ENGINE - KINNER R-5.

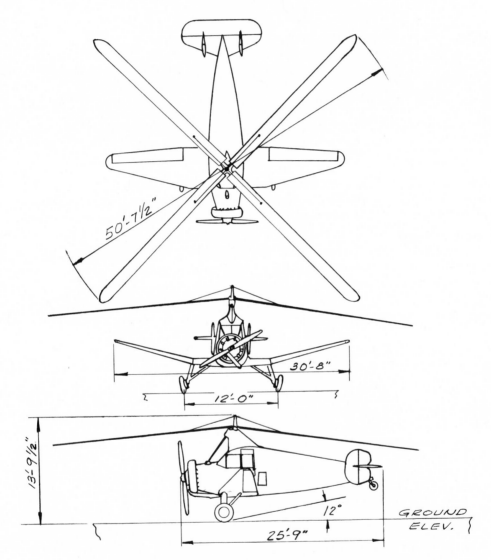

50'-7½"

30'-8"

12'-0"

13'-9½"

12°

25'-9"

GROUND
ELEV.

PITCAIRN AIRCRAFT, INC.
PHILA., PA.
CABIN AUTOGIRO   PA-19  (4-PLACE)
ENGINE - WRIGHT WHIRLWIND 420

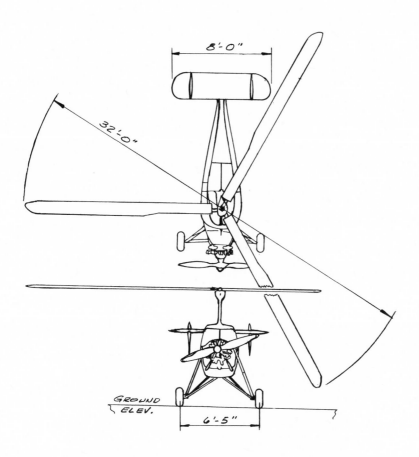

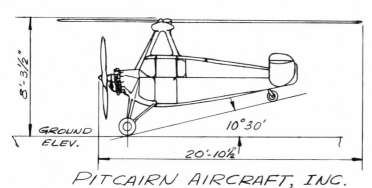

PITCAIRN AIRCRAFT, INC.
PHILA., PA.
AUTOGIRO (EARLY VERSION)   PA-22 (2-PLACE)
ENGINE —   POBJOY 90 H.P.

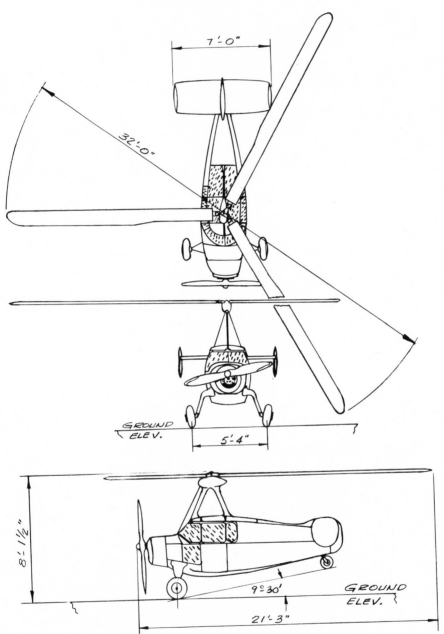

7'-0"

32'-0"

GROUND
ELEV.

5'-4"

8'-1½"

9°30'

GROUND
ELEV.

21'-3"

PITCAIRN AIRCRAFT, INC.
PHILA., PA.
AUTOGIRO (FINAL VERSION)  PA-22A (2-PLACE)
ENGINE - POBJOY 90 H.P.

## PITCAIRN AUTOGIROS

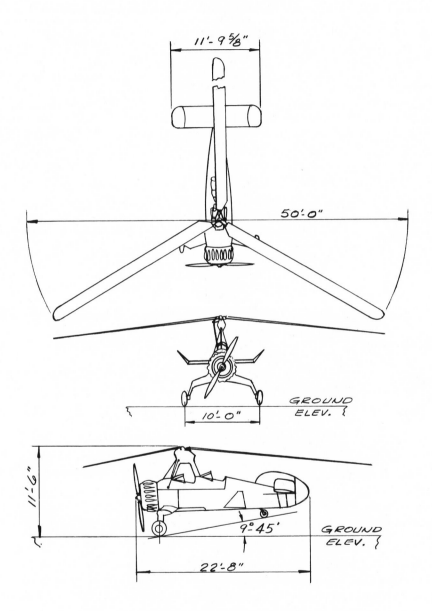

PITCAIRN AIRCRAFT, INC.
PHILA., PA.
(ARMY YG-2) AUTOGIRO    PA-33 (2-PLACE)
ENGINE – WRIGHT WHIRLWIND 420 H.P.

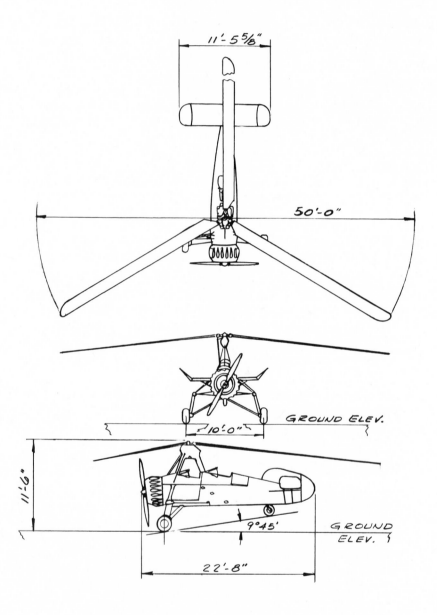

11'-5⅝"

50'-0"

GROUND ELEV.

10'-0"

11'-6"

9°45'

GROUND
ELEV.

22'-8"

PITCAIRN AIRCRAFT, INC.
PHILA., PA.
(NAVY XOP-2) AUTOGIRO     PA-34 (2-PLACE)
ENGINE — WRIGHT WHIRLWIND 420 H.P.

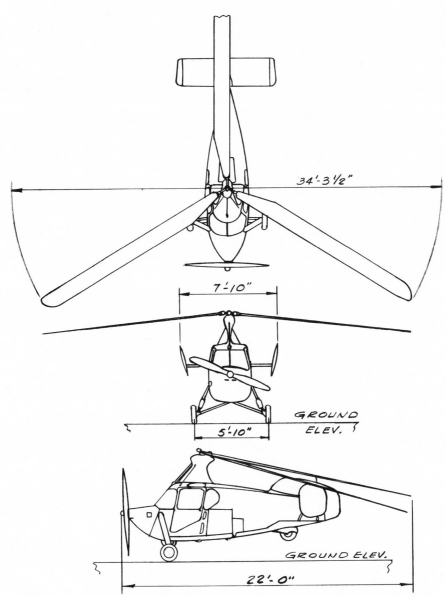

34'-3½"

7'-10"

GROUND
ELEV.

5'-10"

GROUND ELEV.

22'-0"

PITCAIRN AIRCRAFT, INC.

PHILA., PA.

AUTOGIRO          AC-35 (2 PLACE)

ENGINE -      POBJOY 90 H.P.

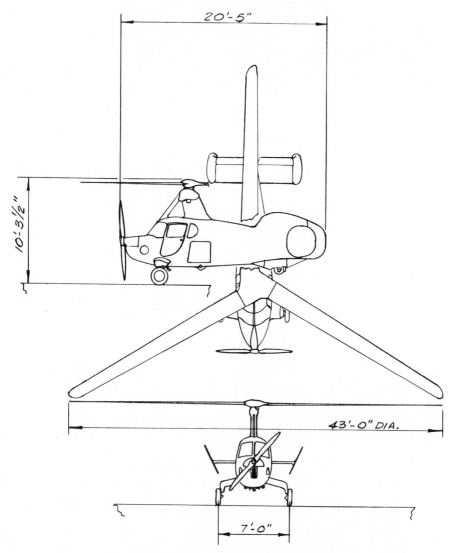

PITCAIRN AIRCRAFT, INC.
PHILA., PA.
AUTOGIRO (ALL METAL)   PA-36 (2-PLACE)
ENGINE — WARNER SCARAB 165 H.P.

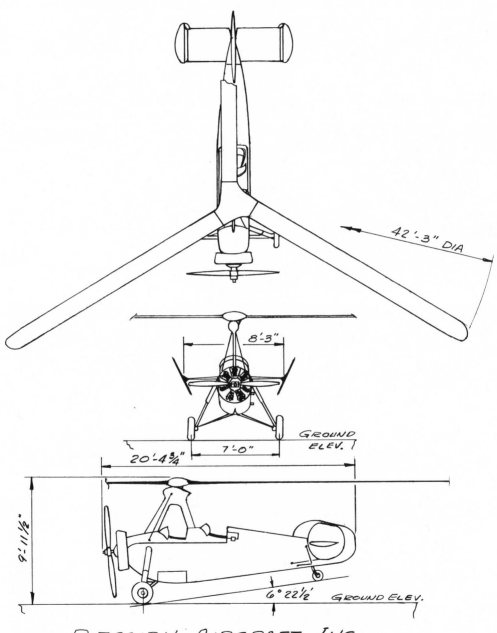

42'-3" DIA

8'-3"

7'-0"

20'-4¾"

9'-11½"

GROUND ELEV.

6° 22½'   GROUND ELEV.

PITCAIRN AIRCRAFT, INC.
PHILA., PA
AUTOGIRO              PA-39
ENGINE —   WARNER SCARAB 165 H.P.

## PITCAIRN AUTOGIROS S.G.T.A. DESIGN CONCEPT
### SUBMERGED GAS TURBINE AUTOGIRO

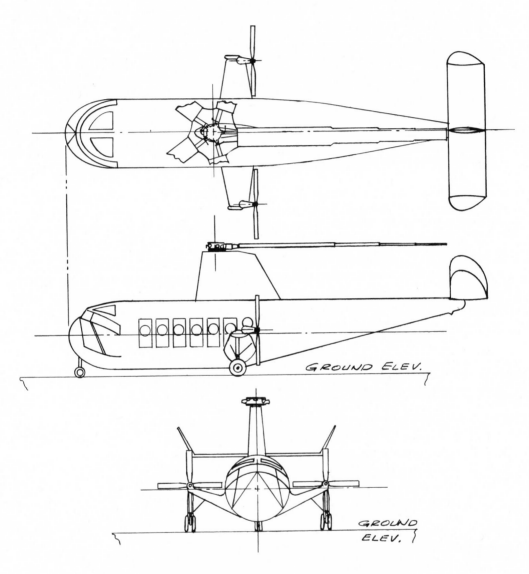

GROUND ELEV.

GROUND ELEV.

PITCAIRN AIRCRAFT, INC.
PHILA., PA.
AUTOGIRO          SGTA-3

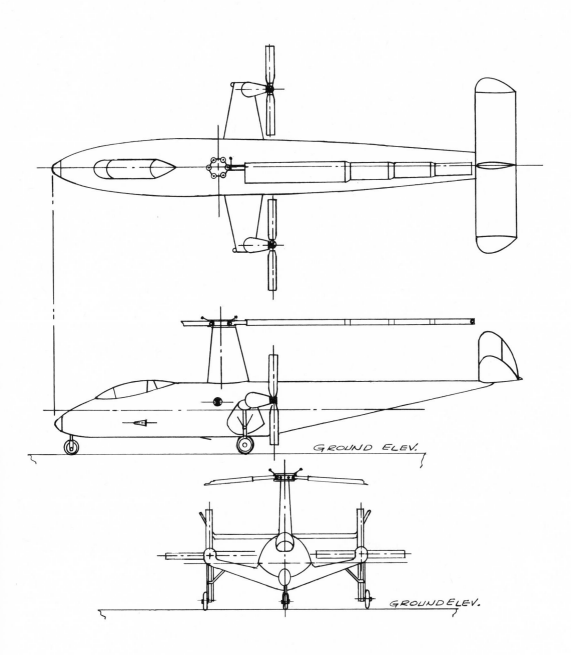

GROUND ELEV.

GROUND ELEV.

PITCAIRN AIRCRAFT, INC.
PHILA., PA.
AUTOGIRO        SGTA-5

## C. F. A. DESIGN CONCEPT
# CRUISE FAN AUTO-GIRO

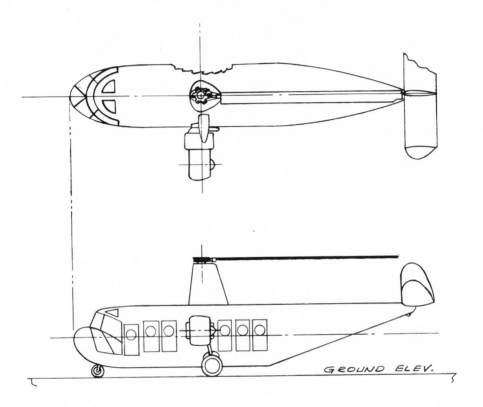

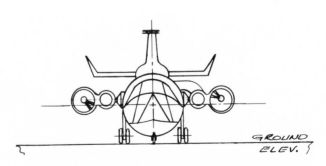

PITCAIRN AIRCRAFT, INC.
PHILA., PA.
GYRODYNE          CFA-3

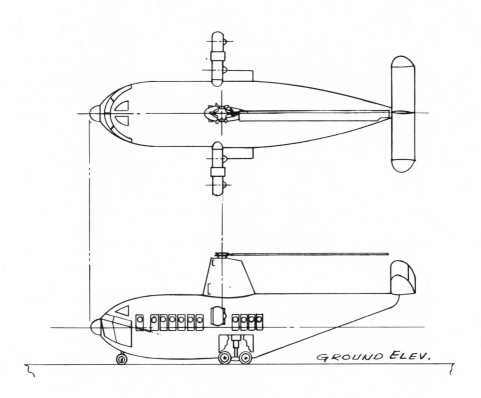

GROUND ELEV.

GROUND
ELEV.

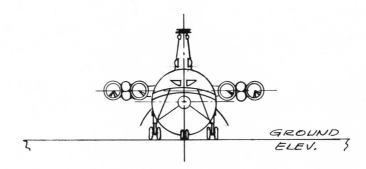

PITCAIRN AIRCRAFT, INC.
PHILA., PA.
AUTOGIRO CFA-4

# Index